WORLD STEAM
IN THE
TWENTIETH CENTURY

WORLD STEAM IN THE TWENTIETH CENTURY

E. S. COX
C.ENG., F.I.MECH.E., M.I.LOCO.E.

LONDON
IAN ALLAN

First published 1969

Published in the United Kingdom by Ian Allan Ltd,
Shepperton, Surrey, and printed by R & R Clark Ltd
Edinburgh 3. S.B.N. 7110 0079 4

Contents

List of Tables

LIST OF TABLES

Preface

THIS IS A BOOK about locomotive design which attempts to trace the common thread of Stephenson's original concept through the railways of the world during the present century. It identifies five recognisable broad schools of locomotive design, those of America, Britain, France, Germany and Central Europe, and, after describing under what influence design in those countries arrived at the form which it did, it explains how these strains have spread and intermingled in all countries. Far from having pursued their own design variations in isolation, each administration has been influenced to a greater or lesser extent by the practice of others. In the various books which have been published on world steam, none to the author's knowledge has explored this aspect in a comprehensive manner.

To state such a subject is easy, but to accomplish it satisfactorily is far otherwise. Superman himself could hardly attain the omniscience needed to do full justice to the matter. Any general presentation within a single volume is bound to be vulnerable to the superior knowledge and detailed investigation of those who have studied a particular sector of the whole field. The author's only competence to make the attempt is that for forty years it was one of his professional tasks to make himself aware of and to measure the relative importance of all locomotive developments as they arose in order that their suitability for adaption to the design needs of his own administration could be considered. To this congenial task was added a lifelong interest in what the other fellow was doing, and an inability to be interested solely in the products of his own country. These qualifications, such as they are, have been supplemented by the good fortune of being able to visit the railways of some twenty countries abroad.

To make the treatment of so wide a subject readable or indeed possible, some short cuts are necessary. Much of its presentation must owe something to the literature of the subject, a selection of which is presented in the bibliography. Less than justice has to be done in tracing developments in those few administrations which have been little influenced by the 'big five', and, for reasons of space, narrow gauge railways, and experimental departures from the normal locomotive format, are only occasionally referred to. Then, too, descriptions of particular engineering features must be limited, and for wider or more technical treatment of many of the aspects touched upon together with appropriate drawings, the reader is referred to the technical press, to other more authoritative books, and to the proceedings of engineering societies in the different countries.

An attempt has been made to present an impartial picture in that no more space is given to the practice of the author's own country than to that of other countries which have had a similarly important influence upon the development of the art. Well-established facts speak for themselves but impartiality breaks down when the facts are missing to the extent that conjecture has to be employed to fill the gaps. A story such as this would be rather dull without some opinions and judgements, but, where the author has ventured these out of his own professional experience and observation, it must be stressed that they are the purely personal views of one man only. Enough information has not yet emerged, and may indeed never do so, to enable a completely accurate and detached verdict to be pronounced upon this vast kaleidoscope.

The definitive treatise on world steam has still to be written. It is to be hoped that this study will add something to the source material when that encyclopaedic work is eventually, if ever, undertaken.

In a work such as this an author's acknowledgments have to be numerous, but to name them all individually would produce too long a list. Collectively a word of thanks must go first to the many locomotive engineers encountered abroad during the author's professional visits over a long period who have provided information and data from which a corpus of records has gradually been built up. This has for the most part only supplemented and confirmed information available from published literature. Even the most industrious writer could hardly follow up all the references in that remarkable work published by Henschel GmbH in Germany in 1941, *20,000 Publications on Railway Technology*, but the bibliography at the end of this work lists the sources which the author has most used to support his own data.

This must be supplemented by special reference to Herr Othmar Bamer of Vienna who kindly answered some outstanding questions, and to Herr Ernst Glenk of the Vereinigung Deutsche Locomotivfabriken, Frankfurt, who provided authentic information as to the total numbers built in each class of German standard locomotives since 1925. A special word of thanks is also due to M André Chapelon who, through the intermediary of Mr George Carpenter, provided authoritative information on some aspects of French practice not hitherto accessible to British engineers.

The first two of the above-named gentlemen also assisted in the provision of photographs, as did Charles Shorto, J. M. Jarvis, Dr P. Ransome-Wallis, George Curry of LAMA and Maurice Crane late of Beyer Peacocks. Where possible hitherto unpublished pictures have been used to illustrate the text, but a yawning scarcity for some classes makes this ideal impossible of total fulfilment.

Lastly a word on numerical equivalents. Weights are shown either in English tons of 2,240lb or as metric tonnes of 2205lb. The metric cheval-vapeur (CV) equals 0·986 of the British and American horsepower (hp). The equivalence is so close that where horsepower is referred to in the text only one figure is shown. On the other hand the true relationship has been allowed for in converting lb of steam or coal per hp hour into kg per cheval-vapeur heure.

E. J. COX
Stoneleigh
Redwood Road
Sidmouth
Devon

CHAPTER ONE

Initial Survey

THE CONSIDERABLE FRATERNITY that is interested in the steam locomotive either professionally or as enthusiasts has always been aware of the differences which have existed in the appearance and the technical content of engines in the different countries in the world. Because of a common heritage stemming from the work of George Stephenson and the early British builders there was at first a measure of similarity in the aspect of the iron horse. As railways began to spread, this soon became blurred as the need to meet all kinds of varying natural conditions to say nothing of the ideas and fancies of contemporary engineers, began to play upon the original basic form. It was possibly around the beginning of the present century that national differences attained their most distinctive shape, and the years between 1900 and 1904 are perhaps as good a time as any to begin a study of the interplay of these national characteristics, one upon the other, which has continued ever since.

The observer is naturally more aware of the engines to be seen upon the railways of his own country, but as time has passed, there have been more and more domestic locomotive designs which have been influenced, in whole or in part, by practices originating from abroad. At the same time it is noticeable that foreign railways have nearly all, at some stage, been influenced in their locomotive practice by imports, whether of engines or of ideas, from other countries. It was in the last half-century of steam that design became less and less a closed shop, and it is possible to trace an increasing intermingling of nationally distinct patterns. To the stern individualist this was no doubt to be deplored, but in all fields of engineering, air, marine and terrestrial, national frontiers have crumbled before the onset of expanding technology, and the art has gained far more than it has lost by well-chosen invention and practice from outside the engineer's own country.

It was not to be expected, having regard to the variety of natural and human conditions, that this interchange would be of equal incidence everywhere. In the steam locomotive field there have been countries, such as the USA, which have absorbed practically nothing from outside, while at the same time themselves exerting a world-wide influence; there are others, of which perhaps Spain could be cited as an example, which have accepted influences from many other countries and have developed an industry of their own, but which have themselves contributed next to nothing to the global sum of exportable knowledge.

In attempting a survey of world steam locomotive practice in the present century, it may enhance the interest of mere description to identify and measure the extent to which the practice of particular countries has influenced that of others, and has in turn been influenced by those others.

Although clothed in the widest differences of dimensions and outside appearance, it is well to remember that the similarities between steam locomotives in use in different countries were far greater than their differences. This is a remarkable tribute to George Stephenson, a practical mechanic with little book learning who so fashioned the *Rocket* and its immediate successors that no better first principles or layout of basic components found acceptance during the whole century and a half of the steam era on railways.

Wherever the steam locomotive was encountered, from the most ancient shunter puffing around some works sidings to its last full flowering, capable of moving 1,000 tons at 100mph, it was apt to consist of the same components. A cylindrical boiler barrel was joined to a water sheathed firebox from which products of combustion passed inside multiple fire tubes to a smokebox at the other end. Here a combination of blastpipe and chimney permitted steam exhausted to the atmosphere from two, three or four cylinders to produce a draught upon the fire which was accurately and automatically geared to the rate at which the engine was working. The steam thus produced fed the cylinders which in turn drove the road wheels directly through coupling and connecting rods. Boiler and engine were mounted on longitudinal framing on which fuel and water could also be carried in suitable containers, but, more usually, these supplies were carried on a separate vehicle behind the locomotive. Travelling by rail at any time over the years of steam traction, whether from Manchester, Milwaukee, Moscow or Madras, would produce many widely differing apparitions to the observer, but only one *modus operandi*, for steam locomotives were all brothers under the skin.

It is, of course, well known that engineers in all lands were little content to remain in thraldom to a conception which produced and could produce little more than 9 per cent thermal efficiency at the traction drawbar, which progressively fouled its environment, to say nothing of its own inside, with the waste products of combustion and of ebullition, and whose unbalanced forces were destructive alike to itself and to the track on which it ran. At recurring intervals up to the very last days of steam relief was sought by borrowing from power station and marine practice, by water tube boilers, condensing turbines, high speed geared engines, and by electric transmission. In no country the world over were these technically superior features, applied to single, or at most two or three experimental units, found to be economically viable, however, and none have ever been reproduced in quantity for revenue-earning service, even to the limited extent of double figures.

So universal a circumstance, seemingly flying in the face of scientific progress in other fields, must have had a reason, and a strong reason at that. The answer is to be found when one ceases to think of the locomotive as an isolated unit, and regards it as part of a transport machine, of a railway in fact, manufacturing for sale and public acceptance effective traction ton miles. From this point of view low thermal efficiency and a primitive technology receded into a position of relatively minor importance, and other factors such as reliability, availability, first cost, fuel cost and cheapness of maintenance were of greater importance to the final economy. The simple fact is that for all those long years the steam locomotive was fully at home in its environment and produced traction ton miles at an acceptably low cost. It was only when improved generation and transmission permitted bulk supplies of electricity to be justified both technically and economically for the more intensively operated rail services, and later when the diesel by its lower fuel and operating costs became able to blanket all its other disabilities, that the bell at last tolled for steam traction as we have known it. It was by such alien agencies that it was finally overcome and displaced, and not by any dramatic change in its own nature.

Having stressed the universality of the main theme, it must be conceded that an infinity of variations have been played thereon by generations of locomotive engineers in different countries. Wheel arrangements have run from 0–4–0 to 4–14–4, and for articulated engines up to 2–8–8–8–2. Appearance has boxed the compass from real works of art whose beautifully shrouded and splashered assemblies were marred by no external pipework or unseemly excrescences, to stark and naked-seeming engines with much daylight to be seen under the boiler and above the coupled wheels, and hung about with a wild excess of exterior devices connected by a tangle of pipework. Every single detail from chimney to brake, shoe from smokebox door to regulator handle, has burgeoned forth into shapes both seemly and fantastic, while the sound of the exhaust has provided evidence to the knowledgeable ear of the whole gamut of freedom for the passage of steam through the cylinders from near strangulation to a full free flow. Throughout the period of steam, compounding in all its forms has appeared and disappeared from the passing scene, now in this country or that adopted as the salvation of the railway's economy, now abandoned as a useless complication, and this sometimes even in those very countries which had adopted it widely in the first place. Thus, given a common heritage of first principles, the steam locomotive in its detailed design and layout might at first sight be thought to be infinite in its variety, only consistent in its inconsistency.

Nevertheless the student of world practice can discern certain common denominators in this mass of individual effort. There have been five major trends of locomotive design, which, besides influencing one another in varying degree, have determined the shape and aspect of steam engines throughout most of the rest of the world. These were in alphabetical order, American, British, French, German and Middle European, the last-named comprising practice in the old Austro-Hungarian Empire and its successors.

It can be argued as to which of these has had the most widespread influence, but in any such consideration, the American school of design must be a strong contender. Not only a massive distribution of such engines during two world wars, but a widespread export during the years of reconstruction which followed, brought administrations in many countries into contact with transatlantic ideas. These ideas favoured conditions of maximum power operation, pooled working, good accessibility, ease of passage over inferior track, and the possibility of servicing by less skilled personnel. At the beginning of the century these conditions had seemed more particular to North America, but by the time World War I was over they had more nearly approximated to the daily needs which railways scattered all over the world found they had to meet. Thus on Russian, Indian, South African and Australian practice the pure American entity became increasingly grafted in the last days of steam, while there were few European railways indeed, not excepting the British, whose continuing development of their own previous practice did not include some measure of American features. At the same time it was American practice itself which has been least influenced by ideas from other countries, so that from the 4–6–0s and 2–8–0s at the turn of the century, up to the 4–8–4s and huge articulated engines of the final stage, there has been a consistent and almost uncontaminated line of development hardly attained anywhere else.

This latter circumstance seems to have arisen from two sources. Firstly it is a fact, well known to film producers, that there are hardly any natural features in other lands which are not found, in some measure, in parts of the vast United States. This has meant that in meeting the extremes of heat and cold, in overcoming mountains and desert, distance and weather, by motive power which has had to be run and serviced by the great human melting pot, there has been little if anything in practical railroading which experience in the Old World could usefully contribute to the New. The other factor stems from the pioneering spirit which lies deep within the make-up of even modern Americans. The assurance which the overcoming of their own obstacles and problems has bred has tended to make them uncurious and unreceptive regarding solutions from outside, not least so far as railway work is concerned.

British design was, of course, the father of all, and many are the countries whose first locomotive came from the land of John Bull. With a mature civilisation, with centres of population lying short distances apart, and with a commerce calling in the main for small individual consignments, traffic developed in the direction of 'little and often' for both passenger and freight so that locomotives of only moderate size and power sufficed. The form which the typically British locomotives took crystallised into an entity in which excellent workmanship assured long life, while economy of line, amounting in the best cases to sheer beauty, was reinforced by a Victorian trend to sweep all irregular excrescences and pipework out of sight. Good coal and a docile labour force combined for long years to permit design in which good accessibility and versatility were less than universal. Rather more because trade follows the flag than due to any particular suitability of the layout for overseas conditions, the British 'line', enlarged in size where necessary, became widespread over the world. In India, South America, Africa, Australia and on scattered individual railways in five continents, wherever British capital was deployed in railway construction and operation, wherever British trained engineers fanned out, there British design was transplanted with all its excellences and its limitations.

With their long tradition of free movement about the world, and with the need to export to live, the British became in time more receptive to the needs and practices of others. Domestically, too, eyes began to be lifted from contemplation only of what had gone before, and from World War I onwards, and at an accelerating pace, the pure British school which had been so completely exemplified by the products of Johnson and Whale amongst the engineers and by Kitson's and the North British Locomotive Co amongst the builders, to name some obvious examples, became increasingly affected by the need for better accessibility and more economical maintenance. Thus American, French and German ideas were examined and assimilated affecting both internal and external assemblies. The later steam locomotives of British design, both those on the home railways and those exported overseas, were in the best cases immeasurably improved technically as a result of this open-mindedness notwithstanding the fact that enthusiasts have never ceased to deplore the falling away from Victorian standards of beauty which resulted.

Besides receiving, British design has given out in these recent years, and the invention and development of the Garratt principle for articulated locomotives, one of the few really original departures from the accepted form, has by its inherent merit, spread over wide sections of the globe, and has greatly extended the value of steam traction to many emergent as well as to a number of historic countries.

From a race of individualists such as the French, it was inescapable that its indigenous locomotives would appear like no others. Although so clearly visible that it was hardly possible to mistake a locomotive of French origin wherever it was seen, the characteristics which defined this particular school of design are especially difficult to capture in words. The logic of having everything which needed attention hung outside the engine was combined with a certain insouciance as to how it was disposed, and as true artists their designers did not mind a little orderly disorder in the disposition of their exterior fittings so long as the overall effect they sought either consciously or unconsciously was achieved. This latter took the form of a certain gracefulness, of fineness of line, if one dares to use the word, a certain femininity. Thus, encumbered with external impedimenta, the most typically French engines were handsome in a special kind of way, and in spite of massive importations of other locomotives from the New World, the final domestic designs, both those which matured and those which never advanced from the drawing-board, were as typically Gallic as any which had gone before.

At first sight it is tempting to ascribe part of the typically French aspect to compounding and to the disposition of cylinders which resulted. This view can hardly be sustained, however, when one recollects how very un-French Churchward's four-cylinder engines looked on the Great Western Railway in England, notwithstanding on outside cylinder disposition similar to that of de Glehn. On the other hand, the simplest and most straightforward two-cylinder simple French design was totally unlike any of its British, German or American counterparts and could not possibly be mistaken for any of them. So we are left appearance-wise with no better commentary than that the French had 'a certain something'.

Whilst these lineaments have also in their time spread into some other countries around the world, although to a lesser extent than those of America or Britain, it is not in externals that French influence has had an almost universal effect, at any rate over the last thirty years of steam, but rather from the technical work of one of the giants of the steam age, André Chapelon. His work on the opening out of the whole steam circuit, directed especially towards freeing the compound engine of its internal restrictions, has been picked up in many other countries and has greatly enhanced the performance and efficiency of simple expansion engines as well.

On the other hand, as we shall see when we come to examine the matter in more detail, French designers have not been totally impervious to ideas from other countries, and some features from the massive post-war importations of American and German locomotives whether by way of purchase or of reparation, have 'rubbed off' on the home product.

The German school of design, as clearly marked and consistent through the years as any others, both gave and received to and from its contemporaries. The form of fire tube superheater first developed by Schmidt was one of the few locomotive departures to become fully world-wide in its application, and the fact that so many national engineers tinkered about with its details, and particularly with the element fastening to the header, does not detract from its Germanic origin. As in the case of Chapelon in France, Wagner and Nordmann of the Reichsbahn had an unseen effect upon countless designs in other countries as a result of their work on the Grünewald experimental station upon combustion, evaporation, and boiler proportions. For the most part pleasingly symmetrical in shape, German engines were draped about with hardly less external hangings than were the French but they seemed able to wear them in a more harmonious manner, while in the products of the Munich firm of Maffei and in the mainstream of Reichsbahn designs after 1923, bar frames and boiler-mounted running-boards shed a transatlantic cast upon their final appearance.

It was particularly the series of 29 types of standard Reichsbahn locomotives for service over the whole of Germany starting with the well-known 01 class of 1925, which crystallised a purposeful and, in the larger engines at any rate, a majestic appearance which was most satisfying to the beholder. With Teuton thoroughness these engines were thoroughly designed, alike in the care and thought obviously put into proportions and layout, as in the meticulous attention which had been paid to the smallest details. While the pre-war Reichsbahn engines cannot have been cheap to build, they indicated, down to the least of them, that they had been designed by people who really cared.

Between the wars, versions of these engines modified as to wheel sizes and arrangement but not in their typical appearance or detail work flooded into the countries of Eastern Europe, either built by the great exporting firms of Henschel, Krupp, etc., for Turkey, Yugoslavia, Bulgaria and Rumania, or, as in the case of Poland, designed and built by domestic manufacturers in the full German idiom. As the aftermath of two world wars German engines also became scattered by way of reparations across the whole of Europe, and in this way some of their features became acceptable to and were sometimes adopted by their recipients.

After 1945 with the country split in two, both the Western Bundesbahn and the Eastern Reichsbahn provided some new steam types still of distinctive Germanic aspect, and contemplated a post-war standardisation akin to that undertaken by British Railways after 1948. Only small quantities and in some cases only prototypes were achieved, however, for their production was too late in relation to the upsurge of dieselisation and electrification.

These last efforts unlike their predecessors had little influence elsewhere, and in some indefinable way failed to continue the striking consistency and admirable looks of their predecessors.

The last of the five distinctive design groups which have been referred to earns its inclusion with this select company, less from any striking technical content or from the breadth of its dissemination about the world, than from its especially individualistic lay-out and appearance. The old Austrian Empire spread over much of South-Eastern Europe before 1918 and blanketed territories which were liberated into independent states after the war was over. Dr Karl Gölsdorf was in charge of locomotive design for all of this area between the years of 1891 and 1916 and he initiated and then developed so distinctive a format that it has been retained not only by his successors in the truncated Austria of the 1920 peace treaties, but in Hungary and Czechoslovakia as well. Once again the massive redistribution of rolling stock after 1945 has spread examples of this particular school into Yugoslavia and into the borders of Russia itself, but on the other hand it never appeared outside Europe in any recognisable form.

As has been suggested above there was nothing technically striking or novel about these engines but they were in a special degree the engineer's answer to unusually severe conditions of operation—exceptionally light permitted axle-loads, indifferent track, poor coal, often mountainous terrain, and a generally lower level of wellbeing and traffic density in the territories in which they worked as compared with Western Europe. The only feature especially favourable to locomotive design indeed was a generous loading gauge, and the total effect of all the above factors together produced aspects which were unusual to say the least, and which in a number of cases resulted in some very ugly ducklings.

It is possible that some 80 per cent of the steam locomotives built in the present century could, by simple inspection, be ascribed to the influence of one or other of these five groups. Naturally the division between them was not clear-cut, and on different railways and at various times they tended in individual cases to shade off one into the other. But the main streams persisted, and in the forthcoming chapters we shall look more closely into what they consisted of, and how they affected one another.

And what of the other 20 per cent of world steam? The existence of individual and strongly marked design trends was not confined to the 'Big Five' but only they had any considerable influence outside the boundaries of their own territories. The engines of a small and select band of other countries also achieved national personalities and easily recognisable appearance which remained largely domestic in its extent. The rough terrain and local industry of Spain produced a breed which however much it borrowed from outside, nevertheless retained something distinctive in its more modern locomotives. Scandinavian countries, Norway, Sweden and Denmark, retained a certain kinship of thought in their products, and stood to some degree apart from all other countries in the manner in which they assembled and detailed the normal ingredients of locomotive design. In Italy too during the whole period after the once-scattered individual railways were taken over by the State, steam motive power was instantly recognisable by a consistent but very plain appearance, and by a technique which for some unexplained reason tended to lag behind current European achievement in both performance and efficiency.

In Russia, carrying in stock the largest number of locomotives owned by any single administration in the world from the 1930s onwards, the vast distances, the climate, and the available manpower were bound to produce distinctive features. Although borrowing much from American sources in later years, a Russian steam locomotive was still not quite like anything else, and the almost unrestricted loading gauge and the remarkably uniform conditions over such a vast area of the earth in traffic density, in terrain and in operating conditions, called forth only a limited number of separate engine classes, some running to several thousand identical units, which no interested person who has visited that country is ever likely to forget.

For reasons which will be presently discussed, hardly any of the locomotive practice in these latter countries, Spain, Scandinavia, Italy or Russia, spilled over to affect administrators or even to influence one another.

Before we proceed with our study and get down to more detail there are a few other comments of a general nature which it is convenient to make at this point.

There is hardly a locomotive of the slightest importance in any country which has not at some time been described and illustrated in the technical press, and, where sufficient lay interest exists, in railway books and enthusiasts' publications. It is possible therefore with sufficient research to amass tables of dimensions, lists of numbers and drawings and photographs. Since the number of different classes of locomotive which have appeared on the railways of the world, even in the present century, runs into thousands, it would be a gigantic task, and rather an unprofitable one, to list them all, so that every book on the subject such as the present one can at best only present that sample which the author considers to be most characteristic and which serves best to illuminate the points which he wishes to make.

The outward shape and the engineering details of the locomotives' design and construction are only part of the whole story, and another part resides in the thinking which produced the original conception, the considerations which led to the choice of this or that feature, and in the success or otherwise in performance and economy which attended the outcome. In this latter sphere our information on an international scale is far from complete and must remain so. Few indeed are the chief mechanical engineers or even designers who have gone beyond mere description and have let their hair down and published a blow by blow description of the travail which brought forth their products, and few are the countries in which information on locomotive performance, official or unofficial, is widespread.

England has probably been the most fortunate country in this respect. There was, it is true, a long period of great reserve in which design officers closely guarded their secrets not only from the public but from one another. A thaw set in after the 1920s, however, and in succeeding years up to the last days of steam more and more information and commentary became available until in the case of the British Railways Standard Locomotives of 1951 onwards no facet of their conception, design, construction or performance remained unrecorded. Then again the fraternity of those lay enthusiasts who observed performance on the line, and who commented in an informal manner upon practice and its implications, has contributed a rich harvest of information to supplement official data, a harvest without parallel in other countries.

As regards France and Germany, in the pages of *La Revue Générale des Chemins de Fer*, *Glasers Annalen* and such-like technical publications, chief engineers and their senior henchmen have published most detailed descriptions, and have presented the results of tests on stationary plants and on the road, set out in a meticulous and painstaking manner. More rarely than in England, however, have innermost thoughts been laid bare, or the failures or shortcomings on which further progress was based been brought to light. Then too, although there has been a measure of lay interest, more especially in France, it has not brought forth anything like the same volume of supplementary comment and information as in England. The same remarks are broadly true of the United States, so that while the Pennsylvania Railroad's *Altoona Test Bulletins* exist, the pages of the *Railway Age* and the *Railway Mechanical Engineer* abound with descriptions, and such books as Ralph Johnson's *The Steam Locomotive*, and Bruce's *The Steam Locomotive in America* discuss the later days of steam, there are enormous gaps in the available information necessary to achieve a full understanding of all that has been done in the New World.

Faced with this unequal and incomplete record of the facts behind the scenes, an author is thrown back upon engineering analogy for his explanation of much of what has been done. Steam is steam and metal is metal everywhere, and the laws of mass, of motion and of thermodynamics are universal. Thus where a chain of technical causes and effects are well attested in one country, it is at least probable that the same considerations have operated in other countries more reticent as to their experiences. Thus we may go a long way towards deducing such matters as freedom of running or otherwise, measure of economy, effective adhesion, freedom from hot boxes and other mechanical ills, and many of the other facets which define the whole locomotive as distinct from its externals alone. There only remain, shrouded in impenetrable mystery, the personal preferences and prejudices of individual engineers, where in their wisdom or otherwise they have preferred to keep these locked in their bosoms. Dr Gölsdorf, for instance, the well-known locomotive engineer and designer of the Austrian State Railways for 25 years, was ahead of his time in seeking publicity for all that he did, and the pages of the English publication *The Locomotive* attest how frequently he volunteered descriptive matter on all his new creations. But his communications were descriptive only, and all the inwardness which lay behind what he did, and all the more enthralling accounts of what resulted from them in performance efficiency and maintenance, must remain for ever unknown.

In this account it is sought to make comparison and to point trends of development by reference to a series of tables setting out the leading dimensions of the engines concerned, but when this seemingly straightforward exercise is attempted on an international scale certain difficulties arise. Cylinder dimensions, wheel diameters, working pressures, grate areas and weights as built, as well as external dimensions, could be expected to be factual, whether expressed in English or in metric units. But the question arises, factual at what point in time? Successive batches of the same design of engine often contain changes in some or all of these values and the information available from different sources can vary according to which particular batch within a series is being described. Translation of English measurements into metric and vice versa is a further source of divergence according to the constants which are used in the conversion and the manner in which figures are rounded off. Thus as many as five different versions of these basic values may be found in respect of the same locomotive class in the different records and publications available. These differences are not usually so great as to invalidate any comparison being made, but they must be borne in mind in that our comparisons are of necessity of a general rather than of a meticulous kind.

Unfortunately starting tractive effort and boiler heating surface, which at first sight ought to be equally useful measures of locomotive capacity, are even more suspect. The effort available at the wheel rim at the point of initial movement depends upon the proportion of full boiler pressure which is available at the pistons to exert the thrust necessary to achieve movement, and on this proportion there was no common agreement. In Britain and America 85 per cent of the designed boiler pressure has been a usual measure, but in other countries percentages as low as 60 per cent have been officially adopted, with various other values in between. Moreover, whatever the nominal value, a host of factors conspired to vary the true effort obtainable in practice, of which valve events, cross section and resistance of steam pipes and passages, cylinder port areas and the onset of condensation all had their effect. If these considerations rendered the true starting effort unclear in simple expansion engines, it was doubly opaque in the case of compounding.

Many are the complex but not necessarily truthful formulae which have been devised to take account of the still more devious labyrinths through which the incoming steam must pass, starting valves, reducing valves, receivers and so on, before entering the low-pressure cylinders of double expansion engines. Thus the calculated value for starting tractive effort was always a dubious one, even within a single administration where a common formula was used; as a means of comparing potential power from one railway to another the figure was wellnigh useless. Since on the other hand test results which would give the true starting effort were seldom available, and even when available were also subject to all kinds of inconsistencies as between test procedure in different countries, it has been decided to omit this often published but always unreliable figure from the present tabulations. Solace may be taken from the fact that important French and German books also making international comparisons omit values for the starting tractive effort, doubtless for the same reasons.

Similar care is needed in using published figures for boiler-heating surfaces as a measure of the steam-raising capacity of different boilers. Even within a single railway successive engineers may have had different ideas on how best to obtain a given steam production, by long tubes or short, by spacing them well apart or by packing them in regardless, and by different proportions between flue tubes and small tubes. Comparison of one engine with another can be misleading in that a lesser surface with good design could usually produce more steam than would a larger surface with poor design. Internationally the comparison was further vitiated in that some administrations measured their heating surface on the gas side of the tubes and firebox, while others based it upon the area on the water side.

It must not be deduced from the above that no figure means anything and that the student must throw overboard all attempt at comparative analysis, but the more one lived with and understood the steam locomotive the more one realised that dimensions published in good faith always required a little consideration before their full acceptance.

It is a matter for regret that while ambivalent figures such as the above were included as a matter of course in every official locomotive description, from no matter what country, there were other values bearing upon the very heart of locomotive power potential which were seldom made available. Of such were the free area for the hot gases to pass through the tube bank, and its relationship to the grate area, and the relation between cross sectional area and total internal surface area of the tubes. These proportions were vital for maximum steam production and high boiler efficiency and their values gave a remarkably accurate assessment of the power potential of a given boiler. Similarly, diameter and steam lap of the piston valves and the maximum travel were indices of how expansively it was possible to use the steam produced and were thus a measure of relative economy in working. Other vital figures, only obtainable from extensive testing work, were maximum steam production and steam consumption per indicated horsepower hour.

Values such as are outlined above are not available to us on an internationsl scale, even although they may be readily forthcoming in particular countries at particular periods in history. It is for these reasons that seeking to compare an American 4–8–2 with a Russian 2–8–4, or a British Railways' Britannia with a German 03 class Pacific, for example, needs a measure of patience and perspicacity.

Finally, in these introductory remarks there is the matter of steam locomotive speed limits on which there was such a profound difference of outlook as between European countries on the one hand, and British and American thought on the other. The former placed a speed limit individually on every class of locomotive, whereas the latter put the speed limit on the route rather than on the engine. Throughout the steam era on the Continent, a limit of maximum speed was decided for each and every type as it was built, a limit derived from a consideration of wheel diameter and piston speed, number of cylinders, balancing and hammer blow. No matter that a certain route had a weight of rail, depth of ballast, alignment and bridge strength suitable for 90mph (144kph), a particular engine once designated by the design office as 'Maximum Speed 50mph (80kph)' was not permitted to exceed that figure other than possibly on special test runs.

In England and America, it was the nature of the track and natural features of a particular route which settled the maximum speed; the mechanical engineer never, except in the most abnormal circumstances, superimposed a further engine limit as such, so that any type of engine could run as fast as it was able within the track limits. This permitted a much greater measure of operating flexibility and could result on occasion in 2–10–0 locomotives with 5ft diameter wheels running at 90mph (144kph) on passenger trains. No harm was done by such running of which any record remains, and indeed, so long as civil engineering restrictions were rigidly observed, the mechanism of the well-designed steam locomotive was perfectly capable of coping with any intermediate speed up to the track limit.

Of course continental railways had route speed limits as well, some of them having the force of law, and it was in order to deal with this double set of limits, those imposed by the mechanical engineer as well as those of his civil engineering colleague, that speed recorders as distinct from speed indicators were an obligatory fitting. This 'belt and braces' philosophy as regards speed was perhaps not without sound motive, for Latin *élan*, left to itself, was capable of more extravagant action in this sphere than was British phlegm, for example. This tempting theory fails, however, when one recollects that the orderly German driver was just as closely hedged around with these double safeguards as were his colleagues of sunnier and more carefree lands, and in Table 23, Chapter 6, an example is given of the kind of 'engine' speed limits which were applied in that particular country.

With the advent of electric and diesel locomotives this duality of outlook has ceased and all administrations have had to come into line with continental practice. Unlike the driving mechanism of steam, that of the new motive power consisting of diesel engines, gearboxes or traction motors in whatever combination, must not be overspeeded lest it burst, and maximum locomotive speed is now uniformly posted up within the cabs of all non-steam power wherever it is found. Only the age-old argument remains as to whether such maxima are better enforced by use of speed indicators or speed recorders. Here the cleavage is as deep as ever.

CHAPTER TWO

What makes Foreign Locomotives so Foreign

WHETHER LOCOMOTIVES in another country seem 'foreign' to the observer depends of course upon the nature of practice in his own country. If, for example, he lives in Belgium or Spain where design through the years has borrowed a great deal from outside, his journeys to other parts of Europe to America, and about the world generally will not disclose to him much which he cannot see in his own country apart from differences in mere size. On the other hand, to these who dwell in the homelands of any of the five distinctive national schools of design outlined in the last chapter, engines in any of the other four, or in overseas countries, which derive their practice from such sources, will certainly appear foreign-looking. The engineer will recognise and appreciate the different history, personalities and natural features of the countries concerned which have thrown up this or that characteristic. The enthusiast will be guided in his appreciation or otherwise by the competence with which the foreigner tackles its work, by its fitness for its purpose, by what he knows of its efficiency, and of course by the standards of appearance and sound which he has acquired through pursuit of his enthusiasms.

It could be asked in view of the same basic form and arrangement of steam locomotive being used everywhere, why there should have been such wide national differences, even allowing for the fact that ever-widening dissemination of knowledge and technology has tended to break down barriers as this century has progressed. The differences, however, have stemmed from perfectly logical causes, only diversified and made more interesting by the application of the ideas of individual designers.

Let us take a look at some of these influences which can be classified as arising from loading gauge, profile and curvature of the line, nature of the track and bridges and the loads they will carry, climate and terrain, nature and cost of fuel, quality of water, tradition of mechanical competence on the part of the staff and the nature of the servicing facilities which are provided.

Size and, in the last resort, power depend upon the loading gauge, the height and width which the construction of the line has permitted rolling stock to attain. The really controlling factors in any locomotive's steam production and therefore power output are the diameter of the boiler barrel and the free area for the passage of the hot gases of combustion which that diameter makes possible. Neither grate area on the one hand nor cylinder dimensions on the other can escape from the effects of the ceiling which this factor places upon the maximum evaporation of the boiler. In Europe and the older civilisations, the first railways entered an already mature society, and in the towns through which they had to thread their way, the bridges and tunnels, which were scaled down to keep costs within financial possibilities, led to moderate cross sectional dimensions, fully adequate at the time, but placing a considerable design burden upon posterity. In the new world on the other hand, and in overseas countries of late development, the railway was built through relatively empty terrain. Indeed as the lines pushed west in the USA, it was often the railway which arrived before the towns were established. In these circumstances there was no obstacle to acceptance of a loading gauge which was far less restrictive. Thus while British locomotive development has had to take place within a cross section 9ft

(2750mm) wide and 13ft (3960mm) high in round figures, Western Europe has been able to design within 10ft (3050mm) by 14ft (4270mm) while American design could deploy itself within an area 11ft (3350mm) wide by 16ft (4880mm) high. The effect of height and width limitations was emphasised where, as was usual, the boiler barrel was placed above coupled wheels. Only the Garratt form of articulated locomotive broke away from this latter restriction by having boiler and firebox carried entirely clear of the wheels. This permitted power outputs to narrow gauge and other dimensionally restricted lines which would have been unattainable in a conventional layout.

Besides the height and width of the loading gauge its shape has had an influence upon national characteristics. Of all major countries, Great Britain has been the worst served in this respect, for the adoption of high station platforms from the earliest days led to a restriction in permissible width, usually 8ft 8in at all points below 3ft 6in above rail level. This had a big influence at first towards use of inside cylinders. Where technical advantage led to the placing of the cylinders outside, they had usually to be inclined, and, as power demand increased, use of multi-cylinders in the larger sizes became common unless higher working pressures permitted retention of the simpler two-cylinder arrangement. The almost universal use of the rail-level platform at stations throughout the rest of the world has permitted larger horizontal outside cylinders, and has favoured equally compounding and the retention of two simple cylinders for high powers, and the adoption of outside valve gears, and it has permitted use of crankpin bearings appropriate to the needs of these developments.

In some countries, of which Germany, Russia and some parts of America were the principal, steaming capacity of the boilers, and certainly appearance, have been affected by a kind of super loading gauge in the form of an upwards extension in the region of the chimney, only applicable to certain routes. The stovepipe chimneys standardised by the pre-1945 Reichsbahn were split halfway up their height, and the upper extension, removable at the sheds should the engine have to traverse restricted routes, was an eye-catching if not exactly beautiful adornment. In Russia, too, a similar feature, differently applied, graced the ubiquitous 2–8–4 and 2–10–2 types which could be seen at work both with and without this extension in different parts of the country. On the Atchison, Topeka and Santa Fe Railroad in the United States a more sophisticated even if more repellent-looking way of doing the same thing was to be seen. On this system steam operation had reached what was probably the ultimate level of high power output before the diesel took over, and its stud of 4–8–4 locomotives ran through the 1,762 miles (2819km) from Los Angeles to Kansas City with passenger train loads up to 1,500 tons (1523 tonnes) on tight schedules. The chimney height could be doubled at will over the divisions where this was permissible, particularly in the mountainous regions of the west, by a contraption of wire ropes and pulleys which gave the engines a remarkable appearance when so operating. The object of the exercise here, as it was elsewhere but to a milder degree, was to squeeze out the very last pound of steam which the boiler would produce by permitting some increase in draught due to the greater height of the chimney providing more effective entrainment of the hot gases by the exhaust. That at least was the theory, but it was not universally accepted, and other administrations seemed able to reach maximum output by manipulating the arrangement and proportions of the exhaust system within the normal available height.

Even where wheel diameter was small and the need for boiler power only moderate, administrations favoured by ample loading gauge have tended to pitch their boilers high because of the freedom they could thus gain for ashpan design and entry of sufficient air for good combustion. This was the most sensitive, but by some designers least appreciated, vital spot in the chain of events leading to prolonged good steaming. It was the taking advantage of this freedom in back-end design which more than anything else permitted that large gap of daylight above the wheels and under the boiler which characterised the appearance of all American and many European engines.

The nature of the available track and bridges, their strength and state of maintenance, have had a powerful influence upon locomotive characteristics. Broadly stated, while permitted loads of 30 tons (30·5 tonnes) per axle were general on American railways for many years, and 18 to 20 tons (18·3 to 20·3 tonnes) on British lines, on much of the European continent 17 (17·3 tonnes) and even 16 tons (16·2 tonnes) have been all that could be permitted. Indeed some railways in South-Eastern Europe could not rise above 14 tons (14·2 tonnes), and arrears of bridge maintenance could lead to performances such as that seen by the author in 1949 in which the Irun to Lisbon through 'express' came to a halt by the big viaduct near Salamanca, to allow a diminutive 0–6–0 pilot engine to run over the bridge by itself, to be followed after due delay by an equally diminutive 0–6–0 hauling the rest of the train. These considerations have powerfully affected the kind of motive power which could be operated both in number of wheels and in total weight and sometimes even in age. Thus in American and British practice, four-coupled engines for passenger work and six-coupled for freight had a long reign, being displaced as the twentieth century dawned by six- and eight-coupled engines respectively. Only latterly were eight- and ten-coupled wheels required for these duties, in general use in the USA and in more limited use in England. In Europe the need for sufficient adhesion with lower permitted axleloads tended to require the spreading of the coupled wheelbase over more wheels at any given stage of development, ten-coupled freight engines appearing in Austria as early as 1900. Even twelve-coupled engines were designed for Austria, Bulgaria and Wurtemberg.

On lines which have been cheaply constructed and whose bridges are not the strongest, it is not only the axleload itself which is critical, but also the disposition and spacing of the axles. Whatever the total weight, it can be important for this to be evenly distributed along the wheelbase, and this is the reason why sometimes the leading bogie is seen to be tucked back under the boiler, with the centre line of chimney and smokebox coincident with the centre line of the leading bogie wheel or truck. By this means more weight is carried by the bogie and less by the coupled wheels, a loss to adhesion it is true, but an essential factor in gaining acceptance for the engine over lightly constructed permanent way. With or without this particular feature, the wheelbase must be spread out sufficiently to produce a low bending moment per foot run on the bridge girders. Since such railways, particularly in mountainous territory, will abound in curves, European engineers, to a far greater extent than American or British, have had to learn the difficult art of making a long wheelbase flexible laterally. This is the reason why so many forms of truck exist in continental designs, combining the leading guiding wheels with the first coupled axle, giving controlled sideplay at both these positions appropriate to the curves to be traversed.

A most difficult design problem was posed where to the above requirements of low axle weight and long wheelbase was added the need for a large boiler to meet difficult operating conditions in conjunction with poor coal. A powerful engine could only be obtained in these circumstances by paring every ounce of weight off main frames and superstructure, and this is one of the reasons for the absence of low footplates and splashers, and the generally naked look of so many engines subject to these conditions. The frames were thus designed of shallow depth and with a minimum of cross bracing, whether of plate or bar construction, and were by simple inspection very flexible and 'whippy'.

Little factual information is available to us on so technical a subject as the integrity or otherwise of the frames of such engines against cracking or fracture, but it is a fortunate engineering fact, well attested by experience in Great Britain, that freedom from frame trouble was attainable not only by a strong box-like construction which flexed very little in service in a lateral direction, but also by a light and elastic frame so long as the sideways freedom was uniformly distributed along its length. The Americans ultimately found salvation from frame trouble in the rigid cast steel integral frames of later practice. On the other hand it is possible that many central European engines which had frames so slender that is was a marvel why they did not crack up in quick time, were in fact relatively trouble free, on the principle of the bamboo which bends but does not break. The long vale of tears in which frame troubles of all kinds resided during the steam era, was carved out by the persistent use of frames which were neither sufficiently rigid nor sufficiently flexible, but were a mixture of both, and fatigue flaws grew with great gusto where the rigid and the flexible portions met.

Very naturally terrain and climate produced strongly marked characteristics in countries where these natural manifestations took an extreme form. In mountainous territory the compound flourished, and it lasted there long after it had disappeared from more level routes. It permitted expansive working at full tractive effort in a manner denied to single expansion, while the low speeds of operation in toiling up long gradients, permitted free steam flow through the somewhat restricted and tortuous passages which were usual in pre-Chapelon days. Small coupled wheels and more of them were clearly a help in crossing the mountains, and it was of crucial importance that the engines should keep their feet when rail conditions became slippery.

The possibility of track irregularities causing the coupled wheels to be left in the air as it were while leading and trailing carrying wheels took more than their share of the weight, had at all costs to be avoided. To this end, rear coupled engines 2–8–0s, 2–10–0s, 4–8–0s and even 4–10–0s were widely popular, and where the required grate area and ash disposal conditions demanded a trailing truck, transfer of weight off the coupled on to the truck wheels was inhibited by connecting the springs through compensating beams.

The more severe continental type climate of Northern Europe and North America demanded shelter for the footplate staff, and side-window cabs with roofs which extended back over the firing platform towards the tender had become obligatory early on those administrations whose winter conditions were severe. Injectors and associated piping had to be tucked up in cabs and under clothing, and this is the reason too why mechanical lubricators often found themselves inside the cab also. In Russia the front end of the tender was built up to produce a totally enclosed cab, a practice also usual in Scandinavian countries, while in Canada the engine cab had a full back, and communication with the tender was made through a flexible corridor-type gangway. In Russia, too, for many years a full set of stanchioned railings was obligatory all round the external footplating, because of accidents to the type of labour which serviced the engines when out in the open, working on surfaces encrusted with solidified snow and ice. At the other end of the scale, the perpetual sunshine of Egypt for long called for no more than a tasselled roof and a spectacle plate to form a rudimentary cab affording the maximum air circulation round the footplate staff while running and standing. In countless other hot countries American-style cabs sported large side windows permanently open, while front hinged doors on both sides of the boiler were held open for the same purpose. In India, and countries which combined great heat with monsoon rains, compromise was necessary. Cabs were provided on both engine and tender with open sides for dry weather operation, and louvres were provided, normally carried outside the cab side-sheets, which could be slid back on runners to close the gaps when the torrential rain drove in while still maintaining a measure of ventilation. The author's personal experience can attest that this arrangement was not productive of much comfort, but then nobody is very comfortable anywhere in the monsoon.

From these climatic effects we turn to the nature of the available fuel which was at the root of design and performance everywhere. The steam locomotive grew up and developed into its final form on the use of coal, and although in some parts of the world other fuels such as oil and wood were more accessible or cheaper, their combustion was accomplished by adaptations of the coal-burning firebox, rather than by any radical departure tailored to the special characteristics of the alternative fuel itself. Thus coal was king, and its nature, calorific value and ash content have had a great influence on design.

With good coal, 30,000lb (13650kg) of steam per hour could be generated from a fire-grate of 30sq ft (2·79m²) or just over and this output sufficed for moving the traffic which offered over much of Northern Europe and Great Britain into modern times as well as in the countries which they influenced in locomotive matters. Thus in Prussia up to World War I and in England up to World War II, with a few exceptions, the largest engines could be successfully operated with narrow fireboxes disposed between the frames and over the coupled axles. Scandinavian and Dutch design was similarly satisfied, and the French Nord Railway never provided itself with any other kind of firebox during its independent existence other than on experimental types. The advantages of clinging to this form of firebox were the economy in weight and first cost which resulted from avoiding the need for trailing carrying wheels and the saving in fuel burned during periods of preparation and standby. The disadvantages were the structural difficulties of providing adequate air inlet and ash carrying capacity, and the poor combustion which resulted if for some unforeseen reason bad coal had to be substituted for the good coal on which the whole arrangement was primarily based.

With coal of low calorific value, obviously more coal had to be burned for the same heat release, and since there was a limit to the rate at which coal could be burned on each square foot of grate if high loss of unburned fuel ejected up the chimney was to be avoided, then larger grates had to be provided, and if this factor, or the need for still larger steam production than 30,000lb/hr (13650kg/hr) called for more than 36sq ft (3·34m²) of grate area, the largest which could reasonably be accommodated between the frames, then a wide firebox was resorted to. This was either carried over a trailing truck or, in the case of countries having a high loading gauge, above the coupled wheels. In Europe 40 to 50sq ft (3·72 to 4·65m²) was the usual grate area on the larger engines, but in America, maximum power operation demanded areas approaching 150sq ft (13·9m²) which, disposed in a length of 16ft (4880mm) and a width of 9ft (2750mm), produced an inner firebox equal in volume to a good-sized living-room! With coals having high ash content exceptional ashpan capacity was necessary if length of run between stops for servicing was not to be unduly limited. Thus we see in many European designs the trailing truck disposed very far behind the trailing coupled wheels in order to leave unobstructed space underneath the grate for provision of a large deep ashpan, easy to get at for cleaning out, and allowing ample entry of air for combustion.

It was not only the quality of coal which led to differing modes of design, but its price in relation to the other expenses of locomotive operation. Where coal was available and relatively cheap as in USA and Great Britain, auxiliary devices to save coal had to be inexpensive indeed if the value of the economy produced was to be sufficient to exceed the interest on the increased capital cost, and the added cost of maintenance of the device itself. In these countries, by and large, the coal-saving devices most ready to hand, compounding and feed water heating, have made only moderate impact. The other great coal-saver, superheating, had the exceptional merit of raising first and maintenance cost so little in relation to its substantial savings that it has been acclaimed and adopted all over the world.

In Europe where coal was usually dear, often not too plentiful, and sometimes almost a precious material, things were otherwise, and compounding wove its way from first to last through the texture of design thought, both before and after the advent of superheating. Here the two sides of the balance sheet were more closely matched, however, and the advantage was rarely decisive, as will be seen when we come to look at things more closely. Compounding for new design only survived substantially in the last days of steam in a single country, France, and for this there were psychological as well as practical reasons.

Feed water heating devices of all kinds festooned the exteriors of numerous European locomotives, and became standard equipment in the form of pumps and heaters in France and Germany and others which followed their practice. It was the disposition of these items around the outside of the engines which gave so many continental engines a 'Christmas tree' effect, still acceptable if the units and connecting piping were symmetrically laid out, quite horrifying in appearance if they were strewn all over the exterior with complete abandon as was sometimes the case.

After coal, water. It was only comparatively lately in steam locomotive history that fully effective water treatment became available and, as is well known, chemical treatment of the feed water either individually on each engine, or through bulk supply from the lineside, eventually became able to assure completely scale-free boilers without associated foaming or priming. But it was a long and stony road to reach this goal, and even when it was reached, lack of means or lack of faith prevented its universal adoption before steam itself had disappeared.

Without such treatment or with only partial treatment, the effect of much of the natural water in many countries was terrible, in corrosion and scaling up of the internal surfaces of the boiler, and various devices were sought to collect some of the scale or sludge from the incoming water in trays before it escaped into the interior of the boiler, trays disposed in additional domes or drums on the top of the boiler which could be taken out periodically and cleaned. The additional impedimenta on top of the boilers which resulted greatly affected the appearance of the engines concerned. It was German Reichsbahn practice to provide an extra dome for the purpose while Hungary was the protagonist of the separate cylinder behind the chimney. On the other hand, English and American engines and their derivatives seldom went in for such excrescences, and if trays to catch incoming scale were used, they were tucked away discreetly inside the boiler barrel, only the top feed clacks being visible externally. Likewise were the French, but on some of their tank engines having the TIA water treatment applied individually to each locomotive, the small tank containing the mixture for doping the incoming water was perched up on the boiler top with an effect upon the appearance which would give an industrial designer nightmares!

Then again, in earlier times the importance of having a sufficiently large water surface inside the boiler for disengagement of steam, and a sufficient volume of steam space above the water line was not recognised and this led to persistent and seemingly inexplicable carry over of water into the cylinders. This was the reason for the appearance on some designs, mainly of German or Austrian origin, for two domes connected by a steam pipe of large diameter external to the boiler itself. The available steam space was thus increased, and there was a chance that the steam delivered to the regulator head in the second 'dry steam' dome had lost some of its moisture on the way. As boilers grew larger these deficiencies cured themselves and the double domes disappeared, but in the final days of American maximum power operation this problem once again reared its ugly head, but no real remedy had been found before the advent of other forms of motive power.

The foreign-ness of locomotive design was also a function of the manner in which the water supply was carried in the case of tank engines. Common practice was to have the bulk in side-tanks disposed on either side of the boiler, with a small further quantity below the coal space in the rear bunker, and this arrangement was usual in England and France. In Germanic and Scandinavian countries there was a liking to dispose some of the water in tanks carried between the frames and underneath the boiler, but the most dramatic effect upon appearance was where the whole supply was carried behind the cab over the trailing truck or bogie. There was a very good reason for this latter disposition, in that there was little change in weight on the coupled wheels as the water supplies became used up during the journey. For duties where a constant maximum adhesion was considered essential this layout was sometimes adopted, even if at some sacrifice to the total amount of water carried. Examples of this kind were the Dutch 4–8–4 4-cylinder tank engines built specially for mineral traffic, and the German Reichsbahn Type 62 4–6–4 tanks and when a number of Bundesbahn Type 38 4–6–0s were converted post-war into 4–6–4 tank engines for push and pull working, again the whole of the coal and water was carried over the trailing bogie.

The customs that grew up in different countries regarding methods of servicing and maintaining their motive power have naturally had their influence on the product. A deep cleavage existed in the case of sand, that somewhat incongruous substance which still, after all the years, remains the best means of establishing the grip of smooth wheel on smooth rail when conditions of adhesion are bad. Over most of the world, sandboxes, one or more in number according to the number of coupled wheels to be served, were placed on top of the boiler. Following the reasonable thought that if coal had to be supplied over the top of the tender coal spaces and bunkers, the feeding of sand into boxes above the boilers could equally well be achieved by one means or another, there was the undoubted advantage that the sand was kept in a warm place, and the valves and pipes leading therefrom could be kept equally free from the effects of condensation and moisture and of freezing in bad weather. Sometimes both neatness of appearance and still further assurance of dry sand were obtained by combining dome and sandbox under a continuous elongated casing, a feature much followed in Scandinavian countries. On British locomotives on the other hand, and their progeny overseas, sandboxes were always placed low down adjacent to the wheels they served. The low footplate was retained longer in Britain than elsewhere, a feature which favoured this particular sandbox position, and the position remained even after footplating was raised up to the boiler flanks. Shed equipment and custom were geared to the supply of sand manually by means of suitable spouted buckets, and this conservative way of doing lasted as long as steam in the British Isles. Although conducive to a neat aspect, and reducing to a minimum the length of sand piping which had to be maintained, troubles with moist and clogged sand were on the whole more prevalent with this second alternative.

This was one example of the logic of accessibility which was variously displayed about the world. Few would deny that everything requiring regular attention by the engine crew or at the depot should be placed so accessibly that it can be reached, and if need be taken down with a minimum of disturbance to adjacent ironmongery. And yet this aim has at all times and places conflicted not only with the artist which lurks deep within all true engineers, and which seeks a pleasing and orderly exterior aspect, but also with the sheer difficulty of finding a place for everything within a restricted space, of squeezing a quart into a pint pot as it were. American locomotives, whether at home or abroad, have usually carried the provision of accessibility to its utmost, a process which, as it has turned out, has not prevented the appearance of many strikingly handsome machines. For the locomotives of the rest of the world, as for its womenfolk, the past century has been one long saga of winning progressive freedom from the cult of seemliness, of covering everything up, of undue primness which in England was dubbed Victorian, and was no doubt described by similarly suitable nomenclature elsewhere. A glance through Charles Lake's *The World Locomotives* of 1904 shows, other than on its American pages, low footplates, splashers and an economy in outside embellishments, which was typical of its time. The pace at which design has become emancipated towards a transatlantic freedom, with consequential improvement in accessibility, has varied greatly, the products of the firm of Maffei of Munich, having already burst their bonds by the turn of the century, while in England on the other hand the process was painfully slow, and only really broke free in the last days of the LMS Railway and on the standard locomotives of the nationalised British Railways after 1951.

The extent to which the available labour force was prepared to do awkward work comes in here. Outside cylinders and valve gears and everything else visible and ready to hand was important where both supervisors and men had a non-technical background without any tradition of fine workmanship or meticulous care as was the case in America while mass immigration provided the bulk of the labour force. For the mechanics of England and Western Europe on the other hand, and especially those who had graduated into supervisory positions, it was an expected part of the day's work that men would have to take down the external coverings which masked the 'works' and to squeeze themselves into uncomfortable positions in order to reach complex machinery. Only thus could many of the earlier French compounds have been serviced, for example, whilst the practice at one time on a certain English railway of demanding that the inside of main frames be painted white, the better to show up the cleanliness and good maintenance of inside valve gear, was only an extreme example. The progress of locomotive engineering has seen the gradual averaging out of the human conditions which originally gave rise to such differences and the various stages in between have produced design and appearance variations which are manifest to the onlooker.

The training traditionally given to drivers and firemen, and their ability or otherwise to meet complex controls and to make adjustments to their engines while in service would clearly have an influence in what they were given to drive and adjust, and again, design processes emerged geared to these factors and to the existence of pooled or individual engine allocation. Once more a division took place between American and English practice on the one hand, and European practice and its derivatives on the other. The whole trend in the first of these sectors has been to keep the engines as simple as possible to drive, and so to design them that the increasing efficiency which advance in knowledge made possible was obtainable without any additional technical call upon the driver's skill. Similarly, adjustments to motion and running gear have been taken out of the hands of the driver altogether, so that in England as a case in point, he was latterly left with a single spanner as his sole tool, and that only for undoing lubricator caps. These features were necessary prerequisites to the extension of pooled working which at the expense of a measure of reliability in timekeeping, brought about a large reduction in operating costs, or more accurately speaking enabled them to remain at a low level against a background of ever-increasing wages and material costs. In this area all such features as wedge adjustments to axlebox and connecting and coupling-rod brasses, adjustable blastpipes, fine screw adjustments to valve rods, and in the case of compound engines, independent hp and lp valve gear and manually controlled intercepting valves have been discarded one by one.

The continental engineer, and more particularly his French colleague, has been less frightened of complication, and his training and mental equipment caused him to seek the theoretically perfect even if it gave rise to complexities calling for special training of the enginemen, and a high degree of individual allocation of motive power if the intended results were to be obtained. Thus the French crew was able to keep the wedges in the driving gear of their engines in such close adjustment that a knocking box or clanking rod end was seldom heard. Each run was a virtuoso performance in which the driver by fine adjustments of high- and low-pressure cylinder cut-offs, and by the judicious use of entry of high-pressure steam to the low-pressure cylinders while starting and even on the run, was able to coax a power output which per unit size of locomotive was unsurpassed elsewhere. The Gallic temperament was less suited by simplicity, and until the American 141R class engines came along post World War II, it was definitely less at home with, and less able to get brilliant performance from, simple expansion engines. Thus the locomotive designs of these two national schools of thought and behaviour, the American and the French, reflected the temperament and background of their peoples, with many gradations in between as other countries arrived at a position appropriate to their native disposition.

These then are some of the more important considerations which have influenced design practice from one country to another, in each case providing a valid reason, free from purely personal considerations, as to why something was done in such a manner by one administration but not by another. They do not between them, however, suffice to cover all of the items which can make a particular aspect of design look foreign. Take chimneys, for example, the feature which more than any other determines the aspect and character of any locomotive. The truly functional chimney is the stovepipe, and nothing more than its stark shape, correctly proportioned, is needed to get the best from any engine. But the shapes it has assumed throughout the world are legion with lip and base expressing the fancy of the individual designer. Before the American self-cleaning smokebox and internal spark arrester came along, or rather before it was generally accepted elsewhere, spark arresters were sometimes incorporated in the chimney itself in the form of inverted cones or the mushroom-shaped tops of the Gölsdorf era. Chimneys have been made fat to accommodate multiple blastpipe nozzles or to conceal ejector and pump exhausts, long and fat for double and triple blastpipes and long and thin to cope with the seven in line ejectors of Dr Adolf Giesl-Gieslingen. No feature is more characteristic than the chimney, a glimpse of which alone can usually allow the observer to judge the parentage of any given engine.

In like manner all kinds of shapes and profiles have been adopted on locomotives to cheat the effects of the wind. Leaving aside full stream-lining which became a widespread but thinly adopted fashion in the 1930s, many European administrations at the beginning of the century believed that some benefit to wind resistance came from conical smokebox doors and 'windcutter' cab fronts, and extreme examples of this were to be seen on the PLM in France and in Baden and Bavaria. As boilers increased in size and chimneys shortened, and more expansive use of the steam extended, the tendency of the exhaust to beat down and obscure the driver's vision called for use of deflector plates, some, uniformly useless, attached to the chimney itself and others, in the form of sideplates alongside the smokebox, of all kinds of sizes and shapes, doing in varying degree the job for which they were intended.

A miscellany of minor items must conclude our survey of 'foreign' features. Headlamps assumed a size and importance in inverse proportion to the civilised nature or otherwise of the terrain traversed, unfenced wide open spaces calling for a powerful searchlight to light the way ahead, with graduations downwards through a bright array to indicate clearly the approaching train at level crossings and low level platforms, to the almost pinpoint lights of British engines whose purpose was not to illuminate but to indicate train categories to traffic staff. The sounds which the steam engine produced while standing and running could be very national indeed. The sharp, deep-throated but choppy exhaust sound of a simple expansion engine working in short cut off with long travel valve gear has tended to characterise modern engines everywhere, but there were notable exceptions. Many older simple engines with short travel gear and poor steam passages emitted a kind of confused and strangulated roar, whilst modern French compound engines signalised their ultimate efficiency by light and feeble exhaust sounds whether at starting or lifting 500 tons up heavy grades. On the other hand, maximum power operation in America produced a dramatic thunder, the like of which we shall not hear again on railways. So with whistles, the high-pitched squeak emitted by a huge French 4–8–2 seeming as incongruous as the marvellous sounding American chime whistle emerging from some quite lowly engine type in Spain. Latterly the chime whistle spread widely over the world, but it was in its own country that it became typical of a way of life almost, and through travel and through films the characteristic wail sounding across city block, prairie or mountains became for many one of the basic sounds of the New World. In Russia, which also adopted the chime whistle, the designers managed to inject a raw and harsh note into the music, which was somehow more appropriate to that vast and unfriendly land.

Lastly there were the running numbers of the engines displayed on cabsides, buffer beams or smokeboxes. The systems of numbering adopted by different administrations have been legion, but they divided into four broad categories. First there was the random school, typified by the practice of the Pennsylvania Railway in America and by various English railways such as the London and North Western in England before 1925. Here new engines were allocated the numbers of previous old engines as they were withdrawn for scrapping. Numbers bestowed upon a given class were thus quite random and out of series, and they could not be used in any way for recognition purposes. The second group bestowed numbers in continuous series to each class so that the number of any individual engine at once signified to the initiated the group to which it belonged. The figures making up the numbers did not in themselves have any special significance. Of such were most American engine numberings, and this system also spread across Britain from 1923 onwards.

A third group, of which Germany was a principal example, used a prefix number before the consecutive running number of the engine itself. The prefix, which might be anywhere from 01 to 99 to designate the class, did not have any intrinsic meaning.

Finally there was the sophisticated group which sought to arrange things so that the engine number conveyed all kinds of information besides numerical order. Thus in France the first figure might indicate number of coupled axles or wheel arrangement, followed by a letter indicating the stage of design development, followed by the serial number. The ultimate was reached in Czechoslovakia, where the first digit gave the number of coupled axles and the second had to have three added to it so that when multiplied by ten it gave the maximum permitted speed in kilometres per hour. Then the third figure added to ten gave the axleload in metric tons. The fourth digit indicated the sub class if any, and then came the serial number proper of the engine within the class.

What has been described in this chapter, and more also, has served to build up the infinite variety of form, arrangement and detail which has been superimposed upon the basic steam locomotive concept. Whether selected by choice or necessity, still further diversification has been assured by the personal ideas and tastes of the many chief mechanical engineers or designers in private firms who have been responsible for the provision of motive power to meet traffic needs. To anyone like the present author who assembles data for an overall review, the similarity of dimensions and power output of innumerable engines is nearly as striking as the infinite diversity of their proportions, features and appearance.

CHAPTER THREE

America

THE AMERICAN STEAM LOCOMOTIVE scene was a gigantic one, alike for the extent of the United States' railroads, the numbers of locomotives in service and produced by individual builders, the relative size of the engines in any given epoch, and for its influence upon world trends. Route mileage, 192,000 (307200km) by the beginning of the twentieth century reached a maximum of 257,000 (411200km) in 1915. Bruce estimates that a total of 176,750 steam engines were built up to 1950, 105,500 in the last fifty years to 1950, and 59,000 of them by the largest single manufacturer. At their most numerous in 1924 there were 70,000 in stock on the different US railways, and in a single year, 1905, 6,300 locomotives were ordered. The largest engine of the steam era had sixteen coupled wheels divided into two groups, was 131ft (39·95m) long, had a grate area of 150sq ft (13·9m^2), and a starting tractive effort of 135,375lb (61300kg). It weighed with tender 519 English tons (528 tonnes). About 37,000 locomotives or 21 per cent of the total built were exported all over the world, and American practice had an increasing influence on the domestic locomotive designs in a number of countries of which Russia, India, South Africa and Australia were the principal. One million two hundred thousand employees served the home railways in 1949.

As has already been mentioned, the railroads opened up the country, and for long years the nation depended almost exclusively upon them for its continued growth of trade. Ever-increasing head end power was thus called for, and in a land of vast natural resources and an open-handed attitude to life, power and performance was held, from first to last, as of much greater importance than economy and high efficiency. Over much of the country the railroad came first with its low lineside platforms at stopping points. Grade crossings, whether in city or country, were the rule, and when these became intolerable to road traffic, the resulting bridges had to accommodate themselves to locomotive dimensions already well established. In this way high power provision was facilitated by a generous loading gauge 15ft (4572mm) high in the east, up to 16ft 5in (5000mm) in the west, with widths up to 11ft (3350mm). In a similar way bridges and permanent way would accept 24-ton (24·4 tonnes) axleloads as far back as 1904, and in later stages of development as much as 35 tons (35·5 tonnes) was permitted.

Locomotive design remained throughout an extraordinary mixture of individuality and conformity. The railways of the country were divided up into 132 systems classified by the Interstate Commerce Commission as Class I and almost innumerable minor ones, and unless, as occurred at rare intervals, a common financial management controlled the destinies of several lines, each railroad clung tenaciously to the layout and details which suited it best, and any imposed standardisation from without was resisted resolutely. On the other hand the majority of administrations had their engines built by one or other of the great private locomotive manufacturers which by 1905 had dwindled to three in number as far as main line engines were concerned, Baldwins, the American Locomotive Company and the Lima Locomotive Company. The price benefits of quantity production and quick deliveries were only obtainable by permitting these firms a big say in the design. Thus a considerable degree of hidden standardisation had to be swallowed in effect: a builder's rather than a customer's manifestation; only four railroads built any large proportion of their engines in their own workshops. The broad aspect of all American locomotives thus contained a strong family resemblance, to a much greater extent than was found in Europe, but the manufacturers were unable to reach their goal of maximum efficiency because every railway demanded its own detailed variations on the main theme. Neighbouring lines would thus demand small differences in dimensions and detail layout on engines destined for the same kind of service, with the result that in the final stages of steam when the 4–8–4 wheel arrangement as an example was almost universally accepted for high power mixed traffic operation, the more the engines of the different railroads approached one another in capacity, the greater were the detail variations which were demanded.

There was another influence which, far more than was the case in other countries, added to this complex of standardisation and individuality. This was the existence of a large and vigorous supply industry, auxiliary to the main builders, which sold proprietary fittings of all kinds, not only injectors and brake equipment as elsewhere, but almost every accessory fitting which a locomotive required or which its owning administration could be induced to buy. Of such were cast steel main frames, cylinder and valve liners and rings, drawgear, bearings and lubricating pads, power reverse gears, every kind of stop-cock and indicator, and a host of other things too numerous to mention. Successive batches of very similar engines for different railroads at a given makers would thus have to be equipped with an entirely different range of fittings, but it did mean that any given railroad could, if it remained faithful to its own accessory suppliers, achieve a measure of domestic standardisation of small parts and fittings. The typical American locomotive was in the outcome more of an assembly job, not necessarily any the worse for that and with a few notable exceptions, of which the Pennsylvania was the principal, it owed more to operating and management demands than it did to pure engineering. On the representative road there was a vice-president in charge of engineering at executive level, and there was a superintendent of motive power whose main preoccupation was getting the best out of the head end power from day to day. The chief mechanical engineer, so strong and individual an influence upon engine design in England, for example, was seldom to be found.

Conditions tended to be rugged, and locomotives congenitally shy of steam, or which needed nursing or specially skilled attention in one way or another, were liable to be discarded in quick time whereas in the old world quite a number of types displayed both these properties during a long and respected life. In this connection also the trend to paradox was seen in that ability to surmount severe operating conditions with a minimum of skilled attention made American designs very attractive to less sophisticated and emergent countries. On the other hand, even Americans themselves could hardly claim that their builders paid the same attention to close fits, meticulous workmanship and beautiful finish as was a matter of course in England or France, for example, and although in later years the gap narrowed almost to vanishing point, there were long years in the present century when an American locomotive as delivered was a fairly rough-and-ready job.

Finally in these general remarks, it is to be noted that engine classes seldom built up into large numbers, partly because of the continual pressure in each succeeding batch to achieve just that little bit more specific power, but mainly because of the large number of independent railways which shared the nation's traffic. In this chapter there will be no account of large-scale amalgamations, and even nationalisation, which elsewhere concentrated administration and produced large and sometimes even huge studs of the same design. In 1948 there were about 34,000 steam locomotives at work but the railway with

1 American design. Illinois Central Railroad 4–8–2 No 2452 [J. M. Jarvis

2 British design. Ex-London & North Eastern Railway Class B1 4–6–0 No 61167 [E. S. Cox

3 French design. Former Est Railway 4-cylinder de Glehn compound 4–6–2 No 31022 [*C. Shorto*

4 German design. Ex-Prussian State Railways Class P8 4–6–0 No 38.3086 [*E. S. Cox*

5 Austrian scene. Inside cylinder compound 4–6–0 No 917 in foreground. Tank engine behind has 'flower pot' type spark arresting chimney [*O. Bamer*

6 Backbone of Pennsylvania passenger services for thirty years. K4S Class 4–6–2 No 3740. Note lightweight Walschaert valve gear and Belpaire firebox, the latter unusual in US practice [*P. Ransome Wallis*

7 New York Central JIA Class 4–6–4 No 5280 heading the "Empire State Express"; Harmon (NY) to Chicago—962 miles without engine change [*J. M. Jarvis*

8 American Giant. Lehigh Valley 4–8–4 No 5101 at New Jersey, 1941. Coupled wheels 6ft 5in dia; whistle body inclined near chimney is 28in long, excluding valve; axle weight 30 tons [*P. Ransome-Wallis*

the largest route mileage, the Atcheson, Topeka and Santa Fe, had only 1,730 steam units in stock, and the New York Central and Pennsylvania systems which served the biggest centres of population, had 3,473 and 4,467 respectively, with diesels at this date hardly as yet building up to appreciable numbers. By contrast Russia had a single class of locomotive which totalled more than the motive power stock of these three railways put together.

I. 1900–1905

Let us now look at the state of the art in the United States as the century opened and in the first few years thereafter. Table 1 sets out a selection of the principal types which were running up to 1905. The 4–4–0, 2–6–0 and 4–6–0 types which had started life in 1840, 1860 and 1850 respectively were now on the way out, their capacity being no longer sufficient despite low cost and extreme simplicity. Over 50,000 of these machines had served the previous century well, and in particular the three-point suspension, consisting of bogie pivot, and one point on each side of the engine at the centre of the coupled wheel equalising system, had assured stable if lively riding over the relatively indifferent track which was common. The bar frames were originally introduced because no facilities existed at first within the country for rolling suitable plates, while smiths of average skill could produce a frame from moderate lengths of bar subsequently bolted together. These two features, suspension and frames, so suited the native conditions in which the engines had to operate that they remained with American practice to the end of steam.

For passenger work the 4–4–2 was the favoured type, with the 4–6–2 for the first time appearing on the horizon after a very short-lived phase in which a small number of 2–6–2s had been constructed. From the point of view of mere size, weight and tractive effort it is interesting to note how closely the Union Pacific 4–6–2 of 1903 (entry No 8) approximated to the dimensions of the British Britannia Pacific of 1951.

The 2–8–0 introduced in 1866 was still the principal type for freight haulage, and was currently being ordered in large numbers. Although first built experimentally as far back as 1870, the 2–10–0, unlike the case in Europe, did not find lasting favour, and while the Santa Fe introduced it in 1902, it was repeated only sporadically thereafter. On the other hand, the 2–10–2, built for the first time in 1903 for the Santa Fe, was the harbinger of a fairly wide adoption ultimately. The latest 'largest locomotive in the world' had at this time just been built in the form of a 0–6–6–0 Mallet articulated engine, forerunner of yet another basic type which in the years to follow spread over most American railways.

Although a tank engine is shown in the table, it was a rarity on the American scene, both before and afterwards, and until electrification or the diesel took over, most administrations preferred to operate their morning and evening 'commuter' services by demoted main line engines of earlier vintage, which, however unsuitable, had already largely paid for themselves and did not therefore weigh so heavily on the overall capital costs of operation as did purpose-built engines. Shunting work, unlike the case in Europe, was usually undertaken by 0–6–0 tender engines, the tender tank being sloped off to give good rearward vision. Without leading trucks they were considered unsuitable for line service, and again unlike Europe and particularly England, these engines were hardly ever seen on the main line in freight service and never on passenger trains.

Superheating was yet to come, but working pressures had risen to around 200lb/sq in (14kg/cm^2) and a number of railways obtained batches of compound engines usually alternative to similar engines with simple expansion. No railway adopted compounding universally, and of the four different systems in use none became pre-eminent and only one found any continuance. Although relatively high pressures were in use, the typical saturated simple expansion locomotive of the day could hardly better 25lb of steam per lhp hour (11·2kg per cheval-vapeur) but the best compound was found able to attain a steam rate of 21lb (9·4kg). There were quite a number of tandem compounds with hp and lp cylinders bolted end-on with the two pistons sharing the same piston rod and driving gear. This was not a very happy arrangement and some of the larger engines carried permanently a small crane on the smokebox side whose purpose was to assist in moving the hp cylinder aside after it had been unbolted from the lp cylinder, in order to service the lp pistons and valves. Another arrangement was the Vauclain in which hp and lp cylinders were disposed one above the other in a single casting on each side of the engine, the two pistons meeting in a combined crosshead whence the drive to the wheels was the same as on an ordinary two-cylinder engine. The Mallet compound articulated system was introduced into the US in 1904 and unlike the other compounds, continued in being to the end of steam. It carried two outside lp cylinders on the leading unit, and two outside hp cylinders on the trailing unit. The foregoing three systems, which retained outside drives only, commended themselves because with the class of labour available proper attention to and lubrication of motion between the frames was almost impossible to assure, and the level of precision in the machine and fitting shops was simply not up to making a durable job of the crank axle. It was for these reasons that the fourth system, the four-cylinder in line 'balanced' compound, although paying a bonus in reduction in destructive forces, and giving a 16 per cent steam saving over the saturated non-compound, was no more popular than the others. Compounding was gladly thrown overboard when the advent of superheating in 1905 was found to give by simpler and static means savings of 25 per cent and more. Only the Mallet type survived, and then only because on the maximum tonnage slow speed freight services on heavy grades for which this type was used in compound form some further economy was obtainable, even with superheated steam when full regulator full cut-off working was the order of the day.

Apart from the inescapable need for a starting valve for admitting steam direct to the lp cylinders, American designers resolutely resisted all thought of applying those further refinements of separate valve gears, independent cut-offs and independent hp exhaust which led to higher efficiency in Europe, and the single de Glehn compound of typical French design supplied to the Pennsylvania Railroad in 1906 had absolutely zero influence upon later development.

Very large boilers were already appearing at this time, and grate areas of 50sq ft (4·54m^2) and larger were becoming usual on engines having wide fireboxes fired with bituminous coal. Indeed American railways were coming to realise that it was not the engine but the fireman which represented the upper limit of available power at that time. Although there seemed an inexhaustible supply of husky immigrants whose bulging muscles were able to fire 5,000lb (2270kg) of coal per hour, a serious problem was arising which was only solved by the later advent of the mechanical stoker. A few railways served territory adjacent to anthracite mines, and to use the available slow-burning fuel, grates had to be enlarged into the region of 80sq ft (7·43m^2), although the amount of coal the fireman had to handle per hour was no greater, comparing like for like in the use of the two kinds of coal. These huge fireboxes, splayed out over the trailing wheels to the width of the loading gauge, produced for a time a curious phenomenon where the driver's cab was placed over the boiler ahead of the firebox, the fireman occupying a rudimentary second cab in the usual position. With successive increases in boiler diameter, this position became ultimately untenable, and in later and larger anthracite-burning engines the driver resumed his usual position.

These first years of the century were days of enormous industrial expansion, reflected in continuously increasing traffic on the railways. It was in one of these years, 1905, that, as already mentioned, no less than 6,000 new locomotives were ordered by the different lines. It was also a period of 'Boom or Bust' as a means of commercial progress, only 2,500 engines having been built in 1903, and orders were down to 1,000 in 1908, but by 1912 they had sprung up to 4,500. Hard-faced superintendents drove their motive power and their men to ever-increasing effort. In those free-wheeling days it was results that counted, and rather sketchy standards of inspection and workmanship gave rise to many homeric breakdowns, the full story of which is, alas, unlikely ever to be told. The boiler explosion, seldom experienced in the old world, in these years was still a dreaded and all too frequent occurrence. While mainly due to human carelessness, nevertheless it sometimes had its origins in the workshop and even on the drawing-board. So far as can be traced, foreign practice was neither studied nor countenanced, and by the same token, when the typical American product was exported to the old world, usually on the basis of quick delivery to some overseas administration whose domestic builders were for the time being full up, it was apt to be welcomed for its strong pull with plenty of steam, but to be rather sniffed at for its rough finish and moderate economy.

To the discerning there were some admirable features in American design, however, and although no engine was ever built in the United States for the Great Western Railway of England, Churchward, who became the Chief Mechanical Engineer of that system in 1902, introduced some of their features into his standard practice. The first was the casting of each outside cylinder with half the smokebox saddle, the two parts being bolted up the middle, a construction which gave a very secure anchorage against piston thrusts and a firm base on to which the front end of the boiler could be bedded, but at the expense of a certain weakness in the forward extension frames which had to be stiffened by massive stay rods from the smokebox. A second was the taper boiler barrel in conjunction with a Belpaire firebox sloping inwards and downwards at the back, with easy radii rather than flat surfaces and with a generous distance between the crowns of the inner and outer fireboxes to give maximum area of water surface to promote lively steam disengagement. K. J. Cook when Mechanical and Electrical Engineer of the Western Region read a paper on Churchward's developments,* and in it he showed a drawing of an Illinois Central Railroad boiler, booked into the Swindon Drawing office in 1902, which contained every feature subsequently adopted, and the parenthood of the GW series of standard boilers was effectively established, the prototype No 1 boiler with all these advantageous points of design emerging in February 1903. Apart from this, Canada and Mexico followed United States' practice *in toto*, and there was a scattering of the unadulterated home product round the world into countries not economically bound to any European sources. The German firm of Maffei of Munich, possibly as a result of a Baldwin importation of a Baldwin locomotive on to the Bavarian State Railways in 1900 (Table 7, entry 15), adopted the bar frame and the high running plate above the coupled wheels at the beginning of the century and all its products were so equipped thereafter.

II. 1906–1926

The next phase of American development can conveniently be taken as the years 1906 to 1926, including the time of World War I. The conventional still reigned supreme; road competition had hardly yet raised its head to galvanise administrations towards higher speeds, lighter weights, more intensive user, or refinements in design towards longer runs

* The late G. J. Churchward's *Locomotive Development on the Great Western Railway*. K. J. Cook, Proc Inst Loco Engrs No 214, 1950.

and repair periods. Increase in size and power went steadily forward, but in this period came two developments which revolutionised engine performance—the superheater and the mechanical stoker. There also became available the results of work on the stationary locomotive test plant of the Pennsylvania Railroad at Altoona, which not only greatly influenced design at home, but for the first time spread the substance of modern American thinking and practice into many design offices in other countries.

An overall glance at Table 2 will show how greatly power output had been stepped up. The 4–6–2 reigned supreme in passenger work with the 4–8–2 as yet relegated to fast freight services with smaller coupled wheel. The 2–8–2 had become the customary wheel arrangement for general freight, but ten-coupled engines were multiplying and the Mallet articulated engine had expanded from the single 0–6–6–0 for pusher service in 1904 to a plethora of different sizes and wheel arrangements working on the main line by 1926.

The German Schmidt return bend element type of superheater was brought to America at the beginning of this period, and, as in other countries it soon established its worth and superiority over other early attempts at the same thing. By 1910 the domestic superheater Co had been formed for its exploitation and no locomotive of any importance was built thereafter without it. It was the only foreign importation since the arrival of the earliest complete locomotives from England in the 1830s which has had any universal effect upon American practice. As a result of tests it was possible to report that for representative American applications, savings ranged from a minimum of 23 per cent to a maximum of 46 per cent, the economy increasing with the increased power required. It was found that 30 per cent higher capacity was derived from a given locomotive using superheated steam than from the same size and type of locomotive using saturated steam. With such a vista in front of them all administrations joyfully threw compounding overboard with its unwanted complications, except only in the case of slow-speed Mallets. So little had inside cranks and starting valves been to the liking of their engineers that no serious attempt was made, as was done in other parts of the world, to combine compounding with superheating, and only two such essays are on the record, a 4–8–2 experimental three-cylinder engine designed by the eminent designer Lawford Fry in 1926, and three very unconventional eight-coupled freight engines built for the Delaware and Hudson system between 1924 and 1933. None was sufficiently successful to warrant any continuance.

It was the mechanical stoker which removed the limitation on output imposed by the capacity of the fireman, and permitted the ultimate development of steam power, at first at home but ultimately all over the world. First introduced in 1905, it appeared in several forms, but by 1925 had settled down to the ultimate very simple but rugged combination of two-cylinder driving engine on the tender, screw conveyers into the cab, and steam-jet delivery of the coal on to the firebed from a table plate just inside the firehole. It was appreciated that this method of firing was more wasteful, not only because a lot of the coal was crushed into fine dust during its passage along the conveyors and was apt to get drawn straight through the firebox by the draught and ejected up the chimney unburned, but also due to the fact that the fireman, sitting at his ease with only a row of steam valves to control, was less likely to worry about efficiency of combustion than he did when every pound of coal had to be lifted by his muscles alone. On the other hand, the mechanical stoker enabled the fire to be carried in a much thinner bed, and it provided better combustion at high firing rates. It was easily able to cope with firing rates up to 40,000lb (18200kg) per hour, and could meet the needs of even the largest steam locomotives which it was feasible to build. A grate area of 50sq ft (4·54m^2) has usually been taken as the dividing line below which use of the stoker could hardly be justified, and from 1938 the American Interstate Commission ordered that all coal-burning engines must be fitted if the total weight on drivers exceeded 71½ tons (72·6 tonnes) for passenger engines and 101½ tons (103 tonnes) for freight.

Wherever operating conditions have approximated to those in the United States, as for instance in Russia, stokers have been fitted as a matter of course, but there were many other administrations whose traffic requirements put their engines on the border line of justification. Thus application was tentative in England and Germany, and it appeared only on a few classes in France, Australia and South Africa.

On the whole, engineers outside America were rather wary of the stoker because whatever its virtues, it used 20 per cent more coal at moderate output than did hand firing on the same engine as was established from Test Plant Results in America and in England, so hand firing tended to continue to be used wherever it was possible to do so. On the other hand, at very high output calling for firing rates of around 150lb (730kg/m²) of coal per sq ft of grate area there was little to choose between the two methods of firing, for the draught required to burn the coal in either case under these circumstaces was so great as to sweep a large proportion of the fuel straight up the chimney unburned.

Table 2 shows the arrival of two other developments, namely the re-introduction of three simple expansion cylinders for fast freight engines, and the use of four simple expansion cylinders instead of compound cylinders on the articulated engines. The three-cylinder arrangement had been used in tentative form on a few engines on the Philadelphia & Reading RR as far back as 1910, but in 1922 the American Locomotive Company converted a 4–8–2 locomotive for the New York Central. The reduction in crankpin loads through the division of the drive on to two axles, and the more even turning moment were at first acclaimed as the dawn of a new era. Dislike of inside valve gear led to the use of the Gresley conjugated gear to drive the inside valve, and some very big engines were built on this plan, including the remarkable 4–12–2s of the Union Pacific of which no less than 90 were put to work (entry No 7). Only what might be termed mixed traffic engines, of moderate speed, were thus equipped, but by 1930, after some 250 had been built in total, this bright dawn turned to stormy weather, for it was found quite impossible to design and maintain a crank axle in the space available which would stand up to the forces involved on these huge machines. The Gresley gear was another of the very rare importations of European ideas into American practice. Knowing the shortcomings of this gear in its own country of origin when maintenance facilities were reduced during the last war, it can be imagined how it was unlikely to commend itself across the Atlantic for long.

The use of simple expansion on articulated engines was introduced in the first place to get more reliable traction on heavy duty at the expense of a somewhat lower efficiency, because the compounds could be absolute brutes where one of the two independent units slipped, and choked receivers were the order of the day. No Mallet type engine could run faster than about 30mph(48kph) at this time due to the unstable riding of the front unit, and it was only much later in 1940 when improvements to boiler bearing and side control made speeds as high as 60mph (96kph) acceptable, that the four-cylinder simple expansion arrangement came into its own. Before leaving articulated engines in this period, attention is drawn to the so-called 'Triplex' (entry No 14) type in which besides the two power trucks under the boiler of the conventional Mallet a further truck was placed under the tender, the three main frames being connected by knuckle-joints. All six cylinders were of the same size, those in the centre being the hp, and the four at the outer ends being the lp, the engine under the tender exhausting straight to the atmosphere. Only four engines of this kind were ever built and this ambitious attempt to get something for nothing, as it were, was defeated by insufficient steam-producing capacity.

In following chapters we shall see a good deal of locomotive standardisation, not only of details but of complete series of engines, but as pointed out above, the regimentation which this implied was repugnant to the American way of life. It is of the more interest to refer therefore at this juncture to the only series of standard locomotives which was ever produced in the USA for service on the railways as a whole. That country entered World War I in 1917 and in 1918 all the railways were taken over by the Government under a body known as the United States Railroad Administration. Before a return to private ownership was effected in 1920, a Standardisation Committee had been set up comprising builders and users and a standard series of twelve locomotive types was born. These are set out in Table 3 and it will be seen that they paralleled the principal varieties being offered by private industry up to the time its output was sawn off in the interests of military production. They were a thoroughly workmanlike series and 1,830 were built, the 2–8–2 type accounting for nearly half the total. It is to be feared that the use of common details left something to be desired, and it was clearly a field day for the supply trade. This is exemplified by the fact, seen in the table, that two proprietary valve gears sponsored by accessory firms were specified for ten out of the twelve classes in place of the royalty-free Walschaert's gear. After 1920 the Standardisation Committee was disbanded, and all the parties went their own ways, so that the whole thing caused no more than a ripple on the surface of locomotive history in the New World.

Not so visible to the naked eye were some further improvements of this period, the booster in 1914, inverted rocker side control for bogies and trucks in 1915 and the one-piece cast steel bed in 1923. None of them had any wide use abroad, but the two last mentioned proved indispensable features in the ultimate development of steam in America, the first because it was the only way to apply adequate lateral guiding force to the extremities of such vast engines and the latter as the solution to intolerable frame troubles as axle weights and piston thrusts grew to gigantic values.

Problems of the increasing size and power output of boilers were ash disposal and adequate air inlet to the firebed. These will be enlarged upon later, but they account for the general unpopularity of coupled wheels under the firebox, and only a trailing truck with its smaller wheels either two or four in number would leave space for an acceptable ashpan design. This truck was unproductive in that the weight it carried was not available for adhesion. Thus was born the booster, a small two-cylinder auxiliary steam engine whose crankshaft was geared through an idler wheel to one axle of the truck. The idler wheel could be engaged or disengaged by an air cylinder whose control was interlocked in such a way that the driver could only bring the booster into use when the main engine was set in or near full gear. It contributed from 10,000 to 14,000lb (4550 to 6380kg) additional tractive effort at starting and could be left in gear up to a running speed which at first did not exceed 15mph (24kph), but which after further development could be left in up to 30mph (48kph). It was an obvious help in starting heavy tonnage freight trains out of difficult places, and in passenger service it was an aid to rapid acceleration particularly on heavy trains with frequent stops. The little engine could, however, be making 300rpm at a road speed of 15mph (24kph), and the getting of it into and out of gear was a somewhat crude process so that maintenance was heavy. Its acceptance therefore was somewhat mixed, some roads such as the New York Central using it on all of its modern types up to 1937, whilst others like the Pennsylvania did not use it at all. In the really large engines in the last phase of steam with eight or more coupled wheels its use was gradually abandoned. Abroad it attracted the interest of Sir Nigel Gresley of the British London and North Eastern Railway, and he fitted successively an Ivatt Atlantic, two three-cylinder 2–8–2 freight engines and a Robinson 0–8–4 tank engine, the latter used on hump shunting. With some adjustments to the original design it did what was intended, but its use was given up when first cost and maintenance was set against the more moderate advantages it gave under British conditions. Elsewhere applications have similarly only been in small numbers and with like results.

In World War I, large numbers of engines were built for the different theatres, and in particular a moderate-sized 2–8–0 designed to the British loading gauge was used by the US Army, of which large numbers remained behind in Belgium and France at the war's end (Table 7, entry 1). This was hardly a typically modern product, having a narrow firebox, and it had no influence on further practice in those countries. None worked in England of which any record remains. The large and typical 2–10–0 engines built at the same time for Russia and shipped from West coast ports to Vladivostok, introduced that country for the first time to American practice in modern form, and the seeds thus sown bore fruit in future years, since there were many obvious similarities between Russian and American operating conditions. Table 7 indicates further exports in the immediate post-war which enlarged the acquaintance of the Old World with the products of the New. Having short travel valves and straightforward but none too generous steam ports and passages these engines did not distinguish themselves efficiency-wise, as will be seen in Chapter 5, but all were competent to do a good traffic job. The author encountered one of the Madras and Southern Mahratta Pacifics when on a visit to India in 1938, and although everything rattled and pounded, its lively progression along the track contained no tendency to build up lateral oscillations such as were bedevilling its British designed counterparts to the point of acute danger at the same time.

The arrival in South Africa of prototype 4–6–2 and 4–8–2 engines from Baldwins in 1925 introduced the SAR to the American way of doing, and although thereafter its main intake was from Britain and Germany, future deliveries displayed an unmistakable transatlantic content in their design. The first three entries in Table 8 witness a similar introduction into the Australian continent. Here it was not a case of prototypes and proven merit, but arose from the appointment of Americans to the leading engineering posts on the South Australian Railways. It never occurred to them to do otherwise than use 100 per cent American design for their new motive power, and the three classes introduced in 1926 were as typical as any running in their home country, except for the rather remarkable fact that they were all built by the firm of Armstrong Whitworth in Great Britain.

Of much greater influence abroad than these various exports was the work of the stationary test plant owned by the Pennsylvania Railroad. Originally built in 1904 and set up at the St Louis Exhibition of that year, it was transplanted thereafter to Altoona, adjacent to that railroad's main workshop, and from 1906 onwards, it undertook performance and efficiency tests of successive locomotive developments over the next thirty years. Not only so, but it made the results available to the world through publication of a series of Test Bulletins, and the results obtained been have studied in design offices, and analysed by commentators in many other countries. Since French and German examples were brought over to be tested for comparison alongside native products at St Louis and since the last published results covered the T_1 class of 4–4–4–4 high speed passenger engines built as late as 1942, the sum total of the information which was released offers a remarkable running commentary upon the comparative course of American locomotive development in the present century.

Because the Altoona plant was owned by the Pennsylvania, it rather naturally only tested engines belonging to its own administration and having made the results generally available it did not feel disposed to find time on its rollers for engines belonging to other lines or for prototypes from the big outside builders. Moreover Pennsylvania engines were a little untypical in that they were usually designed and built by the railroad itself, and they tended to be of moderate size even at the expense of double heading, while other railroads maintained an unbroken advance in size and power. This said, however, they were sufficiently representative, and Table 4 sets out some of the results obtained, showing for each class of engine figures applicable to the point of highest steam production as well as to the point of lowest steam consumption per Indicated horsepower hour. A number of aspects emerges from this survey. Firstly, superheating brought down the steam consumption per Ihp from the order of 24lb (10·8kg/cv) to around 17lb (7·6kg/cv), a gain of almost 30 per cent, greater by this relatively cheap fitting than compounding had effected at more cost and complication. Secondly, the nature of the prevailing traffic requirements is seen in deflecting design towards making minimum steam consumption coincident with a relatively high power output. Even with the very big grate areas provided, the firing rate at lowest steam user tended to be high, so that boiler efficiency was rather low. Thus even with the refinements in design which the Pennsylvania in particular introduced up to the 1920s onerous operating demands tended to blanket the gains from technical improvement, and the analysis thus provided permitted administrations everywhere to appreciate something of the realities of locomotive economics. This trend continued to the end of American steam and in the case of the final Pennsylvania design, with 200° F (94° C) more steam temperature, poppet valves and enlarged ports and passages à la Chapelon, 5,000hp was obtained with the very creditable minimum steam consumption of 13·6lb (6·10kg/cv) per hp hour and cylinder efficiency of around 14 per cent but with boiler efficiency sunk to little more than 50 per cent.

Another point visible from the table is the manner in which freight engines were designed in the 1912–16 period for low-speed operation, with their lowest steam consumptions being reached at high output round about 20mph (32kph). The characteristics of the curve of steam consumption with power was very flat, which itself encouraged the hanging of everything behind the tender which the engine could move, and it was to ameliorate such conditions that the idea of 'limited cut-off' was developed. In the I1s class of 2–10–0 engines the cylinders were enlarged and valve events rearranged so that full tractive effort was obtained at 50 per cent cut-off, and the driver could no longer work at 70 per cent or more as in conventional machines. As will be seen in the table, this pulled steam consumption down from 20·2 to 16·4lb/1hp (9·06 to 7·36kg/cv) at maximum steaming capacity, a saving of 19 per cent compared with the L_1s class with the normal arrangement. The advantages of this device were mitigated by starting difficulties, insufficiently overcome by the provision of small auxiliary ports which admitted additional steam at the blind spots in the turning moment diagram, and the whole thing was of decreasing use at higher speeds of operation. Although applied to a few freight designs on other railways, limited cut-off never became widely popular on two-cylinder engines.

Now it can be asked, if the Altoona plant results so thoroughly illuminated American conditions of working, how can it be stated that they had a world-wide influence? The answer is twofold. In the more obvious case, the ability to isolate the variables one by one whilst keeping other factors constant led to an understanding of the interrelation of the different aspects of locomotive design which had not hitherto been available and which could be applied in a fully valid manner to other schools of locomotive thought and practice elsewhere. The second answer is that testing was not confined to measurement of the overall performance of complete locomotives, but covered a multitude of specialised aspects such as size and type of piston valves, mechanical versus hand firing, different kinds of superheater and level of superheat, blastpipe and chimney proportions and many others. Here again, there was much to be learned from this in countries not themselves having access to stationary test plants. Much to be learned it is true, but certainly not everything, for Altoona and American design generally was not interested in the short cut off high efficiency working which the traffic and economic conditions in Europe rendered useful and necessary. In the whole of the Test Bulletins, for example, there is no mention or analysis of the importance and effect of steam lap and valve travel, a factor which turned out to be as important as superheating itself in the improvement of locomotive efficiency in Europe. It was to fill these gaps that there was a long agitation for the building of test plants elsewhere, leading to eventual construction at Vitry in France and Rugby in England.

The active years of Altoona and of Pennsylvania locomotive development were from 1904 to 1917. Afterwards things became more sporadic, and with the production of the M_1 4–8–2 type in 1923, no more new designs were produced until the 'Duplex' locomotives of 1942–4, and the plant became correspondingly underemployed. In the great slump of the late 'twenties, and with the increasing effect of road and air competition thereafter, a management unsubsidised from any external source drew the purse strings tight upon research and development.

On a visit to Altoona at the end of 1945 the Test Plant was seen to be neglected and forlorn. Having been the mecca of countless locomotive engineers from many countries through the years it was sad indeed to see its approaching end. It is true that the Q class 4–4–6–4 engine had recently been tested and had produced the phenomenal steam output of 137,476lb/hr (62500kg/hr), but no Bulletin of which there is any record here was published for external study.

III. 1927–1949

The last phase of American steam ran from the late 1920s to the building of the last of the species in 1949 and Table 5 sets out the principal land marks in this period. The appearance of the first lightweight high speed diesel trains here as in Germany alerted the steam interests to do something about it, and between 1935 and 1938 there appeared a few engines of moderate size with large coupled wheels specifically aimed at competing with the newcomers. The first entry in the table is typical. The moderate cylinder dimensions and resultant tractive effort were at a European rather than an American level, but grate areas of over 60sq ft (5·6m²) and axleloads of more than 30 tons (30·5 tonnes) claimed them for the New World. Just as with diesel traction, so with the early steam hauled lightweight flyers, it was soon found that the public would not patronise sub-standard accommodation, and a second and last phase of this specialised effort called for head end power hardly less than for ordinary service, and the streamlined Milwaukee 4–6–4 in the fourth entry marked the end of this short-lived manifestation.

Another change was the increase in the size of the coupled wheel for freight operation. Against the onslaughts by the sprightly motor truck the low speed of steam railroad freight haulage would no longer suffice to retain the traffic. After a disastrous period in which existing engines were speeded up with much rail distortion and breakage due to insufficient balancing of the moving parts, a new generation of locomotives for this service became essential, capable of at least 60mph (96kph) not only by virtue of increased wheel size but also because the revolving and reciprocating parts were properly balanced across the locomotive, a practice formerly more evident in the breach than in the observance. By the same token, money being short in the hard times of the early 'thirties, quite a number of existing engines was rebuilt to include these features.

Some notable 4–6–4 engines were built in the period and the manner in which the New York Central developed the type form the J_1A class of 1927 to its final manifestation the J_3A class in 1938 (entries 2 and 3) indicates the advances in design which were applied in varying degree to all American construction at this time. These are the items in order of their application which were adopted on successive batches and often applied retrospectively at major repairs: Large volume steam chest with enlarged ports and passages; feed water heater recessed into smokebox with centrifugal boiler feed pump; full dynamic balancing of lightweight reciprocating parts; multiple valve front end regulator; cast steel beds with integral cylinders; increased boiler pressure, and roller bearings to all wheels. A few engines had a streamline casing for publicity reasons but it was soon—and thankfully—removed.

Retaining virtually the same starting tractive effort and grate area, the J_3A developed a maximum indicated hp of 4,725 and drawbar hp of 3,880, as against corresponding figures of 3,900 and 3,240 respectively for the J_1. Steam and coal per 1hp (cv) were 14·76 (6·60) and 1·84lb (0·82kg) as against 15·44 (6·92) and 1·94lb (0·87kg). The original J_1A engine weighed, as will be seen in the table, 153 tons (155·7 tonnes) in working order. The various improvements as listed above which were applied in stages caused its final manifestation, the class J_1E to weigh 157·5 tons (160 tonnes). The J_3A with its increased power output weighed only 3 tons more, so that there was a betterment of specific weight per indicated horsepower of 15·5 per cent. This last achievement was also the result of a vigorous weight-saving campaign in the design which included such features as nickel-steel boiler plates, corten steel air reservoirs, aluminium cab, running-boards and boiler clothing, and lightweight valve gear.

The foregoing epitomises the kind of advances in equipment which were made over the last two decades of American steam, but it was the advance to and development of the 4–8–4 type which brought it to its final form for passenger and mixed traffic service. Table 5 picks out two classes of this type in order to set them alongside development generally, but the 4–8–4 is worth a rather closer look, for it represented a last fling on the part of the railroads in asserting their individuality before the diesel imposed a take-it-or-leave-it policy with only manufacturers' standard designs available to choose from. Table 6 lists thirty separate designs of 4–8–4 which were produced for twenty-six of the principal railroads between 1929 and 1946. There were only about 1,000 engines of this wheel arrangement produced in the whole period, but however small the series, each railway must have something different from the others, even although the level of power provision in this traffic category seems to have levelled out. The similarity in general size and power disclosed in this table is almost as remarkable as the fragmentation of dimensions of the principal components.

Twenty-three of the engines had nominal tractive efforts between 60,000 and 69,800lb (27170 and 31650kg) and the widest span was from 57,000 to 73,000lb (25830 to 33200kg). Nineteen engines had adhesive weights between 120·6 tons (122·6 tonnes) and 129·5 tons (131·6 tonnes), and yet, to produce this very similar head end power, there were twelve different cylinder sizes, ten-coupled wheel diameters between 5ft 10in and 6ft 8in (1778mm and 2032mm) and ten different working pressures from 225 to 300lb/sq in (15·8 to 21·1kg/sq cm). Grate areas shaded off in no less than twenty-three variations between 77·3 and 115·0sq ft (7·17 and 10·67m²), and no two boilers had exactly the same linear dimensions or heating surfaces. When it is realised that except for a tiny number built in railroad shops, the classes listed were the products of only the three principal manufacturers, the design cost per locomotive must have been considerable.

But this was not all. To accompany these steps in principal dimensions there were even greater variations in details fɹom class to class. To mention only some, there could be Baker or Walschaert valve gear, and with the latter open or box-type expansion links, with the reversing rod lifting the valve rod in front of or behind the link. While the single top slidebar with multiple bearing surfaces was preferred, the Laird two-bar type was also found. Bogies and trailing trucks had various wheelbases, the former having either inside or outside axle bearings, and the latter with or without a booster. The boiler top presented every aspect from separate dome and sandbox through a combined casing covering both, to a continuous streamline casing enveloping the chimney as well. Sand pipes and boiler feed pipes ran the gamut from total exposure to complete disappearance behind the clothing. Such was the luxuriance of American steam in its last stages, and yet each and every machine was as typical of its land of origin as any other, and despite the variations which have been described the whole collection were somehow extraordinarily alike in external appearance and in basic technical content.

It is indeed tempting to the outsider to conclude that not more than three standard designs with common details and fittings could have done the work of the whole of this surfeit of variety; but such a thought would have been abhorrent to the men in charge at the time in question.

Before passing on, the magnitude of the American scene is emphasised when it is realised that there were four more and different designs of 4–8–4 on the Canadian railways which narrowly followed the practice of their southern neighbours to say nothing of another such design for the Mexican Railways which did likewise. Then there were at least eighteen more Class 1 railroads in the States, not mentioned in the table because they had no 4–8–4s, using instead 4–8–2s or other appropriate wheel arrangements for comparable traffic. Amongst these were such well-known names as the Pennsylvania, New York, New Haven & Hartford, Illinois Central, Baltimore & Ohio, and Southern Railway.

Brief mention was made above of 'Duplex' locomotives, or to give them their proper name, four-cylinder rigid frame engines. It has also been described how difficulties with spring centering devices and the hinged connection between front and rear units held down the speed capabilities of articulated locomotives. To overcome these troubles the Baldwin Locomotive Company since 1932 had tried to interest various railways in a rigid framed alternative without result, but in 1937 the Baltimore & Ohio had a 4–4–4–4 prototype constructed in its own shops. The Pennsylvania also became interested and in collaboration with all three builders produced a 6–4–4–6 experimental engine in 1938 which was a striking exhibit at the World's Fair in 1939. This very large engine was of greater capacity than was needed and a rather smaller 4–4–4–4 edition was built to the extent of two prototypes by Baldwin in 1942. Fifty more were constructed half by Altoona and half by Baldwin in 1945 (entry 7 in Table 5) and this T_1 class became the Pennsylvania's answer to the 4–8–4 development elsewhere.

During the last war this railway found itself without a freight engine design of maximum power, having nothing bigger than the 2–10–0 of 1916 vintage already described.* Exceptional traffics had to be met and the unusual course was taken of having Altoona build 125 2–10–4 engines of Chesapeake & Ohio design (entry No 8). With this holding operation under way, the Juniata workshops, having built a 4–6–4–4 prototype in 1942, proceeded to construct a series of 25 of the 4–4–6–4 type but different cylinder arrangement, the Q2 class of 1942 (entry No 14) which was directly comparable in size with the 2–10–4. The reason for going to the Duplex arrangement in both passenger and freight applications was mainly to reduce the piston thrust which on the C&O type of engine amounted to 178,300lb (80900kg) per cylinder. Splitting up the wheelbase into two driven units produced thrusts of only 92,000 and 133,000lb (41800 and 60500kg) in the two and three axle units respectively. Another advantage favouring high power at speed was the possibility of having larger valves, ports and passages *pro rata* in each of the four smaller cylinders compared with the two large ones. These two designs, the T_1 and the

* It is true that there was an experimental 2–8–8–0 simple expansion articulated engine, but this was never repeated.

Q2, were of exceptional power output. While the T_1 produced a maximum of 6,666 lhp at 100mph (160kph) on the plant the Q2 reached nearly 8,000 lhp with a 40 per cent cut-off at 57mph (91kph). It is sad to relate that all this brilliant achievement failed to live up to its first promise in daily service for the fact that the two groups of wheels were uncoupled had a fatal effect upon reliable adhesion in the arduous running conditions the engines had to undertake. No other locomotives of this kind were built at home or abroad.

No further twelve-coupled non-articulated engine was attempted and the 2–10–4 of the Atcheson, Topeka & Sante Fe remained the largest of its kind, being in two respects the biggest engine in America, with its 30in × 34in (762 × 864mm) cylinders and its boiler pressure of 310lb/sq in (22kg/cm²) with normal firebox construction. This giant with five pairs of 6ft 2in (1880mm) diameter coupled wheels carried a boiler 8ft (2438mm) diameter, 41ft 9in (12725mm) long, to which the smokebox added another 12ft 6in (3810mm). The firebox crown sheet was 18ft (5486mm) long and the grate measured 13ft 6in (4115mm) long by 9ft (2750mm) wide.

The full flowering of the simple expansion articulated engine began about 1928 and the rest of Table 5 indicates the most notable examples. No one design was 'biggest' in all respects, but maximum dimensions reached 28in × 32in (711 × 814mm) for the four cylinders, 300lb (21·1kg/cm) working pressure, 182sq ft (16·9m²) of grate area, and 146,000lb (62500kg) of starting tractive effort. Maximum axle load was 37½ tons (38·1 tonnes), and the greatest adhesive weight 247 tons (251 tonnes) with a maximum engine weight in working order of 344 tons (350 tonnes), 519 tons (527 tonnes) including the tender. Compounding practically died away as the unstable riding habits of this kind of engine were overcome by use of flat front boiler bearing surfaces and introduction of a four-wheeled leading bogie so as to permit higher speeds. Even 60mph (96kph) and above became commonplace with such machines as the Union Pacific 4–6–6–4 (entry 10). No test plant was capable of taking these monsters, so we are without much factual information as regards their performance and efficiency, although we do know that some would burn as much as 18 tons (18·3 tonnes) of coal per hour in daily service. The question of the ultimate limitations of locomotive power is discussed in another chapter but it may be said here that it is difficult to foresee what further development in power output could have been possible for conventional steam, had the diesel not appeared at this particular juncture. The end, when it came in 1949, was rather an anticlimax in that the last steam locomotive which was built was a compound Mallet of moderate size for the Chesapeake & Ohio, a rather strange reversion against the general trend.

The thirteen volumes of the publication sponsored by the Mechanical Division of the American Railway Association and its predecessors, known first as the *Locomotive Dictionary* and then as the *Locomotive Cyclopedia*, give what is probably the most complete record, from 1906 to 1947, with illustrations and drawings of all aspects of steam-engine design, available in any country in the world. Therein the student can trace step by step not only the burgeoning forth of the modern American locomotive as a whole of which this chapter can give no more than a skeletal impression, but also practice down to the smallest details and fitments. To summarise so vast a cornucopia in any intelligent manner is wellnigh impossible, and there is only space here to refer to a few of the principal features which not only brought home practice to its final high level, but also commended themselves for adoption by railways in other parts of the world.

The heart of a boiler is of course the inner firebox and this was universally made of thin steel plate in America and traditionally of rather thicker copper plates in Europe and other parts of the world following European practice. While power outputs were moderate, available water of mixed quality, and where riveting was the only method of joining the plate overlaps, there was little to choose between the two materials, notwithstanding loud arguments by protagonists on either side. Gradually, however, the balance of advantage swung towards use of steel and this material was progressively invading erstwhile copper box territory as steam drew to its end. The developments which supported this trend were almost exclusively of American origin starting with the use of welding, first to repair cracks which developed from stayholes, then continuing with the butt welding of sides to backplates and tubeplates. Repairs were greatly facilitated by the ability to weld in patch plates and half sides to replace thin and corroded sections. This could be done if desired *in situ* without lifting the boiler since removal of the trailing truck, grate, and built-up ashpan typical of US design left only the two thin rear bar frame extensions in the way when firebox repairs were undertaken from floor level. These arrangements were naturally very welcome to a number of other countries with rudimentary shop capacity. It was however when maximum power operation became essential that the steel box really came into its own, for once again ease of welding permitted better securing of the tubes into firebox tubeplate, wide use of the flexible staybolts, and introduction of thermic syphons or arch tubes to improve circulation, all factors which resisted, without rapid deterioration, the enormous thermal stresses of high output from the Stephenson boiler, and the methods of servicing which intensive user made necessary. Use of 100 per cent lineside water treatment wherever applied was removing the bogeys of corrosion and overheating and wasting of the plates under scale, so that the ultimate attainment of the all welded boiler, cautiously introduced in 1938, was at last becoming a practical reality, and its application was developed and widely extended in Germany during and after the last war.

The frequently lower grades of coal plus the need for high output brought American practice far earlier up against the limitations of the simple bar type grate than was the case in Europe, and a grate made up of rocking sections became necessary so that the ash and clinker could be shaken out of the fire at intermediate points. At a later stage such grates were arranged so that the sections could be turned through 90° at will, thus decanting a spent fire into the ashpan at the end of a trip, and the ashpan in turn was equipped with bottom doors through which ashes and dead fire together could drop into the disposal pit on the depot. The hopper type ashpan as it was called was adopted early in the century in Europe especially where coal was poor, but it was only quite late in the day that these devices became standard practice in Great Britain. Use of wartime WD locomotives brought over by the American Army paved the way, and from 1945 onwards first the LMS Railway and finally the nationalised British Railways adopted them as standard.

At the same time the American self-cleaning smokebox was adopted by these administrations as well as in Australia, South Africa, India and many other places responding to American practice. In a pioneer country such as the USA the fire hazard could not be tolerated from hard-worked locomotives spreading incandescent cinders over the countryside, and in 1905 the Master Mechanics' front end solved the problem by a system of plates across the smokebox which compelled the hot cinders issuing from the tubes to be bounced at high velocity against full width netting, with the final result that the grit and char emerging from the chimney-top was black and harmless while the smokebox itself was kept free of accumulations of the products of combustion. This device did not commend itself to many European engineers partly because of the debit upon efficiency which the extra draught to work it called for by way of higher exhaust pressures, and partly because the blatant scattering of fine ash over the adjacent customers and property was considered anti-social.

Bar frames and their derivative, the integral cast steel bed, were another American feature which spread widely over the world.* At moderate piston thrusts and power output they tended to be more resistant to cracking due to lateral bending than were the plate frames general in the Old World, this advantage also arising from the central position of the former in relation to springs and axleboxes. This advantage, never more than marginal if the respective designs were right, fell away as powers increased, the bar frame in its turn becoming prone not only to cracks and fracture but also to wear and loosening of the bolts which connected the various members together. Ultimate levels of operation in the States would have become quite uneconomic but for the development of the locomotive bed, combining in one huge casting, cylinders, saddle, side frames and all cross stretches. First introduced in 1925, foundation beds of this kind were exported to form the backbone of super power engines in many parts of the world, notably in Australia and South Africa.

To run coupled axleboxes free of heating and wear remained for many years the number one problem on most railways everywhere in that the usual form of journal axlebox was ill-fitted to take lateral and piston thrusts, while its running cool upon the journal demanded a completeness of lubrication and an accuracy of machining and alignment which was at first unattainable. The Americans soon found that the combination of their heavy loads, rough service conditions, and coarse machining methods were best met by axleboxes presenting only brass surfaces to the load, lubricated not by oil but by hard grease, applied in the form of sticks or cakes of soap-like consistency, pressed by springs against the journal. This gave very high resistance to rotation when cool, and bearings so lubricated ran at considerable temperatures by deliberate intent. Side rods and connecting rod big-ends were also grease lubricated, and the need to recharge the grease every 150 miles or so was a big obstacle in the way of long non-stop runs. But it worked well enough to impress other railways about the world suffering severe climatic or operating conditions, and experiencing insufferable trouble with their oil lubricated bearings, so that the system was seen on parts of the indigenous stock of India, South Africa, Australia and of course on engines exported from the USA itself. It was as late as 1930 that the Timken Company perfected a system of large roller bearings suitable for locomotive coupled axleboxes, and the famous demonstration 4–8–4 locomotive No 1111 was sent all over the country to show what could be done. Although expensive, these bearings transformed running conditions in fast heavy service, and they were widely applied both domestically and abroad in the last twenty years of steam. They were not universally acclaimed, however, in countries where traffic demanded lower powers, because development had also been continuous there with the normal type of oil lubricated journal bearing, and so far as coupled bearings were concerned, the hot box had disappeared for all practical purposes, and mileage between repairs had climbed to a level which challenged the roller bearing on all-in cost. Steam, however, came to an end before the best choice was finally resolved in such countries as England, France or Germany.

These were some of the bigger items which crossed the Atlantic from West to East, and there were of course many others from automatic couplers to chime whistles. An interesting study too would be to examine those other ingredients of American steam which failed to transplant successfully or in any quantity to other climes, such as Baker valve gear, dual metal piston and valve rings, cast steel beds for tenders and roller bearing side rods, but space forbids.

Reference has already been made to the comparative indifference of American designers to refinements in valve events. This is not to say of course that they did not receive some share of attention, and indeed two books on the subject found their way to England and were by this author's side when it was his task to lay out the valve gear for a new

* It can be claimed that bar frames originated in England with the first Bury locomotives of 1830, but all the real development of this kind of frame was American.

2–6–0 design in 1924. But references to the effects of variations in steam lap and lead and valve travel are rare in the generality of railway engineering literature on the other side of the Atlantic and it is clear that no such revolution in effectiveness and efficiency due to manipulation of these factors took place as was the case in England and Germany. Indeed it is very difficult to find out what were the prevailing steam laps at any given period, but the Pennsylvania M1 class 4–8–2 of 1923 had 27in × 30in (686mm × 762mm) cylinders, 12in (305mm) diameter piston valves, steam lap $1\frac{7}{16}$in (36·5mm) lead $\frac{9}{32}$in (7·1mm) exhaust clearance $\frac{7}{16}$in (11·1mm) and a valve travel of 7in (178mm), and it is possible that these events were representative of more enlightened practice over a fairly long period. It was only at the very end of steam that, in desperation to achieve a long delayed higher cylinder efficiency in the face of the approaching diesel, steam distribution was seriously attacked, and trials with poppet valve gears of one kind and another opened the eyes of the designers as to what more was possible. By that time, however, it was much too late. In considering the above it is only fair to add that due to the insatiable power demands, engines were rarely worked below 35 per cent cut-off, and often at 50 per cent and more, and under these circumstances the niceties of obtaining full-bodied indicator cards at 15 to 20 per cent cut-off were largely academic.

Let us finish this chapter with a glance at the final exports of complete steam locomotives from America together with a number of types clearly derived from American thinking. Tables 7 and 8 set out examples of the massive outward pouring of locomotives into the war zones, and of replacements of much needed motive power after hostilities ceased, together with engines in the American style designed and built elsewhere. As in World War I, a moderate-sized 2–8–0 was designed for army supply in Europe, but this time it was a far better product with wide firebox boiler (Table 7, entry 8) and unlike its predecessor it was used widely in England before being drawn off after the invasion of France. Some of these engines, suitably modified as to gauge, were also sent to Russia, while after the war and the division of Europe by the Iron Curtain, many found themselves on the Eastern side and they are to be seen to this day hard at work in large numbers, especially in Hungary and Poland. A small and very American-looking 0–6–0 tank also appeared in smaller numbers, some of which remained at work on the Southern Region of British Railways up to the very end of steam. It was experience with the 2–8–0s which as mentioned above so powerfully influenced British Railways towards adoption of some of the front and back end features with which they were equipped.

A larger 2–8–2 (entry 9) was sent to Iran, India and Australia, and some of this design ended up in Portugal and Turkey. Lastly, as purely wartime products, the Russians ordered further large numbers of the same design and size of 2–10–0 which they had had sent to them in the first war (entry 2). In this they exhibited a characteristic trait which has underlined through many years their attitude to things mechanical, namely to cling to something they know well and which will work under their particular conditions, even if it is out of date and of less than modern potential. The lessons learned with these engines really sank in, and aided by experience with two experimental 2–10–2 and two 2–10–4 engines obtained from Baldwins and Alco respectively in 1931, this administration went over to a purely American technique with the appearance of the J.S. 2–8–4 and F.D. 2–10–2 home designed and built classes of 1931–2. Further notable designs, the L class 2–10–0 of 1945 and the P36 4–8–4 of 1950, confirmed this trend and their dimensions are included in the table (entries 10–13 of Table 8).

India was another country which during the war changed over to American-style design. The time was ripe, not only because of interruption of its former source of supply from England, but because of recent unfortunate experiences with English design of which more will be recounted later. In the first of the subsequently numerous class of WP 4–6–2 engine* sent over from Baldwins in 1942, all the principal features were American in inspiration: boiler, steel firebox, archtubes, self-cleaning smokebox, grate, ashpan, bar frames and 'Boxpok' wheels. The Indian administration, however, called for some other features, alien to US practice, with which they had had good experience on British engines, such as 7½in (190·5mm) valve travel with 1¾in (44·5mm) lap, narrow ring piston valves and leading bogie with LMS-type lateral spring control. The corresponding WG Class 2–8–2 freight engine, the design and prototypes of which were worked out in England, combined most of the same features (Table 8, entry 6).

Back in Europe, the most notable post-war export was the group of 1,323 141R class 2–8–2 locomotives ordered early in 1944 and delivered to the French National Railways from 1945 (Table 7, entry 7). Of moderate dimensions by American standards, they were of high capacity for European conditions, and equipped in different batches with coal and oil firing, plain and roller coupled wheel bearings, and spoked and Boxpok wheels, they formed a hard and very effective core of motive power which brought a new look to French operation particularly as regards intensive pooled working. While giving the home produce a stiff run for its money, these engines cannot be said to have influenced domestic thought and design to any extent. The same can be said of the effect of the 300 all-purpose 2–8–0 engines built by Alco and Canadian firms and sent to Belgium in 1946, a design very closely based upon the WD 2–8–0 previously mentioned.

A notable and, for Europe, very powerful 2–10–0 design was produced for Poland in 1947, 100 being built by the three major US builders. This engine with 25in × 27½in (635mm × 697mm) cylinders and 20·3 tons (20·7 tonnes) axleload was, like the two other series for France and Belgium above described, very successful and more than 200 to the same design were later built domestically by Polish firms. Another massive but not quite so large 2–10–0 was built to the extent of 88 units for the Turkish Railways in the same year. Unlike all other American exports of other than small size, these engines were not built by one of the 'Big Three' manufacturers but by the relatively small Vulcan works of Wilkes Barre, Pennsylvania, which had had very little previous experience of building such giants. Clumsy-looking machines, they were banished to the eastern part of the country and clearly were held in far less regard by their owners than were the more ubiquitous 2–10–0s of German descent.

Finally in this all-too-brief survey of overseas influence must be mentioned trends in Australia. Apart from the introduction of purely American designs on the South Australian system in 1926 as mentioned above, as far back as 1922 the New South Wales Railways had begun to study and then introduce such features as rocking grates, self-cleaning smokeboxes and grease lubrication of main bearings. Each successive new design from that time contained more transatlantic content even although maintaining a generally British aspect. With the appearance of the D57 class 4–8–2 in 1929 and of the C38 4–6–2 class in 1943, the changeover was complete, these engines having integral cast steel beds in addition to all other typical US features. The engines were, however, designed and built in Australia, only the cast beds being imported† (Table 8, entries 8 and 9). Ten years later than the C38s and three years after the last steam engine had been built for American railroads, the now combined Baldwin-Lima Corporation built for New South Wales a series of 20 2–8–2 freight engines of 100 per cent US design with cast steel beds (Table 7, entry 14). These must have been amongst the very last products of an industry first established in 1831, and they were as typical and true to national form as any of the nearly two hundred thousand which had preceded them.

* *Introduction and Development of the Pacific Type Locomotive for the Broad Gauge in India*, by J. N. Compton; Proc Inst Loco Engrs No 212, 1949.

† *Some Notes on the C38 class 4–6–2 Locomotive*, by H. Young; Proc Inst Loco Engrs No 182, 1944.

9 Ultimate refinement in American design. New York Central Niagara Class 4–8–4, built 1945. Note Baker valve gear, roller bearing main and side rods, tidy disposal of all auxiliaries [*New York Central RR*

10 Canadian Pacific 4–6–2 No 2469, in which it can be detected that Canadian design followed American practice in all respects [*J. M. Jarvis*

1378
I. C.R. R.
13

1503

11 Most numerous modern American wheel arrangement to which 14,000 engines of various designs were built for US Railroads, 1905–1930; Illinois Central 2–8–2 No 1376 [*J. M. Jarvis*

12 Delaware & Hudson 4–6–6–4 simple expansion Mallet No 1503. Note firebox extending over rear coupled wheels. The forward part forms a combustion chamber and the grate occupies only the part above the trailing bogie. Note also traces of British influence; lipped chimney and covering up of external pipework [*P. Ransome-Wallis*

13 One of numerous American 2–8–0 locomotives supplied to Europe during World War I. This one was taken over by Nord Railway after the war and became No 4.1356 [*C. Shorto*

14 Typical American 4–6–2 exported to Paris–Orleans Railway in 1922. No 3639 at Paris (Austerlitz), 1925. Note chimney, cab and tender as only French features [*C. Shorto*

15 SNCF No 141R1272, one of the later of 1340 American-designed and built engines ordered after World War II. Fitted with mechanical stoker and roller bearings on all wheels [*E. S. Cox*

16 No 29.177 one of 300 2–8–0 locomotives built in USA and Canada for Belgian State Railways from 1946. Derived from similar design built for US Army in World War II [*P. Ransome Wallis*

18 New South Wales Railways C38 Class 4–6–2 No 3801. Designed and built in Australia with many American features including cast steel bed and roller bearings throughout
[*New South Wales Government Railways*

19 New South Wales D57 Class 3-cylinder 4–8–2 No 5713. Transatlantic features include Americanised Gresley gear operating the inside valve, cast steel bed and power reverse [*New South Wales Government Railways*

17 Although designed and built in Russia, this engine is essentially American in conception and detail; JS Class 2–8–4 No 20–297 at Voronesh [*E. S. Cox*

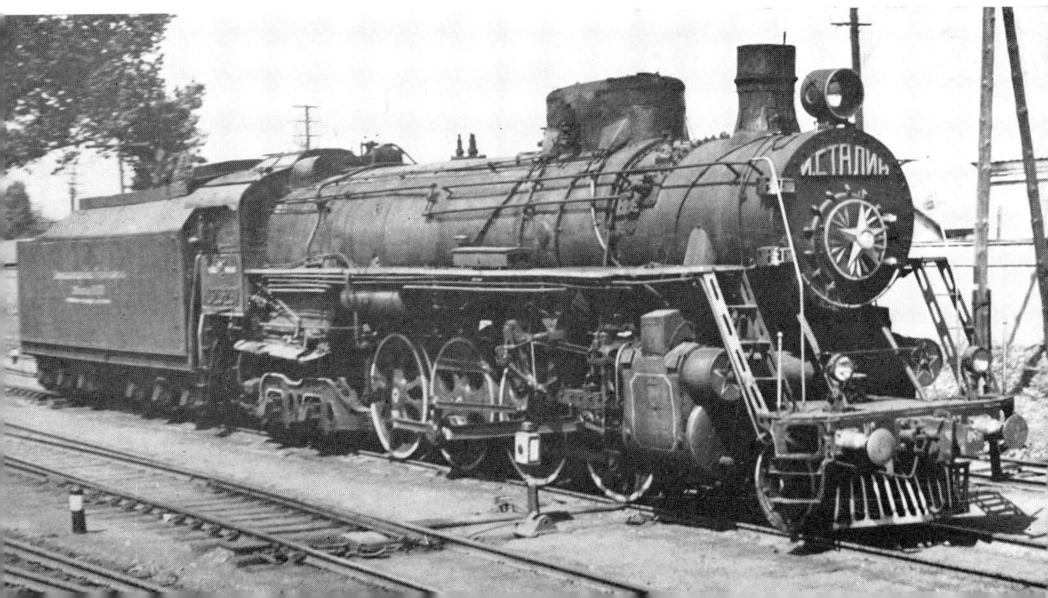

20 Typical of best British practice at the beginning of the twentieth century. Caledonian Railway 4–4–0 No 897, designed by McIntosh and built in 1900

21 The only British compound design to reach appreciable numbers; 4–4–0 No 40931, one of 240 3-cylinder engines built first for the Midland and later for the London, Midland & Scottish Railway between 1901 and 1932

[*E. S. Cox*

22 Typical Churchward design for Great Western Railway incorporating American features in front framing, cylinders and boiler—2–6–2T No 6142 [*E. S. Cox*

23 British inside cylinder 0–6–0 engines were used on passenger as well as freight duties. Ex-LMSR No 44348, one of a class of 772 engines built between 1911 and 1940 [*E. S. Cox*

24 The only Garratt design used for main line freight duties in Great Britain. No 4998, one of 33 built from 1927 for the LMSR and photographed during dynamometer car trials [*E. S. Cox*

26 Ex-Southern Railway 4-cylinder simple 4–6–0 No 30850 *Lord Nelson* built in 1926. Some of this class had cranks set at 135deg to give eight exhaust beats per revolution. Note outside valve gear which became general from about this period [*E. S. Cox*

Needless to say there are many other countries which received locomotives and ideas from the USA; Canada and Mexico have been only briefly referred to because, although following American practice 100 per cent in the present century, they displayed no feature worthy of additional mention. There was too the tremendous efflux both of whole locomotives and of trends to narrow gauge railways all over the world, of which, for reasons of space, it has been necessary to forgo mention in the present volume. Enough has been said here, it is hoped, to portray in highlights what the American theme consisted of, how it developed in its own country, and the extent of its influence elsewhere on standard and broad gauge railways. That it also displayed in its final developments the ultimate power possibilities of steam traction will have already become evident.

AMERICAN RAILROADS. REPRESENTATIVE LOCOMOTIVES 1900–1905

Entry	Year	Wheel Arrangement	Railroad	Cylinders Diameter × Stroke inches / mm	Coupled Wheels Diameter feet / mm	Working Pressure lb/sq in / kg/cm²	Grate Area sq ft / m²	Weight Engine Working Order: Axle tons / tonnes	Adhesive tons / tonnes	Total tons / tonnes
1	1900	4–4–0	New York, New Haven & Hartford	20 × 26 508 × 660	6′ 6″ 1981	200 14·0	30·3 2·83	20·4 20·6	40·8 41·2	62·0 63·0
2	1904	4–4–2	Pennsylvania Cl E2A	$20\frac{1}{2}$ × 26 521 × 660	6′ 8″ 2032	205 14·4	55·5 5·16	24·5 24·8	49·0 49·6	82·3 83·6
3	1904	4–4–2	New York Central *	(4) $15\frac{1}{2}$: 26 × 26 394 : 660 × 660	6′ 7″ 2006	220 15·5	56·2 5·22	24·5 24·8	49·0 49·6	90·0 91·5
4	1904	4–4–2	Philadelphia & Reading †	(4) 15 : 25 × 24 381 : 635 × 610	7′ $0\frac{1}{4}$″ 2134	200 14·0	80·7 7·50	18·1 18·4	36·2 36·8	
5	1903	4–6–0	Delaware & Hudson	21 × 26 533 × 660	5′ 9″ 1753	200 14·0	84·8 7·87	19·6 19·9	58·7 59·7	78·2 79·6
6	1903	4–6–0	Union Pacific †	(4) $15\frac{1}{2}$ 26 × 28 394 : 660 × 711	5′ 3″ 1600	200 14·0	47·5 4·41	21·0 21·4	62 1 63·2	83·0 84·5
7	1901	2–6–2	Lake Shore & Michigan	$20\frac{1}{2}$ × 28 521 × 711	6′ 8″ 2032	200 14·0	48·5 4·50	21·2 21·6	63·7 64·8	84·7 86·2
8	1903	4–6–2	Union Pacific	22 × 28 558 × 711	6′ 5″ 1956	200 14·0	49·5 4·60	21·0 21·4	63·1 64·2	99·3 101·0
9	1900	2–6–0	Boston & Maine	19 × 26 482 × 660	5′ 3″ 1600	200 14·0	30·3 2·83	18·9 19·2	56·8 57·8	64·8 65·9
10	1900	2–8–0	Big Four	22 × 30 558 × 762	4′ 8″ 1422	200 14·0	35·0 3·25	18·7 19·0	74·7 76·0	83·8 84·9
11	1902	2–10–0	Atcheson, Topeka & Santa Fe ‡	(4) $17\frac{1}{2}$: 30 × 34 444 : 762 × 863	4′ 9″ 1448	225 15·8	59·5 5·53	20·7 21·2	103·8 105·6	116·0 117·8
12	1903	2–10–2	Atcheson, Topeka & Santa Fe ‡	(4) 19 : 32 × 32 482 : 813 × 813	4′ 9″ 1448	225 15·8	59·5 5·53	20·9 21·5	104·7 106·5	128·2 130·1
13	1904	0–6–6–0	Baltimore & Ohio §	(4) 20 : 32 × 32 508 : 813 × 813	4′ 8″ 1422	235 16·5	72·2 6·71	24·0 24·4	144·2 146·7	144·2 146·7
14	1904	2–6–4T	Philadelphia & Reading	20 × 24 508 × 610	5′ $1\frac{5}{8}$″ 1562	200 14·0	68·5 6·36	18·0 18·3	54·0 54·9	90·0 91·5
15	1900	0–6–0	Central New England ¶	20 × 24 508 × 610	4′ 3″ 1295	180 12·7	23·4 2·17	18·0 18·3	54·0 54·9	54·0 54·9

Entry	Year	Wheel Arrangement	Railroad		Cylinders Diameter × Stroke inches / mm	Coupled Wheels Diameter feet / mm	Working Pressure lb/sq in / kg/cm²	Grate Area sq ft / m²	Weight Engine Working Order: Axle tons / tonnes	Adhesive tons / tonnes	Total tons / tonnes
1	1914	4–4–2	Pennsylvania	Cl E6S	23½ × 26 596 × 660	6′ 8″ 2032	205 14·4	55·8 5·18	29·7 30·6	59·4 60·3	107·2 109·0
2	1907	4–6–2	New York Central	Cl K2A	22 × 28 558 × 711	6′ 7″ 2006	200 14·0	56·5 5·24	25·7 26·2	77·0 78·2	119·4 121·3
3	1914	4–6–2	Pennsylvania	Cl K4S	27 × 28 685 × 711	6′ 8″ 2032	205 14·4	70·0 6·50	30·0 30·5	90·0 91·4	138·5 140·8
4	1926	4–6–2	New York Central	Cl K5B	25 × 28 635 × 711	6′ 7″ 2006	200 14·0	67·8 6·29	27·5 27·9	82·6 84·0	135·0 137·2
5	1911	4–8–2	Chesapeake & Ohio		29 × 28 736 × 711	5′ 2″ 1575	180 12·7	66·5 6·17	26·6 27·1	106·6 108·4	147·3 149·7
6	1923	4–8–2	Pennsylvania	Cl M_1	27 × 30 686 × 762	6′ 0″ 1829	250 17·6	69·9 6·48	30·2 30·7	121·0 123·0	174·3 177·0
7	1926	4–12–2	Union Pacific		(3) 27 × 31 & 32 686 × 787 & 813	5′ 7″ 1702	220 15·5	108·3 10·00	26·6 27·1	159·5 162·0	221·3 225·0
8	1914	2–8–2	Pennsylvania	Cl L1S	27 × 30 686 × 762	5′ 2″ 1575	205 14·4	70·0 6·50	26·2 26·7	105·0 106·7	140·7 143·0
9	1922	2–10–0	Pennsylvania	Cl I1S	30½ × 32 774 × 813	5′ 2″ 1575	250 17·6	70·0 6·50	31·3 31·8	157·5 160·0	172·3 175·0
10	1925	2–8–4	Boston & Albany		28 × 30 711 × 762	5′ 3″ 1600	240 16·9	100·0 9·29	27·7 28·2	110·8 112·7	172·0 174·7
11	1906	2–6–6–2	Great Northern *		(4) 21½ : 33 × 32 545 : 838 × 813	4′ 7″ 1397	200 14·0	78·0 7·24	23·5 23·9	141·0 143·2	158·2 160·8
12	1924	2–8–8–2	Chesapeake & Ohio †		(4) 23 × 32 584 × 813	4′ 9″ 1448	205 14·4	112·9 10·47	27·4 27·8	219·2 223·0	254·3 258·5
13	1918	2–10–10–2	Virginian *		(4) 30 : 48 × 32 762 : 1219 × 813	4′ 8″ 1422	215 15·1	108·7 10·10	27·5 27·9	275·0 279·4	305·0 310·0
14	1914	2–8–8–8–2	Erie ‡		(6) 36 × 32 914 × 813	5′ 3″ 1600	210 14·8	90·0 8·35	28·0 28·5	336·5 342·0	377·0 383·0
15	1907	0–10–0	New York Central §		24 × 28 610 × 711	4′ 3″ 1295	210 14·8	56·5 5·24	23·7 24·1	118·3 120·0	118·3 120·0

* Mallet Compound † Mallet Simple ‡ 'Triplex' § Switcher

UNITED STATES RAILROAD ADMINISTRATION—TWELVE STANDARD LOCOMOTIVE TYPES 1919–1920 Table 3

Entry	Wheel Arrangement		Number Built	Valve Gear	Cylinders Diameter × Stroke inches / mm	Coupled Wheels Diameter feet / mm	Working Pressure lb/sq in / kg/cm²	Grate Area sq ft / m²	Weight Engine Working Order: Axle tons / tonnes	Adhesive tons / tonnes	Total tons / tonnes
1	0–6–0		255	Baker	21 × 28 533 × 711	4′ 3″ 1295	190 13·4	33·2 3·08	24·0 24·4	72·8 74·0	72·8 74·0
2	0–8–0		175	,,	25 × 28 610 × 711	4′ 3″ 1295	175 12·3	47·0 4·36	23·9 24·3	95·6 97·2	95·6 97·2
3	4–6–2	Light	81	,,	25 × 28 610 × 711	6′ 1″ 1829	200 14·0	66·7 6·19	24·1 24·5	72·3 73·5	123·7 125·7
4	4–6–2	Heavy	20	,,	27 × 28 686 × 711	6′ 7″ 2006	200 14·0	70·8 6·58	29·4 29·9	88·1 89·6	136·7 138·8
5	4–8–2	Light	47	,,	27 × 30 686 × 762	5′ 9″ 1753	200 14·0	70·8 6·58	25·0 25·4	100·0 101·6	144·2 146·5
6	4–8–2	Heavy	15	,,	28 × 30 711 × 762	5′ 9″ 1753	200 14·0	76·3 7·08	27·0 27·4	108·0 109·8	157·2 159·8
7	2–8–2	Light	625	Walschaert	26 × 30 660 × 762	5′ 3″ 1600	200 14·0	66·7 6·19	24·5 24·9	98·2 99·8	130·3 132·5
8	2–8–2	Heavy	233	,,	27 × 32 686 × 813	5′ 3″ 1600	190 13·4	70·8 6·58	26·7 27·1	106·7 108·5	143·0 145·3
9	2–10–2	Light	94	Southern	27 × 32 686 × 813	4′ 9″ 1448	200 14·0	76·3 7·08	24·6 25·0	123·2 125·2	157·2 159·8
10	2–10–2	Heavy	175	,,	30 × 32 762 × 813	5′ 3″ 1600	190 13·4	88·2 8·19	26·2 26·6	131·0 133·2	170·0 172·8
11	2–6–6–2		30	Baker	(4) 23 : 35 × 32 584 : 889 × 813	4′ 9″ 1448	225 15·8	76·3 7·08	26·6 27·0	160·0 162·6	200·0 203·2
12	2–8–8–2		80	,,	(4) 25 : 39 × 32 610 : 991 × 813	4′ 9″ 1448	240 16·9	96·0 8·92	26·6 27·0	213·0 216·7	237·0 242·0

Entry	Wheel Arrange-ment	Class	Date Built	Condi-tion of Test	Steam Evapor-ated lb/hr kg/hr	Speed mph km/hr	ihp cv	Steam lb/ihp kg/cv	Steam Temp. °F °C	Exhaust Pressure lb/sq in gms/cm²	Cut-off %	Cylinder Eff. %	Coal lb/hr kg/hr	Coal (grate) lb/sq ft/hr kg/m²hr	Smokebox Vacuum in mm Water	Coal per lb/ihp/hr kg/cv/hr	Boiler Efficiency %
							Cylinders							Boiler			
1	4–4–2	E2A	1904	A	30,700	38	1,200	26·5	388	—	30	—	5,580	101	8·7	—	42·4
					19000	61	1216	11·87	198				2540	495	223		
2				B	28,900	67	1,130	23·8	388	—	15	—	5,012	90	8·0	—	45·2
					13120	107	1146	10·67	198				2280	440	203		
3	4–4–2	E6S	1912	A	44,400	47	2,450	18·5	500	12·7	50	13·0	8,000	143	15·0	3·0	47·5
					20150	75	2480	8·30	260	892			3640	700	381	1·34	
4				B	30,000	75	1,800	17·0	500	6·0	25	12·7	3,500	63	7·2	2·1	75·0
					13600	120	1825	7·63	260	421			1590	317	183	0·94	
5	4–6–2	K4S	1914	A	67,000	47	3,250	20·0	600	18·5	65	11·0	12,000	171	18·8	3·2	50·0
					30450	75	3295	8·97	315	1300			5350	838	477	1·43	
6				B	34,000	66	1,750	16·1	550	3·9	25	14·3	3,800	54	6·2	1·8	76·0
					15460	107	1774	7·22	290	274			1730	264	157	0·81	
7	4–4–4–4	T_1	1942	A	105,475	100	6,666	15·6	728	25·9	20	—	24,000	252	22·5	3·5	43·0
					48000	160	6760	7·00	385	1820			10900	1235	571	1·57	
8				B	77,113	76	5 535	13·6	746	11·1	22	—	13,131	144	14·7	2·5	52·5
					35010	122	5610	6·10	395	780			5920	706	373	1·12	
9	2–8–0	H9S	1912	A	34,500	22	1,800	18·5	570	8·0	50	—	7,500	135	8·0	3·5	40·0
					15650	35	1825	8·30	300	562			3400	661	203	1·57	
10				B	25,800	22	1,450	17·6	550	4·2	30	—	3,750	83	4·7	2·7	56·5
					11720	35	1470	7·90	290	295			1810	407	119	1·21	
11	2–8–2	L1S	1914	A	58,000	29	2,800	20·2	580	16·0	65	11·5	12,000	171	17·2	4·2	45·0
					26400	46	2838	9·06	304	1125			5350	838	437	1·88	
12				B	38,000	18	2,000	19·0	540	5·5	50	12·5	5,000	71	7·2	2·7	67·5
					17270	29	2028	8·52	283	386			2270	346	183	1·21	
13	2–10–0	I1S	1916	A	58,000	25	3,500	16·4	660	18·0	45	14·6	12,000	171	17·0	3·2	47·5
					26350	40	3545	7·36	350	1265			5350	838	432	1·44	
14				B	41,000	22	2,500	15·3	630	9·2	40	14·7	6,000	86	8·5	2·4	67·0
					18650	35	2534	6·86	332	646			2730	422	216	1·08	

(A) At maximum evaporation (B) At minimum steam consumption

AMERICAN RAILROADS. REPRESENTATIVE LOCOMOTIVES 1927–1949

Table 5

Entry	Year	Wheel Arrangement	Railroad	Cylinders Diameter × Stroke inches / mm	Coupled Wheels Diameter feet / mm	Working Pressure lb/sq in / kg/cm²	Grate Area sq ft / m²	Weight Engine Working Order: Axle tons / tonnes	Adhesive tons / tonnes	Total tons / tonnes
1	1935	4–4–2	Milwaukee	**19 × 28** 482 × 711	**7′ 0″** 2134	**300** 21·1	**69·0** 6·41	**31·7** 32·4	**63·4** 64·4	**127·6** 129·5
2	1927	4–6–4	New York Central Cl J1A	**25 × 28** 635 × 711	**6′ 7″** 2006	**225** 15·8	**81·5** 7·56	**27·0** 27·4	**81·3** 82·6	**153·0** 155·5
3	1938	4–6–4	New York Central Cl J3A	**22½ × 29** 560 × 737	**6′ 7″** 2006	**275** 19·3	**82·0** 7·61	**30·0** 30·5	**90·0** 91·5	**160·6** 163·0
4	1938	4–6–4	Milwaukee	**23½ × 30** 596 × 762	**7′ 0″** 2134	**300** 21·1	**96·5** 8·96	**32·2** 32·7	**96·5** 98·0	**153·0** 155·5
5	1938	4–8–4	Atcheson, Topeka & Santa Fé	**28 × 32** 711 × 813	**6′ 8″** 2032	**300** 21·1	**108·0** 10·03	**32·0** 32·5	**128·0** 130·0	**223·2** 227·0
6	1945	4–8–4	New York Central	**25½ × 32** 647 × 813	**6′ 7″** 2006	**275** 19·3	**101·0** 9·38	**30·7** 31·2	**122·8** 124·8	**210·0** 213·5
7	1942	4–4–4–4	Pennsylvania Cl T_1	**(4) 19¾ × 26** 501 × 660	**6′ 8″** 2032	**300** 21·1	**92·0** 8·54	**30·0** 30·5	**120·0** 121·9	**223·5** 227·2
8	1930	2–10–4	{Chesapeake & Ohio / Pennsylvania}	**29 × 34** 737 × 864	**5′ 9″** 1753	**260** 18·3	**121·7** 11·30	**33·3** 33·9	**166·5** 169·2	**253·0** 257·0
9	1938	2–10–4	Atcheson, Topeka & Santa Fé	**30 × 34** 762 × 864	**6′ 2″** 1880	**310** 21·8	**121·5** 11·28	**33·1** 33·7	**165·7** 168·4	**243·0** 247·0
10	1936	4–6–6–4	Union Pacific	**(4) 22 × 32** 559 × 813	**5′ 9″** 1753	**255** 17·9	**108·2** 10·03	**28·7** 29·2	**172·2** 175·0	**255·0** 259·0
11	1945	2–6–6–6	Chesapeake & Ohio	**(4) 22½ × 33** 560 × 838	**5′ 7″** 1702	**260** 18·3	**135·2** 12·55	**37·5** 38·1	**225·0** 228·5	**335·0** 340·0
12	1929	2–8–8–2	Great Northern	**(4) 28 × 32** 711 × 813	**5′ 3″** 1600	**240** 16·9	**126·0** 11·70	**30·4** 30·9	**243·3** 247·5	**282·0** 286·4
13	1928	2–8–8–4	Northern Pacific	**(4) 26 × 32** 660 × 813	**5′ 3″** 1600	**250** 17·6	**182·0** 16·90	**30·9** 31·4	**247·0** 251·0	**320·0** 325·0
14	1944	4–4–6–4	Pennsylvania Cl Q2	**(2) 19¾ × 28 (2) 23¾ × 29** 501 × 711 590 × 737	**5′ 9″** 1753	**300** 21·1	**121·7** 11·30	**34·4** 35·0	**172·2** 175·0	**277·2** 281·5
15	1941	4–8–8–4	Union Pacific 'Big Boy'	**(4) 23¾ × 32** 590 × 813	**5′ 8″** 1727	**300** 21·1	**150·3** 13·95	**30·4** 30·9	**243·2** 247·0	**344·4** 350·0

AMERICAN RAILROADS. THIRTY 4–8–4 DESIGNS BUILT 1929–1946

Table 6

ry	*Railroad*	*Date*	*Cylinders* inches mm	*Coupled Wheels Diameter* feet mm	*Working Pressure* lb/sq in kg/cm²	*Grate Area* sq ft m²	*Tractive * Effort* lb kg	*Adhesive Weight* tons tonnes	*Tota Engine Weight* tons tonnes
1	Northern Pacific	1938	28×31 711×787	6′ 5″ 1956	260 18·3	115·0 10·67	69,800 31650	131·6 133·7	227·2 231·0
2	Chicago North Western	1929	27×32 686×813	6′ 4″ 1930	275 19·3	100·0 9·27	71,800 32500	128·6 130·9	222·8 226·2
3	Denver Rio Grande	1929	27×30 686×762	5′ 10″ 1778	240 16·9	88·0 8·17	63,700 28850	112·4 114·2	200·0 206·2
4	,, ,,	1937	26×30 660×762	6′ 1″ 1854	285 20·0	106·0 9·84	67,200 30450	124·6 126·6	213·8 217·1
5	Great Northern	1929	28×30 711×762	6′ 1″ 1854	250 17·6	102·0 9·48	67,000 30350	121·2 123·0	210·8 214·0
6	,, ,,	1930	29×29 737×737	6′ 8″ 2032	225 15·8	97·7 9·07	58,300 26400	110·5 112·3	206·8 210·0
7	Nashville, Chattanooga & St Louis	1930	25×30 635×762	5′ 10″ 1778	250 17·6	77·3 7·17	57,000 25830	101·6 103·3	178·3 181·0
8	Wabash	1930	27×32 686×813	5′ 10″ 1778	250 17·6	96·2 8·94	70,817 32100	122·3 124·2	202·5 205·0
9	Milwaukee	1930	28×30 711×762	6′ 2″ 1880	230 16·2	103·0 9·56	60,000 27170	122·7 124·6	201·0 204·2
0	,,	1937	26×32 660×813	6′ 2″ 1880	285 20·0	106·0 9·84	70,800 32200	126·1 128·1	217·5 221·0
1	Burlington	1931	28×30 711×762	6′ 2″ 1880	250 17·6	106·5 9·88	67,500 30600	125·5 127·5	212·5 215·8
2	Lehigh Valley	1931	26×32 660×813	5′ 10″ 1778	255 17·9	88·3 8·20	66,700 30220	122·7 124·6	201·3 204·5
3	,,	1935	27×30 686×762	6′ 5″ 1956	275 19·3	96·5 8·96	66,500 30140	120·6 122·6	197·2 200·1
4	Lackawanna	1934	28×32 711×813	6′ 2″ 1880	250 17·6	88·2 8·18	72,000 32600	122·1 124·0	199·5 202·7
5	Chesapeake & Ohio	1935	27½×30 698×762	6′ 0″ 1829	255 17·9	100·3 9·32	68,300 30950	129·5 131·6	224·5 228·1
16	Richmond, Fredericksburg & Potomac	1936	27×30 686×762	6′ 5″ 1956	260 18·3	86·5 8·03	62,800 28430	119·0 120·9	185·0 188·0
17	Southern Pacific	1937	25½×32 647×813	6′ 8″ 2032	300 21·1	90·4 8·48	64,760 29400	123·2 125·2	212·0 215·7
18	Union Pacific	1937	28×31 711×787	6′ 8″ 2032	300 21·1	100·2 9·31	63,800 28900	131·7 133·8	219·0 222·6
19	St Louis Southwestern	1937	26×30 660×762	5′ 10″ 1778	250 17·6	88·3 8·20	61,500 27850	110·6 112·4	210·5 218·4
20	Atlantic Coast	1938	27×30 686×762	6′ 8″ 2032	275 19·3	97·7 9·07	63,900 28920	117·5 119·4	205·5 208·7
21	Atcheson, Topeka & Santa Fé	1938	28×32 711×813	6′ 8″ 2032	300 21·1	108·0 10·02	66,000 29900	131·2 133·2	227·5 231·2

* Calculated at 85% Boiler Pressure

Table 6 *continued—*

Entry	*Railroad*	*Date*	*Cylinders* inches mm	*Coupled Wheels Diameter* feet mm	*Working Pressure* lb/sq in kg/cm²	*Grate Area* sq ft m²	*Tractive* * *Effort* lb kg	*Adhesive Weight* tons tonnes	*To Eng Wei* to tonr
22	Soo Line	1938	26 × 32 660 × 813	6′ 3″ 1905	270 19·0	88·3 8·20	66,000 29900	117·4 119·3	199 202
23	Delaware & Hudson	1943	24½ × 32 622 × 813	6′ 3″ 1905	285 20·0	96·2 8·93	62,040 28100	120·6 122·5	210 213
24	St Louis,—San Francisco	1943	28 × 31 711 × 787	6′ 2″ 1880	255 17·9	88·0 8·17	71,200 32250	125·0 127·0	206 209
25	Central of Georgia	1944	27 × 30 686 × 762	6′ 1½″ 1866	250 17·6	90·2 8·38	62,300 28200	116·2 118·0	199 202
26	Chicago, Rock Island & Pacific	1944	26 × 32 660 × 813	6′ 2″ 1880	270 19·0	96·3 8·94	67,000 30350	125·0 127·0	208 211
27	Missouri Pacific	1944	26 × 30 660 × 762	6′ 1″ 1854	285 20·0	106·0 9·84	67,200 30450	125·0 127·0	221 211
28	Norfolk & Western	1945	27 × 32 686 × 813	5′ 10″ 1778	275 19·3	107·7 10·00	73,300 33200	128·5 130·6	220 223
29	New York Central	1945	25½ × 32 647 × 813	6′ 7″ 2006	275 19·3	101·0 9·38	61,500 27850	122·7 124·7	210 213
30	Philadelphia & Reading	1946	27 × 32 686 × 813	5′ 10″ 1778	240 16·9	94·5 8·77	68,000 30800	124·2 126·2	197 200

* Calculated at 85% Boiler Pressure

REPRESENTATIVE AMERICAN LOCOMOTIVE EXPORTS 1916–1953 — Table 7

Entry	Year	Wheel Arrangement	Railway	Cylinders Diameter × Stroke inches mm	Coupled Wheels Diameter feet mm	Working Pressure lb/sq in kg/cm²	Grate Area sq ft m²	Weight Engine Working Order: Axle tons tonnes	Adhesive tons tonnes	Total tons tonnes
1	1916	2–8–0	US Army World War I	21 × 28 533 × 711	4′ 8″ 1422	190 13·4	32·7 3·03	16·7 17·0	67·0 68·1	74·3 75·6
2	1916	2–10–0	Russian	25 × 28 610 × 711	4′ 4″ 1321	180 12·7	64·7 6·00	16·0 16·3	80·5 81·8	90·8 92·4
3	1919	2–8–2	PO Ry France	24⅜ × 27½ 620 × 700	5′ 5″ 1650	171 12·0	50·6 4·70	16·9 17·2	67·7 68·8	89·4 90·9
4	1922	4–6–2	,, ,,	24⅜ × 25⅝ 620 × 650	6′ 4¾″ 1950	171 12·0	50·6 4·70	17·5 17·8	52·6 53·5	91·8 93·3
5	1924	4–6–2	Madras & Southern Mahratta—India	22 × 28 559 × 711	6′ 2″ 1880	180 12·7	48·0 4·45	17·0 17·3	51·0 51·8	82·4 83·8
6	1931	2–10–2	Russian	27½ × 30 697 × 762	5′ 0″ 1524	200 14·0	79·0 7·33	22·6 23·0	113·0 114·8	149·8 152·4
7	1945	2–8–2	SNCF France	23½ × 28 596 × 711	5′ 5″ 1650	220 15·5	55·5 5·15	19·7 20·0	78·8 80·2	111·5 113·3
8	1942	2–8–0	US Army World War II	19 × 26 483 × 660	4′ 9″ 1448	225 15·8	41·0 3·80	15·6 15·9	62·5 63·5	71·9 73·1
9	1943	2–8–2	Indian & Portuguese	21 × 28 533 × 711	5′ 0″ 1524	200 14·0	47·0 4·36	15·6 15·9	63·0 64·0	88·5 90·0
10	1942	4–6–2	Indian WP Class	20¼ × 28 514 × 711	5′ 7″ 1702	210 14·8	46·0 4·27	18·0 18·3	54·1 55·0	97·2 98·8
11	1947	2–10–0	Polish	25 × 27½ 635 × 697	4′ 9″ 1448	227 16·0	67·8 6·29	20·3 20·7	101·3 103·0	117·2 119·0
12	1946	2–8–0	Belgian	22 × 28 559 × 711	5′ 0″ 1524	225 15·8	47·5 4·41	19·1 19·4	76·5 77·8	91·5 93·0
13	1947	2–10–0	Turkish	23⅝ × 28 600 × 711	4′ 9″ 1448	250 17·6	57·8 5·36	18·2 18·5	91·0 92·5	109·0 110·8
14	1953	2–8–2	New South Wales	21 × 28 533 × 711	5′ 1½″ 1561	210 14·8	45·0 4·17	18·5 18·8	73·6 74·8	101·8 103·5
15	1900	4–4–2	Bavarian Class S2/5	(4) 13 : 22 × 26 330 : 559 × 660	5′ 11½″ 1816	199 14·0	30·0 2·80	15·7 16·0	31·4 32·0	62·5 63·8

LOCOMOTIVES FOLLOWING AMERICAN FORMAT BUT DESIGNED AND BUILT OUTSIDE THE NEW WORLD — Table 8

Entry	*Year*	*Wheel Arrangement*	*Railway*		*Where First Engine Built*	*Cylinders Diameter × Stroke* inches / mm	*Coupled Wheels Diameter* feet / mm	*Working Pressure* lb/sq in / kg/cm²	*Grate Area* sq ft / m²	*Weight Engine Working Order* Axle tons / tonnes	Adhesive tons / tonnes	Total tons / tonnes
1	1926	4–6–2	South Australia		Britain	**24 × 28** 610 × 711	**6′ 3″** 1905	**200** 14·0	**55·0** 5·10	**24·2** 24·8	**72·8** 74·0	**116·9** 118·8
2	1926	4–8–2	,,	,,	,,	**26 × 28** 660 × 711	**5′ 3″** 1600	**200** 14·0	**66·6** 6·18	**22·8** 23·4	**91·1** 92·6	**154·8** 157·5
3	1926	2–8–2	,,	,,	,,	**22 × 28** 559 × 711	**4′ 9″** 1448	**200** 14·0	**47·0** 4·36	**18·5** 18·8	**74·1** 75·3	**100·0** 101·6
4	1933	2–8–4	,,	,,	Australia	**22 × 28** 559 × 711	**4′ 9″** 1448	**215** 15·1	**59·5** 5·53	**19·6** 19·9	**77·2** 78·5	**124·5** 126·5
5	1944	4–8–4	,,	,,	,,	**$20\frac{1}{2}$ × 28** 520 × 711	**5′ 6″** 1676	**215** 15·1	**45·0** 4·18	**15·0** 15·2	**60·0** 61·0	**104·3** 106·0
6	1950	2–8–2	India	Cl WG	Britain	**$21\frac{7}{8}$ × 28** 555 × 711	**5′ $1\frac{1}{2}$″** 1561	**210** 14·8	**45·0** 4·18	**18·5** 18·8	**73·6** 74·8	**101·8** 103·5
7	1955	4–6–2	India	Cl WL	,,	**$19\frac{1}{4}$ × 28** 489 × 711	**5′ 7″** 1702	**210** 14·8	**38·0** 3·53	**16·5** 16·8	**49·5** 50·3	**88·0** 89·5
8	1943	4–6–2	New South Wales		Australia	**$21\frac{1}{2}$ × 26** 545 × 660	**5′ 9″** 1753	**245** 17·2	**47·0** 3·86	**22·4** 22·8	**67·2** 68·2	**112·2** 114·0
9	1929	4–8–2	,,	,,	,,	(3) **$23\frac{1}{4}$ × 28** 590 × 711	**5′ 0″** 1524	**200** 14·0	**65·0** 6·04	**22·3** 22·7	**89·2** 90·7	**134·9** 137·0
10	1932	2–8–4	Russia	Cl JS	Russia	**$26\frac{3}{8}$ × $30\frac{3}{8}$** 670 × 770	**6′ $0\frac{3}{4}$″** 1850	**213** 15·0	**75·7** 7·04	**20·4** 20·7	**80·9** 82·2	**133·1** 135·1
11	1931	2–10–2	Russia	Cl FD	,,	**$26\frac{3}{8}$ × $30\frac{3}{8}$** 670 × 770	**4′ 11″** 1500	**213** 15·0	**75·7** 7·04	**20·0** 20·3	**100·0** 101·6	**135·0** 137·0
12	1945	2–10–0	Russia	Cl L	,,	**$25\frac{9}{16}$ × $31\frac{1}{2}$** 650 × 800	**4′ 11″** 1500	**199** 14·0	**64·5** 6·00	**18·2** 18·5	**91·0** 92·4	**103·8** 105·2
13	1950	4–8–4	Russia	Cl P36	,,	**$22\frac{5}{8}$ × $31\frac{1}{2}$** 575 × 800	**6′ $0\frac{3}{4}$″** 1850	**213** 15·0	**72·6** 6·74	**18·0** 18·3	**72·0** 73·3	**135·0** 137·2
14	1949	2–8–8–4	Russia	Cl P38	,,	(4) **$22\frac{5}{8}$ × $31\frac{1}{2}$** 575 × 800	**4′ 11″** 1500	**213** 15·0	**115·0** 106·8	**20·0** 20·3	**160·0** 162·6	**214·9** 218·5
15	1927	4–6–2	Victoria	Cl S	Australia	(3) **$20\frac{1}{2}$ × 28** 520 × 700	**6′ 0″** 1829	**200** 14·0	**50·0** 4·54	**23·5** 23·9	**70·5** 71·6	**112·2** 114·0

CHAPTER FOUR

Great Britain

THERE COULD HARDLY BE a greater contrast than that between locomotive design and operation in North America and in Great Britain. From maximum tonnages over vast distances in open territory we turn to conditions of small consignments, short runs and a railway system which had to be built into an already established pattern of town and country. The inventiveness of the early engineering fathers and the enterprise of its merchants gave Britain a head start in the industrial revolution, and the form of locomotive pioneered by George Stephenson became the pattern, in principle if not in details, to which the steam engine all over the world conformed. As befits such a pioneering record there has through the years been a most active lay as well as professional interest in the locomotive in that country to an extent hardly paralleled elsewhere, and in direct consequence more has been written on every conceivable aspect of the Iron Horse in England than in other countries. The two volumes alone of *The British Steam Railway Locomotive* written respectively by E. L. Ahrons and O. S. Nock* convey in some 700 pages a most detailed account of design development from 1825 to 1965 and these are only a drop in the ocean compared with the vast literature, both periodical and in book form, which has grown up in the present century and is available to the student. If it seems, therefore, that this chapter need only consist of selected references to what has been written by others, it can be pleaded that because even British design did not exist in a vacuum, there may be a little more which can be said, viewing things first with perhaps a more detached and impartial eye than is customary and secondly in the context of the theme of this book which endeavours to trace the cross-fertilisation of ideas which has existed between different countries.

The periods into which we shall divide our consideration are set for us by political events. From 1900 until the end of 1922, eighteen major and a further number of smaller independent railways spanned the country. By Government initiative, these were amalgamated into four large groups in 1923—the London Midland and Scottish, London and North Eastern, Great Western, and Southern. Each grappled with the task of bringing some sense and order into the variegated collections of rolling stock which they had inherited, and each, as the 1930s wore on. had established an individual pattern of standard locomotive designs compatible with their inheritance and well suited in most cases to the traffic requirements they had to meet. In 1948, again by governmental intervention, the four grouped Railways were resolved into a single entity, the nationalised British Railways, and once again the pattern of assimilation and then of new standard designs repeated itself until other forms of motive power prevailed and the last new steam locomotive was built in 1960. In spite of, or perhaps because of, this ferment, and certainly as a result of seeking to maintain its position as an exporting country, British design underwent a remarkable change in this period. At the opening of the century, practice had become highly hidebound and conservative, however much contemporary scribes sought to point to individual differences in design. By the end of our period, it had become

* *The British Steam Locomotive 1825–1925*, by E. L. Ahrons; Locomotive Publishing Company, 1927. *The British Steam Railway Locomotive 1925–1965*, by O. S. Nock; Ian Allan, 1966.

open-minded and aware, and it progressed in time with, and made use of, advances in the art, regardless of source.

A feature of the British school of design was the overwhelming position of the Chief Mechanical Engineer. It has been explained how in America he hardly existed, and, as will be seen in succeeding chapters, in many foreign countries he had to share his design function with operators, manufacturers and even with professors of engineering in the universities. In Great Britain he reigned supreme, answerable only to a non-technical or at most a semi-technical board of directors, and he was monarch of all he surveyed, being responsible for design, testing, manufacturing, repairs and in many cases even the running of the locomotives out on the line. This led to many blessings and some evils. With such a strong central command things got done, and done quickly. Parkinson's law operated in reverse and many large departments were run on a shoe-string in a manner which would astonish the modern 'organisation man'. If he was a first-class engineer, and many of them were, he was already prepared to look around him and select for his purposes the best of practice from both home and abroad to which he added the essence of what was in him, in invention and innovation. But because CMEs were also human beings they were not all capable of sustaining this high level. Like the kings of old, power corrupted some of them, and, surrounded by avid courtiers, they pursued an unfruitful and autocratic way. Others had reached their position for all kinds of other reasons than ability to design, being more interested in production, metallurgy, or finance. These were apt to be content to see their names coupled with the latest product; for the rest, all the real work was done by often faceless chief draughtsmen and assistants, whose names, as the true begetters of many a well-known locomotive type, were only disclosed in later years and occasionally even posthumously.

The besetting sin of this hierarchical structure was its isolationist nature. New designs were nursed in secrecy, and information and drawings were only grudgingly if at all dispensed to brother CMEs. It is true that since 1890 there had been an Association of Railway Locomotive Engineers, whose infrequent meetings the CMEs attended, as at an exclusive club. But for all the talk little was given away, and, even if it were, each was sufficiently set in his own ways not to be unduly influenced.

Thus, very largely, were things up to 1922, but with amalgamation into four groups, a change set in. No longer could boards of directors be content only with substituting like for like in succeeding incumbents, but the man in charge did now really have to amount to something, in order to organise and run the much larger departments. Moreover, in three out of the four groups, the running of the engines was divorced from the CMEs' sole control, and independent and very vocal motive power departments were set up whose complaints and criticisms brought a breath of realism and practicability into design operations. In the private manufacturers' world of exports also, no longer was it acceptable as in the past merely to design versions of basic British types for use by overseas railways, but increasing attention had to be paid to climatic and human conditions far removed from those of England, and to what competitors from America, France and Germany were offering.

I. 1900–1923

If we turn now to the period from 1900 to 1910, Table 9 sets out only a fraction of the new types that were designed, but sufficient for comparison, with corresponding tables in other chapters and for the making of certain points. At this time, the 4–4–0 for passenger and the 0–6–0 for freight traffic reigned supreme, with the 4–4–2 and 4–6–0 on the one hand, and the 0–8–0 and 2–8–0 on the other, just beginning to made a substantial appearance. In each wheel arrangement there was close agreement in dimensions, nominal power and speed capacity. Nevertheless as a result of the personal views of the respective designers and due to boiler proportions, steam passages and valve events which as yet had not been influenced by rational investigation, the most astonishing differences in behaviour were forthcoming from engine types of almost identical size. It was these differences which, first in the writings of Rous-Marten, and subsequently in those of Cecil J. Allen and O. S. Nock, formed that unique corpus of literature by which it was possible to judge the 'form' of all kinds of locomotives in daily service on the line, in a manner unparalleled in other countries, a facility not only of interest to the lay enthusiast, but of real value to the discerning professional designer.

The representative locomotive of 1900–10 used saturated steam at 175 to 200lb/sq in (12·3 to 14·1kg/sq cm), had a narrow firebox between the frames, deep in the case of 4–4–0s and 4–4–2s, shallow with 4–6–0s and 2–8–0s. Slide, or sometimes piston, valves carried no more than 1in (25·4mm) steam lap or 5in (127mm) valve travel. Hindrances to free steaming and running existed in narrow and tortuous steam passages, and often in firegrates and ashpans so obstructed by coupled axles as to limit proper air inlet or ash disposal. Inside cylinders were in the majority often by reason of loading gauge restrictions, but at the expense of a congested layout for motion and valve gear, and of high axlebox loadings due to a piston thrust greater, like for like, than with outside cylinder machines. Even with the latter arrangment, valves and valve gear were disposed between the frames, and as late as 1914 there were very few engines in the whole country with their valve gear accessibly mounted outside. This, together with use of low running platforms, deep splashers, and an absence of external piping and accessories, consummated a trend dating from mid-Victorian times in which each designer vied with his fellows to produce the purest and most uncluttered outline and appearance for the locomotive as a whole. Enhanced by vivid colour schemes individual to each railway, sometimes productions of sheer beauty resulted, but in other cases there was nothing to draw the eye away from the gangling or lumpy proportions which mistaken aesthetics had bestowed.

The suburban services in many large cities, as well as duties on short country branch lines, found use for numerous tank engines, which followed their tender counterparts in all but self-contained provision for coal and water, but few as yet ran very fast or very far.

Already, however, this uniform façade was cracking from within and British design would never be the same again. Leading iconoclast was G. J. Churchward of the Great Western Railway, who was courageous enough to borrow good things from America and from France, and to combine them with his own genius into a standard range of locomotive type, so original and effective that it was thirty years before the bulk of British design at home or overseas caught up. This two-cylinder 2900 class and four-cylinder 4000 class 4–6–0s of 1902 and 1907 respectively, so often illustrated and described, were the true harbingers of modern British practice with long travel valve gear, straight steam ports, American-style cylinder construction, and greatly improved boiler performance (entries 6 and 7).

Superheating, too, made its appearance from Germany, the high degree Schmidt apparatus being first applied to some Lancashire & Yorkshire 0–6–0 engines in 1906. As elsewhere its use spread like wildfire, and after 1910 few more saturated engines were built. Strangely, high steam temperature with its attendant benefits was one of Churchward's blind spots, and first-rate engineer as he certainly was, he and his successor continued to ignore its blessings and soldier on with moderate temperatures until the very last days of the Great Western in 1948.

Table 10 gives a bird's-eye view of the kind of engines which were being designed for the home railways in the post superheating era up to the end of the independent railways. Use of 4–4–0 and 4–4–2 had fallen away and the 4–6–0 had emerged as the basic passenger type with the 'Pacific' appearing for the first time in 1922, other than Churchward's abortive and solitary *Great Bear* of 1908. The freight scene was much as before except for some increase in size, but products of great significance resided in the three 2–6–0 engines shown in the table (entries 9, 10 and 11). The GW4300 class engine was the true prototype of the moderate-sized mixed traffic machine, equally at home with passenger trains up to 70mph (112kph) as with fast and slow freight working. This versatility, denied to previous candidates by reason of wheel diameter, valve events and lateral stability while running fast, was to prove of such value in increasing utilisation as running costs mounted, that in the last resort when British Railways launched its final range of 12 standard steam types in 1948, eleven of them were specifically designed for mixed traffic, and increasing use was made of such machines in the intervening period.

The second 2–6–0, inspired by Pearson and designed in 1917 by Clayton at Ashford for Maunsell of the Southern Railway, was the first application of Churchward's principles away from the Great Western Railway itself, and those principles found their way after the war by devious means and at a varying pace into the design practice of the three other grouped railways.

The third 2–6–0 (entry 11) typifies the increasing use of simple expansion multiple cylinders, not only for larger powers, but because this arrangement was held by some to have advantages in its own right compared with use of two cylinders only. Gresley, CME at this time of the Great Northern Railway, was one such, and his large three-cylinder 2–6–0 of 1920 paved the way for his first Pacific of 1922, and of a whole range of locomotives for different traffic purposes down to quite small sizes. He was by no means the pioneer of this system of propulsion, the North Eastern Railway having become considerable users before him, but by developing an elegant and simple system of lateral rocking shafts introducing a two to one proportion in its relative movements he was able to use the two outside valve gears to operate the inside valve. His work in this connection was widely studied and this form of inside valve operation was adopted at one period in America, as we have already seen, and in Australia and different parts of Africa and Asia, although inherent defects caused its ultimate abandonment everywhere.

The advantages claimed for multiple cylinders were more even turning moment and therefore greater sure-footedness in starting heavy trains, a reduction in loads at axleboxes and motion pins, and a more even draught upon the firebed reducing losses from incomplete combustion. Three cylinders were claimed to produce all these advantages, but four cylinders could only do so by setting the cranks at 135 degrees apart and producing 8 exhaust beats per revolution. The validity of the above claims and the relative merits of using two, three or four cylinders were hotly debated in design offices and in the proceedings of engineering societies in different countries for many years, but the results were quite inconclusive, and the best commentary upon them is to observe that in nearly every country in the world except France, the last stage of steam development witnessed a reversion to use of two simple expansion outside cylinders except where loading-gauge conditions made this prohibitive, preference being given to increasing the steam pressure to obtain the required power rather than to multiplying the moving parts.

Notwithstanding this trend towards multiple cylinders, compounding with or without superheating found little favour in British practice in the present century, and Table 12 lists the few engines of this kind which were introduced in our first period. There is no doubt that the obvious failure of the series of compound engines designed by Webb for the London and North Western Railway at the end of the previous century had had a profound effect upon all the other CMEs and CMEs-to-be watching from the side-lines. This was not a failure of compounding as such, but of a defective application arising from one of the worst cases of blind Victorian autocracy on record, and the story has often been told. The second entry in the table indicates the last sorry specimen of this ill-starred brood, and Webb's successor swept away all traces of multiple expansion as quickly as possible, replacing them by simple and infinitely more effective machines in the main stream of British design. There was another system, appearing first on the North Eastern Railway in 1898, and then on the Midland in 1901 which, using a single high-pressure cylinder between the frames and two low-pressure cylinders outside, obtained a satisfactory relationship between hp and lp cylinder volumes, and was both as simple and effective as any simple expansion three-cylinder locomotive. This system was the work of W. M. Smith, Chief Draughtsman of the first-mentioned railway above, and, as subsequently simplified by Deely of the Midland as to starting arrangements, was applied to forty-five of the principal main-line passenger engines of the Midland System as well as to four 4–4–2 engines on the Great Central. Its use was subsequently expanded by the LMS after 1923 as will presently be seen, and it was the only compounding system to find itself on more than a handful of engines built in England in the present century. This arrangement of cylinders reappeared in 1932 on the Great Northern Railway of Ireland and in isolated examples, of which the most notable was a series of five 4–8–2 locomotives, series 476, built in 1950 for the Czechoslovakian State Railways. Strangely enough the cylinder dimensions of this machine of $19\frac{5}{8}$in (500mm) hp and $22\frac{7}{8}$in (580mm) lp × 26in (660mm) stroke were very close to those of the Midland series of more than forty years before which were 19in (482mm) and 21in (533mm) × 26in (660mm), the difference in power output between the diminutive 4–4–0 and the vast 4–8–2 being accounted for by the size of the boiler and a difference in working pressure of from 200 to 285lb/sq in (14·1 to 20kg/cm^2).

Chapter 5 will outline how the de Glehn system of compounding caught the attention of the world, and of various examples constructed at the turn of the century for different administrations, three were brought over by Churchward for the Great Western Railway in 1903–5. Although he learned so much of valve events and steam distribution from these imports, he was not tempted to adopt the system after he had found the way to obtain equal if not better performance and thermal efficiency from simple expansion, as exemplified by his Star class of four-cylinder simple engines introduced in 1907. The sole other de Glehn application, a 4–4–2, built by the Vulcan Company for the Great Northern Railway in 1905, had no aftermath, for in some carefully conducted trials a year later the newcomer showed no advantage over the native Ivatt two-cylinder simple engine.

In France, as steam neared its end, and traffic requirements of loads and speeds were increasing after 1945, the four-cylinder compound reached its dimensional limitations, not only in finding room for the cylinders themselves but in bearing and crank axle dimensions as well. Relief was found by turning over to the three-cylinder compound with cylinders arranged on the Deeley principle, and as Chapter 5 will also tell, had steam continued it is upon this initially British system that further development would have had to be based.

World War I had far less effect upon the domestic locomotive stud than in other European countries. No invasion occurred and few bombs fell in England, and only moderate numbers of some unimportant locomotive classes were collected from the railways and sent to serve the armies in France and elsewhere. The War Office did, however, select the Great Central 2–8–0 (entry 8 in Table 10) for construction by private builders to the extent of 521 units for the same purpose. This simple massive engine without frills was found very acceptable, and after the war the considerable numbers of survivors found their way back to service on the newly formed London and North Eastern and

Great Western Groups. Ninety-two of them lived to serve their country abroad a second time in World War II.

The engines built for home service between 1911 and 1922 followed for the most part the same tradition of appearance and content as had their forerunners of 1900–10. Just here and there as in the case of the SECR 2–6–0 already mentioned, and the LSWR 4–6–0 (entry 6) there began to appear those changes in aspect and accessibility consisting of raised running plates and outside valve gear which were destined to become universal. The later examples continued to be just as variable in their performance as had the earlier types, but superheating had introduced a fuel saving of some 20 per cent for a given amount of work done. Bearing in mind that outside the Great Western, long steam lap and valve travel and straight and unrestricted steam ports were practically unknown, and the importance of such matters unappreciated, astonishing performances were coaxed out of some of the engine classes of this era, notably the George V 4–4–0s of the LNWR, the Director class 4–4–0s of the GCR and the 1500 class 4–6–0s of the Great Eastern. In such machines, combustion rates of 120lb/sq ft (588kg/m^2) of grate and more were still within the capacity of a single fireman and with plenty of steam thus available, devices such as trick ports and ample exhaust clearance where applied, managed to turn a great deal of it into power at the wheel rim, even if rather wastefully as regards thermal efficiency. Other engines again, which shall be nameless, were so antiquated as to valve events, so constipated as to steam flow and so strangulated as to air supply to the grate and draught through the boiler tubes, as to be unable to run satisfactorily at all, and it is one of the wonders of this era, that certain railway managements could be bamboozled into continuing for long years with engine classes so manifestly inferior to their fellows.

Such were the highlights of domestic development up to the year 1922. Outside the Great Western, and with the exception of the introduction of the Schmidt superheater, foreign practice had had a negligible effect upon British design, notwithstanding periodic visits of the officers of various railways to America and elsewhere. What then of the influence of British practice and design outside those offshore islands? It was widespread, but in saying it was due more to political and financial interests than necessarily to inherent technical advantages, one must not underrate its appeal to engineers in charge of distant administrations who had been trained in the British school and who desired only to practise with what was familiar to them. Its solid worth in simplicity and good workmanship were very important where less than normal maintenance facilities were available. Table 14 lists some representative exports.

India as part of the Empire drew its motive power both in thought and deed exclusively from the mother country. At the beginning of the century, the locomotive manufacturers of England complained to the Secretary of State for India that one of the reasons they found it difficult to meet the upsurge of requirements was the large number of different designs which were required. It was pointed out that many 4–4–0 and 0–6–0 classes were on demand, all more or less of the same general dimensions, but differing in almost every detail. The Locomotive Superintendents Committee of the Indian Railway Conference Association considered this stricture in 1901, as an outcome of which, there being no new locomotive design capacity in India itself, the British Engineering Standards Association in London was asked in 1903 to design a range of standard types for Indian requirements. The early result was six very typically British designs for the broad gauge lines having narrow fireboxes and plate frames, three, the 4–4–0, 0–6–0 and 2–6–4 tank types, having inside cylinders and three, the 4–4–2, 4–6–0 and 2–8–0, having outside cylinders. By 1910 orders had been placed for 840 of these engines mainly by the State-owned lines, but the railways still operating as independent companies such as the Great Indian Peninsula and the Bengal Nagpur made many alterations of detail to their own orders, and added

25 Although designed by his successor, this class enshrined every Churchward feature, and provided backbone of express services on Great Western Railway from 1923 until the end of steam; 4-cylinder simple 4–6–0 No 5014 *Goodrich Castle* [*E. S. Cox*

27 Former London & North Eastern Railway 3-cylinder simple 4–6–2 No 60017 *Silver Fox* designed by Gresley, who applied certain Chapelon features. This class held the world steam speed record of 126mph (200kph) [*E. S. Cox*

28 Ex-Southern Railway 3-cylinder simple 4–6–2 No 34044 *Woolacombe*. Originally designed by Bulleid with external streamline casing and three internal valve gears enclosed in oil bath, it was subsequently rebuilt with three normal Walschaert gears and streamlined casing removed

29 Ultimate British Railways Standard design; 3-cylinder simple 4–6–2 No 71000 built in 1954. Fitted with Caprotti valve gear, it had the most economical steam consumption of any simple expansion design [*E. S. Cox*

30 Last steam locomotive to be built for British Railways—2–10–0 No 92220 *Evening Star*, completed at Swindon in 1960. Although primarily for freight duties, this class on occasion ran passenger trains at up to 90 mph(144kph)
[*R. D. Tuck*

32 Belgian version of Caledonian Railway 0–6–0 No 2868 of Type 30 as running in 1931. Major change from original was adoption of longer firebox, placing cab further back
[*C. Shorto*

31 Belgian adaptation of Caledonian Railway Dunalastair Class 4–4–0 originally designed by McIntosh. No 3267 of Type 18, photographed at Ghent in 1931. Note cab with three side windows and uncharacteristic chimney fitted later [*C. Shorto*

33 Dutch version of a typically British form of 4–4–0 No 2124, built in Germany 1914 as seen at Roosendaal in 1930 [*C. Shorto*

further types outside the standard list. Superheating brought a first modification to the basic standards and soon larger boilers were found desirable to the 4–4–0 and 2–8–0 classes, and even the State-owned lines began to demand variations to meet their own alleged differences in operating conditions. Still, on the whole, this series was successful and served India well for moderate outputs, particularly the 4–6–0 which continued to be built until as late as 1947, although as will presently be seen there was a change in policy towards a new series of standard designs in 1921.

It is interesting to think that because of endless variety on the same basic theme, manufacturers might have succeeded in obtaining a similar measure of standardisation on the independent railways in Great Britain, had it not been for the fact that most of these railways designed and built their own engines. Then, too, in India, unlike the case in England, military considerations had a powerful influence, and if the much discussed invasion from the north ever took place, the facility of using any engine in any locality with a common provision of spares was thought to be essential.

The countries of South America also accepted a large quota of British design, particularly Argentina, where the principal railways were British built and owned, and their motive power policy directed by British engineers. Between 1901 and 1920, 2,053 steam locomotives were imported into the Argentine from British builders, but here, with no overriding governmental intervention, no standardisation was attempted, and the major lines, Central Argentine, Buenos Aires Great Southern, Buenos Aires Western and Buenos Aires and Pacific, as well as the Sao Paulo Railway in Brazil, maintained their own distinctive designs, none of which would have looked out of place had they miraculously been encountered between London and Leicester in their spiritual home. Working on the 5ft 6in rail gauge, enjoying a generous loading gauge, and with operating conditions favouring long hauls on fairly level routes at moderate speeds, there were some quite large engines, and the Pacific type first appeared in 1905, well before its emergence in the home country. The above-mentioned operating features also favoured a curious survival in the form of the two-cylinder cross compound, not seen in England in the present century. Engines of this kind continued to be ordered for the Argentine until 1930, one strange by-product being a large 4–8–4 tank engine delivered in 1928 for suburban services on the Central Argentine Railway.

Australia was another country which, until 1922, accepted the unadulterated British product and followed British design in locomotives built in its own workshops. There, 4–4–0, 4–6–0 and 2–8–0 of conventional size and aspect proliferated of which several entries in Table 15 give some examples. Only the 0–6–0 was missing, a wheel arrangement hardly seen, possibly because track conditions in the outback where such engines might normally expect to work, did not favour the absence of guiding wheels. In Egypt too a succession of British CMEs reproduced the unmistakable shapes varied only in earlier specimens by having cabs with open sides and a roof with a fringe of perforated metal attached to its underside looking like nothing so much as fretwork.

We have only space to refer to broad gauge overseas lines, but in the same period there was a vast export of engines of British design to narrow gauge lines, the most notable of course being South Africa, which even as early as 1902 had introduced the Pacific and which continued to progress with sizes of engine comparable with those on the broad gauge notwithstanding its own 3ft 6in (1067mm) rail spacing.

In all this vast output, British lay-out in its conservative form was accepted with hardly any intrusion from the outside world, excepting possibly the single series of 17 4–4–2 compound engines of pure de Glehn lineage built by the North British Locomotive Company for the Bengal Nagpur Railway in 1909 (entry 8, Table 12). The only rumblings were concerned with the difficulties of burning of low-grade coal on narrow grates with its consequential need for ready ash disposal, and of proneness to hot boxes and frame fracture, indigenous to British experience at home and often cruelly accentuated under the conditions in which the overseas engines had to work.

Indeed hot axleboxes were the hidden plague of locomotive operation at this time, not only due to insufficient bearing surface to meet vertical load and horizontal piston thrust, but also, even where surfaces were adequate, due to faulty lubrication and defective alignment and machining which the repair methods and equipment in shops and sheds of the day found it impossible to correct. Up to 1922, passenger and freight locomotives in Britain were each experiencing at least one case of coupled-wheel hot boxes per annum. This was the average, but for the bad types, of which there were not a few, the incidence was much worse. Having regard to the total number at work this placed a tremendous burden upon the maintenance facilities. By simple inspection of drawings, and use of reasonable analogy, it is to be suspected that many foreign railways suffered in a similar manner, and certainly in such countries as India, where climate and a low grade of labour added to the disabilities, hot boxes used sometimes to assume nightmare proportions.

II. 1923–1947

From 1923 until the outbreak of World War II in 1939, British design awoke, and whereas up to the former years only the Great Western had really stepped into the new century technically, now the other three newly grouped companies, at a varying pace related to the personalities in power, bestirred themselves and first caught up with, and in the case of two at any rate finally surpassed, their earlier mentor. The main lines of development on each of the four newly formed railways have been very well documented and there must be few with any interest in locomotives at all who have not seen or read of the principal engine types which were produced and know something of their history and exploits. For comparison's sake, Table 11 lists the dimensions of those engines which may be considered most typical of the different categories. Rather than describe yet again their individual features, it is proposed to deal now with those collective aspects which best epitomise British practice, which reached its summit of achievement in 1939. Although much was done thereafter there were few things which did not have their technical roots in those very live and formative years before the last war.

To the end, the size of locomotives used in Great Britain was moderate, and nothing approaching maximum power operation as known in America or even in France was ever called for. On the passenger side terminal stations in heavily built up areas in the major cities presented a finite length of platform, which it was prohibitively expensive if not impossible to extend. Moreover, smaller frequent trains suited the commercial requirements of the country better than long trains at widely spaced intervals. Train length was thus limited to the region of 15 coaches which the combination of loading gauge and curvature kept within a length of 63ft (19202mm) each and in which the required degree of equipment and amenity could be provided with a weight of about 33 tons (33·5 tonnes). Thus the general maximum passenger train load was 550 tons (560 tonnes) as compared with 750 tons (763 tonnes) in France and over 1,000 tons (1016 tonnes) in the United States, speaking of course in the most general terms. With an allowable axleload of 20 tons (20·4 tonnes) normal, and 22½ tons (22·9 tonnes) on the most important main lines, sufficient adhesion was obtained from six coupled wheels, and the eight-coupled engine for express passenger work was not generally required.

On the freight side, the heaviest trains, those conveying bulk coal, were limited by the length of sidings, by the strength of the three link couplings in normal use, and by the brake power available on the engine at the front and the guard's van at the end of the train, the intermediate load-carrying wagons being unbraked. For the fast freight, power brakes were fitted to each vehicle, but the system of vacuum operation produced problems of propagation and shock with increasing length of train. Thus for mineral trains, 1,500 tons (1523 tonnes) was exceptional and 1,000 tons (1016 tonnes) of trailing load was a customary maximum, with faster vacuum brake-fitted van trains running at about 750 tons (763 tonnes). None of this, either passenger or freight, called for more than about 40,000lb (18200kg) of steam per hour maximum from 50sq ft (4·65m²) of grate area, and hand firing with its better efficiency remained sufficient to the end, for operating at the speeds associated with the loads in question.

Whereas on main-line passenger operations the nature of the track and its alignment permitted speeds up to 90mph (144kph), and in special trails up to 125mph (200kph), fast automatic brake-fitted freight trains could not readily exceed 60mph (96kph) because of the poor stability of the kind of short wheelbase four-wheel wagon still in general use. Unbraked mineral trains were limited to 40mph (64kph) due to the sheer impossibility of stopping within any reasonable distance from anything faster. While at first different types of engine were designed and built for each of these kinds of traffic, rising costs introduced the need to obtain continuous utilisation from the motive power, and this forced the production, as has already been noted, of mixed traffic types able to turn their hand successfully to any class of traffic. This trend did not reduce the number of engine types so much as might be expected, however, because the axle weights which the different routes spread over the country would accept remained widely different. Thus, even in 1948 at the time of nationalisation, after a great deal had been done over many years by the civil engineers to improve uniformity, it was still necessary to recognise and design for six different levels of permitted axleload, 22½, 21, 19, 17, 16 and 13½ tons (22·9, 21·3, 19·3, 17·3, 16·2 and 13·7 tonnes) respectively.

Inheriting a vast variety of motive power from its former owners, in 1923 the four new companies were faced with an obvious need to eliminate some of this variety for the future. The LMS alone found 393 different classes in the 10,316 engines which it took over. In the next ten years there was to be a great slaughter of old and feeble machines, and each company sought to bring some rationalisation into what it had built for replacements. It was here that the personalities of the chief mechanical engineers, still strong powers in the land, produced different interpretations of the act of standardisation. To the Great Western, still retaining its existing lines with the addition only of some minor railways in Wales, there was no problem; it simply carried on as before, applying its already highly standardised taper boilers and certain other of its own fittings to such of its newly acquired stock as it wished to retain. The London and North Eastern had Gresley for mechanical chief, who, since he had inaugurated standard outlines in his Pacific, 2–8–0 and 2–6–0 engines for the erstwhile Great Northern Railway, already had a proven pattern on which to go forward. For reasons, however, which have never been very clearly explained, he confined his further development of new standard types to one 4–6–0, two 2–8–2 and two 2–6–2 designs, one in each of the two last categories remaining on the ground with only two units built. There was also a 2–6–2 tank engine. For the rest he was content to perpetuate selected types from one or other of the former companies, standard neither with one another nor with his own personal designs. Between these two extremes were some 4–4–0 and 0–6–0 engines, new designs it is true, but perpetuating many features of the old North Eastern Railway.

The Southern Railway embraced the former South Eastern & Chatham, Brighton, and London & South Western companies. Maunsell, the new CME of the group, had held this position on the first mentioned of the constituents and until 1939, continued to build engines to two different kinds of standards in parallel. His smaller engines followed his own practice on the SECR, while his larger ones were based on London and South Western practice, and there was very little common ground in between.

The London Midland and Scottish got off to a false start and had to standardise its new locomotives twice over. Circumstances had caused it to have four CMEs in its first ten years of existence. The first two, Hughes and Fowler, were overborne by a Motive Power Superintendent, Anderson, who forced the standardisation of erstwhile Midland Railway practices and details and by 1932, 2,002 new engines had been built in this style of fourteen different designs, some being former Midland types altered only in detail, and the rest being larger improvisations upon the basic theme as in the case of the well-known Royal Scot class of 4–6–0. The third CME, Lemon, only held office for a year, and Stanier was brought in in 1932 from the Great Western by a management unconvinced that the existing regime was producing the best in traffic effectiveness and utilisation potential. Stanier amalgamated the best in former LMS and GW practice and turned out 1,225 engines to eleven further designs in seven years forming a second complete series of standard machines having little interchangeable with the previous standards.

These experiences illuminate a problem of locomotive design all over the world. Not to standardise is to carry a hidden but very real burden of increased first and maintenance costs. If, on the other hand, one sets out to standardise, how far does one go, how cope with the infiltration of new requirements, new developments, how permit the free play of individuality so potent for progress? How, above all, to measure the results of such a policy where the life of the product is over thirty years? No country and no administration has ever answered these questions satisfactorily.

Turning to design features, the indigenous operating conditions already referred to permitted a wider gap between average and maximum power than was general elsewhere, so that locomotives could be operated for the most part in their range of maximum efficiency. This emphasised the importance of early cut-off working, and rendered obligatory a measure of attention to valve events, and freedom for steam to enter and leave the cylinders long before Chapelon in France published his monumental work. First introduced effectively in 1903 by Churchward as a result of his studies with the imported French de Glehn compounds, the long lap, long travel piston valve was taken up, as already shown, by Maunsell on the SECR in 1917 and its use was introduced by Hughes to the LMS in 1924. Maunsell extended the application to the Eastleigh sector of his fleet in 1925, and finally, as a result of a famous interchange trial with a GWR locomotive, Gresley used it for the first time on his Pacifics in 1926. Under British conditions this seemingly tiny modification of using 1½ to 1¾in (38 to 45mm) steam lap instead of 1in (25mm), of employing a valve travel increased from between 4½ and 5in (114 and 127 mm) on the one hand to 6 to 7in (152 to 178mm) on the other brought about reductions in steam and coal consumptions of the order of 20 per cent not incompatible with the benefits of superheating itself. Many existing engines, particularly on the LNER and SR, were modified in this way to their lasting benefit, while the gospel soon spread to the British manufacturers and the products they exported overseas.

There was much variety of thought in boiler design and differences in practice were tenaciously held, but a long time elapsed before the general availability of stationary test plants permitted the contestants to be put to the question. The LMS favoured the Belpaire firebox, greatly improved in shape and steam space by Stanier. Gresley on the other hand used only the round top box and even converted the Belpaires which he had inherited to that form. Maunsell on the Southern used both alternatively in successive designs. There was no difference of view in these years, however, as regards material for the inner firebox, copper being universally adopted. With absence of consistent water treatment and sufficiently weldable grades of steel not yet developed, this was probably a wise practice, but it found its ceiling as greater power was called for.

Until the results of Wagner's work in Germany filtered in, heat absorption and gas flow in the Stephenson boiler were not widely understood, and the resultant variations in tube proportion produced both free steaming and very reluctant boilers almost at random, an effect much emphasised by rule-of-thumb proportions of blastpipe and chimney established before stationary test plant work could isolate the variables. Here, although the work at Altoona in the USA was readily available, American conditions were so widely different as to shed little light on the problem in Britain, and an undoubted weakness in the home product was the variability of steaming quality even with good coal from one class to another.

Very great strides were made in the 1930s with axlebox design, manufacture, repair and lubrication. This was one of Stanier's big contributions to progress, taking the basic Churchward box of the GW and so improving its lubrication that the liability of any given locomotive to running a hot box rose from the two years which it had attained on the Fowler Standard engines to ten years average for all the Stanier designs; no less than sixteen years in the case of the five best classes. For all practical purposes the hot-box problem with plain bearings was vanquished by 1939 so far as further new design was concerned. Where, however, existing engines carried insufficient bearing surface or facilities for lubrication, or where large inside cylinders imposed crippling loads on portions of the bearing ill fitted to take them, then there was no way out, and the sins of the fathers were visited upon the children in full measure.

Outside or multi-cylinders with raised running plates and outside Walschaert's valve gear became universal for the more important new designs on the LNE, LMS and Southern Railways, but the Great Western retained inside Stephenson's valve gear and low running plates for its two cylinder engines until the end of its separate existence. In spite of its manifest drawbacks, the inside cylinder engine for secondary or freight services was only reluctantly abandoned. Older existing designs were multiplied in large numbers and new 0–6–0 designs, albeit often assembled from many already existing components, were produced on all four railways up to 1937. Thus British conservatism had its last fling and machines compact and cheap in first cost were obtained at the price of substandard repair performance and traffic versatility. For its larger engines, the GW used four cylinders and the LNE three. The other two railways used both three and four cylinders for different designs, and as already stated it is clear that neither system had any marked merit over the other. The LMS also built 195 three-cylinder compound 4–4–0s on the Smith system between 1924 and 1932 to a design closely based upon that of the 45 such engines already running the principal services on the Midland Railway before amalgamation. More economical by some 20 per cent than contemporary simple expansion machines having short travel valves, these engines were shown in their turn to be less economical by about the same proportion than simple expansion engines having modern valve events. Within this period a single four-cylinder 4–6–0 of Hughes design was in 1926 converted to compound by renewing the inside cylinders, this by way of a forerunner to the greatest non-event of the inter-war period, namely the abortive development of a four-cylinder compound Pacific under Fowler's auspices which never saw the light of day.

In the concluding years up to 1939 increasing attention was paid to the work of Chapelon in France, who by opening out the steam circuit all the way from regulator intake to blastpipe tip, had disclosed new vistas of performance and efficiency not only for compound but for simple expansion as well. Gresley and Stanier in particular took note in a practical manner of the possibilities involved and in their final Pacific designs paid close attention to ease of passage for the steam through the cylinders which contributed greatly to the brilliant performance of which the A4 class 4–6–2 and the Coronation 4–6–2 were capable, the two designs having maximum speeds of 125mph (200kph) and 114mph (182kph) respectively standing to their credit.

The various developments outlined above were gradually applied to engines designed and built for overseas use, and the design offices of the principal manufacturers, in close touch with progress on the home railways, had much to contribute when, as was usually the case, they were asked to collaborate with the engineers of overseas railways in the preparation of new designs. Table 14 also lists a number of representative classes exported between 1923 and 1939, and apart from increase in dimensions, introduction of the various features described much increased the value of these engines to their owning administrations. While there is little which calls for special comment as regards developments for the Argentine, experiences with those for India had a powerful influence in giving British design a final twist in the direction of a more international outlook in what it provided for railways abroad.

It has been explained how various modifications had been introduced in a random manner on the BESA standard engines in India, and a Locomotive Standards Committee was set up by the Railways Board at Delhi in 1924 in order to revise the BESA designs, introducing long travel valve gear, improved smokeboxes and other features, and also to recommend new and more powerful types for future building—above all more suitable for the burning of low-grade coal. Three of the Indian railways had already taken the initiative in ordering pairs of experimental Pacific designs with wide fireboxes, from England for the Bombay, Baroda and Central India Railway and the East Indian, and for the Madras and Southern Mahratta from America. The new Standards Committee recommended wide firebox engines only and thus were born the X series of standard engines of 4–6–2 and 2–8–2 wheel arrangements, as set out in entries 3 to 6 in Table 14. These engines designed by the Consulting Engineers in London, Messrs. Rendel Palmer and Tritton, and built from 1926 onwards, expressed faithfully in all their main features the second phase of typical British design—outside cylinders, long travel Walschaert's valve gear, plate frames and partly raised running plates with rudimentary splashers. They were un-British only in using a three-point suspension system with compensating levers on the American model. It is unnecessary to enlarge upon the story, so often told, of how these engines proved to be unstable on the track and prone to derailment due to insufficient guiding forces at leading bogie and trailing truck. It is sufficient for our study of national inter-relationship to say that the inspiration for the measures which cured the trouble came from France, whose railways had had long experience of running by Pacifics on indifferent track, and that the correct values of side control finally arrived at in India, had repercussions back in England. There a few of the bigger engines had shown something of the same unstable tendencies even if without the same disastrous results, and there was on the LMS and LNE Railways in particular a general stiffening up of control spring values on the more important engines used in high speed service.

This series of engines showed its unsuitability for overseas conditions in other ways as the Pacific Locomotive Committee Report indicated. The 284 engines of the XA, XB and XC classes had experienced 501 cases of frame fracture up to mid-1938, while 205 firebox tubeplates had had to be changed due to cracking in the radius of the top flanges. Steaming capacity particularly of the XB was limited because the available free area through the tubes could only pass less hot gases than the firegrate was capable of generating. The onset of war caused the search for cures to be laid aside, but plenty of thinking and investigation was going on with the result that when the need for new motive power became pressing in 1942, an entirely new Pacific design was produced in conjunction with the Baldwin Company, and major American features were incorporated such as bar frames, steel firebox with syphons, a boiler with very free steaming qualities, self-cleaning front end, and so on. This WP class had been multiplied greatly since the war, and two following classes, a corresponding WG 2–8–2 in 1950 and a lighter Pacific class WL in 1955, although designed and built in the first place in Great Britain, have retained those American features which so well suit the natural conditions in the sub-continent (Tables 7 and 8).

Before leaving the Indian scene, it is interesting to note that the Bengal Nagpur Railway, rebellious as ever against direction from the State, had called for a four-cylinder compound version of the standard XC Pacific in 1929. In this it was encouraged by its good experience with the non-standard de Glehn compound Atlantics which had been running since 1908, and this system of compounding was repeated in the larger engines. Pre-Chapelon as they were there is no record that they surpassed the normal XCs in any material aspect, and the author's only encounter with them when visiting India with the Pacific Locomotive Committee in 1938 was quite a hair-raising experience. Whether the intercepting valve which could direct the hp exhaust into the blast pipe for starting was defective, or whether the Eurasian driver had some quirk of his own in leaving it half open, a long experience of footplate work has never produced such irregular and muffled exhaust noises as emanated from that engine. Truly like the chariots of the Egyptians, it drave heavily!

Some reference has already been made in Chapter 3 to the gradual Australian trend towards adoption of leading American features, starting with grease lubrication, self-cleaning smokeboxes, rocking grates and hopper ashpans on quite British seeming engines, and then after 1943 veering away towards steel fireboxes, syphons and cast steel beds in the home-produced locomotives. If ever a companion volume of this comes to be written covering narrow-gauge developments, exactly the same trend as in India and Australia would be seen in South Africa, which administration after taking delivery of a few trial engines from America in 1924, thereafter found their features so suitable to their conditions, that a subsequent influx of even larger and more powerful engines through the years, almost exclusively built in England or Germany, retained the preferred features in full measure.

To some extent we have here overrun our story into the post-war period, but the gradual transition from British thinking to American thinking in Britain's overseas sphere of influence is an interesting one. It was by no means a betrayal of basic British design which had so well served the home railways and, indeed the world, for many decades, nor was it a take-over by aggressive Yankee salesmanship. It arose from within the administrations concerned mainly from Englishmen for whom the facts of locomotive life in their own territory had become all too apparent. Many of them would have resented keenly the charge that they were 'going American' and a number of admirable British features remained after the changeover had been made. The plain fact was, however, that in important aspects, the natural and operating conditions which had given rise to American development were also present in many overseas countries, and some at any rate of the American features now adopted would have had in the long run to be invented, even if the New World had never been discovered. In discussing all such trends, however, it must be remembered that the work of many independent hands is seldom clear cut. The above seeks to identify a trend, but there were naturally exceptions due to engineers who looked askance at these alien innovations. If this trend obtruded on the larger and highly developed overseas railways, how much more did it apply to the lesser but more 'difficult' lines in remoter parts of the world on which British engineers found themselves in charge? Few men had more experience in the steam era than P. C. Dewhurst who for a time had to provide motive power for tortuous heavily graded lines in high altitudes in the Andes. His summing up of the requirements for overseas design was of universal application. 'The characteristics of the line and track must be properly met,' he said. 'It is no use placing a more or less normal locomotive on a line of special characteristic and then saying, "The line is abnormal", or "The track is inadequate". The locomotive has to be made to fit the line.'*

During the 1939–45 war, new design work for railways in Britain was damped down, except only for the appearance of a new three-cylinder simple expansion 4–6–2 engine in 1941 for the Southern Railway (entry 15, Table 11) which combined the American style of steel inner firebox and French Le Maitre blastpipe and chimney arrangements with a novel chain-driven valve gear totally enclosed in an oil bath between the frames. This latter novelty was unsuccessful and the engines, of which 140 units of two varieties were built up to 1957, were subsequently rebuilt in normal form. Once again war requirements called for the design and construction of no less than 1,462 engines of 2–8–0, 2–10–0 and 0–6–0 tank types of basic British design for the War Department but, like the German 'Krieglokomotivs', shorn of all frills and designed to save man-hours and scarce materials in their building. Some 833 were acquired by British railways after the war, and some of them are still at work at this writing in the last pockets of steam operation still extant. The remainder played a brief part in the immediate post-war on Dutch, Belgian and French railways and in the Middle East. More popular abroad was the Stanier design of 2–8–0 for the LMS Railway, which had been adopted at the beginning of hostilities as the official 'war locomotive', until the simpler War Department engines referred to above were put into production. So well did the Egyptians like them that in 1952, long after the war was over, 20 engines were ordered from the British Vulcan firm on which the chassis was pure Stanier LMS, but the parallel boiler was one more closely standard with those used on other Egyptian engines (Table 14, entry 13).

As the war drew to a close a curious case of international co-operation arose in the conception and design of an engine for use in the territories expected shortly to be liberated, and sponsored by UNRRA. British industry worked up a 2–8–0 design with the assistance of representatives of seven European countries, and the resulting 'Liberation' locomotive, as it was called, was built in 1946 to the extent of 110 units, and delivered to Czechoslovakia, Poland, Yugoslavia and Luxemburg. With 19 tons axleload and plate frames, they exemplified a strange mixture of national features, but while thankfully received, they started no new trend in the hands of their recipients.

In the three years between the end of the war and 1948, the railways in Britain set about reinvigorating their fleets in an individual manner, and none of them remained quite what they had been before. Although Hawkesworth, who became CME of the GWR in 1941, produced a further 4–6–0 mixed traffic design, this was almost entirely in the tradition of his predecessors, but some work was initiated with the tardy application of high degree superheat, with blastpipe and chimney proportions and with the whole air-gas-steam circuit in the boiler which raised the performance and efficiency of existing GWR engines to much higher levels.

On the Southern Railway, Bulleid continued with his unconventional Pacifics, to which he now added a similar and further class having an 18-ton (18·3-tonnes) instead of a 21-ton (21·3-tonnes) axleload. On the LNER, Gresley had died in 1941, and his successor Thompson did what had been a commonplace with the old autocratic CMEs of pre-1923, namely completely reversed the Gresley line of development, and proceeded to design new engines, type for type no more powerful and rarely better than what had gone before. The conjugated valve gear for three cylinders was, however, replaced by

* *Locomotive design for Overseas Service*, by P. C. Dewhurst, Proc Inst Loco Engrs No 98, 1930.

34 Every feature in this Dutch inside cylinder 4–6–0 had some counterpart in British practice. No 3501 at Eindhoven in 1930 [*C. Shorto*

35 British design for East Indian Railway at the turn of the century. 4–6–0 No 1105, as running in 1938 [*E. S. Cox*

36 Largest of the X series of standard Pacifics designed in England for general use on Indian Railways. East Indian XC Class engine No 614 [*E. S. Cox*

37 De Glehn 4-cylinder compound version of XC Class Pacific built in Britain in 1928 for Bengal Nagpur Railway [*E. S. Cox*

39 Postwar Indian Class WG 2–8–2 locomotives newly constructed at Chitteranjan workshops

38 Representatives of seven European countries assisted British designers in producing this engine for service in liberated countries after World War II. 110 units were distributed between Czechoslovakia, Poland, Yugoslavia and Luxemburg. Yugoslav State Rly 2–8–0 No 38.029 [*English Electric Co*

41 Last phase of British design for the Argentine Railways; a 3-cylinder simple 4–6–2 engine with Caprotti valves and gear. Built by Vulcan Foundry, for Central Argentine Railway

UNRRA

1119

40 Preferred Argentine wheel arrangement for freight duties. 2-cylinder simple 4–8–0 No 4210 for Buenos Aires Great Southern Railway built in England of typical British design

42 Ultimate development of Garratt articulated locomotive. New South Wales Railways 4–8–4 + 4–8–4 No 6003, fitted with cast steel beds and roller bearings on all axles. Note extreme freedom for firebox and ashpan design

43 1900 design of de Glehn 4-cylinder compound mixed traffic 4–6–0, built primarily for Nord Railway. No 362 was photographed in 1931 allocated to Nord–Belge System [*C. Shorto*

44 Non-superheated Henry compound of 1906. Paris Lyon Mediterranée 4–6–0 No 230 B 112 at Paris (Lyon) in August 1925 [*C. Shorto*

; Nord de Glehn com-
)und 2–10–0 No 5.031, of
e earliest series introduced
1913. Note length of
ısing covering dome and
ndboxes [*C. Shorto*

6 Last design of express
ıssenger 4–6–0 in France.
st No 230 K 193, originally
esigned in 1924. Wide
ıimney indicates later fitting
ith Le Maitre multiple jet
astpipe [*E. S. Cox*

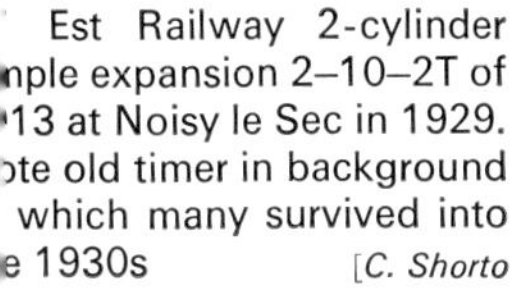

Est Railway 2-cylinder
nple expansion 2–10–2T of
'13 at Noisy le Sec in 1929.
ote old timer in background
which many survived into
e 1930s [*C. Shorto*

48 Nord 2-cylinder simple expansion 2–8–2T for heavy suburban traffic at Paris (Nord). Note Cossart valve gear [E. S. Cox

49 Est de Glehn compound 4–8–2 No 241–014 photographed in original condition in 1930 [C. Shorto

50 PLM 4-cylinder compound 4–8–2 No 241–A–31 at Laroche in 1929. Note LP cylinders outside driving leading coupled axle [C. Shorto

three independent gears, and two instead of three cylinders were applied to all the smaller types. Although Thompson has been much criticised, what he did in these respects was technically right and in keeping with world trends, and when at the eleventh hour of this railway's independence, Peppercorn succeeded in 1946, there was little time to do more than tidy up the somewhat rambling appearance of Thompson's Pacifics and produce the final and very successful A_1 and A_2 4–6–2 classes.

On the LMS, two developments of some importance were introduced in these years by Ivatt on whom the mantle of Stanier had now fallen. First there was the application of self-cleaning front ends, rocking grates and hopper ashpans to all new construction. Excellent experience with these features had been gained with the several hundreds of US designed and built WD 2–8–0s which had been operating in England in 1943–4. Although engines in Britain had got on very well without these features since the beginning, wartime inability and post-war disinclination to cope with time-consuming rough work, rendered this mechanisation of disposal duties entirely opportune. The second step was to borrow from the American roller-bearing manufacturers the idea of using manganese steel rubbing surfaces on axlebox sides and the horn guides in which they worked, and of applying this to plain bearing axleboxes. This attacked locomotive deterioration between repairs at a key point, and lifted repair performance to an altogether higher plane. It was in Ivatt's time too that roller bearings were applied for the first time in England to reciprocating steam locomotives, and he undertook some purposeful and large-scale experiments with rotary cam poppet valve gear. A really decisive move was also made to eliminate splashers and redundant footplating and to carry the running boards from the boiler flanks.

III. 1948 and after

Many of these post-war developments found themselves reproduced in the range of Standard locomotives initiated by Riddles to meet the steam requirements of the unified British Railways after nationalisation in 1948. The inception, design, building and experience with these engines has been most fully described,* and they can be said to epitomise the final stage of British locomotive design practice. It was the original intention that the larger of them, those with leading bogies and trailing trucks, should have bar frames, for the same reasons of security against premature fracture which had led to their widespread adoption in the rest of the world. This proved to be impracticable, however, not only because their added weight would have sacrificed boiler capacity within the permitted axle loading, but also because no equipment and facilities existed within railway as distinct from private manufacture workshops, not only for the building but also for the repair of frames of this kind.

Nine hundred and ninety-nine of 12 classes of these BR standard engines were built until 1960, in which year the last steam engine for domestic use took the rails, thus bringing to a close a phase in engineering history. Although, as has been described, British design had moved closely towards that of other major world trends, so that there was now little difference in principles, efficiency and general arrangement, even if not in size, between the products of America, Germany and England, there still remained something distinctively British even in the appearance of the BR standard engines. To thumb through the pages of one of the many excellent picture books which have been produced in recent years, setting out side by side illustrations of locomotives in many countries, is to recognise at once in the pages devoted to Britain, an economy in line, an absence of

* *British Railways Standard Steam Locomotives*, by E. S. Cox, Ian Allan.

excrescences, even in the later examples which is entirely characteristic. A few other countries have tried from time to time to capture this 'something'. The firm of Borsig in Germany went through a 'British' phase shortly before World War I. The Dutch railways, arising from the fact of so many of their earlier engines had been designed and built by Beyer Peacocks of Manchester, ordered locomotives from their own builders and from Germany which were nearly, even if not quite, British in appearance. Belgium, too, had acquired 4–4–0s, 0–6–0s and 4–6–0s of British design at the opening of the century. And of all unlikely places in the world, even in America on the Delaware & Hudson and the Baltimore & Ohio Railroads in particular, the attempt was made to capture this distinguished but elusive nuance. In the 1930s, not unconnected with the visit to the USA of the GWR locomotive *King George V* in 1927, some attempts were made to simplify the typical American outline, to pack away all air pumps, feed heaters, pipes and rods out of sight to combine dome and sandbox under a single cover, and of course to provide a lip round the chimney rim. Alas for such good intentions, the result was more often lamentable than beneficial, such borrowed clothes ill becoming the more robust and muscular torso of the American iron horse, and to the student of locomotive good looks there can only be a feeling of thankfulness that this particular phase was short lived.

British design development undoubtedly suffered from not having available earlier means for scientifically testing locomotive performance and efficiency under exactly controlled conditions. Ordinary dynamometer car testing under variable speed conditions left many questions unanswered, and while the LNER had initiated a limited amount of work at constant speed using a brake locomotive, it was not until after World War II that the Rugby Stationary Test Plant initially sponsored by Gresley was built, that the Electrical Mobile Test units inaugurated by the former LMSR became available, and that the remarkable testing procedures developed by Ell at Swindon were applied to controlled road tests and to test-plant procedures. The British Railways' standard engines were under design at the same time that the results of this new wave of testing began to be available, and they benefited to a certain extent from this work, as did some of the more important engines from the former companies still in service. But it came in many respects too late, not only for a full application of what was currently being ascertained, but also in respect of completion of many investigations still unfinished when the onrush of the conquering diesel locomotive swept away all further development of steam.

We have left to the last what was perhaps the biggest contribution to the art since the emergence of the Stephensonian steam locomotive itself, namely the Garratt principle, a contribution entirely British in conception and development. In 1907 H. W. Garratt, an Inspecting Officer for locomotives then under construction at Gorton Foundries for the New South Wales Government, outlined his ideas for a new type of locomotive to the management of Beyer Peacock and Company. Following the granting of a patent, the firm purchased the invention, and became the sole licensees for its exploitation. Like most great inventions, this one was basically simple. Its essence was that the boiler was carried in its own separate frame and slung clear of all the coupled wheels, the latter with the appropriate main frames, running gear and fuel and water tanks forming separate engine units at either end, on which the boiler unit was pivot mounted. At a stroke three most desirable features were fully assured for the first time. First, absolute freedom in boiler, firebox and ashpan design, the restrictions imposed by the coupled wheels in all other types of engine being entirely absent. Secondly, however great the total weight, axle weights and weights per foot run could be held moderate, and thirdly there was ease of passage round the most sinuous of curves without sacrifice in steadiness of riding either on curves or on the straight. This last feature in particular brought the Garratt engine wide use on narrow gauge and 'difficult' railways, whose design problems were met with a satisfaction never seen before. But the other advantages, and especially that of boiler design, made the Garratt a candidate for the solution of the problem of providing maximum power even on wide gauge and conventional railways. Since it is these latter with which this book has principally to do, Table 16 gives particulars of Garratt engines on a number of broad gauge railways around the world, culminating in the huge 4–8–4 + 4–8–4 for the New South Wales Government Railways (entry No 7).

Unfortunately the Garratt was little used in its country of origin, the 'retail' nature of the general traffic not calling as a rule for head end power greater than could readily by provided by conventional design. The 33 2–6–0 + 0–6–2 engines bought by the LMSR in 1927–30 (entry 1) for heavy coal traffic were a poor advertisement for the breed in that the purchasers demanded old-fashioned valve events and undersized axleboxes to the extent that satisfactory performance was crippled—a remarkable example of destructive conservatism. For applications abroad, however, the Garratt could and did have applied to it every worth-while development as it arose, bar frames or cast steel bed, long travel valve gear, roller bearings, mechanical stoker, the lot. From first to last, however, there was a certain chariness in using it for high speed passenger service. Giving a ride like a carriage there seemed no reason why it should not be habitually used at speeds over 60mph (96kph), but in practice it was rarely found running above that speed, and the courage of the Algerian Railways in purchasing 12 engines in 1936 having the 4–6–2 + 2–6–4 wheel arrangement with 5ft 11in (1803mm) diameter coupled wheels, and of the French Nord Railway in running them on trial up to 87mph (140kph), was noteworthy. Similar engines were ordered by the Spanish Central Aragon Railway and the Sao Paulo Railway in Brazil, but in neither case did the permitted speed exceed 60mph (96kph).

A final and intriguing question is whether the Garratt principle could not have been used instead of the Mallet in ultimate expansion in size and power on American Railways before the extinction of steam by the diesel. It certainly could have offered great advantages in boiler proportions. The largest Garratt ever built, a single unit for Russia, had four 22⅞ × 28in (580 × 711mm) cylinders, 4ft 11in (1500mm) coupled wheels, 220lb (15·5kg) pressure, 85·5sq ft (7·94m²) of grate area, and weighed 262½ tons (265 tonnes). It will be seen from some of the entries in Table 5, Chapter 3, that this was still a small engine in comparison with those weighing up to 500 tons complete. But there was no aspect of the Garratt principle which was not capable of further enlargement, and there was a time when the American Locomotive Company showed some interest in acquiring rights to build the Garratt but it all fell through. Apart from an inbred resistance to the incorporation of locomotive ideas from Europe, the engineering fact which probably weighed most heavily with the Americans against the Garratt was the diminution of adhesive weight as supplies of coal and water became used up. Maximum power operation as practised in America demanded every pound of adhesion all the time.

British practice thus absorbed from and gave out to the current of steam locomotive design in full measure, and an innate conservatism did not prevent its end-products, both domestic and exported, from reflecting much of world trend.

GREAT BRITAIN. REPRESENTATIVE LOCOMOTIVES 1900–1910 Table 9

Entry	Year	Wheel Arrangement	Railway	Cylinders Diameter × Stroke inches mm	Coupled Wheels Diameter feet mm	Working Pressure lb/sq in kg/cm²	Grate Area sq ft m²	Weight Engine Working Order: Axle tons tonnes	Adhesive tons tonnes	Total tons tonnes
1	1904	4–4–0	London & North Western 'Precursor'	(A) 19 × 26 483 × 660	6′ 9″ 2057	175 12·3	22·4 2·08	19·0 19·3	38·0 38·6	59·7 60·3
2	1904	4–4–0	Caledonian 140 Class	(A) 19 × 26 483 × 660	6′ 6″ 1981	180 12·7	21·0 1·95	19·0 19·3	37·7 38·3	56·5 57·4
3	1902	4–4–2	Great Northern 251 Class	(B) $18\frac{3}{4}$ × 24 477 × 610	6′ $7\frac{1}{2}$″ 2018	175 12·3	30·9 2·87	18·0 18·3	36·0 36·5	65·5 66·6
4	1903	4–4–2	Great Central	(B) $19\frac{1}{2}$ × 26 495 × 660	6′ 9″ 2057	180 12·7	26·0 2·42	18·5 18·8	37·0 37·6	68·5 69·6
5	1906	4–6–0	Caledonian 'Cardean'	(A) 20 × 26 508 × 660	6′ 6″ 1981	200 14·1	26·0 2·42	18·5 18·8	55·0 55·8	73·0 74·1
6	1902	4–6–0	Great Western 2900 Class	(B) 18 × 30 457 × 762	6′ $8\frac{1}{2}$″ 2044	225 15·8	27·0 2·50	18·2 18·5	54·2 55·0	70·2 71·2
7	1907	4–6–0	Great Western 4001 Class	(4) $14\frac{1}{4}$ × 26 362 × 660	6′ $8\frac{1}{2}$″ 2044	225 15·8	27·0 2·50	18·6 18·9	55·4 56·2	75·6 76·8
8	1908	4–6–2	Great Western 'Great Bear'	(4) 15 × 26 381 × 660	6′ $8\frac{1}{2}$″ 2044	225 15·8	41·8 3·88	20·2 20·5	60·6 61·6	97·2 98·8
9	1903	2–8–0	Great Western	(B) 18 × 30 457 × 762	4′ $7\frac{1}{2}$″ 1419	225 15·8	27·0 2·50	15·5 15·7	61·9 62·8	68·3 69·4
10	1910	0–8–0	Lancashire & Yorkshire Large Boiler	(A) 20 × 26 508 × 660	4′ 6″ 1372	180 12·7	25·6 2·38	17·5 17·8	66·8 67·8	66·8 67·9
11	1901	0–8–0	North Eastern	(B) 20 × 26 508 × 660	4′ $7\frac{1}{4}$″ 1413	200 15·8	21·5 2·00	16·0 16·2	58·3 59·2	58·3 59·2
12	1904	0–6–0	Midland 'Deeley'	(A) $18\frac{1}{2}$ × 26 469 × 660	5′ 3″ 1600	175 12·3	21·0 1·95	17·0 17·3	43·8 44·5	43·8 44·5
13	1900	0–6–0	Caledonian 812 Class	(A) $18\frac{1}{2}$ × 26 469 × 660	5′ 0″ 1524	160 11·2	20·6 1·91	16·7 17·0	45·7 46·4	45·7 46·4
14	1903	4–4–2T	Great Central	(A) 18 × 26 457 × 660	5′ 7″ 1702	160 11·2	19·8 1·84	16·0 16·2	31·6 32·2	62·8 63·8
15	1910	4–6–2T	London & North Western	(A) 20 × 26 508 × 660	5′ 8″ 1727	175 12·3	24·0 2·23	17·0 17·3	45·0 45·7	78·0 79·2

Entry	Year	Wheel Arrangement	Railway	Cylinders Diameter × Stroke inches / mm	Coupled Wheels Diameter feet / mm	Working Pressure lb/sq in / kg/cm²	Grate Area sq ft / m²	Weight Engine Working Order: Axle tons / tonnes	Adhesive tons / tonnes	Total tons / tonnes
1	1913	4–4–0	Great Central 'Director' Class	(A) 19½ × 26 495 × 660	6′ 9″ 2057	180 12·7	26·0 2·43	19·8 20·1	39·6 40·2	61·0 62·0
2	1911	4–4–2	North Eastern Z1 Class	(3) 16½ × 26 418 × 660	6′ 10″ 2083	160 11·2	27·0 2·50	20·0 20·3	40·0 40·6	77·1 78·2
3	1911	4–6–0	Great Eastern 1500 Class	(A) 20 × 28 508 × 711	6′ 6″ 1981	180 12·7	26·5 2·46	16·0 16·2	44·0 44·7	64·0 65·0
4	1913	4–6–0	London & North Western 'Claughton' Class	(4) 16 × 26 406 × 660	6′ 9″ 2051	175 12·3	30·5 2·83	19·7 20·0	59·0 60·0	77·7 79·0
5	1921	4–6–0	Lancashire & Yorkshire	(4) 16½ × 26 418 × 660	6′ 3″ 1905	180 12·7	27·0 2·50	19·7 20·0	59·3 60·3	79·1 80·4
6	1918	4–6–0	London and South Western	(B) 22 × 28 559 × 711	6′ 7″ 2007	180 12·7	30·0 2·78	18·7 19·0	56·5 57·4	75·0 76·2
7	1922	4–6–2	Great Northern 'Gresley'	(3) 20 × 26 508 × 660	6′ 8″ 2032	180 12·7	41·2 3·83	20·0 20·3	60·0 61·0	92·4 93·9
8	1911	2–8–0	Great Central 04 Class	(B) 21 × 26 533 × 660	4′ 8″ 1422	180 12·7	26·0 2·43	17·1 17·4	66·0 67·0	73·0 74·2
9	1911	2–6–0	Great Western 4300 Class	(B) 18½ × 30 470 × 762	5′ 8″ 1727	200 14·1	20·6 1·91	18·0 18·3	52·6 53·4	62·0 63·0
10	1917	2–6–0	South Eastern & Chatham 'Maunsell'	(B) 19 × 28 483 × 711	5′ 6″ 1676	200 14·1	25·0 2·32	18·0 18·3	50·9 51·8	59·4 60·4
11	1920	2–6–0–	Great Northern 1000 Class	(3) 18½ × 26 470 × 660	5′ 8″ 1727	180 12·7	28·0 2·60	20·0 20·3	60·0 61·0	71·7 72·8
12	1911	0–6–0	Midland Class 4	(A) 20 × 26 508 × 660	5′ 3″ 1600	175 12·3	21·0 1·95	18·0 18·3	48·7 49·5	48·7 49·5
13	1920	0–6–0	Great Eastern	(A) 20 × 28 508 × 711	4′ 11″ 1498	180 12·7	26·5 2·46	18·8 19·1	54·7 55·6	54·7 55·6
14	1911	4–6–2T	Great Central	(A) 20 × 26 508 × 660	5′ 7″ 1702	160 11·2	21·0 1·95	18·0 18·3	54·0 54·8	86·0 87·4
15	1914	4–6–4T	London, Brighton & South Coast	(B) 22 × 26 559 × 660	6′ 9″ 2057	170 12·0	26·7 2·48	19·5 19·8	56·5 57·4	98·0 99·6

(A) Inside cylinders (B) Outside cylinders

GREAT BRITAIN. REPRESENTATIVE LOCOMOTIVES 1923–1947 — Table 11

Entry	Year	Wheel Arrangement	Railway	Cylinders Diameter × Stroke inches / mm	Coupled Wheels Diameter feet / mm	Working Pressure lb/sq in / kg/cm²	Grate Area sq ft / m²	Weight Engine Working Order: Axle tons / tonnes	Adhesive tons / tonnes	Total tons / tonnes
1	1926	2–6–0	London Midland & Scottish 'Horwich'	21 × 26 533 × 660	5′ 6″ 1676	180 12·7	27·5 2·55	19·6 19·9	55·8 56·7	66·0 67·0
2	1927	4–6–0	London Midland & Scottish 'Royal Scot'	(3) 18 × 26 457 × 660	6′ 9″ 2057	250 17·6	31·2 2·90	20·9 21·2	62·5 63·5	84·8 86·2
3	1934	4–6–0	London Midland & Scottish Stanier Class 5	18½ × 28 469 × 711	6′ 0″ 1829	225 15·8	28·6 2·66	18·2 18·5	54·2 55·0	72·2 73·4
4	1935	2–8–0	London Midland & Scottish Stanier Class 8	18½ × 28 469 × 711	4′ 8½″ 1434	225 15·8	28·6 2·66	16·0 16·3	63·1 64·1	72·2 73·4
5	1938	4–6–2	London Midland & Scottish 'Duchess'	(4) 16½ × 28 418 × 711	6′ 9″ 2057	250 17·6	50·0 4·65	22·4 22·8	66·9 68·0	105·2 107·0
6	1935	4–6–2	London & North Eastern A4 Class	(3) 18½ × 26 469 × 660	6′ 8″ 2302	250 17·6	41·2 3·82	22·0 22·4	66·0 67·0	102·9 104·5
7	1936	2–6–2	London & North Eastern V2 Class	(3) 18½ × 26 469 × 660	6′ 2″ 1880	220 15·5	41·2 3·82	22·0 22·4	65·6 66·6	93·1 94·6
8	1942	4–6–0	London & North Eastern B_1 Class	20 × 26 508 × 660	6′ 2″ 1880	225 15·8	27·9 2·59	17·7 18·0	52·5 53·3	71·2 72·4
9	1947	4–6–2	London & North Eastern A_1 Class	(3) 19 × 26 483 × 660	6′ 8″ 2032	250 17·6	50·0 4·65	22·3 22·7	66·9 68·0	105·0 106·8
10	1923	4–6–0–	Great Western 'Castle' Class	(4) 16 × 26 406 × 660	6′ 8½″ 2044	225 15·8	30·3 2·82	19·7 20·0	58·8 59·8	79·8 81·2
11	1927	4–6–0	Great Western 'King' Class	(4) 16¼ × 28 412 × 711	6′ 6″ 1981	250 17·6	34·3 3·09	22·5 22·9	67·5 68·6	89·0 90·4
12	1928	4–6–0	Great Western 'Hall' Class	18½ × 30 469 × 762	6′ 0″ 1829	225 15·8	27·0 2·51	18·9 19·2	56·5 57·4	75·0 76·2
13	1926	4–6–0	Southern 'Lord Nelson'	(4) 16½ × 26 418 × 660	6′ 7″ 2007	220 15·5	33·0 3·07	20·7 21·0	62·0 63·0	83·5 84·8
14	1930	4–4–0	Southern 'Schools' Class	(3) 16½ × 26 418 × 660	6′ 7″ 2007	220 15·5	28·3 2·63	21·0 21·3	42·0 42·7	67·1 68·2
15	1941	4–6–2	Southern 'Merchant Navy'	(3) 18 × 24 457 × 610	6′ 2″ 1880	280 19·7	48·5 4·50	21·0 21·3	63·0 64·0	94·7 96·2

Entry	Year	Wheel Arrangement	Railway	Compounding System	Number Built	Cylinders Diameter × Stroke inches / mm	Coupled Wheels Diameter feet / mm	Working Pressure lb/sq in / kg/cm²	Grate Area sq ft / m²	Weight Engine Working Order: Axle tons / tonnes	Adhesive tons / tonnes	Total tons / tonnes
1	1902	4–4–0	Midland	Smith later Deeley	†	(3) 19 : 21 × 26 482 : 533 × 660	7′ 0″ 2134	195 13·7	26·0 2·42	19·6 19·9	38·8 39·4	59·5 60·4
2	1903	4–6–0	London & North Western	Webb	30	(4) 15 : 20½ × 24 381 : 520 × 610	5′ 3″ 1600	200 14·1	20·5 1·91	16·0 16·2	44·0 44·7	60·0 61·0
3	1905	4–4–2	Great Northern	de Glehn	1	(4) 14 : 23 × 26 356 : 584 × 660	6′ 8″ 2032	200 14·1	31·0 2·88	18·5 18·8	37·0 37·6	71·0 72·1
4	1905	4–4–2	Great Central	Smith	4	(3) 19 : 21 × 26 482 : 533 × 660	6′ 9″ 2057	200 14·1	26·3 2·44	18·5 18·8	37·0 37·6	74·0 75·2
5	1906	4–4–2	North Eastern	Smith	2	(4) 14¼ : 22 × 26 362 : 559 × 660	7′ 1¼″ 2165	225 15·8	29·0 2·69	19·6 19·9	39·2 39·8	73·6 74·8
6	1907	0–8–0	Lancashire & Yorkshire	Hughes	20	(4) 15½ : 22 × 26 393 : 559 × 660	4′ 6″ 1372	180 12·7	23·0 2·14	16·4 16·7	60·8 61·8	60·8 61·8
7	1926	4–6–0	London Mid-land & Scottish	Hughes	1	(4) 15½ : 22 × 26 393 : 559 × 660	6′ 3″ 1905	180 S 12·7	29·6 2·75	19·7 20·0	58·8 59·8	78·6 79·8

† 5 Smith System 1902/03. 40 Deeley System 1905/09 for Midland Railway. 195 Deeley System for LMS Railway 1924–32. Dimensions shown are for original engines. Later output had 6ft 9in (2057 mm) Diameter Coupled Wheels, 200 lb/sq in (14·1 kg/cm²) Pressure, 28·4 sq ft (2·64 m²) Grate Area and were superheated.

S—All saturated steam except those marked thus

Entry	Year	Wheel Arrangement	Railway	Compounding System	Number Built	Cylinders Diameter × Stroke inches / mm	Coupled Wheels Diameter feet / mm	Working Pressure lb/sq in / kg/cm²	Grate Area sq ft / m²	Axle tons / tonnes	Adhesive tons / tonnes	Total tons / tonnes
8	1909	4–4–2	Bengal Nagpur (India)	de Glehn		(4) 13 : 21½ × 26 330 · 545 × 660	6′ 6″ 1981	220 15·5	31·7 2·94	17·2 17·5	34·5 35·0	72·2 73·3
9	1928	4–6–2	,, ,,	,, ,,		(4) 16½ : 25 × 26 418 : 635 × 660	6′ 2″ 1880	250 S 17·6	51·0 4·73	21·5 21·9	64·3 65·3	105·0 106·8
10	1909	4–6–2	Central Argentine	Two-cylinder Cross Compound		19 : 27½ × 26 482 : 698 × 660	5′ 8″ 1727	180 12·7	29·5 2·74	16·0 16·2	46·1 46·8	77 5 78·7
11	1918	4–8–0	,, ,,	,, ,,		21 : 30 × 26 533 : 762 × 660	4′ 7½″ 1409	180 S 12·7	32·5 3·00	16·0 16·2	60·7 61·7	80·1 81·3
12	1927	2–8–2	,, ,,	,, ,,		21 : 31½ × 26 533 : 799 × 660	5′ 2″ 1575	200 S 14·1	28·0 2·60	16·5 16·8	64·0 65·0	85·0 86·4
13	1928	4–8–4T	,, ,,	,, ,,		22½ : 31½ × 26 571 : 799 × 660	5′ 2″ 1575	200 S 14·1	28·0 2·60	15·9 16·1	63·1 64·1	110·2 120·0

Table 13

BRITISH RAILWAYS STANDARD LOCOMOTIVE TYPES BUILT 1951–1960

Entry	*Year*	*Wheel Arrangement*	*Power Class and Number*	*Number Built*	*Cylinders Diameter × Stroke* inches / mm	*Coupled Wheels Diameter* feet / mm	*Working Pressure* lb/sq in / kg/cm²	*Grate Area* sq ft / m²	*Weight Engine Working Order* Axle tons / tonnes	Adhesive tons / tonnes	Total tons / tonnes
1	1954	4–6–2	Cl 8 71000	1	(3) **18 × 28** 457 × 711	**6′ 2″** 1880	**250** 17·6	**48·6** 4·52	**22·0** 22·3	**66·0** 67·1	**101·2** 102·7
2	1951	4–6–2	Cl 7 70000	55	**20 × 28** 508 × 711	**6′ 2″** 1880	**250** 17·6	**42·0** 3·90	**20·3** 20·6	**60·7** 61·7	**94·0** 95·4
3	1951	4–6–2	Cl 6 72000	10	**19½ × 28** 494 × 711	**6′ 2″** 1880	**225** 15·8	**36·0** 3·35	**19·0** 19·3	**56·8** 57·8	**88·5** 89·9
4	1951	4–6–0	Cl 5 73000	172	**19 × 28** 482 × 711	**6′ 2″** 1880	**225** 15·8	**28·7** 2·57	**19·7** 20·0	**57·1** 58·0	**76·0** 77·2
5	1951	4–6–0	Cl 4 75000	80	**18 × 28** 457 × 711	**5′ 8″** 1727	**225** 15·8	**26·7** 2·48	**17·2** 17·5	**51·5** 52·3	**67·9** 69·0
6	1952	2–6–0	Cl 4 76000	115	**17½ × 26** 465 × 660	**5′ 3″** 1600	**225** 15·8	**23·0** 2·14	**16·9** 17·2	**50·4** 51·2	**59·7** 60·8
7	1952	2–6–0	Cl 3 77000	20	**17½ × 26** 465 × 660	**5′ 3″** 1600	**200** 14·1	**20·3** 1·89	**16·2** 16·5	**48·9** 49·7	**57·5** 58·3
8	1953	2–6–0	Cl 2 78000	65	**16½ × 24** 418 × 610	**5′ 0″** 1524	**200** 14·1	**17·5** 1·63	**13·7** 13·9	**40·5** 41·2	**49·2** 50·0
9	1953	2–10–0	Cl 9 92000	251	**20 × 28** 508 × 711	**5′ 0″** 1524	**250** 17·6	**40·2** 3·73	**15·5** 15·8	**77·5** 78·8	**86·7** 88·1
10	1951	2–6–4T	Cl 4 80000	155	**18 × 28** 457 × 711	**5′ 8″** 1727	**225** 15·8	**26·7** 2·48	**17·9** 18·2	**53·1** 53·9	**86·6** 88·0
11	1951	2–6–2T	Cl 3 82000	45	**17½ × 26** 465 × 660	**5′ 3″** 1600	**200** 14·1	**20·3** 1·89	**16·3** 16·6	**48·7** 49·5	**74·1** 75·3
12	1952	2–6–2T	Cl 2 84000	30	**16½ × 24** 418 × 610	**5′ 0″** 1524	**200** 14·1	**17·5** 1·63	**14·0** 14·2	**41·2** 41·9	**66·5** 67·6

Entry	Year	Wheel Arrangement	Railway	Cylinders Diameter × Stroke inches / mm	Coupled Wheels Diameter feet / mm	Working Pressure lb/sq in / kg/cm²	Grate Area sq ft / m²	Weight Engine Working Order: Axle tons / tonnes	Adhesive tons / tonnes	Total tons / tonnes
1	1905	4–6–0	Indian State BESA type	**19 × 26** 483 × 660	**6′ 2″** 1880	**180** 12·7	**32·0** 2·97	**17·0** 17·3	**50·5** 51·2	**69·0** 70·0
2	1905	2–8–0	Indian State BESA type	**20 × 26** 508 × 660	**4′ 8½″** 1434	**180** 12·7	**32·0** 2·97	**15·9** 16·2	**63·5** 64·5	**71·5** 72·6
3	1926	4–6–2	Indian State XA Class	**18 × 26** 457 × 660	**5′ 1½″** 1562	**180** 12·7	**32·0** 2·97	**13·1** 13·3	**39·3** 39·8	**67·1** 68·2
4	1926	4–6–2	Indian State XB Class	**21½ × 28** 545 × 711	**6′ 2″** 1880	**180** 12·7	**45·0** 4·18	**17·0** 17·3	**51·0** 51·8	**90·2** 91·6
5	1926	4–6–2	Indian State XC Class	**23 × 28** 584 × 711	**6′ 2″** 1880	**180** 12·7	**51·0** 4·73	**19·7** 20·0	**59·1** 60·0	**98·8** 100·4
6	1928	2–8–2	Indian State XE Class	**23½ × 30** 597 × 762	**5′ 1½″** 1562	**210** 14·8	**60·0** 5·51	**22·3** 22·7	**89·2** 90·6	**119·1** 121·0
7	1912	4–6–2	Brazil–Sao Paulo Ry	**21½ × 26** 545 × 660	**5′ 6″** 1676	**200** 14·1	**28·5** 2·65	**17·5** 17·8	**52·4** 53·2	**80·0** 81·3
8	1926	4–6–2	Buenos Aires Great Southern	**(3) 19 × 26** 483 × 660	**6′ 6″** 1981	**200** 14·1	**29·3** 2·72	**17·2** 17·5	**51·5** 52·3	**87·7** 89·1
9	1949	4–8–0	General Roca (formerly Buenos Aires Great Southern)	**19½ × 28** 495 × 711	**5′ 8″** 1727	**225** 15·8	**32·6** 3·03	**15·6** 15·9	**62·4** 63·4	**82·3** 83·7
10	1950	4–6–2	General Mitre (formerly Central Argentine)	**(3) 19½ × 26** 495 × 660	**6′ 2½″** 1893	**225** 15·8	**43·0** 4·00	**18·0** 18·3	**54·0** 54·8	**99·7** 101·5
11	1926	4–4–2	Egyptian State	**20 × 26** 508 × 660	**6′ 6″** 1981	**160** 11·2	**31·2** 2·90	**18·0** 18·3	**36·0** 36·6	**76·7** 77·9
12	1949	4–6–0	,, ,,	**21 × 28** 533 × 711	**6′ 0″** 1829	**210** 14·8	**31·2** 2·90	**20·7** 21·0	**62·1** 63·1	**84·3** 85·6
13	1952	2–8–0	,, ,,	**18½ × 28** 479 × 711	**4′ 8½″** 1434	**225** 15·8	**30·0** 2·79	**16·5** 16·8	**66·0** 67·0	**75·6** 76·8
14	1946	2–8–0	UNRRA 'Liberation' Type	**21⅝ × 28** 550 × 711	**4′ 9⅛″** 1450	**227** 16·0	**44·0** 4·09	**18·5** 18·8	**74·0** 75·2	**84·3** 85·7
15	1953	2–8–2	Spain RENFE	**22⅜ × 28** 570 × 711	**5′ 1½″** 1560	**213** 15·0	**50·6** 4·80	**17·4** 17·7	**69·6** 70·8	**99·8** 101·5

LOCOMOTIVES FOLLOWING BRITISH FORMAT BUT DESIGNED AND BUILT OUTSIDE GREAT BRITAIN Table 15

Entry	Year	Wheel Arrangement	Railway		Cylinders Diameter × Stroke inches mm	Coupled Wheels Diameter feet mm	Working Pressure lb/sq in kg/cm²	Grate Area sq ft m²	Weight Engine Working Order: Axle tons tonnes	Adhesive tons tonnes	Total tons tonnes
1	1903	4–4–0	South Australian		18 × 24 457 × 610	6′ 6″ 1981	160 11·3	21·0 1·95	13·2 13·4	26·2 27·0	39·4 40·0
2	1904	4–4–2T	Belgian State	Type 15	$17\frac{1}{4}$ × 24 440 × 610	5′ $10\frac{7}{8}$″ 1800	170 12·0	19·4 1·80	15·5 15·7	30·5 31·0	61·5 62·5
3	1914	4–6–0	New South Wales	NN Class	$22\frac{1}{2}$ × 26 571 × 660	5′ 9″ 1753	180 12·7	30·5 2·83	20·7 21·0	57·9 58·8	78·3 79·6
4	1918	2–8–0	New South Wales	K Class	22 × 26 559 × 660	4′ 3″ 1295	180 12·7	28·7 2·67	16·5 16·8	66·1 67·2	72·9 74·0
5	1918	4–6–0	Victorian	A_2 Class	21 × 26 533 × 660	6′ 1″ 1854	200 14·1	29·0 2·69	17·0 17·3	51·0 51·8	71·0 72·2
6	1939	2–8–2	Victorian	X Class	22 × 28 559 × 711	5′ $1\frac{5}{8}$″ 1564	205 14·4	42·0 3·90	18·5 18·8	74·2 75·4	102·9 104·5
7	1914	4–4–0	Dutch State (formerly Holland Ry)		$20\frac{7}{8}$ × 26 530 × 660	6′ $0\frac{7}{8}$″ 2100	176 12·5	25·8 2·40	17·0 17·3	33·5 34·2	58·8 59·8
8	1929	4–6–4T	Dutch State		(4) 16 × 26 406 × 660	6′ $0\frac{7}{8}$″ 1850	176 12·5	30·5 2·86	16·6 16·9	49·8 50·6	108·0 109·8

REPRESENTATIVE GARRATT LOCOMOTIVES FOR STANDARD AND BROAD GAUGE Table 16

Entry	Year	Wheel Arrangement	Railway	Cylinders	Coupled Wheels	Working Pressure	Grate Area	Axle	Adhesive	Total
1	1927	2–6–0, 0–6–2	London Midland & Scottish	(4) $18\frac{1}{2}$ × 26 479 × 660	5′ 3″ 1600	190 13·4	44·5 4·13	21·0 21·3	122·1 123·5	155·5 157·2
2	1936	4–6–2, 2–6–4	Algerian State	(4) $19\frac{1}{4}$ × 26 489 × 660	5′ 11″ 1803	284 20·0	58·0 5·38	18·2 18·5	109·2 110·3	212·6 215·0
3	1932	4–8–2, 2–8–4	Russian State	(4) $22\frac{7}{8}$ × 28 580 × 711	4′ 11″ 1500	220 15·5	85·5 7·94	19·5 19·8	156·0 157·6	262·5 265·0
4	1930	4–6–2, 2–6–4	Central Aragon, Spain	(4) 19 × 26 482 × 660	4′ $8\frac{7}{8}$″ 1750	200 14·1	53·0 4·92	15·4 15·6	92·3 94·2	180·5 182·4
5	1929	4–8–0, 0–8–4	Bengal, Nagpur	(4) $20\frac{1}{2}$ × 26 520 × 660	4′ 8″ 1422	210 14·8	69·8 6·48	20·0 20·3	159·4 161·0	234·0 236·5
6	1930	4–8–2, 2–8–4	Buenos Aires Pacific	(4) $18\frac{1}{2}$ × 26 479 × 660	5′ 0″ 1524	200 14·1	49·4 4·57	14·2 14·4	113·0 114·4	194·0 196·0
7	1952	4–8–4, 4–8–4	New South Wales	(4) 19[illegible] × 26	4′ 7″	200	63·4	16·0	127·7	254·7

CHAPTER FIVE

France

Anyone who attempts to survey French steam locomotive practice objectively, but is not himself a Frenchman, is met by certain difficulties of presentation. Compounding has been almost a national religion in France in the present century, and not only has the majority of French engines worked on compound expansion, down to and including the final and most powerful units of the last days of steam, but there is a mountain of literature explaining and justifying the retention of this form of mechanism at the summit of which stands the redoubtable figure of André Chapelon, doyen of European locomotive designers, who, in his famous book *La Locomotive à vapeur*, in numerous papers and articles, and even in replies to this author's questions as recently as the writing of this chapter, has unflinchingly upheld the benefits of compounding which he holds to be incontrovertible.

As against this monolithic attitude the student cannot help but notice two things *per contra*. In the first place it is abundantly clear that compounding has not 'caught on' over the rest of the world. As the other chapters of this book portray, eminent engineers elsewhere have been almost unanimous in rejecting compounding, once superheated steam became available, and when, as will presently be described, the genius of Chapelon found the way to double the power output of existing compound designs, engineers outside France pounced with gratitude upon his improvements in the air/gas/steam cycle and applied them in their own practice almost exclusively to simple expansion engines. Secondly an examination of locomotive design inside France itself discloses the continued existence of an underground resistance movement on behalf of simple expansion which has broken surface at intervals throughout the period we are considering. By no means so well documented as has been the case for compounding, its existence and continuance has nevertheless indicated the presence of serious questionings inside the very citadel of compounding itself as to the wisdom of the accepted doctrine.

It is with such a paradoxical background that we must approach our examination of the French contribution to world practice, and try to deal as fairly as we can with these opposing views. Unlike the countries hitherto dealt with, France at no time experienced a plethora of independent railway companies; many of such as existed had been absorbed into six major administrations as early as 1857, Nord, Est, Ouest, Paris–Orléans, Paris–Lyon–Méditerranée and Midi, and those which remained, mostly in the west of France, were formed into a seventh unit of State-owned and run lines in 1878. In 1908 the Ouest was absorbed into the State-owned system, and thus matters remained until 1938 when the Société Nationale des Chemins de Fer was organised to take over the six systems, and to operate them as quasi-independent Regions covering roughly the same territory as before.* Although at all times subject to close governmental supervision, the different systems had their own chefs de matériel et de traction who pursued an individual line of locomotive development, closely supported by an active manufacturing industry, but at all times recognisably French.

On the other hand, the products of the various designers and builders retained a

* There was a smaller seventh system, that of Alsace-Lorraine, which came, however, under French control only before 1870 and after 1918.

measure of kinship in that, with the exception of the PLM, use of the de Glehn system of four-cylinder compounding was almost universal until, at the very end of steam power, there was a crumbling of the true faith in the appearance of variations which even included the heresy of three cylinders.

With such a background it is not easy to detect such relatively clear-cut stages in locomotive development as elsewhere, and for the purposes of this record it is proposed to divide the whole period into two phases only, pre-Chapelon and post-Chapelon. This great engineer, in charge of locomotive development on the Paris–Orléans system, brought new thought to bear upon conventional steam locomotive design, and between 1929 and 1934 introduced and demonstrated to engineers everywhere modifications which, as already mentioned, were capable of doubling the power output and greatly increasing the economy of designs thought hitherto themselves to be in the van of technical progress. This revolution rang round the world and affected in varying degree practice in all lands, whether of simple or compound expansion.

Before dealing in chronological order with the stages of design development through the present century, there are some general matters to which it is convenient at this point to refer, and it will be as well, too, before considering the locomotives themselves, to come to grips with the nature of the simple versus compound controversy, so important to understand if we are to assess truly the French position in the steam locomotive world.

The French loading gauge, to which engine outlines had to conform, had neither the freedom of America nor the undue constriction of Great Britain, but allowed a height of the order of 14ft (4267mm) and a width of 10ft 4in (3150mm) down to 1ft 3in (380mm) above rail level, thus permitting considerable latitude to the disposition of outside cylinders and motion. Permitted axle weights were rarely above 18 tons (18·2 tonnes) until the late 1930s when some main lines began to accept 20 tons (20·3 tonnes). A very few individual engines at the end of steam development ran with 23 tons (23·4 tonnes). A further restriction, unknown in the two above-mentioned countries, was a governmental decree limiting maximum speed everywhere to 120kph, that is 75mph. For eighty years this incubus lay upon French operation, with the obvious effect that fast overall timings were only obtainable by raising the average running speed as nearly as possible to the maximum, adverse gradients notwithstanding, and this put a premium upon design features which favoured fast hill climbing. In 1937 the limit was raised to 130kph (81mph) over favourable sections of some of the regions, but until the coming of electrification, little more was vouchsafed.

A practice which differentiated French from Anglo-Saxon ways, was to give their enginemen engineering training as fitters, and this, in conjunction with the custom of allocating the more important engines each to individual crews or at most to a pair of crews, reversed the trend elsewhere to eliminate running adjustments as far as possible between depot attention, and encouraged designers to introduce theoretically desirable complications in the knowledge that those who handled the engines were able and were expected to give the necessary day-to-day attention to obtain reliable running. Then again in these general considerations was the officially recognised policy of encouraging the footplate crews to regain any time lost through traffic delays. Safeguarded by the fitting of speed recorders, whose charts indicated unambiguously the observance of all speed restrictions, this measure was recognised by the Ministry of Public Works as specifically conducing to safety, in that liability to accident was logically considered to be far less when the timetable was working as intended. Premiums were awarded to drivers for their prowess in making up lost time, a courageous practice little followed elsewhere. This also had its effect upon design, for means had to be given to the men to do what was expected of them, which predicated the need to extract super power from the engines under emergency conditions.

As regards compounding, the salient features appear to be the following:

(1) Expanding the steam through more than one cylinder, intelligently carried out, must, and did, always lead to a lower steam and fuel consumption, where like was strictly compared with like. This is because:

(*a*) The total number of expansions of the steam which were possible was greater, leading to a reduced steam demand for a given output. Wasteful working was impossible, for even at full cut-off a measure of expansion was assured which was absent in simple cylinder working in the same manner.

(*b*) The range of pressure and temperature drop in each cylinder was less, with lower losses due to leakages and condensation. Moreover, such steam leakage as passed the high pressure valves was not wasted but did work in the low pressure cylinders.

(*c*) The lower final exhaust pressure, discharged to the chimney through suitable orifices, could promote more efficient combustion of the fuel especially if this was of poorer quality.

(2) While the above economic advantages were potentially common to all compounds, two operating advantages, more reliable starting and higher power during periods of acceleration, were only noteworthy on particular kinds of compounds such as the de Glehn. Other kinds of compound in general showed no advantage over simple expansion in these respects.

(3) To obtain these operating advantages, a measure of mechanical complication, and a special expertise on the part of the engine crew, were essential. These features rendered compound engines, designed to exploit their operating advantages to the full, less amenable to pooled working and optimum utilisation.

(4) The disadvantages from the use of compounding which were special to steam locomotives, with their relatively restricted dimensions in relation to power output, could take the form of lower availability, lower potential utilisation, inferior reliability, and higher man-hours and cost of servicing and repairs. All of these drawbacks were not present in all compounds, but it was rare indeed that at least one of them was not clearly present.

(5) Every railway administration and all mechanical engineers sought to combine in their motive power high performance with low specific fuel cost and low costs of servicing and repairs per mile of revenue service. Minimum fuel costs came from compounding, but minimum maintenance costs were achievable in most countries by simple expansion, and preference for one or the other usually rested upon the relative value which different administrations placed upon one or other of these factors.

I. Locomotive practice before Chapelon

Turning to the locomotive scene in the 1900–30 period, the de Glehn system of compounding dominated the field, being applied to the principal engine classes on the Nord, Est, État, PO, and Midi Railways, application to passenger machines being wellnigh universal, but to freight and tank engines varying from one administration to another. The PLM Railway was the most compound-minded of all, as a result of some experiences shortly to be related, but while also using four cylinders, its starting arrangements and system of controlling the cut-offs in hp and lp cylinders were different from the de Glehn.

At the very beginning of our period, and following experience with several types of

4–4–0 engines, there appeared in 1900 on the Nord system what was to become the archetype of French locomotive in the present century. It was a 4–4–2 de Glehn compound engine (entry 1, Table 17A) and its performances on the Nord attracted attention from all over the world. Replicas in one form or another were built for British, Egyptian, German, Indian, Spanish and Swiss railways, and an example even found its way on to the Pennsylvania Railroad in the USA. In France it not only proliferated on its own railway but its design was closely followed in 4–6–0 and 4–6–2 versions of increasing size, as well as in freight and tank engines on the other railways above-mentioned. Let us therefore pause to observe what were the principal features of this notable locomotive family. With two outside hp cylinders disposed well behind the bogie centre line, and two inside lp cylinders placed well ahead, drive was divided between two axles, connecting rods of roughly equal length providing a natural balance for the reciprocating parts, and dividing the thrusts and stresses evenly over axleboxes and frames. Then in place of the simple means, usually automatic, employed elsewhere for admitting live steam at reduced pressure to the lp cylinders for starting only, a much more complex arrangement characterised the de Glehn system.

In the first place there were two regulators admitting steam direct to hp and lp cylinders respectively. Then there were intercepting valves which at the driver's will shut off the passage between hp exhaust and lp steam chest, thus permitting the hp exhaust to pass directly into the blastpipe and chimney without traversing the lp cylinders first. Finally there were independently controlled valve gears for hp and lp engines. Four methods of working were thus made available to the driver:

(1) With hp and lp regulators both open and intercepting valve shut, live steam reached all four pistons, and each cylinder exhausted direct to chimney. A safety valve limited the pressure in the lp steam chests. This was the usual position for starting.

(2) With intercepting valve shut, opening either the hp or lp regulator alone, would operate the engine as a two-cylinder simple using either hp or lp cylinders respectively, the pistons in the other cylinders to which steam was not admitted merely floating. This position might be used for manœuvring light engine, or in case of failure, but it would hardly cope with service starts.

(3) With hp regulator only open, and intercepting valves open, exhaust from hp cylinders passed through the receiver to lp steam chests and the engine worked as a compound. Thus was the position for normal running..

(4) With the conditions as (3) above the lp regulator could be opened to bring the lp steam chest pressure up to the maximum permitted by the receiver safety valve. This permitted what was called reinforced compound working, and was available for increasing tractive effort during acceleration or on gradients for as long as the boiler would stand the increased demand.

With all these variables at his command, aided by pressure and temperature gauges indicating their effect, an intelligent and well-trained driver could do two things to an extent denied to his brothers on simple expansion machines. He could achieve excellent starting on engines having poor factors of adhesion, by using his two regulators, and the independent reverse gears to keep the tractive effort at all times just below the point of slipping. Secondly, again by manipulating the independent cut-offs, and by the judicious use of 'reinforced' working he could hold his power output to the uppermost edge of what boiler and fireman could produce by way of steam, drawing upon the heat reservoir capacity in fuel bed and water volume in the boiler to give exceptional outputs for limited periods.

The most astounding performance in relation to the size of the engines resulted from these tactics, and locomotive superintendents and railway managements everywhere sat up and took notice, the more so as these fireworks were accompanied by a modest consumption of often rather inferior coal. Enthusiasms were kindled in the minds of lay observers as well and from that day to the end of steam there were never lacking those who complained bitterly when it was found that their own home railways did not set their stalls out unreservedly likewise.

There was of course another side of the matter, as there always is in engineering, and this was found out in due time both in France itself and in other interested countries. A remarkable breed of drivers was needed to obtain clear melody from this orchestra of diverse instruments, and without an almost superhuman keenness of 'feel' for what was going on in all its inter-related parts, errors of judgement could quickly produce cacophony and throw away the intended advantages. Few foreigners, and certainly not the run of American and English drivers, were either trained or able to assure a consistent best from the de Glehn system. Secondly, such complex machines had to be kept up to concert pitch, and one has only to contemplate the woes resulting from a leaky or maladjusted intercepting valve, to realise how important close and devoted individual attention was before even the best drivers could coax these super performances out of the engines. More serious than the above were the growing pains. The Nord Atlantic abovementioned and its sisters were probably the most beautifully proportioned locomotives ever designed. As bigger and more powerful machines became necessary to meet increasing traffic, cylinder sizes had to go up, but with a finite distance between the backs of tyres, axlebox and crank web widths were unable to grow in proportion, with the result of a decreasing service and reliability from these members. Following the traditional design of the period, steam ports and passages did not grow *pro rata* to cylinder volume, and it became increasingly difficult to get power increases in proportion to engine size.

This last difficulty was presently to be brilliantly solved by Chapelon, but in the meantime, with certain notable exceptions, the generality of compounds tended to lose something of the original sparkle as their size increased.

In the mainstream of this first phase of compound design Table 17 lists some of the best known engines of this kind built in France between the celebrated Nord 4–4–2 of 1900, and various huge 4–8–2s constructed in the 1920s. After 1930 hardly anything was designed for important main-line service which was not touched by the magic hand of Chapelon. The Nord group of engines were perhaps the best of their kind, at any rate so far as travellers' observations are to be relied upon. Whereas other administrations remained very conservative in the manner in which they applied the valve events and steam circuits of earlier designs to their later and larger engines, there is evidence that as early as 1907 Nord engineers were beginning to sense the value of freer entry and exit for steam through the cylinders, and in successive series of Pacifics, in 4–6–0 mixed traffic engines, and in the very effective 2–8–0 and 2–10–0 freight engines, a competent and handsome family of designs was produced and many accounts have been published of their prowess.

On the Est, alone of the 'Grandes Lignes', the 4–6–0 was retained for front-line duty until as late as 1924, and the next step in power was not to the 4–6–2 but to the 4–8–2, Pacifics not being acquired until later. This ponderous design is referred to in entry 13 and illustrated in Plate 49. The great advance in size was evidently a little ahead of its time, for a number of modifications were found necessary at first and the prototype was not multiplied until 1929–31 when 40 more were built. These were followed by 49 for the État Railway, who were so uneasy with them that they disposed of them to the Est, on whose main lines they continued with the original batch until the end of steam. They represented in acute form the de Glehn system growing out of its clothes and were certainly not a very elegant design.

The basic de Glehn compound Pacific was to be seen in greatest numbers on the PO, Midi and État lines and at a later date on the Est of which entry 4 is typical. Direct descendants of the original Atlantics, their extremely neat and well proportioned appearance shrouded a disturbing relative diminution in their power and speed capabilities, which Chapelon's studies and tests were presently to disclose.

The PLM Railway, alone of French lines, did not use the de Glehn system. On 4–6–0s and Pacifics, the four cylinders were set in line across the engine above the bogie, but with very unequal connecting rod lengths to achieve a divided drive. No intercepting valve was provided to permit starting using live steam direct from the boiler in all four cylinders in simple expansion, but, as was the case with many non-French compounds, the driver had a starting valve under his command by which he could augment the pressure in the lp cylinders to produce initial movement, the engine working as a compound at all times. Another departure was that although four independent valve gears were provided, the cut-off in the lp cylinders was fixed at 63 per cent for all conditions of working while the hp cut-off could be varied in the ordinary way from full gear to mid gear at will.

As the 1920s progressed, the Pacifics were experiencing difficulty in getting away fast enough with heavy trains, if delayed on up grades, because of insufficient adhesion, and 4–8–2s were introduced for the first time on the PLM having an adhesive weight one-third greater than the 4–6–2s. There were some novel and rather peculiar features on these new engines. Faced with the need for lp cylinders 28in (720mm) in diameter, and the impossibility of providing an adequately dimensioned crank shaft with the cylinder centres so wide apart if they were inside the frames, the cylinder position was switched, and the lps were placed outside driving the leading axle with a very short connecting rod while the hp cylinder block, now inside the frames, was placed far back, behind the trailing bogie axle, and its pistons drove the cranks on the second coupled axle.

While four valve gears had been standard hitherto a simplification was introduced which was widely applied thereafter on the PLM in that the inside eccentrics and expansion links were suppressed, only the lap and lead levers remaining, Thus the leads which were the constant components of the hp and lp valve travel were independent, each being obtained from its own proper crosshead. The variable element was derived from the oscillation of the outside expansion link affecting adjacent pairs of valves simultaneously through rocking shafts. The upshot of this arrangement was that hp and lp cut-offs varied together, but with constant bias towards longer lp values. A total of 145 of these 4–8–2 engines were built between 1927 and 1932. In spite of 5ft 10½in (1790mm) diameter coupled wheels they were not very free running engines, and were restricted to the Laroche–Dijon and Marseilles–Nice sections of the main line. A single version with 6ft 6¾in (2000mm) wheels was produced in 1930 and formed the prototype for some infinitely more effective 'Mountain' type engines built in the post-Chapelon era.

The PLM family of locomotives, using this form of compounding at this time, ran the railway presumably to the satisfaction of their owners, but no records which the author has seen indicate performance or efficiency which surpassed these features on the de Glehn system.

We must now consider the repeated attempts in this period to break away from compounding and revert to simple expansion and Table 18 lists a variety of such engines built for French railways. The first revolt was rather surprisingly on the PLM itself, a railway so steeped in compound propulsion that of 845 locomotives ordered between 1870 and 1907 no fewer than 835 were in that form. At the prevailing working pressure of

213lb/sq in (15kg/cm²) and with the techniques available in those days, a lot of firebox and stay trouble was being experienced, and when in 1907 a new four-cylinder Pacific design was in contemplation to replace existing 4–6–0s, it was decided to try out the newly available Schmidt superheater on a simple expansion version having 171lb/sq in (12kg/cm²) pressure, as well as to continue the traditional saturated compound form with 227lb/sq in (16kg/cm²), the latter because weight restrictions would not at the time permit superheating and compounding together. Systematic trials were carried out of the first two engines turned out in 1909 and the four-cylinder simple showed a steam consumption of 21·4lb/Ihp hr (9·10kg/cm²), as against 25·17lb (11·28kg) for the compound. As a result, 70 of the simple Pacifics were ordered and put to work. Very naturally the question was asked in the meantime, what about superheating combined with compounding? By 1912 it had been found possible to make such weight adjustments as would permit the latter, and 20 such engines were ordered together with 20 more simples with their pressure raised to 199lb/sq in (14kg/cm²). No record of steam consumption per Ihp hour was made available on the tests carried out with these latter engines, but over a total distancc run of around a quarter of a million miles in each case, coal consumption was stated to be 0·169lb per ton mile (0·121kg per tonne km) for the compound versus 0·189lb for the simple, a betterment of 10 per cent. Only compounds were ordered thereafter and the simples were all rebuilt to come into line. The wide publicity given to these trials had a tremendous effect and confirmed mightily the convictions of those who believed in compounding and even shook some of those who did not. In 1931 M Vallantin, the engineer responsible, came to London and told the tale all over again to the assembled Institute of Locomotive Engineers.*

For a time after this contest, acceptance of compounding was almost but not quite universal, the waverer being the État who in 1911 made its extraordinary purchase of 50 locomotives to the exact designs of Peter Drummond's two-cylinder simple 4–6–0s on the Highland Railway in Scotland. It followed this up in 1912 by the introduction of three further classes of simple expansion engines, this time built by French firms, consisting of four-cylinder 4–6–0 express, two-cylinder 4–6–0 mixed traffic and two-cylinder freight types. Granting, however, that even so large a rebellion as this was untypical, experiences during and immediately after World War I reopened the whole question in an extensive way. The means and expertise essential for getting good service from complex compound engines fell away, while massive importations of American WD engines, as well as some 500 ex-Prussian State engines delivered in 1919 as reparations, gave French engineers first-hand experience of the possibilities of much simpler assemblies than those to which they had been accustomed. This encouraged the majority of those in charge of motive power to advocate the standardisation and simplification of their steam locomotives.

As early as 1919, the Nord Railway, another citadel of two-stage expansion, had built two little known 2–6–0 mixed traffic engines (entry 1) which were evidently intended to be simplified successors to the four-cylinder de Glehn 4–6–0s of 1911. For reasons which are veiled from us this very straightforward, and in all other essentials typical Nord, design did not multiply but the germ remained.

About this time the central rolling stock and design office (OCEM) was established in Paris and its first task was to prepare, on behalf of all French railways, designs for standard locomotives, all of which were to be superheated two-cylinder simples. This was too much for the PLM administration, however, and when proposals matured for 4–6–2 and 2–8–2 units of the intended series, it persuaded the OCEM to carry out comparative trials in normal service between recent existing compound and simple expansion types of these

* *Compound Locomotives on the PLM Railway*, by R. G. E. Vallantin; Proc Inst Loco Engrs No 100, 1931.

wheel arrangements. In 1922, the Paris–Orléans Railway had taken delivery of 50 two-cylinder simple Pacifics of almost 100 per cent American design, and five of these engines were sent to the PLM while the same number of PLM 6201 class compound Pacifics invaded the PO lines, all the engines in this case being superheated. On each line the newcomers were teamed up in special links with five of their opposite numbers, and a similar exchange was arranged between PO and PLM 2–8–2 engines, simple and compound respectively. Set as far as practicable common daily tasks as to speeds and loads, observations were taken over four months for the Pacifics and over six months for the Mikados, of ton-kilometres worked and coal consumed.

Although these trials were far from being the fully controlled tests of later times, their indications over such a broad spectrum could not be expected to be far astray. The results showed a coal saving in favour of the compounds of from 12 to 27 per cent for the Pacifics and from 4 to 20 per cent for the Mikados, there being a marked reduction in the saving when the compounds were running on the PO as compared with the compounds running on their own home ground. M Vallantin reported that, as is so often the case in such circumstances, violent recrimination broke out between the contestants and a third party had to be called in to clear the air. The final report stated, 'These trials have made evident the fact that double expansion does procure a definite saving in fuel consumption over simple expansion, even with superheated steam. This saving appears to be in the order of 10–12 per cent for the PLM engines.'

These trials were a great heartener for the 'establishment', and the results were not lost upon André Chapelon whose investigations into the scope for general improvement were in progress about this time. Indeed the PO American Pacifics clearly became fixed in his mind as the criterion for the behaviour and possibilities of simple expansion, as references testify in his ultimate great book, *La Locomotive à vapeur*.

In these, as in the former confrontations between compound and simple on the PLM in 1910–12, it was very necessary to ask, however, what compound was being compared with what simple. These were the days when best use of steam in locomotive cylinders was waking up from its long sleep, and the 25lb of steam per Ihp hour for simple expansion, and 23lb for compound, both using saturated steam, common at the turn of the century, came tumbling down to half those values by the end of steam development as a result of superheat, better valve events, larger steam ports and passages, and the other improvements of a half-century of intensive endeavour in many lands. Lowest published figures were ultimately 11·2lb per Ihp for four-cylinder compounds, rather naturally in France, and 12·2lb per Ihp for a three-cylinder simple expansion engine in England. It all depended therefore at what point in this descending scale one caught the simple and compound engines which were to be compared. For example, the PLM four-cylinder simple Pacifics of 1910 used 21·4lb of steam per Ihp hour, even although superheated, which indicated very poor valve events and cylinder design. The American-built PO Pacifics, although not tested scientifically, would, on the analogy of very similar engines mounted on the Altoona test plant in the USA, be using of the order of 18lb of steam per Ihp hour minimum, again testifying to the fact that they were a long way behind the thermal performance of which simple expansion would presently be capable. Thus while so many of these early confrontations were absolutely accurate in the relative placing of particular locomotives as regards fuel consumption, they were often far from pronouncing accurately upon the relative overall merits of simple and compound expansion as such.

In 1932 the Nord turned out the first of its two-cylinder simple suburban passenger tank engines with 'Cossart' valves (entry 4). These machines made an immediate impression with their lively performance and ease of maintenance, and in 1933 schemes were publicised by the Nord for a complete changeover in new construction to this kind of engine. Two of the current compound Pacifics were rebuilt with the cylinders and valve gear of the 2–8–2 tanks. Diagrams were published at the same time showing further 4–8–2, 2–8–2 and 2–10–2 tender designs which it was proposed to develop on these lines. When it came to the crunch, the features of the de Glehn compounds which appealed so strongly to the French and particularly the lower fuel consumption, won the day and no more was heard thereafter of simple expansion for main line services on the Nord until 1940 as will presently be seen.

Of the other railways, the Est did not waver in its allegiance to compounding for express passenger work, but before the First World War it had already begun to abandon double expansion for freight and secondary duties. This railway, however, clearly took a lot of notice of the practical advantages of simple expansion for freight working as demonstrated by the German engines it acquired after 1919. So much was this so, and so impressive was the behaviour of the German G12 class of three-cylinder simple 2–10–0s which came to it as reparations, that from 1925 onwards this administration had no less than 195 similar engines built for it in France, to almost identical dimensions, but with a definitely French aspect and detail design. This railway thereafter clung to simple expansion with either two or three cylinders for its requirements of freight and tank engines.

The État railway acquired 250 two-cylinder 2–8–2 fast freight engines with 5ft 5in diameter coupled wheels between 1921 and 1923, and in 1928 they rebuilt one of their four-cylinder compound Pacifics as a three-cylinder simple with Renaud poppet valve gear. In 1933 they went to the unprecedented length of having a huge 4–8–2 engine built, also with three simple expansion cylinders and Renaud gear (entry 5). Although the latter was known to be capable of some 2,800hp at the drawbar, it is clear that neither of these two engines proved themselves as successful applications of the simple expansion principle. The Midi too registered its revolt in 1925 by having a series of otherwise typical French Pacifics built as two-cylinder simples (entry 13). On the Paris–Orléans line, 70 two-cylinder 4–6–0s were built from 1917, some of them in England, having 5ft 9in coupled wheels, a general utility class obviously inspired by the German P8 class. There was also the curious circumstance on this same railway that, having in 1908 had 30 typical de Glehn Pacifics built for them by Alco in America to French drawings, they took delivery in 1922 of 50 two-cylinder simple Pacifics, of American design as above mentioned. They had also acquired in 1918, 150 2–8–2 locomotives from Alco, based upon the French design used on the État, but with many American features.

As a final commentary on this uneasy groundswell of attempts to get away from compounding, there is the occasion when in October 1925 emissaries from England under the leadership of Sir Henry Fowler, Chief Mechanical Engineer of the London Midland & Scottish Railway, visited French Railways to seek guidance regarding the design of important 4–6–2 and 2–8–2 locomotives on which it was proposed to employ compound expansion.

To the surprise of the visitors, they did not find 100 per cent acceptance of the compound principle, Bachellery of the Midi, Lacoin of the PO and Nasse of the État dissenting. On the other hand Vallantin of the PLM, Buchâtel, Est and Collin, Nord, plus the recently converted Dubois of the Central Design Office spoke in favour with strong, if somewhat diverse, voices.

Turning now to more detailed considerations, a striking feature of all French engines in this country was the light and elegant design of the Walschaert's valve gear which was almost universally in use. Such economical sections of return crank, valve and combination rods could only avoid buckling and failure if the loading at the valve spindle was consistently low enough to permit movement by such slender intermediaries. This meant effective lubrication and absence of unbalanced steam loads, and French engineers seemed more skilled than their contemporaries in assuring these desirable features.

Unique too was the trend to very short cabs and footplates. While in America, Germany and eventually in England roomy and well-protected cabs became general with the controls arranged around a seated position for the driver, French cabs even on some of the latest and largest tended to remain rudimentary and spartan and to demand that the driver stand rather than sit. On the pioneer Nord Atlantic there was hardly room to stand in front of the boiler faceplate, whilst very short side sheets to the cab afforded little protection from side winds and gangway doors were usually unthought of. Things were not much different in the 4–6–4 engines working on the same line forty years later, while arrangements on other railways departed little from this general effect. The swirling air currents generated within cabs while running, combined with the usually dusty nature of the coal used, required the wearing of goggles on the part of the crew and, as many travellers will testify, French enginemen could look dirtier at the end of their journey than did their fellows anywhere else in the world. It is difficult to account for this continuing insistence on discomfort, except to observe that cabs always had been rudimentary, and a study of French locomotive design in the nineteenth century discloses some almost unbelievable cases where there hardly seems room for a human being on the engine footplate at all.

As if to mitigate this aspect of physical discomfort, smoothness and steadiness of riding was present on the generality of these engines to an extent hardly experienced elsewhere. Springs and spring rigging were designed, made and maintained so that they really did what was intended; they received as much attention on all counts as did any other dynamic parts of the machine, and seldom if ever was that dreadful tooth-chattering vibration to be experienced which on some American and British engines made travelling on the footplate for any length of time a veritable purgatory. Not only this, but as has been mentioned before, the passage at speed of increasingly large engines over, what was in the first quarter of the century at least, not very good track, alerted the designers to the need to understand and provide for lateral stability. As early as 1924 George Marié had summarised work already done in a famous book, in which the need was emphasised to trace sources of instability in both engine and track, and to identify resonances which might build up into destructive oscillations. Amongst other things, a strong spring side control on bogies and trucks was shown to be essential, a lesson which, as has already been seen in Chapter 4, was not universally appreciated. But in France all this was fully understood and few foreigners ventured on to French footplates without remarking upon the exceptional degree of smooth and steady riding which was experienced.

In the boilers, the surfaces inside the tubes through which the hot gases from the grate gave up their heat to the surrounding water, were increased by internally projecting radial fins, the well known 'Serve' tubes which were a general feature for many years, and a Gallic speciality was the trapezoidal grate and firebox, in which the foundation ring, lying between the frames at the front in the ordinary manner for a narrow firebox, splayed outwards towards the rear, the backplate being that appropriate to a wide firebox. By this means good grate area for moderate powered engines was obtained without need for the great length (and weight) of barrel which was otherwise required to carry a wholly wide firebox behind the coupled wheels. Sandboxes on top of the boilers were usual, and between the wars increasing adoption of the ACFI feed water heater provided cylindrical heat exchanger mounted longitudinally on the boiler top abaft the chimney, and a massive horizontal pump unit for which room had to be found at running plate level. These features with their associated pipework, plus Westinghouse pumps, double spindled on the larger engines, plus duplicated reversing rods alongside the boiler for the independent inside and outside valve gears, could, and often did, cause a disordered and 'messy' appearance to the engine as a whole, to which smoke deflecting wing plates of peculiar shapes added only the finishing touch. The Est and PLM 4–8–2 engines were notable examples, but there were other engines typified by the PLM 4–6–2s and 2–8–2s and the Nord Pacifics and 2–10–0s which succeeded in spite of all in presenting a symmetrical and even pleasing appearance. The usually neat and thin lipped chimney and domed smokebox door gave most French engines an elegant and by no means ponderous look at the front end. However disposed, these things together were mounted on a basic disposition and shape which, whether simple or compound, of the new century or of the last days of steam, were unmistakably and characteristically French.

To the enthusiast as distinct from the technician there were two other features of the French locomotive scene which can only be described as distressing, both having to do with the impact upon the auricular senses. The shrill high pitched whistle, which was never departed from throughout the whole era, seemed entirely incongruous emanating from such sophisticated and modern machines, as did the almost complete absence of any exhaust noise at starting, or indeed even at quite appreciable power outputs. While this last was of course connected with the efficient use of the steam, it robbed the observer of that strong bark of the steam locomotive at work elsewhere.

It has already been mentioned how widely the de Glehn compound was studied abroad, and reference has been made in previous chapters to the three examples which were built in France and sent to the Great Western Railway in England in 1902–4, and to the single one to the Pennsylvania Railway in America in 1904, where on the Altoona test plant it registered a minimum steam consumption of 19·8lb of steam per Ihp hour in its original unsuperheated form. The Prussian State Railways had a number built domestically from 1902 onwards in 4–4–0 (class S5) and 4–4–2 (class S7) form, while in Belgium, from 1905 considerable numbers of 4–4–2 engines with 6ft 6in diameter wheels and of 4–6–0 engines with 5ft 11in wheels were built (Type 8)and after the war they were accompanied in 1921 by domestically built 2–8–0s (Type 33) having many common features. In 1905, ten 4–4–2s exactly to the Nord design were supplied to Egypt, and from 1906, seventeen engines of British outline but of full de Glehn content were built by the North British Locomotive Company of Scotland for the Bengal Nagpur Railway. Switzerland and Portugal too had de Glehn engines built for them from 1903 to 1910 but thereafter drifted off towards other fancies. Thus many countries were able on their own lines and under their own traffic conditions to study the new gospel, but it is interesting that in none of those mentioned did it take root and multiply notwithstanding the many lessons which could be picked up, as in England, from this or that aspect of the design as a whole. Only in Spain, principally on the geographically adjacent 'Norte' system, did the pattern really stick, and up to the last days of independent design on that railway development proceeded in step with that in France through Chapelon modifications to the massive 4–8–2 compounds still in service at this writing.

Apart from the above, miniature versions of typical French outlines, usually simple expansion, were exported to Abyssinia, Indo-China, French Equatorial Africa and other regions where French capital had provided and French influence was running these far flung systems, and just across the Mediterranean in Algeria and Tunisia, then firmly under French rule, exact replicas of standard gauge French designs were universally to be seen at work.

II. Locomotive Practice after Chapelon

Enough has been said in the first part of this chapter to indicate that the basic French compound machine was meeting obstacles to its further development as time went on. While conventional design held sway, free running at speed, and a proportional increase in power output in relation to increased size, cost and weight was not being universally obtained. Moreover, optimum steam consumption was taking place only at moderate outputs and economy suffered as the power increased. It was the call for more speed and power to meet post-war conditions which first led André Chapelon to study the thermal cycle of existing engines more closely and in particular the losses of one kind and another which took place therein. By means of close theoretical study backed up by a series of indicating and dynamometer car tests he came to realise that, if only such losses could be tackled one by one and materially reduced, there resided as much opportunity for increased power and effectiveness within the well-tried Stephenson form as was being offered at the time, usually without practical experience, by way of high pressures, turbines and condensers. The current PO de Glehn compound Pacifics built between 1907 and 1914, typical of their kind, were found to suffer considerable pressure drop between the boiler and the pistons, to experience large pressure fluctuations in the steam chests, and above all to attain such low steam pressures in the receiver, that even with full gear working in the lp cylinders, power output in them was only a fraction of what it ought to be. Thus, for example, at a speed of 65mph (104kph) with hp cut-off 55 per cent, lp 82 per cent, out of a total of 1,873 horse power developed, 1,478 was generated in the hp cylinders and only 395 in the lp. Test results of this kind confirmed what had long been suspected, namely that in many four-clyinder compounds the lp cylinders became little more than passengers at the higher speeds.

It is proposed in the remainder of this chapter to recapitulate what Chapelon did to remedy this state of affairs, to refer to the notable new locomotive designs and rebuilding of old ones which followed, to outline something of the results obtained, and finally to discuss why in spite of this shot in the arm, compounding did not thereafter sweep the world and gain adoption everywhere.

The whole initial process of improvement has been faithfully explained and recorded as it happened in the pages of the *Revue Générale des Chemins de Fer*, while in that monumental volume *La Locomotive à vapeur* Chapelon himself told the story again, with detailed exposition of the theory upon which each separate item of improvement was based. It is not an easy book to read because of the wealth of detail provided, but its principal message stands out loud and clear. There were three main lines of attack, a more effective draughting system, higher superheat, and an increase in the cross section of steam ports and passages all the way from blastpipe tip back to regulator head. The first of these was achieved by replacing the former variable orifice discharging into a single narrow chimney, by a double blastpipe and chimney arrangement in which the exhaust steam emerging from two fixed orifices was split up by an arrangement of intermediate cowls into eight separate upward streams, the larger surface area of which much more effectively entrained the hot gases from the tubes. With this arrangement the vacuum in the smokebox was increased more than three times for the same back pressure in the blastpipe. Maximum steam temperatures were increased from the region of 570°F to 750°F by a new design of superheater element (the Houlet) which greatly increased the surface swept by the hot gases for a given free area through the flue tubes. As a result, lp cylinders which had previously been receiving the hp exhaust in saturated condition with all the losses thus entailed, now received steam having up to 100°F superheat.

The biggest and most important change was the third, namely improvement in the steam passages. Chapelon did not claim to be the innovator in this direction and he conceded that a start had been made by the Nord Railway in 1907 when it had improved the steam circuit areas by 25 to 30 per cent on its four-cylinder engines as previously mentioned. Now he decided to do no less than double steam areas all the way through, and thus divide by four losses due to wiredrawing. This not only meant steam pipes and the steam passages in the cylinder casting, but in particular it meant port openings through the valves at both inlet and exhaust.

Various means were sought to achieve the latter effect by increasing the valve travel and the size of the valves. Then there was a stage where piston valves having double inlet and double exhaust outlet functions were employed, but the most fully effective was found to be the employment of horizontal poppet valves cam operated from the normal Walschaert's valve gear. With each part of the engine now giving its full power because freedom of ports, passages and valve events assured a sufficiently high inlet pressure to the lp cylinders, 'reinforced' working by admitting boiler steam to the receiver while running was no longer required and Chapelon in his book makes no reference to this once much-vaunted adjunct to the de Glehn system.

To match the power potential thus afforded, the boiler had to be made capable of sustained high evaporation and a Nicholson Thermic Syphon was fitted into the steel firebox while all the tubes were welded into the tubeplate at the firebox end. Exhaust steam feed water heating on the ACFI principle was also introduced. When the transformation was complete, the maximum drawbar horsepower from these old Pacifics had nearly doubled, that derived from the lp engine having alone *increased* by 1,000hp. Table 20A shows the stages in this Odyssey in which steam consumption per Ihp hour fell from 16lb to 12lb (7·17 to 5·39kg/cv).

Table 19 lists the principal engines of the post-Chapelon era.

The first engine to be dealt with in this way was turned out of Tours workshops in 1929, and some 45 further Pacifics were thus transformed on the PO up to 1934. In 1932 appeared the prototype of a still bolder transformation in which the main frames at the back end were renewed to permit substitution of an additional coupled wheel in place of the trailing truck, thus turning the 4–6–2 into a 4–8–0. At the same time a new design of boiler was provided having a long narrow firebox with 40·8sq ft (3·80m²) of grate area, and a working pressure of 284lb/sq in (20kg/cm²). Weighing 107 tons (109 tonnes), with 75 tons (76·4 tonnes) available for adhesion, as much as 4,172 indicated horsepower was clocked at 84mph (134kph), cut-offs being 37 per cent in the hp cylinders and 57 per cent in the low. Of the total, 2,500hp was produced in the hp cylinders, 1,672 in the low. With indicated powers such as these over 3,000hp was available at the tender drawbar. With cut-offs 30 per cent hp and 40 per cent lp at 56mph (91kph), steam consumption reached bottom at 11·4lb per Ihp (5·11kg/cv) hour whilst exerting 2,300hp. Eleven more of the old Pacifics of 1907 were converted in this way in 1934, and Chapelon was able to report that the rebuilding had increased maximum indicated power by 120 per cent, with a reduction in coal consumption per drawbar horsepower hour of 48·5 per cent.

Naturally such potential permitted some brilliant running in ordinary service, and for the few years remaining before electrification took over, pilgrims came to the PO Railway from far and near to worship at the shrine of this new life for the steam locomotive. Between 1932 and 1936 all the other French railways climbed upon the band wagon, and set about transforming their own compound Pacifics and 4–8–2 engines. Not all applied the whole of the recommended features, but in proportion to what they did apply, so a most gratifying increase in power potential and economy was obtained. The Nord had 20 of the PO transformations sent to it, and in 1936–7 had 28 more engines of the same design built new. As travellers well know, this group displaced all others on the Paris–Calais expresses and so remained until electrification cut steam operation short at Amiens.

The State Railway had 160 Pacifics dealt with up to 1937, and the Est Railway tackled not only its own 40 Pacifics, but acquired 23 similar engines ex-PO and applied some of the modifications to its 4–6–0s and 4–8–2s as well. Similarly the PLM started to break into its large stud of Pacifics. The final stage of the true de Glehn arrangement as modified by Chapelon was to be seen in the 25 further 4–8–0 locomotives transformed in 1940 from the remaining PO Pacifics and sent to the PLM Railway. Besides being tidied up in appearance, these engines were fitted with mechanical stokers, the power outputs of which they were capable being beyond the sustained capacity of any fireman.

Design offices all over the world had paid lively attention to what was going on in France from 1932 onwards, but it did not escape their attention that the three cornerstones of Chapelon's edifice, better draughting, higher superheat and increased steam ports and passages, were not necessarily tied up with compounding as such, and that each and all of them were equally applicable to simple expansion. Thus in America, England and Germany, the major other repositories of steam locomotive development, advances soon began under all three headings which were acknowledged to be due to Chapelon's pioneer investigations and demonstrations. In all three schools of design their application led to notable improvements in performance and thermal efficiency, but for reasons shortly to be discussed this work did not incline the generality of administrations outside France any more towards compounding than they had been before.

In France itself it seems clear that as the 1930s drew to their close, questions were beginning to arise as to the direction locomotive design was to take. The various rebuildings above mentioned sufficed for current traffic needs, and such few new designs as were in contemplation did not mature until during or after the approaching World War II. In the period of the 'phoney' war when France was still as it had been, two eminent engineers, Léguille and Chan, read a paper before the Institution of Locomotive Engineers in London on April 17, 1940. In this paper the authors made it clear that once again economy in running and maintenance costs was becoming a very acute problem, and while compounding was still preferred for coal saving, it was no longer possible to shut the eyes to other solutions including simplification of the mechanical parts. The other growing problem was that traffic now demanded passenger train loads of 650–750 tons (660–760 tonnes) averaging 62mph (100kph) and above over the more level routes, and fast freight loads of 1,000 tons (1016 tonnes) at 50mph (80kph) and that if steam could not cope with these duties it must give place to ever more widespread electrification. To meet this situation several different approaches were made.

By 1938 Chapelon had outlined a solution to the possibility of super steam power by including in his book design projects for 4–6–4 and 4–8–4 passenger, 2–10–4 mixed traffic and 2–12–0 freight engines. Up to 6,000 indicated hp was to be produced on these locomotives by a novel arrangement of six cylinders in which, grouped in different ways, there were to be four cylinders in line under the smokebox driving axles in the usual way, while a further pair of cylinders further back inside the frames drove yet another axle through a second crank axle. Two of the cylinders received high pressure steam and the other four were low pressure. Only one of these projects was ever realised and that to the extent of one unit only. 2–12–0 locomotive No 160A was turned out in 1946 and was in some ways the most remarkable 'normal' steam locomotive ever built. Although nominally a rebuild from one of the PO 2–10–0 de Glehn compounds, it was really a new engine with outside hp cylinders driving the third axle. One pair of inside lp cylinders was disposed under the smokebox driving the second axle while the other pair was placed amidships under the

51 Est 3-cylinder simple expansion 2–8–2T of 1930 design for heavy suburban traffic, No 141 TD 103 entering Paris (St Lazaire) in 1959. Some of the thought and detailing was derived from experience with German reparations locomotives [*E. S. Cox*

52 The basic Chapelon Pacific, PO design, with all that famous engineer's improvements, allocated to Nord system. No 231E40 on "Golden Arrow" train at Paris (Nord) [*E. S. Cox*

53 Etat version of the Chapelon transformation No 231D581 at Paris (St Lazaire). Note ACFI feed pump on footplate and tangle of pipework [*E. S. Cox*

54 "Transformed" PLM 4-cylinder compound 4–6–2 No 231K3 at Abbeville in 1963. Except for double chimney and ACFI feed water heater, appearance is very little changed from 6201 series of 1912 [*E. S. Cox*

55 SNCF 3-cylinder simple expansion 4–6–4 design of 1940. No 232 R001 at Paris (Nord). Note semi-streamlining and Cossart valve gear [*E. S. Cox*

56 World's most efficient steam locomotive. SNCF 4-cylinder compound 2–8–2 designed in 1938 incorporating all "Chapelon" improvements but mostly built after the war. No 141P 137 at Paris Est, 1960 [*E. S. Cox*

57 Pure French design on Spanish Norte Railway. 1911 design of de Glehn compound 4–6–2 No 231–4002 at Avila 1954. Note incongruous American Worthington feed water heater and pump, a later addition

58 Prussian State 4-cylinder compound 4–4–2 Class S9 of 1907, transferred to Belgian Railways in 1919 as reparations and photographed at Liège in 1931. Note roomy cab and generous ashpan below firebox

[*C. Shorto*

59 Bavarian State 4-cylinder compound 4–6–0 to Maffei design of 1904. Originally Class P3/5, No 38.430 when taken over by Reichsbahn. Photographed near Hof, 1929 [*C. Shorto*

dome driving the fourth axle. Poppet valves operated by Walschaert's gears were used throughout, and the lp cylinders were steam jacketed. The boiler contained two superheaters, one of normal type and the other in the lower part of the boiler, reheating the hp exhaust so as to assure steam admission of at least 518deg F to the lp cylinders when working normally. In 1948 trials were carried out in the former PLM main line, and, as was to be expected, notable hauling power was exhibited. Thus Chapelon had produced one solution to the super-power problem, but had made no contribution to the plea for simplicity. The complexity from the maintenance point of view was prodigious and the administration clearly flinched from multiplying monsters of this kind.

Although Chapelon's name has rung through this chapter, that great designer would readily admit that his was not the only influence upon French locomotive design, and in the other two important new classes initiated just before the war other hands had clearly been at work as regards form and layout even if his improvements to the air/gas/steam cycle were fully incorporated. The 141P class of 2–8–2 mixed traffic engine was under design in 1938 and first ran in 1940. This was a re-vamping of the PLM 2–8–2 type of 1914, but increase in the working pressure from 227 to 284lb/sq in (16 to 20kg/cm²) permitted smaller cylinders to be used (entry 9, Table 19) and this in turn allowed the reversal of the previous cylinder arrangement, the 25·6in (650mm) diameter lp cylinders being between the frames on the 141P. To permit better riding at speed the leading pony truck was replaced by an Italian 'Zara' type truck, and ACFI feed water heaters and mechanical stokers were applied. A total of 318 of these locomotives was ultimately built, mostly post-war, for service on all regions. Improvement in mechanical wellbeing was sought by increasing the frame thickness with longitudinal reinforcement between driving axleboxes. This version of an earlier PLM design showed a similar improvement in power output, the maximum of the former on test being 1,850hp at the wheel rim as against 2,835hp for the 141P.

In 1938 there was also under design through the auspices of the OCEM, a series of 4–6–4 express passenger engines specifically for the Nord system, and here again it was 1940 before they took the road. They showed many departures from previous practice in employing bar frames, and a rotary cam poppet valve gear developed by Dabeg. Three of them were *mirabile dictu* three-cylinder simple expansion engines class 232R, and once again that looking over the shoulder towards simplicity which had been such a recurrent theme in French development manifested itself. Four more were four-cylinder compounds having their cylinders reversed from the long standing de Glehn system in that the lp cylinders were outside. All had large boilers pressed at 284lb/sq in (20kg/cm²) with 55·6sq ft (5·17cm²) of grate area and combustion chambers. The Dabeg valve gear on these compounds was found to be less efficient than was the Lentz oscillating cam valve system driven by Walschaert gear on the PO rebuilds and the 232S class was subsequently fitted with the latter arrangement. The last of this batch of eight engines, ascribed to the engineer De Caso, did not appear until 1949, after the war, in the form of the famous four-cylinder compound 232 U1. Into this design was put every ounce of know-how and ingenuity by the devotees of the truly French school of locomotive design. With roller bearings throughout, mechanical stoking and exceedingly large steam passages, a reversion was made to Walschaert's gear driving long travel piston valves. French love of complexity achieved its climax in a galaxy of power-operated intercepting, by-pass and anti-vacuum valves in conjunction with an automatic device permitting 90 per cent cut-off in the lp cylinders for starting. All of this somewhat nullified the contra-simplification of using, in a very un-French manner, two sets of valve gear only to operate four valves, but it did produce simplified operation by the driver, a goal which had never hitherto seemed of much importance to the designers.

The war dealt hardly with French railways, and out of about 15,000 locomotives pre-war, only some 2,500 remained serviceable out of a stock of 10,500 when liberation was achieved. Apart from the superhuman task of getting existing engines into service again, the desperate need for new motive power was met in three ways. The first and obvious one was to requisition such German 2–10–0s as could be obtained of classes 50 and 52 (two-cylinder) and 44 (three-cylinder) some of which had had to be built in French factories during the occupation. These were supplemented as a short term measure by numbers of British and American WD 2–8–0s which had followed the armies in. Secondly was the restoration to peacetime uses of the French locomotive building industry. But most dramatic and as it turned out most effective of all was the purchase in 1945 from the three principal American builders of a total of 1,323 2–8–2 engines of class 141R. These engines, of the same general size as the indigenous 141P class, were two-cylinder simple expansion, and in all respects, except for a few details and fittings, were of purely trans-atlantic design. They have already been referred to with tabulated dimensions in Chapter 3. The first 700 had standard American exhaust arrangements with self-cleaning deflec-tor plates. They burned coal by mechanical stokers, and had bar frames, spoked wheels and coupled axleboxes with plain oil lubricated bearings. Most of the subsequent 623 engines were oil fired and had single Kylchap exhaust arrangements. Of these the first 400 had Boxpok castings and roller bearings on the driving wheels only, the remaining 223 had the same features on all coupled wheels, while the last 200 engines to be con-structed had monobloc cast steel beds.

These engines were a far cry from previous American importations, and they contained everything which American designers had learned about rugged performance with high availability; a minimum steam consumption of 14lb per Ihp hour was recorded. They were eminently suited to pooled working to which French railways were introduced for the first time in conjunction with a special maintenance organisation based on Ameri-can practice. Soon they were to be seen in all parts of France slogging away with that massive and yet thin exhaust sound which was characteristic. Used mostly on freight service, their stint of passenger duties was carried out on more heavily graded lines, and they eventually took over completely traction on the difficult line from Marseilles to Ventimiglia. It was not long after the war that the traveller could witness at such points as Les Arcs between Marseilles and Toulon, large parks of erstwhile PLM 4–8–2s so completely out-classed by the new motive power that it was just not worth while repairing them and setting them to work again.

We now come to what was truly French in the post-war period, but unlike the case in England and Germany, no new standard series was developed, for the national policy to electrify the main lines as soon as possible made it appropriate to meet the needs of lines still to be electrified by transfer of the more modern steam engines from one Region to another. Thus PLM express engines, released as the wires spread through Dijon to Lyon and on to Marseilles, found themselves on Nord and Est and État just as before them PO engines had invaded these same systems. In a similar manner remaining steam suburban lines were infiltrated by redundancies from those electrified, and for a number of years the Gare du Nord in Paris, as an example, displayed Nord 2–8–2 and PLM 4–8–4 tank engines running side by side, and it was possible for the student to study at the same time French breakaway to simple expansion and French cleavage to compounding.

Thus very few brand new engines were built and those only in the highest power bracket. No attempt was made to develop modern low powered types for secondary duties as was done in Britain and Germany. The pure mainstream of French design was, how-ever, leavened to a small extent by importations from abroad as regards components and details. As higher power outputs were demanded a mechanical stoker became a necessity, and a first trial was made on a Pacific locomotive on the Nord in 1931, followed by the fitting of two of its 2–10–0 engines. Thirty of these were equipped in 1937, as was the single 4–8–2 engine built for the État in 1932. After the formation of the SNCF stokers were systematically applied to all new designs for main line service, such as classes 141P and R, 240P, 232R and S and 241P. The stokers used were based upon the American 'Standard' type although later examples were manufactured in France.

Some 335 engines had already been fitted up by 1940 with poppet valve gears, the most numerous being the Lentz type originating in Austria, a form of valve much favoured by Chapelon as contributing to the optimum steam circuit. The Caprotti poppet valve gear from Italy was used in conjunction with simple expansion on the largest and latest engines of the Alsace–Lorraine lines.

There was even to be found on the 141P class a direct derivative from the LMS Railway in England, in that its coupled axleboxes had pressed-in brasses having serrated thin white metal pockets which were clearly the result of collaboration between Stanier and Léguille immediately before the last war. On the whole, however, French design was little affected by other people's practice, and its outward appearance not at all.

The last stage of steam development brought French designers sharply up against the moment of truth so far as compound expansion was concerned. Brilliant performance and power output unsurpassed in the world in relation to size was theirs. Numerous comparative tests with available simple expansion types, of 141P against 141R, of 232S against 232R, of État 'Chapelon' Pacific against Alsace-Lorraine two-cylinder 'Caprotti' Pacific, of the latest Nord 2–10–0 design against the ex-German class 44, all indicated a round increase in fuel consumption of 30 per cent for the simples, or reduction of up to 25 per cent for the compounds whichever way one liked to regard the results. Mechanically, however, all was not well as the compounds grew larger, although little has been written about it. The Achilles heel of French maximum power development was undoubtedly the crank axle. In the four-cylinder system, as soon as inside lp cylinders reached 26in (660mm) diameter on the standard rail gauge, there just was not room, even with the wheel centres dished as far as one dare, for crank web width greater than 4in (102mm), and this was totally insufficient to avoid shaking loose of the related parts if the axle was of the built-up type or early development of fatigue flaws if of the solid forged type. Some easement was sought in such designs as the 232S or PLM 4–8–2 by placing the lp cylinders outside, but even so the increase of crank widths up to 5in (127mm) thus obtainable was still far from sufficient for the reliable transmission of the 2,000 or so horsepower which the inside hp cylinders were capable of producing. The outsider can only imagine the shifts which were necessary to keep these engines at work, but it is a fact that from first to last, and despite some small scale attempts at pooled working with secondary service types, they were never allowed to get out of the hands of single or at most double nominated crews. This coupling of the machine to the man produced a dreadful shortfall in potential utilisation. Chapelon reports, for example, that the 141P class compounds were engaged as to 85 per cent of their running time on express passenger and fast freight duties, whereas the American 141R class only occupied 25 per cent of their time on such jobs, the remainder being ordinary freight working. None the less the latter in pooled working achieved 44 per cent higher annual mileage. It was further to be observed that in the case of the engines having the highest power to weight ratio of all, the Chapelon 4–8–0s of class 240P turned out in 1940, and set to work on the PLM main line, a remarkably short life ensued before the engines had to be taken out of service due to mechanical deterioration, and a series of less heroic but more substantial 4–8–2s derived from the original PLM design but fully modernised was introduced on to this line in 1947 and took over all of the principal passenger duties down to Marseilles until final electrification.

Somewhere in the archives of the SNCF the final balance sheet as regards running costs per kilometre exists, but it is extraordinarily difficult to deduce the situation from the meagre detail which has been published, and still more so to translate French conditions into terms which make any comparison with the experience of other countries possible. For example, in England cost of coal in pence per mile was rarely higher and usually lower than the total repair cost in the same units. Some figures made available in respect of the 141P and R engines on the other hand show that while repair costs per kilometre for the simple expansion 141R were 40 per cent lower than 141P due to greater simplicity and higher annual mileage, even the higher repair costs of the compound engine were still only 63 per cent of its cost of coal per kilometre. Under such a relationship of fuel to repair costs it was possible for French engineers to show a marginal cost advantage for their compond engines overall, but those responsible for motive power elsewhere saw a different picture under their own conditions. They just did not care to sail so close to the wind as regards mechanical reliability as did the French, nor could they tolerate the low utilisation which resulted from the need to nurse these very complex machines. Where applied in full to simple expansion Chapelon's principles had so reduced steam and fuel consumption that the marginal further reductions made possible by compounding were not in those countries considered to outweigh the advantages of simplicity, low maintenance cost and high utilisation for which simple expansion still exerted a strong counter attraction. Thus nowhere outside France was compounding taken up afresh, nor were replicas of the famous Chapelon engines built for foreign service, other than a small number in Spain.

Only in the very last act of steam design did French designers really grasp the nettle of the crank axle problem and during the war at a time when plans were afoot for developing the four-cylinder compound further, a heroic move was made to explore the possibilities of compounding with three cylinders. This kind of engine, although known in England, had been somewhat of a rarity in Europe and, indeed, only a single such machine had previously been constructed in France in 1887 for the Nord Railway. But the presence of only a single cylinder between the frames made it possible for the first time to provide a built-up crank axle having webs 8½in (216mm) thick, which doubling of this vital dimension gave promise of a more acceptable mileage before dissolution set in. Accordingly the unsuccessful 4–8–2 three-cylinder simple which the État had built in 1933 was taken in hand and converted into a three-cylinder compound, appearing as a 4–8–4 in 1946. This remarkable machine whose leading dimensions are shown in entry 9 Table 19 had a single hp cylinder inside the frames and two lp cylinders outside as on the English 'Deeley' system. Unlike that system, two separate regulators were used but there was no intercepting valve as in the de Glehn system. Live steam supplied to the lp cylinders on starting was limited to 199lb/sq in (14kg/cm²), the boiler pressure being 284lb/sq in (20kg/cm²). A by-pass valve was fitted to the hp cylinders to avoid negative thrust at certain positions of the cranks. An unusual feature was that to save space the piston valve below the hp cylinder was duplicated in the form of two 7·8in (200mm) diameter valves side by side. A number of American practices were incorporated such as roller bearings on all axles, Franklin self-adjusting axlebox wedges, and inverted rocker side control for the bogies, in addition of course to the mechanical stoker.

When it became possible to resume testing in 1948, 4,000 drawbar horsepower was recorded at speeds between 44 and 70mph with a maximum of 4,200, 625 tons could be reliably started on a 1 in 70 gradient, and 62mph (100kph) attained with 830 tons (856 tonnes) on a gradient of 1 in 155. Fuel economy was found to be as good as that achieved by the recent four-cylinder compounds of class 141P.

The features of this engine have been dealt with at some length, for at this point in history it is clear that the SNCF authorities, with or without Chapelon's blessing, decided to jettison the de Glehn system and concentrate in the future, if there was to be any future, on the three-cylinder compound for high powers. The design of a corresponding heavy freight engine of 2–10–4 wheel arrangement was put in hand (Table 19, entry 13) and the drawings were complete by 1948. This vast engine with 5ft 5in (1650mm) diameter coupled wheels, 98 tons (100 tonnes) of adhesion and 151 tons (154 tonnes) total weight in working order was never constructed, nor was the 4–8–4 engine multiplied, because the increasing spread of electrification rendered them for ever unnecessary.

With small home production of new steam types went only a tiny output of such engines for other countries after the last war. Chapelon's advice was sought for those which were exported such as 4–6–0 and 4–6–2 engines to Egypt, and some large metre gauge engines for Brazil, but it was noteworthy that in all these cases two cylinders were employed and compounding was not used, Chapelon in his last active work on the steam engine doing what so many of his colleagues abroad had done, namely to apply his principles to simple expansion.

Many writers have described performances and footplate trips with one or other of the great locomotives which spelled out the end of steam for France. It is sufficiently clear that in relation to the size of the machines concerned they were unmatched anywhere else in the world both in their contribution to brilliant running and in the elegance with which it was achieved.

Perhaps the truest 'feel' of French locomotive performance at its best is enshrined in a series of articles written for the English periodical *Engineer* by a Canadian, Edward H. Livesay, who with official blessing and under close supervision roamed the Regions on nearly all the most interesting engines in the last days of steam.* Any who have read these articles must have been struck by the Gallic persistence with which the long-standing compound versus simple controversy was kept alive. Having ridden on France's brightest and best upon which only paeons of praise could be bestowed, with characteristic devilment Livesay's hosts saw to it that when he mounted one of the American 141R class simple expansion engines they provided him with one of the roughest of the flock, made even more horrifying to ride upon by a driver carefully instructed to pull up the gear to 15 per cent and less. Thus at the very end, as at any time before, the student had to be wary of what was being compared with what in the enclosed world of French compounding.

* *Engineer* Vol. 197, 1954.

FRANCE. REPRESENTATIVE COMPOUND LOCOMOTIVES—PRE-CHAPELON

Table 17A

Entry	Year	Wheel Arrangement	Railway	Class	Cylinders Diameter × Stroke inches / mm	Coupled Wheels Diameter feet / mm	Working Pressure lb/sq in / kg/cm²	Grate Area sq ft / m²	Weight Engine Working Order: Axle tons / tonnes	Adhesive tons / tonnes	Total tons / tonnes
1	1900	4–4–2	Nord	2.641	(4) $13\frac{3}{8}:22\frac{1}{16}\times25\frac{3}{16}$ 340 : 560 × 640	6′ $8\frac{1}{2}$″ 2045	227 16·0	29·5 2·74	16·2 16·5	32·3 33·0	65·1 66·5
2	1900	4–6–0	,,	3.122	(4) $14:22\frac{1}{16}\times25\frac{3}{16}$ 355 : 560 × 640	5′ $8\frac{7}{8}$″ 1750	213 15·0	26·5 2·46	16·0 16·3	43·0 43·7	58·0 59·0
3	1910	4–4–4	,,	2.741*	(4) $13\frac{3}{8}:22\frac{1}{16}\times25\frac{3}{16}$ 340 : 560 × 640	6′ $8\frac{1}{2}$″ 2045	256 18·0	38·1 3·54	17·1 17·4	34·2 34·8	76·0 77·2
4	1910	4–6–4	,,	3.1102*	(4) $17\frac{5}{8}\times25\frac{3}{16}:24\frac{3}{8}\times28\frac{3}{4}$ 440 × 640 : 620 × 730	6′ $8\frac{1}{2}$″ 2045	227 16·0	46·1 4·28	17·7 18·0	53·2 54·1	100·3 102·0
5	1911	4–6–0	,,	3.538	(4) $15:21\frac{5}{8}\times25\frac{3}{16}$ 380 : 550 × 640	5′ $8\frac{7}{8}$″ 1750	227 16·0	29·7 2·76	17·5 17·8	50·0 51·0	69·4 70·8
6	1912	4–6–2	,,	3.1151	(4) $16\frac{1}{8}:23\frac{5}{8}\times26$ 410 : 600 × 660	6′ $8\frac{1}{2}$″ 2045	227 16·0	34·7 3·22	16·1 16·4	48·2 49·2	83·9 85·6
7	1912	2–8–0		4.061	(4) $16\frac{1}{2}\times25\frac{3}{16}:22\frac{1}{2}\times27\frac{1}{2}$ 420 × 640 : 570 × 700	5′ 1″ 1550	227 16·0	34·7 3·22	17·7 18·0	70·8 72·3	80·7 82·4
8	1913	2–10–0	,,	5.001	(4) $19\frac{1}{4}\times25\frac{3}{16}:26\frac{3}{4}\times27\frac{1}{2}$ 490 × 640 : 680 × 700	5′ 1″ 1550	227 16·0	34·7 3·22	17·3 17·6	86·6 88·4	97·0 99·0
9	1924	4–6–2	,,	3.1201	(4) $17\frac{3}{8}\times26:24\frac{3}{8}\times27\frac{3}{16}$ 440 × 660 : 620 × 690	6′ $2\frac{3}{4}$″ 1900	227 16·0	37·7 3·50	17·7 18·0	53·1 54·2	92·6 94·5
10	1932	4–6–2	,,	3.1251	(4) $17\frac{3}{8}\times26:24\frac{3}{8}\times27\frac{3}{16}$ 440 × 660 : 620 × 690	6′ $2\frac{3}{4}$″ 1900	242 17·0	37·7 3·50	18·6 18·9	55·7 56·8	104·4 106·5
11	1904	4–6–0	Est	,,	(4) $13\frac{3}{4}:22\frac{1}{16}\times26$ 350 : 560 × 660	6′ $10\frac{1}{4}$″ 2090	227 16·0	30·7 2·85	17·5 17·8	51·0 51·8	70·6 71·7
12	1924	4–6–0	,,	3231	(4) $16:23\frac{1}{4}\times26\frac{3}{4}$ 405 : 590 × 680	6′ $10\frac{1}{4}$″ 2090	227 16·0	33·7 3·13	18·2 18·5	53·6 54·7	77·8 79·4
13	1925	4–8–2	,,	241.002	(4) $17\frac{3}{4}:26\times28\frac{3}{8}$ 450 : 660 × 720	6′ $4\frac{3}{4}$″ 1950	284 20·0	47·7 4·43	18·2 18·5	73·0 74·6	114·8 117·2
14	1914	4–6–2	État	231.501	(4) $16\frac{1}{2}:25\frac{3}{16}\times25\frac{5}{8}$ 420 : 640 × 650	6′ $4\frac{3}{4}$″ 1950	227 16·0	45·8 4·26	18·6 18·9	55·7 56·6	96·5 98·0
15	1910	4–6–2	Midi		(4) $15\frac{3}{4}:21\frac{1}{4}\times25\frac{5}{8}$ 400 : 540 × 650	6′ $4\frac{3}{4}$″ 1950	227 16·0	43·0 4·00	17·8 18·1	53·3 54·1	89·9 91·3

Entry	Year	Wheel Arrangement	Railway	Class	Cylinders Diameter × Stroke inches mm	Coupled Wheels Diameter feet mm	Working Pressure lb/sq in kg/cm²	Grate Area sq ft m²	Weight Engine Working Order: Axle tons tonnes	Weight Engine Working Order: Adhesive tons tonnes	Weight Engine Working Order: Total tons tonnes
1	1903	4–4–2	Paris–Orléans	3001	(4) $14\frac{3}{16}:23\frac{5}{8}\times25\frac{3}{16}$ 360 : 600 × 640	6′ $8\frac{1}{4}$″ 2040	227 16·0	33·9 3·16	17·0 17·3	34·0 34·6	66·0 67·1
2	1902	2–8–0	,,	5001	(4) $15\frac{5}{16}:23\frac{5}{8}\times25\frac{5}{8}$ 390 : 600 × 650	5′ 1″ 1550	227 16·0	33·4 3·10	16·5 16·8	66·0 67·1	73·6 74·8
3	1903	4–6–0	,,	4001	(4) $14\frac{3}{16}:23\frac{5}{8}\times25\frac{5}{8}$ 360 : 600 × 650	5′ $10\frac{7}{8}$″ 1800	227 16·0	33·7 3·13	18·0 18·3	54·0 54·9	72·9 74·1
4	1907	4–6–2	,,	4501	(4) $16\frac{1}{2}:25\frac{3}{16}\times25\frac{5}{8}$ 420 : 640 × 650	6′ $0\frac{7}{8}$″ (A) 1850	227 16·0	46·0 4·27	17·1 17·4	51·2 52·3	89·8 91·8
5	1909	2–10–0	,,	6001	(4) $18\frac{1}{8}\times24\frac{3}{8}:26\times25\frac{5}{8}$ 460 × 620 : 660 × 650	4′ $7\frac{1}{8}$″ 1400	227 16·0	41·0 3·80	15·2 15·5	76·1 77·7	83·6 85·2
6	1906	4–6–0	Paris, Lyons & Mediterranean		(4) $14\frac{1}{2}:21\frac{1}{4}\times25\frac{5}{8}$ 370 : 540 × 650	6′ $6\frac{3}{4}$″ 2000	227 16·0	32·3 3·00	16·3 16·6	48·9 49·7	70·0 71·2
7	1912	4–6–2	,, ,,	6201	(4) $17\frac{3}{8}:25\frac{5}{8}\times25\frac{5}{8}$ 440 : 650 × 650	6′ $6\frac{3}{4}$″ 2000	227 16·0	45·7 4·25	17·9 18·2	53·8 55·0	89·4 91·2
8	1913	2–8–0	,, ,,	4271	(4) $15\frac{3}{4}:22\frac{7}{8}\times25\frac{5}{8}$ 400 : 580 × 650	4′ 11″ 1500	227 16·0	33·0 3·08	15·7 16·0	62·5 63·8	72·2 73·5
9	1914	2–8–2	,, ,,		(4) $20\frac{1}{16}\times25\frac{5}{8}:28\frac{3}{8}\times27\frac{1}{2}$ 510 × 650 : 720 × 700	5′ 5″ 1050	227 16·0	45·7 4·25	17·4 17·7	69·9 71·1	94·7 96·3
10	1914	4–6–4T	,, ,,	5301	(4) $14\frac{3}{16}:22\frac{1}{16}\times25\frac{5}{8}$ 360 : 560 × 650	5′ 5″ 1650	227 16·0	26·7 2·48	16·2 16·5	48·5 49·5	92·2 94·1
11	1925	4–8–2	,, ,,	241A1	(4) $20\frac{1}{16}\times25\frac{5}{8}:28\frac{3}{8}\times27\frac{1}{2}$ 510 × 650 : 720 × 700	5′ $10\frac{1}{2}$″ 1790	227 16·0	53·8 5·00	18·2 18·5	72·6 74·0	112·3 114·6
12	1926	4–8–4T	,, ,,	242A1	(4) $16\frac{1}{2}:24\frac{7}{8}\times25\frac{5}{8}$ 420 : 630 × 650	5′ 5″ 1650	227 16·0	33·0 3·08	15·9 16·2	63·7 65·0	117·6 120·0
13	1931	4–8–2	,, ,,	241C1	(4) $17\frac{3}{4}\times25\frac{5}{8}:26\frac{3}{4}\times27\frac{1}{2}$ 450 × 650 : 680 × 700	6′ $6\frac{3}{4}$″ 2000	284 20·0	53·8 5·00	19·3 19·7	77·2 78·8	123·5 126·1
14	1932	2–10–2	,, ,,	151A1	(4) $18\frac{7}{8}\times25\frac{5}{8}:29\frac{3}{8}\times27\frac{1}{2}$ (B) 480 × 650 : 745 × 700	4′ 11″ 1500	284 20·0	53·8 5·00	18·2 18·5	90·8 92·7	120·0 122·4

(A) Later engines had 6ft $4\frac{3}{4}$in (1950mm) Diameter Coupled Wheels (B) All Cylinders outside frames

FRANCE. REPRESENTATIVE SIMPLE-EXPANSION LOCOMOTIVES 1900–1955

Table 18A

Entry	Year	Wheel Arrangement	Railway	Class	*Cylinders Diameter × Stroke* inches mm	*Coupled Wheels Diameter* feet mm	*Working Pressure* lb/sq in kg/cm²	*Grate Area* sq ft m²	*Weight Engine Working Order* Axle tons tonnes	Adhesive tons tonnes	Total tons tonnes
1	1919	2–6–0	Nord	3.1501	$22\frac{3}{8} \times 26\frac{3}{4}$ 570 × 680	5′ $8\frac{7}{8}$″ 1750	171 12·0	25·7 2·39	18·4 18·8	55·2 56·3	66·9 68·3
2	1930	0–10–0T	,,	5.601	24 × 26 610 × 660	4′ $5\frac{1}{8}$″ 1350	199 14·0	24·7 2·30	17·9 18·3	89·8 91·7	89·8 91·7
3	1931	4–6–2	,,	3.1249	$25\frac{3}{16} \times 27\frac{1}{2}$ 640 × 700	6′ $2\frac{3}{4}$″ 1900	242 17·0	37·7 3·50	18·5 18·9	55·6 56·8	98·4 100·5
4	1931	2–8–2T	,,	4.1201	$25\frac{3}{16} \times 27\frac{1}{2}$ 640 × 700	5′ 1″ 1550	256 18·0	33·4 3·10	20·8 21·2	83·2 85·0	120·0 122·5
5	1925	2–10–0	Est	150.001	(3) 22 × 26 560 × 660	4′ $7\frac{1}{8}$″ 1400	199 14·0	35·0 3·25	16·5 16·8	82·3 84·0	96·0 98·0
6	1913	2–10–2T	,,	5900	$24\frac{7}{8} \times 26$ 630 × 660	4′ $5\frac{1}{8}$″ 1350	199 14·0	33·2 3·08	17·8 18·2	89·0 90·9	118·5 120·8
7	1925	2–6–2T	,,	32.001	$20\frac{1}{16} \times 26$ 510 × 660	4′ $7\frac{7}{8}$″ 1420	185 13·0	22·2 2·06	15·6 15·9	46·6 47·6	75·9 77·5
8	1930	2–8–2T	,,	141.701	(3) $20\frac{1}{16} \times 26$ 510 × 660	4′ $7\frac{7}{8}$″ 1420	227 16·0	30·3 2·80	18·4 18·8	73·5 75·0	104·3 106·5
9	1930	2–10–2T	,,	151.751	(3) 22 × 26 560 × 660	4′ $5\frac{1}{8}$″ 1350	199 14·0	33·0 3·06	18·0 18·4	90·4 92·2	120·2 122·6
10	1917	4–6–0	Paris–Orléans		$19\frac{5}{8} \times 25\frac{5}{8}$ 500 × 650	5′ $8\frac{7}{8}$″ 1750	171 12·0	29·4 2·73	15·9 16·2	47·6 48·6	66·4 67·8
11	1921	2–8–2T	,, ,,		$24\frac{3}{8} \times 27\frac{1}{2}$ 620 × 700	5′ 5″ 1650	227 16·0	30·0 2·79	18·3 18·7	73·5 75·0	104·3 106·5
12	1909	4–6–2	Paris, Lyons & Mediterranean	6101	(4) $18\frac{7}{8} \times 25\frac{5}{8}$ 480 × 650	6′ $6\frac{3}{4}$″ 2000	171 12·0	45·7 4·25	17·8 18·2	53·6 54·6	88·2 90·0
13	1925	4–6–2	Midi		$24\frac{7}{8} \times 25\frac{5}{8}$ 630 × 650	6′ $4\frac{3}{4}$″ 1950	185 13·0	45·8 4·26	17·6 18·0	53·0 54·0	87·2 89·0

FRANCE. REPRESENTATIVE SIMPLE-EXPANSION LOCOMOTIVES 1900–1955

Table 18B

Entry	Year	Wheel Arrangement	Railway	Class	Cylinders Diameter × Stroke inches mm	Coupled Wheels Diameter feet mm	Working Pressure lb/sq in kg/cm²	Grate Area sq ft m²	Weight Engine Working Order: Axle tons tonnes	Adhesive tons tonnes	Total tons tonnes
1	1912	4–6–0	État		(4) 17 × 25$\frac{3}{16}$ 430 × 640	6′ 8$\frac{3}{8}$″ 2040	171 12·0	29·7 2·76	16·0 16·3	48·0 49·0	70·0 71·4
2	1912	4–6–0	,,		21$\frac{5}{8}$ × 25$\frac{3}{16}$ 550 × 640	5′ 8$\frac{7}{8}$″ 1750	171 12·0	29·7 2·76	15·8 16·1	47·3 48·3	66·9 68·0
3	1916	2–8–0	,,		23$\frac{1}{4}$ × 25$\frac{5}{8}$ 590 × 650	4′ 8$\frac{5}{8}$″ 1440	171 12·0	34·0 3·16	16·0 16·3	64·0 65·0	73·2 74·4
4	1918	2–8–2	,,		24$\frac{3}{8}$ × 27$\frac{1}{2}$ 620 × 700	5′ 5″ 1650	171 12·0	40·9 3·80	16·0 16·3	63·9 65·1	84·3 86·0
5	1933	4–8–2	,,		(3) 20$\frac{7}{8}$ × 30 : 22$\frac{3}{8}$ × 25$\frac{5}{8}$ 530 × 760 : 570 × 650	6′ 4$\frac{3}{4}$″ 1950	284 20·0	53·8 5·00	19·8 20·2	79·2 80·8	124·3 126·8
6	1933	4–6–2	Alsace-Lorraine	S16	22$\frac{5}{8}$ × 28$\frac{3}{8}$ 575 × 720	6′ 4$\frac{3}{4}$″ 1950	284 20·0	48·4 4·50	19·6 20·0	58·8 60·0	105·3 107·4
7	1936	2–10–2	,, ,,	G16	(3) 22$\frac{5}{8}$ × 28$\frac{3}{8}$ 575 × 720	4′ 11″ 1500	284 20·0	53·8 5·00	19·6 20·0	98·0 100·0	126·8 129·3
8	1940	4–6–4	SNCF	232R	(3) 21$\frac{1}{4}$ × 27$\frac{1}{2}$ 540 × 700	6′ 6$\frac{3}{4}$″ 2000	284 20·0	55·6 5·17	21·6 22·0	64·7 66·0	121·2 123·6
9	1940	2–10–2T	,,	151TQ	24$\frac{7}{8}$ × 26 630 × 660	4′ 5$\frac{1}{8}$″ 1350	199 14·0	38·2 3·55	17·2 17·5	85·8 87·5	115·2 117·5
10	1948	0–10–0T	,,	050TQ	24$\frac{7}{8}$ × 26 630 × 660	4′ 5$\frac{1}{8}$″ 1350	171 12·0	29·5 2·74	18·5 18·9	92·6 94·5	92·6 94·5
11	1952	4–6–0	Egyptian State		21 × 28 534 × 711	6′ 0″ 1829	227 16·0	38·0 3·53	21·5 21·9	63·2 64·2	87·8 88·8
12	1955	4–6–2	,, ,,		22 × 28 559 × 711	6′ 9″ 2057	227 16·0	— —	22·3 22·7	67·0 68·1	109·0 110·8

FRANCE. REPRESENTATIVE COMPOUND LOCOMOTIVES—POST-CHAPELON

Table 19

Entry	Year	Wheel Arrange-ment	Railway		Class	Cylinders Diameter × Stroke inches mm	Coupled Wheels Diameter feet mm	Working Pressure lb/sq in kg/cm²	Grate Area sq ft m²	Weight Engine Working Order: Axle tons tonnes	Adhesive tons tonnes	Total tons tonnes
1	1932	4–6–2	Paris–Orléans	(A)	231-702	(4) $16\frac{1}{2} : 25\frac{3}{16} \times 25\frac{5}{8}$ 420 : 640 × 650	6′ $4\frac{3}{4}$″ 1950	**242** 17·0	**46·6** 4·33	**18·7** 19·1	**56·2** 57·3	**99·0** 101·0
2	1934	4–6–2	,, ,,	(A)	231-722	(4) $16\frac{1}{2} \times 25\frac{5}{8} : 25\frac{5}{8} \times 27\frac{3}{4}$ 420 × 650 : 650 × 690	6′ $4\frac{3}{4}$″ 1950	**242** 17·0	**46·6** 4·33	**18·7** 19·1	**56·2** 57·3	**101·0** 103·0
3	1934	4–8–0	,, ,,	(A)	240-702	(4) $17\frac{3}{8} : 25\frac{3}{16} \times 25\frac{5}{8}$ 440 : 640 × 650	6′ $0\frac{3}{4}$″ 1850	**284** 20·0	**40·8** 3·80	**18·7** 19·1	**74·8** 76·4	**107·2** 109·4
4	1938	4–6–2	Paris, Lyons & Mediterranean	(A)	231H	(4) $15\frac{3}{4} : 25\frac{3}{8} \times 25\frac{3}{8}$ 400 : 650 × 650	6′ $6\frac{3}{4}$″ 2000	**284** 20·0	**45·7** 4·25	**18·6** 19·0	**55·8** 57·0	**98·1** 100·1
5	1940	2–10–0	Nord	(C)	150P	(4) $19\frac{1}{4} \times 25\frac{3}{16} : 26\frac{3}{4} \times 27\frac{1}{2}$ 490 × 640 : 680 × 700	5′ 1″ 1550	**256** 18·0	**38·0** 3·53	**17·7** 18·1	**88·8** 90·6	**103·0** 105·2
6	1940	4–6–4	SNCF	(B)	232S	(4) $19\frac{7}{8} : 26\frac{3}{4} \times 28\frac{3}{8}$ 455 : 680 × 720	6′ $6\frac{3}{4}$″ 2000	**284** 20·0	**55·6** 5·17	**21·5** 22·0	**64·6** 66·0	**124·5** 127·1
7	1940	4–8–0	,,	(C)	240P	(4) $17\frac{3}{8} \times 25\frac{5}{8} : 25\frac{5}{8} \times 27\frac{3}{16}$ 440 × 650 : 650 × 690	6′ $0\frac{3}{4}$″ 1850	**284** 20·0	**40·8** 3·80	**19·6** 20·0	**78·4** 80·0	**110·7** 113·0
8	1942	2–8–2	,,	(C)	141P	(4) $16\frac{1}{8} : 25\frac{3}{16} \times 27\frac{1}{2}$ 410 : 640 × 700	5′ 5″ 1650	**284** 20·0	**46·3** 4·30	**18·6** 19·0	**74·1** 75·6	**109·2** 111·5
9	1946	4–8–4	,,	(A)	242A1	(3) $23\frac{5}{8} \times 28\frac{3}{8} : 26\frac{3}{4} \times 30$ 600 × 720 : 680 × 760	6′ $4\frac{3}{4}$″ 1950	**284** 20·0	**53·8** 5·00	**20·0** 21·0	**82·3** 84·0	**145·0** 148·0
10	1946	2–12–0	,,	(A)	160A	(6) $20\frac{1}{2} \times 21\frac{1}{4} : 20\frac{1}{2} \times 21\frac{1}{4} :$ $25\frac{3}{16} \times 25\frac{5}{8}$ 520 × 540 : 520 × 540 : 640 × 650	4′ $7\frac{1}{8}$″ 1400	**256** 18·0	**47·3** 4·40	**19·6** 20·0	**117·5** 120·0	**134·7** 137·5
11	1947	4–8–2	,,	(C)	241P	(4) $17\frac{3}{4} \times 26\frac{3}{8} : 26\frac{3}{8} \times 27\frac{1}{2}$ 450 × 670 : 670 × 700	6′ $6\frac{3}{4}$″ 2000	**284** 20·0	**53·8** 5·00	**20·0** 20·4	**80·4** 82·0	**129·0** 131·7
12	1948	4–6–4	,,	(B)	232U	(4) $17\frac{3}{8} : 27\frac{3}{16} \times 27\frac{1}{2}$ 440 : 690 × 700	6′ $6\frac{3}{4}$″ 2000	**284** 20·0	**56·6** 5·26	**22·0** 22·5	**66·2** 67·5	**127·3** 130·0
13	D	2–10–4	,,	(B)	152	(3) $23\frac{1}{4} : 26 \times 30$ 590 : 660 × 760	5′ 5″ 1650	**313** 22·0	**64·2** 5·96	**19·6** 20·0	**98·0** 100·0	**150·8** 154·0

(A) Conversion from existing type (B) New and original design (C) Built new as development of existing design (D) Design completed but engine not built

EXPORTED TO OR BUILT BY OTHER COUNTRIES

Table 20

Entry	Year	Wheel Arrangement	Railway	Class	Cylinders Diameter × Stroke inches / mm	Coupled Wheels Diameter feet / mm	Working Pressure lb/sq in / kg/cm²	Grate Area sq ft / m²	Weight Engine Working Order: Axle tons / tonnes	Adhesive tons / tonnes	Total tons / tonnes
1	1902	4–4–0	Prussian State	S5[1]	(4) $13\frac{3}{8}:20\frac{7}{8}\times25\frac{3}{16}$ $340:530\times640$	6′ 6″ 1980	199 14·0	22·1 2·05	15·1 15·3	30·2 30·8	47·5 48·4
2	1902	4–6–0	Madrid, Zaragosa & Alicante		(4) $13\frac{7}{8}:21\frac{3}{4}\times25\frac{3}{4}$ $350:550\times640$	5′ 9″ 1750	200 14·0	27·4 2·55	14·0 14·2	42·0 42·7	61·0 62·0
3	1903	4–4–2	Great Western (England)	102	(4) $13\frac{3}{8}:22\frac{1}{16}\times25\frac{3}{16}$ $340:560\times640$	6′ $8\frac{1}{2}$″ 2045	227 16·0	29·5 2·74	17·2 17·5	34·5 35·1	65·0 66·1
4	1903	4–4–2	Prussian State	S7	(4) $13\frac{3}{8}:22\frac{1}{16}\times25\frac{3}{16}$ $340:560\times640$	6′ 6″ 1980	227 16·0	32·3 3·00	15·5 15·7	31·1 31·6	62·7 64·0
5	1904	4–4–2	Pennsylvania (USA)	2512	(4) $14\frac{3}{16}:23\frac{5}{8}\times25\frac{3}{16}$ $360:600\times640$	6′ $8\frac{1}{2}$″ 2045	227 16·0	33·3 3·09	19·5 19·8	39·0 39·6	73·0 74·2
6	1905	4–4–2	Egyptian State		(4) $13\frac{3}{8}:22\frac{1}{16}\times25\frac{3}{16}$ $340:560\times640$	6′ $8\frac{1}{2}$″ 2045	227 16·0	29·5 2·74	16·9 17·2	33·8 34·4	66·4 67·5
7	1905	4–4–2	Belgian State		(4) $14\frac{3}{16}:23\frac{5}{8}\times25\frac{3}{16}$ $360:600\times640$	6′ 6″ 1980	227 16·0	33·1 3·07	17·7 18·0	35·5 36·1	71·6 72·8
8	1905	4–6–0	Gothard (Switzerland)		(4) $14\frac{3}{16}:23\frac{5}{8}\times25\frac{3}{16}$ $360:600\times640$	5′ $3\frac{3}{8}$″ 1610	227 16·0	25·8 2·40	16·7 17·0	33·5 34·6	64·0 65·0
9	1911	4–6–2	Norte (Spain)	3001	(4) $14\frac{1}{2}:22\frac{1}{2}\times25\frac{3}{16}$ $370:570\times640$	5′ $8\frac{7}{8}$″ 1750	227 16·0	44·0 4·10	15·3 15·5	46·0 46·7	75·0 76·2
10	1912	4–8–0	,, ,,	4001	(4) $15\frac{3}{4}:24\frac{1}{2}\times25\frac{3}{16}$ $400:620\times640$	5′ $1\frac{3}{8}$″ 1560	227 16·0	44·0 4·10	15·2 15·4	61·0 62·0	78·7 80·0
11	1913	4–8–4T	,, ,,	4201	(4) $15\frac{3}{4}:24\frac{1}{2}\times25\frac{3}{16}$ $400:620\times640$	5′ $1\frac{3}{8}$″ 1560	227 16·0	34·1 3·17	15·4 15·6	61·5 62·5	99·2 100·8
12	1919	4–6–0	Belgian State	8BIS	(4) $15\frac{3}{4}:23\frac{5}{8}\times25\frac{3}{16}$ $400:600\times640$	5′ 11″ 1800	227 16·0	33·1 3·07	19·9 20·2	59·7 60·7	83·5 84·9
13	1921	2–8–0	,, ,,	33	(4) $16\frac{9}{16}:23\frac{5}{8}\times26$ $420:600\times660$	4′ $11\frac{7}{8}$″ 1520	227 16·0	35·0 3·25	18·7 19·0	75·0 76·2	85·0 86·4
14	1925	4–8–2	Norte (Spain)	4601	(4) $18\frac{1}{8}:27\frac{1}{2}\times26\frac{3}{4}$ $460:700\times680$	5′ $8\frac{7}{8}$″ 1750	227 16·0	53·8 5·00	15·7 15·9	62·7 64·0	101·0 103·0
15	1931	4–8–0	Beira Alta (Portugal)		(4) $16\frac{1}{2}:25\frac{3}{8}\times25\frac{3}{8}$ $420:650\times650$	5′ $4\frac{1}{8}$″ 1610	227 16·0	42·7 3·97	14·5 14·7	58·0 58·9	86·0 87·4

Table 20A

PROGRESSIVE IMPROVEMENT IN POWER OUTPUT. PARIS–ORLÉANS RAILWAY 4-CYLINDER COMPOUND 4–6–2 ENGINES AS A RESULT OF CHAPELON'S MODIFICATIONS

		Maximum Drawbar Horsepower at	
		69mph	110 km/hr
Stage	*Engine Condition*	hp	cv
1	As originally built	1,470	1450
2	Increased travel for LP valves	1,500	1480
3	Single KC blastpipe	1,600	1580
4	Improved superheat	1,745	1720
5	LP piston valves with double admission and double exhaust	2,030	2000
6	Increased areas of cylinder ports and passages poppet valves. Double KC blastpipe. Still higher superheat	2,332	2300
7	Increased steam area through LP poppet valves. 10% increase in volume of LP cylinders	2,687	2650
	Improvement Stage 7 over Stage 1 83%		

CHAPTER SIX

Germany

GERMANY, WHOSE NATIONAL characteristics of authority and order have led it furthest amongst nations along the road of standardisation, has nevertheless by the circumstances of its own history and the effects of two wars produced a wide variety of locomotive types of great interest which have had a considerable influence upon design thought elsewhere. There have been within the present century four distinct periods of development, each retaining to a remarkable degree a common thread of technical thinking and of appearance. Between 1900 and 1914 the Prussian State Railways, whose practice had the greatest influence upon what followed afterwards, was only one out of eight major State administrations and of a number of secondary railways within the country, each one following its own 'line', usually supported by one or more specialist manufacturers within its own boundaries. The diversity of engine types thus produced was much akin to that obtaining in England at the same time, and some were similarly exported to other countries in which Germany had a political or financial interest.

From 1914 through World War I and until the formation of the unified Reichsbahn in 1920, a small number of further designs was produced under central direction, to be widely distributed to the still separate State organisations. At the same time, as soon as the war was over and before they were engulfed in the maw of the all-embracing Reich, each State organisation brought out the final expressions of its own design tradition and philosophy amongst which were some excellent and striking machines. In this period the reparations demanded by the peace treaties caused the dispersal of some 5,000 active locomotives of many different types to replace those devastated and lost by neighbouring countries during the hostilities, Belgium and France receiving the largest shares.

As soon as post-war recovery commenced the resulting shortage enabled the central direction of the newly formed Reichsbahn to plan for a series of standard locomotives covering the traffic needs of the whole of Germany, and in the later 1930s reaching out towards new and higher standards of speed and performance. This was the period of Germany's greatest influence in world locomotive affairs, and many were those who made the pilgrimage to Berlin to study form, and numerous were the resulting applications, whether as whole designs or merely as adaptations of the basic thinking.

So widely did the series of 29 standard designs cover the operating spectrum that there was no difficulty in selecting one of them, in drastically simplified form, as a universal work horse for wartime duties in home and conquered territory, and no further new design proved necessary until after the ultimate débâcle in 1945. Once again, huge numbers of locomotives were taken over by the victorious Allies, and distributed throughout the war-torn countries which now emerged from the battle with their transport systems in ruins. Mainly 'Krieglokomotivs' were retained, and few of the other former Reichsbahn types remained with the conquerors.

The final period of steam development commenced after a stricken Germany, now divided by the Iron Curtain into separate Eastern and Western States, was able to embark on the rebuilding of its shattered territories. The Bundesbahn of Federal Germany (Western Germany) and the Reichsbahn of the German Democratic Republic

(Eastern Germany) having divided up the rolling stock which remained usable or repairable at the war's end, commenced in 1950 and 1954 respectively the introduction of a modest post-war steam series. Before these could be developed very far either in variety or numbers, and before they had any chance to influence practice elsewhere, dieselisation and electrification intervened here as in other parts of the world to bring steam development to an end. These post-war engines retained a close kinship in design philosophy both with the mainstream of German practice, and as between the post-war products from each side of the Curtain.

A lively export trade has been maintained through the years by a number of well-known manufacturing firms. These not only between them supplied the whole needs of the home railways but sent their products into every corner of the globe. The great firm of Henschel alone, for example, had built 25,000 locomotives up to 1941, 11,500 for German railways, 6,000 for private industry and 7,500 exported to 27 countries abroad. A considerable number of the latter were to customer's drawings, but as will be seen later in this chapter a substantial quantity also were of pure German design.

I. 1900–1920

Let us look first at some of the principal engine types turned out by the independent State lines other than the Prussian in the period before 1920, as set out in Tables 22A and B. These states of the realm for the most part bordered the Great Prussian plain to the west and south, so that their terrain was more undulating and even mountainous. The best coal, subject to the long haul from the Rhineland, was expensive and that obtainable from coalfields more nearly to hand was often of poorer quality. These circumstances had a marked effect upon the kind of engines which were designed, and explains in part why they were so unlike those built for Prussia where the natural conditions were different.

The need for coal economy favoured compounding, and although the advent of superheating led to a gradual supersession of double expansion in many other quarters, here it was largely retained plus superheating and the last, biggest and best products of these states remained faithful to this condition. The heavy gradients demanded six- and eight-coupled engines for passenger work, and eight-, ten- and even twelve-coupled wheels for freight, while the poorer coal required big grate areas and ample air inlet and ashpan capacity below the grate, features which called for rear carrying wheels, where applied, being placed far back behind the firebox.

The majority of the Bavarian State Railway locomotives were designed and built by the firm of Maffei of Munich, a firm which developed an individual design style which marked out its products clearly wherever they were found at home or abroad. This consisted of four compound cylinders usually all driving the same axle, the low-pressure cylinders being outside. Two valve gears served the four separate valves through rocking levers, or in some examples drove double valves on the same spindle. Maffei was the first European firm to standardise the use of the American style of forged bar frame, which may or may not have been influenced by the purchase by the State Railways of some Atlantic locomotives from Baldwins as early as 1900.* With the bar frames went running boards high on the boiler flanks, and visibility and accessibility unusual by previous European standards in that it was claimed to be possible to see all four big-ends from a suitable position on one side of the engine. Thus were combined a majestic if somewhat un-European appearance with maintenance and servicing

* See Table 7, entry 15.

facilities ahead of their time. Heavy haulage at moderate speeds was well served, but Bavarian passenger trains were not renowned for their sprightliness in those pre-World War I days, and the attention of observers was seldom captured by undue speed.

The best known engines of this administration were the 4–6–2s of class S3/6 in the nomenclature of the original owners, and of class 18.400 upwards of the subsequent Reichsbahn (Table 22A, entry 2). They were built at intervals from 1906 to 1930, in steps of coupled axleload from 15·7 to 17·6 tons (16 to 18 tonnes), and were the only non-Prussian type to be perpetuated by the Reichsbahn in order to meet the operating need for a low axleload Pacific until its own 03 class appeared in sufficient numbers. Plate 62 shows one of the most recently built of these engines, and its compact shape, and very un-German use of a flared chimney-top without the unsightly joint at mid-height, made this type one of the best-looking in this part of Europe.

What has been said of Bavarian engines applies also to those of the neighbouring Baden State, only more so. Maffei's designs for this administration added 'windcutter' cab fronts and conical smokebox doors of more exaggerated shape, and provided an even greater spread of wheelbase under the firebox in the case of Atlantics and Pacifics, these features combining to produce a stark and 'spikey' appearance. Adhering consistently to compounding this administration obtained from Maffei its final swansong in the form of a Pacific (Type IVh), designed in 1918 but only turned out in 1920 at the eleventh hour before unification (Table 22A, Entry 15). This rather ugly machine was made more ungainly by the steam chests for the inside hp cylinders being arranged in tandem with those for the outside lp cylinders, both valves being mounted on the same long spindle driven from the outside Walschaert's gear. With the unusual wheel diameter of 6ft 10⅝in (2100mm) this class was intended for express traffic on the Mannheim to Basle section, and was accorded a permitted maximum speed of 81¼mph (130kph). Incidentally it was the first engine in Germany to be allowed to approach an 18-ton axleload.

The Saxon State Railways, centred on Leipzig and Dresden, were also strongly individual in their locomotive design, but they all had a neatness of assembly and economy in external hangings which singled them out from other German products at the time, their use of the Belpaire firebox, gracefully capped chimneys and neat cabs giving them an almost English aspect. This administration never seemed to make up its mind about compounding, and different series, contemporary in time, might be either simple or compound. This fact was exemplified in the final productions, a Pacific brought out in 1917 and a 2–8–2 passenger engine for heavily graded routes turned out in 1918, both built by the firm of Hartmann of Chemnitz, which also built most of the other Saxon engines in the present century (entries 9 and 10 in Table 22A). The first of these engines was the first European three-cylinder simple Pacific. The valve gear included a conjugated drive for the inside valve on the same lines as that adopted on the Prussian wartime 2–10–0 first built in 1915 of which a number had been drafted into Saxony, and which will be referred to later. The 2–8–2 on the other hand was a compound with four cylinders driving on to the second coupled axle, and with 6ft 3in (1905mm) diameter wheels it was a forerunner of the powerful large-wheeled passenger and mixed traffic Mikados which followed later on many administrations. Both of these fine engines were rare birds indeed to Western observers, but Plate 60 shows one of the 2–8–2s in action near Hof in 1929.

In Württemberg, no axleload greater than 15¾ tons (16 tonnes) was permissible and the Pacific design (entry 1 in Table 22B) to which examples were built at intervals between 1909 and 1921 had to be somewhat smaller than its counterparts elsewhere.

With deep running boards set low enough to require shallow splashers, and a 'wind-cutter' cab front, the combination of dome and sandbox in one casing together with a simple arrangement of auxiliary fittings produced a very neat appearance. Coupled wheels only 5ft 10⅞in (1800mm) diameter befitted the serrated profiles the engines had to travel, and a few of them were to be seen as late as 1955 in the Stuttgart area. Similarly long-lived were the class of 2–12–0 freight engines built between 1917 and 1924 (entry 4 in the table). The only representatives of their wheel arrangement in Europe other than the Austrian 2–12–0 of 1911, unlike the latter, they were built to the extent of 44 units. By dint of using thin flanges on the third and fourth coupled axles, and additional sideplay to the first, third and sixth axles, the last spring controlled, this vast engine was enabled to traverse reasonably sharp curves. Some of these engines turned up after World War II banking trains up the southern flank of the Semmering Pass in Austria, whence they had been drafted during the Anschluss. Beside such major efforts, the rather pretty and very straightforward 2–6–2 tank (Plate 63 and entry 3 in the table) was another survivor into modern times of this almost forgotten independent administration. Most of its engines were built by the Esslingen Locomotive Works located in the town of that name, not far from Stuttgart.

On the Prussian State Railways conditions were generally different from elsewhere in Germany in that the principal routes were more level and the coal available within the Railways' own territory was usually of good quality. This led to the retention of the four-coupled express engine longer than on other German lines and resulted in the narrow rather than the wide firebox being the normal thing. Tables 22B and C list the principal types, which were classified under the letters S for *Schnellzuglokomotiv* (express passenger), P for *Personenzuglokomotiv* (secondary passenger), G for *Güterzuglokomotive* (freight) and T for *Tenderlokomotiv* (tank engines for all duties). In the opening years of the century, 4–4–0, 2–6–0, 0–8–0 tender engines and 2–6–0 and 0–6–0 tank engines of moderate size with axleloads not exceeding 17½ tons (17·8 tonnes) were the most generally used. This era brought to an end a long period in which there had been much havering about compounding, two-cylinder 2–6–0s and 0–8–0s in particular having been turned out in a most random manner either as simples or compounds. Small groups of 4–4–0s and Atlantics were built as pure four-cylinder de Glehn compounds in the French manner (Table 20, entries 1 and 4), or in the form of the so-called 'balanced' compounds sometimes with the cylinders turned the other way round, lp outside instead of inside, based upon Maffei developments. From 1906 onwards, with the 4–6–0 as an added wheel arrangement for the most important passenger and mixed traffic duties, the advent of superheating enabled the administration to make up its mind that single expansion gave it all it needed for the generality of its motive power and only in the S.10^1 class of 1911 (entry 12 in Table 22B) was compounding continued in parallel with other versions of the same general design having three and four simple cylinders.

It is possible to wonder whether the Berlin authorities learned as much about steam distribution from their de Glehn compounds of 1902 as had Churchward in England at almost the same time. From inspection of illustrations, and recollecting the influence German thinking had upon the valve events of the Lancashire & Yorkshire Railway engines in England which were fitted with long lap long travel valves in the 1906–8 period in conjunction with a pioneer application of Schmidt superheating, it is more than probable that the long travel valve had already been standardised on the Prussian State Railways by 1906 at the latest. If this were so it would fully account for the general eclipse of compounding, because there is copious evidence that it retained no advantages for general use over single expansion with long valve travel in this pre-Chapelon era.

The majority of the Prussian engines was not only very uniform in its design approach,

60 The first large wheeled 2–8–2 for passenger duties. Saxony State 4-cylinder compound, originally Class XX and No 19.001 on Reichsbahn stock list. Taken at Hof, 1929 [*C. Shorto*

61 Pure Prussian State design. 2-cylinder simple 0–10–0 originally classified G.10; No 57.3492 at Aachen, 1930 [*C. Shorto*

62 The only Bavarian design subsequently built by Reichsbahn. 4-cylinder compound 4–6–2 No 18616 at Stuttgart, 1956. Originally numbered 18517, it was renumbered 18616 when fitted postwar with new all-welded boiler [*E. S. Cox*

63 A Wurttemburg State Railways' survivor. 2–6–2T formerly Class T5, later No 75 019, built 1910, entering Stuttgart station in 1960 [*E. S. Cox*

64 Survivor of two wars. Ex-Prussian P8 Class 4–6–0 delivered to Belgium as reparations in 1919, now as 64.057 standing at Antwerp in 1956 [*E. S. Cox*

65 3-cylinder simple expansion Prussian Class G12 war locomotive of 1917—later No 58 1393. Note Belpaire firebox and conjugated 2 to drive 1 behind cylinders for inside valve [*Archiv Bellingrodt*

66 French version of Prussian G12 class. The chassis is basically the same, but the boiler is different. Est Railway No 150.E.172 as later fitted with Le Maitre blastpipe and wide chimney [*P. Ransome Wallis*

67 The classic 01 Class Reichsbahn Pacific first built in 1925. No 01 113 at Wurzburg, 1959. Note wide spacing of trailing truck wheels

68 Reichsbahn 2–6–2T for secondary services. Between 1928 and 1940, 520 of these engines were built. No 64 132 at Augsburg; note array of fittings on boiler top

[E. S. Cox

69 A little known class. Only two of the original Reichsbahn Class 23 2–6–2 were built in 1941, before the war terminated all construction other than that of the *Kreiglokomotiven* *[Archiv Bellingrodt*

both in the ensemble and in detail, but the engines were highly standardised amongst themselves, and they laid down a truly national school of design which has permeated subsequent German practice right up to the demise of steam development in the late 1950s. The engines built in largest numbers for passenger work were the 4–6–0s of the P8 and S10 classes. The former, built over the period from 1906 to 1924 (Plate 4 and entry 10 in Table 22B), ran to 3,500 units and were the forerunners of the General Utility 4–6–0 which was to become so numerous and popular in England and elsewhere. With 5ft 8⅞in (1750mm) diameter wheels and a 17-ton (17·2-tonne) axleload they could run anywhere and turn their hands to anything and they have been amongst the most numerous and successful engines of their kind to run in any part of the world. The S10 series were slightly larger machines whose 6ft 5in (1980mm) diameter coupled wheels fitted them for undertaking the fastest duties. Here the administration let itself go in a large-scale exercise to determine once and for all the optimum means of propulsion. The original S10 of 1910 series (entry 11) had four simple cylinders in line, an arrangement already studied in Belgium in 1904 leading eventually to the Type 9 4–6–0 of that administration as built from 1906 onwards. $S10^1$ series commencing 1911 (entry 12) was as already mentioned a compound, the earliest manifestations of which had the hp outside cylinders disposed over the rear bogie wheels with a low running plate and splashers, whereas the later version, of which Henschel's delivered 232 units between 1914 and 1916, had all the cylinders in line with longer outside connecting rods. A raised running plate on the boiler flanks obviated the need for splashers. Although these were sprightly machines, one of which attained a speed of 95mph (152kph) during an experimental run in 1933, it was the final series. Class $S10^2$ (entry 13) of 1914 was, as a three-cylinder simple with separate Walschaert's gears for each valve, the eventual prototype for future development in that no further four-cylinder simple expansion engines were built after 1914, and no three-cylinder simples with conjugated gear after 1924.

The general features and admirable simplicity of the P_8 class of 4–6–0 were reproduced in the G_8 class 0–8–0, G_{10} 0–10–0, T_{13} 0–8–0 tank, T_{14} 2–8–2 tank, T_{16} 0–10–0 tank and T_{18} 4–6–4 tank, classes which were built in huge numbers, the first two amounting to 6,000 and 3,500 units respectively, while the T_{14} and T_{16} reached over 1,000 each and the T_{18} over 500, these figures apart from export orders for the same designs. A peculiarity discernible in this series of engines is that the boilers themselves appear to have been by no means standardised as between outwardly similar classes. It would seem that firebox lengths and distance between tubeplates were tailored to the physical dimensions of each individual design, rather than have one boiler adaptable to several classes as was more usual elsewhere. In view of the large numbers of each standard class which were to be built, interchangeability of the boilers complete between classes was not so important, while on the other hand flanged plates and tube diameters together with all details and fittings were highly standardised.

It is convenient to pause here to consider the merits of the various design features which commended themselves to others, and the influences which led to a wider dissemination of individual types, as these factors affected the spread of German practice abroad before 1914. The biggest contribution thus made was the high degree superheater. Of all the improvements made since George Stephenson outlined the basic form, the superheater remains the principal. Its great success was due to the fact that it attacked the heat cycle at the point where the losses were greatest, namely in the cylinders, by the elimination of condensation during admission and expansion and re-evaporation at exhaust. Commencing with a form of smokebox heater, Wilhelm Schmidt's genius led him to conceive the supremely simple idea of dividing the incoming steam from the regulator into a number of small tube elements each inserted into a suitably enlarged flue tube in the boiler. For the first time a really large superheating surface became feasible, and one moreover which it was easy to manipulate in the initial design to give any desired characteristics of boiler efficiency and superheat temperature. Not only was the bogey of undue cylinder condensation exorcised but a net gain in steam consumption from 20 to 30 per cent was achieved with low cost and little technical difficulty, and only at the expense of an increase in weight of the order of a ton or so. Thus most of the undoubted economy remained as a net gain, not dependent upon some test results published by back-room boffins, but very actual to firemen, inspectors and depot superintendents out on the line. This arrangement, first installed on an engine in its own country of origin in 1902, spread round the world with a most remarkable rapidity first in trial installations, but almost immediately after in bulk application, and after 1914 few indeed were the new locomotives anywhere, including America, which were not superheated on this system. Nothing is perfect, and long years of development lay ahead in improving the joint between element and header, and in assuring longer life to the return bends. Many, too, were the attempted departures from its main features, but in the latter days of steam most of these had fallen by the wayside, and its last form was remarkably true to its initial conception, the mark of the truly great invention.

Turning now to more exclusive features, one part of Germany's export trade in locomotives, as indeed was the case for all countries similarly engaged, was to produce engines to other peoples' designs, and of these were numerous engines of essentially British design for Holland and Egypt, and to a lesser extent in this period for South Africa. There was even one class of typically British inside cylinder 4–4–0 built by Borsig in 1914 for the British South Eastern and Chatham Railway. German design technique itself was exported mainly in two forms, that based upon Prussian State practice and that stemming from Maffei's productions for Bavaria and Baden. The Prussian engines, designed as already mentioned in collaboration with the important private builders, were essentially simple straightforward machines. Universal use of outside cylinders kept resultant axlebox loading to a minimum and permitted adequate bracing of the plate frames throughout their length. The round top boilers were of straightforward design with direct firebox staying and there was at that time an absence of superfluous gadgetry. The practice of providing wedge adjustment not only for the main axleboxes but at every coupling rod crankpin, permitted maintenance staff at the depots, if adequately trained and supervised, to take up wear as it occurred between shoppings and to keep the engines free of clanking and knocking which in turn only produced more wear. On top of all this the favourable valve events led to crisp performance and very welcome economy. Many of these factors were most acceptable to less sophisticated administrations, and this made the German marque easy to sell abroad. On the other hand, none of these Prussian based designs was any more suited than were the British or French at that time in getting the best out of inferior coals, and in dealing with the ash disposal problems associated therewith. We know also that the single wide Schmidt piston valve rings typical of the period could lead to wasteful running unless frequent replacement was budgeted for.

The Maffei ingredients appealed abroad from quite other points of view. To railways which had already had experience of compounding the Maffei arrangement with only two valve gears serving the four valve was a welcome simplification, and the even turning moment of four cylinders eased axlebox loading. The bar frame gave more lateral strength, particularly on engines required to traverse sinuous routes, and afforded a quite remarkable degree of visibility and accessibility. Unlike the North German types, Maffei engines had every facility for the digestion of poor coal. Some Maffei exports are listed in Table 26A, entries 1 to 6.

It has been stated more than once that Kaiser Wilhelm's 'Drive to the East' and his vision of Germanic influence or even dominion stretching through the Balkans and Turkey-in-Asia towards Mesopotamia and eventually to the shores of India itself, gave a political twist to the assiduity with which the bagmen of the home builders fanned out into these countries on the way, and boosted the sale of standards and components which it would be very handy to encounter when, if ever, a Greater Germany swallowed up these lesser breeds without the law. An examination of what was actually sent abroad in this period somewhat modifies this picture, however, because although exports were massive they were far from being standardised on any basis, and with few exceptions, it was during World War I and afterwards that Reichsbahn designs and details made a really massive infiltration into Eastern Europe, and by 1918 dreams of South Eastern conquest had evaporated at least for the next decade.

While 1914 was the end of an era for German locomotives at home, a short interregnum occurred during the war itself and immediately afterwards, not only until the official formation of the all embracing Reichsbahn in 1920, but for several years beyond until the products of the new administration became sufficient in numbers and variety to meet all needs. Table 22C, entries 8 to 12 list these particular types of which there first fall to be considered the wartime ten-coupled locomotives and their derivatives. Actually it was just before the war when Henschel's were put in charge of design work on a 2–10–0 which would be capable of considerably more power than the G10 class 0–10–0. Retaining the same 4ft 7⅛in (1400mm) diameter wheels, the adoption of three cylinders, an axle weight increased from 14 to 16½ tons (14·3 to 17·0 tonnes) and use of a leading truck allowed an increase in starting effort of 37 per cent and of permitted speed from 37½ to 44mph (60 to 70kph). Thus the G12¹ class was first turned out in 1915. Already, however, a more universal route availability became essential and in 1917 the true wartime version, the G12, became the precursor of 1,200 units built progressively up to 1924. The G12 class had a 15·7 ton (16-tonne) axle load, but by clever design both cylinders and boiler were marginally larger (entry 11 in table 22C), and the reduction in weight was achieved notwithstanding the introduction of a wide Belpaire firebox and bar frames, adopted for the first time together into Prussian practice, although already usual on Saxon and Bavarian engines respectively. The inside valve on all of these engines was driven by a system of cross shafting, deriving its initial motion from the two outside Walschaert gears, and arranged with vertical arms disposed in two to one proportion which was a different way of arriving at the same effect that Gresley (or rather Holcroft) achieved subsequently in England by a system of levers working horizontally. It can be said at this point that this conjugated gear did not prove ultimately satisfactory, the curse of all such motions being that small wear or distortion at individual pins was capable of producing an altogether disproportionate error in events at the inside valve itself. Its use was not therefore continued for any new design after 1918.

In 1918 there appeared a three-cylinder 2–8–0 version classified G8³ (entry 10 in the table), identical in all respects with the G12 except for a shorter boiler. Less than 100 of these were built, however, and in 1919 a lighter two-cylinder version Class G8² was turned out. The reasons for the development of either of these engines are very difficult to plumb. With an axleload one ton heavier than that of the G12, no operating advantage is discernible unless there was considerable territory where only shorter turntables were available. Of this class Wagner, Chief of Motive Power of the Reichsbahn, subsequently wrote, 'The G8² type suffered badly from a mistake in design. The idea was to make it identical with the G12 in as many details as possible, and that one of the coupled wheels should be left out and the boiler, firebox and tubes shortened accordingly. Unfortunately the same diameter of tubes was retained and these were consequently very short for their diameter. This attempt at standardisation proved a failure in so far that the boiler showed a very low efficiency. The superheat was excellent, and the general steam-raising capacity good, but the exit temperatures from the tubes was too high, especially from the flue tubes.' This verdict did not prevent over 1,000 of the two-cylinder engines being built up to 1927.

Both the 2–8–0 and 2–10–0 engines above described, although Prussian designs, were widely distributed on to the regional German administrations during the war and immediately afterwards. A slightly modified version of the G12 went to Turkey and Luxemburg, while quantities of the $G8^2$ went to Rumania and Turkey; numbers of these engines were also distributed as reparations, and the allocation of some of both the G12 and $G12_1$ classes to France specifically for working iron-ore trains in the now restored territory of Lorraine had an unusual aftermath. Notwithstanding the existence already of French designs of 2–10–0s, so much were the newly acquired German engines to the liking of their new masters, the Est Railway, that a large new series of three-cylinder 2–10–0s was built between 1926 and 1932 having almost identical arrangement and dimensions and the same conjugated valve gear (Table 18A, entry 5). The harsh Germanic aspect of the G12s was, however, filtered out in the process, and a gentler typically French appearance was grafted on in its place, its essence lying in the chimney, smokebox, running plate and cab design which was substituted. Plates 65 and 66 show the two engines, and locomotive history has few more dramatic examples of the effect of ingrained national feelings as to what an engine should look like. Other lessons were clearly learned from the strangers by the Est administration. While for express passenger work typically French compounds continued to be provided, for freight and suburban services two- and three-cylinder simple tender and tank engines appeared post 1918 which obviously owed something to the favourable maintenance experience gained, and in some cases the discerning could observe cylinders, main crossheads, valve spindle crossheads and slidebars frankly copied from German origins.

The P10 class of three-cylinder 2–8–2 mixed traffic engine, although designed in this period, was not turned out until the first year of the Reichsbahn, and its building was continued until 1927. Its conception probably owed something to the pioneer Saxon 2–8–2s already referred to, and its boiler and Belpaire firebox were akin to those of the G12s. Unlike the latter type, however, it made use of three separate valve gears for the three cylinders, the link for the inside gear being operated from an additional outside return crank. The P10 proved so useful and successful that it was retained by the Bundesbahn on important passenger and fast freight workings into the 1960s. The remaining new classes of this period were the T28 2–8–2 tank of 1921 and the T20 2–10–2 of 1922. The former was the last standard gauge rack rail engine built for the State railways, and thereafter it was found more economical to work heavily graded branch lines by adhesion using very large ten-coupled tank engines of which the T20 class was the harbinger.

With the war over, Belgium, which had been almost completely denuded of rolling stock, received 1,959 engines from Germany in replacement, 1,820 of them of Prussian design comprising 43 different types. This large stud was prominent on the Belgian railway scene for many years, and numerous were their own engines which greeted the invaders when for the second time they overran the country in 1940. Many of this indestructible brood survived again, and Plate 64 shows a P8 class 4–6–0 at Antwerp in 1956. It was in these immediate post-war years, too, that certain eastern European nations began to accept German design on a large scale. The newly independent state of Poland, much of whose territory had formerly been in eastern Germany, naturally took over large blocks of Prussian types in all categories as did to a lesser extent Czechoslovakia, Yugoslavia, Bulgaria, Greece, Rumania, Lithuania and Latvia.

The most numerous classes naturally spread furthest, P8 4–6–0, G7 and G8 0–8–0, G10 0–10–0 and G12 2–10–0 being most prominent. Whereas this German influx had little influence upon subsequent design in Belgium, the French Nord Railway and Czechoslovakia, all further construction in Poland, mainly by native builders, followed closely German design both in general and in detail, while certain existing classes such as G10 were built new in their entirety. This country indeed gilded the lily by fitting a larger wide firebox boiler to the traditional P8 4–6–0 and a large number was built, mostly in Poland, between 1922 and 1934 (Table 26B, entry 1). Rumania, too, took these engines to its heart but did not, like Poland, play variations upon the main theme. Rather it adopted this class plus the G8 0–8–0 and the G10 0–10–0 as national standards, reproduced exactly to the designs of the Fatherland.

Turkey was in a rather different category in that it had been an ally rather than an enemy. Prussian types were drafted in during the war, including some G12 2–10–0s with smaller wheels and other detail alterations as already mentioned. After the unification of the railways in that country in 1927, G10 0–10–0s and a number of T18 4–6–4 tanks were built for the new administration, together with a big batch of 2–8–0s to the $G8^2$ design.

This vast exodus, both of physical machines and of design experience, had two large after-effects. First of all, it created a motive power vacuum in the newly formed Reichsbahn so that after the years of depression were over a big restocking commenced to a new series of standard designs which sought to combine the best features of previous German practice and to bring them up to date. Secondly it confirmed a number of countries in accepting the German format in its entirety for their future locomotive design.

Both of these aftermaths will now be described.

II. 1920–1960

In April 1920 the Reichsbahn was set up to take over and operate on behalf of the unified State all the separate groups existing within the country. A central engineering management was set up in Berlin which proceeded to evolve standard locomotive types for universal use. R. P. Wagner was in charge, and he and his staff inherited and developed the traditions of the Prussian State Railways. Wagner became something of an international figure as the work of his department took shape and emerged to public view. During visits to the author's country in 1929 and again in 1935 he read papers on aspects of recent German locomotive development which had taken place under his guidance,* and return visits were of course made to Berlin where facilities for studying his designs and making trips in the dynamometer car and on the footplate were freely given. Much of the writing about locomotives in German technical journals and society proceedings has by long custom been very academic and erudite, abounding in formulae and meticulous theory. It was a surprise therefore to find Wagner, a big bear of a man, to be earthy and practical and full of that realistic common sense which particularly appeals to railway engineers everywhere. It is to be hoped that no disservice is done to his memory in recalling that he seemed a very perfunctory adherent of the Nazi party which had in due course so completely infiltrated the affairs of the whole country including railways, and unlike some of his henchmen, his 'Heil Hitler' greeting to colleagues and subordinates, then obligatory, lacked a good deal in precision and zest.

* *Some New Developments of the Stephenson Boiler*, Proc Inst Loco Engrs No 93, 1930; *High Speed and the Steam Locomotive*, Proc Inst Loco Engrs No 124, 1935.

No longer would engines only suitable for the great North German plain now suffice, but the new classes must operate in the mountainous south and west with equal effectiveness. Some 284 separate engine classes were absorbed from the old administrations into the new organisation, one of whose first acts was to renumber the whole lot into a system so flexible in its scope that it sufficed not only to cover absorbed stock, and all that was built for the Reichsbahn up to its demise in 1945, but also to meet the needs of the subsequently divided railways of West and East Germany without alteration to the very end of steam. So monumental a scheme, although a trivial detail in locomotive history, merits a few words in passing.

Its main principle was that a locomotive number should consist of two parts. The first part was the class number to which the figures 01 to 99 were allocated in the manner set out in column 1 of Table 21. The second part consisted of the serial number of the engine in its own allocated class. Standard classes were usually left open ended so that the first engine in a numerous class of freight engines might be 52.001, for example, while a later engine could be 52.5620. An exception was made in the case of certain passenger types such as 01 where a variant having three cylinders commenced at 01.1000, and was known as class 01^{10}. This device was also used to deal with small-sized regional classes taken over, and a perusal of the columns headed 'Reichsbahn Class' in Table 22 will give some idea of the process. Thus pre-grouping Pacifics were allocated class number 18, and within this, Saxon engines were classified 18^0 with running numbers below 100, Wurtemberg engines 18^1 with numbers between 100 and 199 and so on. In a similar manner Regional 4–6–0s class number 38 all came within the first thousand running numbers. The very numerous Prussian P8 class 4–6–0 became class 38 numbered between 1000 and 4000. To run ahead of our story, after 1945 the newly formed Bundesbahn picked out for its new types class numbers not already allocated pre-war, and, although politically at odds, the East German administration while following the same system, kept equally clear of what had gone before as Table 25 illustrates.

The 29 Reichsbahn standard classes are set out in Table 23, and these are the engines best known to travellers of this generation in Germany. Several things command attention. Increased axleloads were now permitted up to 20 tons (20·4 tonnes) for main-line duties; the Pacific and the 2–10–0 hitherto only seen on the regional railways now became universal types. Working pressure of the more important classes rose from 171 to 227lb/sq in (12 to 16kg/cm²). After a brief trial with an alternative four-cylinder compound Pacific in 1925, simple expansion with long travel piston valves was standardised for all classes, using two cylinders wherever possible and only resorting to three for the highest powers. Bar frames, so long exemplified by the practice of the firm of Maffei, were universally adopted, and where a wide firebox was disposed behind coupled wheels, the trailing truck was set far back in the manner initiated by the regional lines to obtain optimum air inlet and ash disposal arrangements. The relatively simple silhouette of pre-1914 classes was replaced by an orderly but very 'busy' array along the boiler-top including a pump-operated feed water heater, the tubular heat exchanger for which was set athwart the smokebox with its two ends protruding and there was a second dome under which the feed water from the heater reached the boiler water level through a cascade of trays. There was also a large capacity sandbox—two of them in the case of ten coupled engines. High running platforms were general and splashers discarded. Smoke deflecting sideplates were fitted reaching down to the platform on all passenger and mixed traffic tender types—it was later that they appeared on large boilered freight engines and some tank types, while the separate 'wing' type of plates only proliferated after 1945. All engines were so laid out that they would pass through a universal loading gauge 13ft 9½in (4205mm) high. The very short chimneys that this demanded for the big engines was mitigated by use of a detachable extension 13½in (345mm) high, so that engines allocated to the principal main lines having a permitted height of 14ft 11in (4550mm) wore their 'hats' more or less permanently.

The springs of trailing carrying wheels, where fitted, were compensated through to the coupled wheel springs, so that the designed adhesion was always available. On some such engines the compensating beams had two fulcrum points, so that by means of a minor operation at the shed, axle weights could be varied by as much as two tons each, according to the permitted loading for the routes the engines was required to traverse.

Electric light was provided on all down to the smallest types, with inspection bulbs, suitably protected, disposed permanently above the driving gear to ease the driver's task in oiling round at night.

A number of interesting individual features ran through the series. Where wide fireboxes were used there was no combustion chamber, used generally all over the world; this feature never found favour in German practice until Bundesbahn days, largely for constructional and maintenance reasons which, before fully softened water was available, could be formidable. Superheater headers had physically separated compartments for saturated and superheated steam to avoid heat loss. Blastpipes were unusually low in the smokebox and the caps and chimney chokes were of relatively large diameter. The American self-cleaning front end did not commend itself, and a simple cylindrical 'basket' joining blastpipe and chimney looked after the sparks. Cylinders always had tail rods, and while wedges were retained in the axlebox hornguides, wedge adjustment was no longer provided in the rod ends. The cabs were large and roomy, and on the driver's side were simply laid out. On the fireman's side, however, things were more complex. Besides the controls for the Knorr feed pump there was a lifting injector tucked along the firebox side inside the cab. In addition, two mechanical lubricators were mounted on the faceplate, one above the other delivering through manually controlled valves to sight feeds at eye level. These were refinements in application of these details common in Europe but not usually seen in England or America. The standard firedoor opened inward and had two air ducts on each side controlled by automic flap valves. These were intended to be responsive to the vacuum above the firebed so that when the process of firing produced a thick fuel bed, extra top air was admitted with the effect of reducing smoke production. In 1937 investigation of this contraption was one of the reasons for another visit of a party of LMS officers of whom the author was one. Official reaction on the spot to this device seemed to be rather lukewarm, and the final commentary was provided by a class 39 2–8–2 on which we rode, where we found both ducts carefully stopped up with sponge cloths!

Apart from the foregoing a great deal of former Prussian State detail design was incorporated into the new series, and in spite of so much which was novel, they perpetuated the substance and appearance of Prussian development in a quite remarkable manner. The principal features of the largest engines were repeated faithfully all down the line, including the small fry at the bottom end, 2–6–0s of class 24, class 64 and 71 passenger tanks and even the shunters. To see diagrams of the whole series laid side by side as appears in the folding plates of Niederstrasser's book is to realise the single-mindedness which informed this standardisation.*

Development of this series was continuous up to 1939 both by adding successive types within the original format, and by the construction of modifications and prototypes intended to advance the frontiers of performance and efficiency. Of the former were the 2–8–2 class 41 of 1936 and the 2–10–2 class 45 of 1937, both with 5ft 3in (1600mm) coupled wheel. The latter in particular was a magnificent machine, the very epitome of

* See Bibliography.

all that was best in German design, and it was clearly intended to be the heavy freight engine of the future with a permitted speed of 56mph (90kph). Its building ceased, however, in 1941 after only 28 units had been constructed and wartime and post-war traffic requirements were sufficiently met by 2–10–0 engines. The last of the standard series was type 23, a 2–6–2 engine intended to replace the ubiquitous type 38 4–6–0 of Prussian origin. The first two were not built until 1941, when production of this particular design ceased. It was a handsome engine in the form of a shortened version of the class 41 2–8–2, but there was a modified aftermath in both Western and Eastern Germany after the war as will presently be seen.

In parallel with this cautious development of a central theme varying only in the matter of size and suitability for different traffic categories, the Reichsbahn also undertook from 1935 onward to exploit the utmost possibilities of the Stephensonian layout and a two-pronged attack was made upon speed and efficiency. The exploits of the pioneer 'Flying Hamburger' diesel railcar set had already rung round the world by averaging more than 80mph (130kph) over the 178 miles (285km) between Berlin and Hamburg, and the fact that the morning and evening business expresses between these centres called for more seating capacity than the diesel set could provide put the steam designers on their mettle. The requirements for these heavier trains were average speed 75mph (approx. 120kph), maximum speed 110mph (175kph) trailing load up to 300 tons (309 tonnes), maximum 1hp, 3,000. To meet these conditions an enlarged version of the 01 class was designed with three cylinders, 7ft 6½in (2300mm) coupled wheels, and 284lb/sq in (20kg/cm²) boiler pressure while the grate area of 51sq ft (4·7m²) was set over a trailing bogie thus producing a 4–6–4 type which was enclosed in a fully streamlined casing. Two such engines class 05 were turned out by Borsig in 1934 and on a special test run, a speed of 124½mph (200kmh) was attained on the level. There was a third such engine built in 1937, but turned back to front with the cab leading, an arrangement made possible by the use of pulverised coal firing. For the same high speeds on secondary services two six-coupled tank engines with 7ft 6½in (2300mm) wheels were also produced, No 61.001, a two-cylinder 4–6–4T in 1935 and No 61.002 a 4–6–6T with three cylinders in 1938. These very specialised engines were of course tailored to particular services, and to raise the running speed of the generality of main line services further modified versions of both 01 and 03 Pacifics were built in 1939 with their permitted speed raised from 81 to 94mph (130 to 150kph). For these engines three cylinders were introduced and full streamlining applied, while valve events and cylinder ports and passages were improved. The resultant 01^{10} and 03^{10} classes were built to the extent of 55 and 60 units respectively until new passenger locomotive construction was closed down by the war in 1940. After the war, the streamlining, which had only been applied to the first few engines in each case, was removed, as also from 05.001 and 05.002. The third engine of this class was rebuilt as a conventional engine with its streamlining also removed to match the other two. Plate 73 shows No 05.002 in its post-war condition.

The other development of the conventional layout was to explore the use of higher working pressure. Two 4–6–2s were built by Krupp generally to the design of the 03, but with 355lb/sq in (25kg/cm²) pressure and as four-cylinder compounds the better to exploit the expansive properties of steam at this pressure. Two companion 2–10–0s of type 44, similarly modified, were built by Henschel. Constant speed tests carried out by Nordmann in 1938 produced a minimum steam consumption of 12·6lb/1hp (5·65kg/cv) which, however, only showed a 6 per cent improvement over that of the simpler 01 engine.

Speed and power were combined in two 4–8–4 engines class 06 which, together with those outlined above, completed this massive step forward towards a higher level of performance with conventional steam.

This new generation of locomotives made a considerable impact upon the world locomotive scene. As already mentioned both Wagner himself, in charge of the centralised locomotive department, and Nordmann who dealt with the testing, published numerous descriptive articles and papers. In particular the work of these two engineers went deeply into the question of boiler and tube proportions. On this subject, for long years opinion had taken the place of exact measurement and there was a wide band of tolerance as to what was considered acceptable practice or indeed acceptable steaming capacity. With the assistance of the Grünewald Testing Station, Wagner was able to arrive at sufficiently exact dimensional relationships to eliminate much of the need for inspired guesswork. It thus became possible to lay down a boiler design on the board with much better assurance that the resistance of the tube bank to the flow of hot gases, the exit temperatures of the hot gases from both large and small tubes, and therefore steaming capacity and overall efficiency would achieve optimum values within what was theoretically possible with the Stephenson boiler.

This doctrine spread widely, whether its origin was acknowledged or not, and its lessons were found to be of universal application until power requirement became so great that they could no longer be matched by proportionate increase in boiler diameter. Thus the series of British Railways' Standard locomotives built after nationalisation in 1948 had their boilers successfully proportioned according to this doctrine. On the other hand, limitations of cross section forced American designers of high-powered steam to depart more and more from the optimum proportions, and the resultant shortfall in boiler efficiency was one of the ultimate limitations to steam traction.

Reference has been made above to the countries surrounding Germany which made a massive acquaintance with the products and practice of that country in the years following 1918. Increasingly as the new Reichsbahn types were set to work at home, other countries built or had built for them variations on the main theme particularly suited to their own traffic conditions. Table 26 sets out a selection of these engines which, differing in greater or lesser measure from the exact Reichbahn prototype, were nevertheless designed to the same rules, and for the most part carried the same details.

Poland, Bulgaria, Yugoslavia and Turkey were the main recipients. In Poland nearly all were built by domestic firms. Improvisations upon basic Reichsbahn design were made in all five classes listed in Table 26B. Only three of the 4–8–2s were built, but the 2–8–2s of almost identical capacity became the principal steam passenger engine, and the 110 units of this class were to be seen on all the principal main lines. They can be considered as an improved and simplified version of the Prussian P10 class 2–8–2, and similarly the Ty23 Polish 2–10–0 was originally largely a two-cylinder version of the German wartime G12, and this was modernised in succeeding versions of roughly the same dimensions until the arrival of the 2–10–0 from the USA referred to in Chapter 3 caused Polish design to abandon the German and follow the American layout and details in the final Ty-51 class. The Prussian P8 4–6–0 design which, as already referred to, had a larger boiler applied to it by the Polish designers is indicated in entry 1. It will be seen that a wide firebox over the coupled wheels was achieved with 43sq ft (4·00m^2) of grate area.

Still wider improvisation was undertaken in Bulgaria, this time largely by German manufacturers, since there was no indigenous locomotive industry. Here a greater degree of standardisation of major components was achieved than in Germany itself, and of the eight classes tabulated it will be seen that no less than six carried the same boiler. The 4–8–2s of which there were twelve were rather smaller machines than the Polish, while both these and the later deliveries of 2–8–2s had three cylinders, an arrangement which the Bulgarian authorities came to prefer for its larger power. The two-cylinder 2–8–2s were similar to but not the same as the German class 41, while the 4–6–2s of class 05 were again offbeat versions of the German 03^{10}, having smaller coupled wheels.*

The really remarkable engines were the 4–10–0s and the 2–12–4 tanks. The 4–10–0s, of which there were 22, were 100 per cent German in appearance and details, and they carried the standard boiler. Limited to a speed of 47mph (75kph) they took their share in heavy mineral haulage, and were the only engines of their wheel arrangement to have been built in the present century. The 2–12–4 tanks were not the only twelve-coupled engines owned by this administration, for a number of 0–12–0 tanks of rather hybrid appearance had been built by Hanomag in 1922. However, the larger machines were of pure Reichsbahn design, even although the first two-cylinder batch was built by the firm of Cegielski in Poland in 1931. To get such a crocodile round prevailing curves the leading truck wheels had 5⅜in (135mm) side play each way, and the leading coupled wheels 1⅜in (35mm), the two axles being coupled in a Krauss truck. The third and fourth coupled wheels were flangeless, the sixth axle had 1in (25mm) side play each way, and the trailing bogie 4⅞in (125mm). Following prevailing German practice, piston valves were 12¾in (325mm) diameter with 1½in (40mm) steam lap, ¼in (6mm) lead, and ⅛in (3mm) exhaust clearance. A three-cylinder version came out in 1943, this time built by a German firm, rather surprisingly right in the middle of the war. There were 20 in all of these unusual engines, 12 two-cylinder and 8 three-cylinder, and to see them at work over 1 in 40 grades on coal trains in the neighbourhood of Sofia was one of the sights of the steam era.

Yugoslavia, more than most of its neighbours, had to make do with a hotch-potch of inherited and derived engines from various sources, including Austrian, Hungarian and even British, if the *Liberation* class of 2–8–0s can be so called. The modern German contribution took the form of 110 engines of the three classes shown in the table, all supplied in 1930, to signalise completion of upgrading on certain main lines where 19½-ton (19·9-tonne) axleload could now be supported in place of the previous 14 ton. They do not call for particular comment, except to note that a single boiler served them all, and to wonder what was in the mind of the local engineers who demanded a 26in (660mm) stroke for engines almost identical to those being supplied to Bulgaria where 27½in (700mm) stroke was preferred.

As has been indicated above, Turkey received considerable numbers of identical German types after World War I, but by 1926 it also was improvising on the main theme by the ordering of a 4–8–0 version of the Prussian P8 class. The same boiler with narrow firebox made do for a 2–10–2 engine (entry 10) with a 13¼-ton (13·5-tonne) axleload suitable for use on lightly laid lines. The centrepiece of modern Turkish steam traction lay in the 2–8–2 and 2–10–0 classes of 1937. The former was much akin to the Polish Pt31 class, and had no exact counterpart in Germany itself. Like the Polish version it was a magnificent engine, and while there were only eleven in the class, they were seen by many travellers on principal passenger duties well into the 'sixties. The 2–10–0s were particularly suitable for working mixed traffic over the mountainous routes of Asia Minor. Akin to the Reichsbahn class 43, of which only 35 were built before developing into the three-cylinder class 44, these Turkish two-cylinder engines ran to 166 units to which most German builders contributed, together with Skôda of Czechoslovakia, and the British Vulcan and Beyer Peacock firms who together built 37 in 1948.

For Germany's needs in World War II there was ready to hand one of the 'regular' Reichsbahn standards, a 'light' two-cylinder 2–10–0 of class 50 having a 14·8-ton (15·1-tonne) axleload, designed in 1938. Subject to detail modifications such as eliminating as

* Alone of steam locomotives outside Russia, these two classes were fitted with stanchioned double railings along the outside footplating.

far as possible non-ferrous and special materials, this was built as an interim type until a true 'War Locomotive' was designed suitable for mass production by the principal builders at home and in the occupied territories with the help of sub-assemblies and details from outside industry. With dimensions as shown in entry 2 in Table 23B more than 6,000 locomotives of this class 52 were built from 1942 in most of the countries which came under German control. Austerity features to reduce man-hours in building and use of scarce materials included welded steel firebox with side-stays welded at both ends, fabricated coupling, connecting, and valve gear rods in which drop stamped ends were butt-welded to a rolled section centre portion, elimination of top feed dome, feed water heater and smoke deflector plates, and low tin-bearing materials. To avoid production difficulties in connection with such large numbers, many engines were built with plate instead of bar frames. A very simple design of bogie tender was also introduced in which a semicircular water tank was strong enough to eliminate the need for the conventional underframe. A heavier class 42 on the same general lines but with a 16·8-ton (17·1-tonne) axleload was initiated in 1943, and about 800 were built, in addition to continuance with the already established class 44 three-cylinder 2–10–0. A major wartime service of this vast array was to assist the German conquest of Russia, and when the tide of war receded, many of the class 52 in particular were left behind in sufficiently serviceable condition for the Russians to convert them to the 5ft 0in (1524mm) gauge by setting out cylinders and frames and providing longer axles. In the aftermath of the war, it was these 2–10–0s more than other German types which were principally acquired by the standard gauge northern and eastern European countries which had been overrun, and Plates 70, 71 and 72 show them at work in Austria, East Germany and Russia.

The sorting out of locomotives which either were or could be made serviceable at the war's end is a saga which it is to be hoped somebody will chronicle some day in its entirety. Enthusiastic lay investigators have pieced together various aspects but it was not until 1950 in Western Germany and 1954 in East Germany that further new steam design began to appear again for domestic use, and Tables 24 and 25 indicate the relatively few such products which appeared on the Bundesbahn and the truncated Reichsbahn before new steam building ceased altogether.

As travellers will know well, the post-war Bundesbahn relied upon 01, 01^{10}, 03 and 03^{10} engines for its principal passenger duties, and there was actually a surplus of 2–10–0s of all kinds for freight duties, so that large numbers of the 'Krieglokomotivs', especially those with the plate frames which had proved less satisfactory, could be dispensed with. First needs from the slowly recovering industry was therefore for medium-sized engines for mixed traffic and special duties. Thus the first off the mark was the class 23 2–6–2 (entry 2 in Table 24), out in 1950. The original two class 23 engines built in 1941 had been retained by East Germany, and the revised version now brought out contained some radical departures from pre-war appearance. The top feed dome disappeared, sandboxes departed from the top of the boiler, wing type smoke deflectors were used while a lipped chimney without detachable upper extension was large enough in diameter to encompass not only the central exhaust from the cylinders, but in the outer annulus that from air pump and feed water pump as well. Lessons from wartime production and maintenance favoured steel firebox and welded stays with a welded mainframe which was a cross between bar frame proper and the plate frame of former times. The 2–8–4 tank class 65 (1951) and the light 2–6–4 tank (1955) class 66 included similar features, as did a 0–10–0 shunting tank of 1950, but only 18, 2, and 41 of these engines were built in addition to 105 of class 23, the last appearing in 1959. These engines had no progeny either at home or abroad. Whether their performance and maintenance characteristics were better than those of the earlier types they replaced we shall probably never know.

English people entering Germany from Holland through Venlo were well acquainted with the Class 23 which worked the 'Rheingold' and other trains on to Cologne for a number of years, but speeds were leisurely and the fore and aft shuttling motion which could be felt in the train was reminiscent of that produced by the British Railways' Standard Pacifics before their drawbar springs were given non-resonant characteristics.

The final expression of the long line of German locomotive development was exemplified by the two three-cylinder Pacifics of class 10 built by Krupp in 1957. A more conservative approach was observable than in the pre-war 04, 05 and 06 developments, and moderation was expressed in a wheel diameter of 6ft 6¾in (2000mm) and a working pressure of 256lb/sq in (18kg/cm²). The leading features of class 23 were applied, but roller bearings were fitted to all axleboxes and crankpins and some interesting details appeared such as American chime whistle, rotating 'clear view' screen in the driver's front cab window, luminous indicators in the cab adjacent to the reversing wheel for steam pressure and temperature and cut-off, and a semi-streamlined fairing over cylinder fronts and running plate. Oil firing removed some of the limitations of hand-fired coal, and for the first time more firebox volume became desirable in relation to the intended maximum steam production of 40,000lb/hr (18200kg/hr), so that a combustion chamber was provided. A 21½-ton (22-tonne) axleload, permissible for the first time in Germany, gave a factor of adhesion of 3·9.

From 1951 onwards new boilers with combustion chambers were designed for classes 01 and 03 and their three-cylinder variants, and also for class 41. As these replacement boilers were fitted considerable changes were made to bring the engines as a whole into line with post-war thinking. Sandboxes were taken off the boiler-top and were relocated at running plate level. Large diameter chimneys and wing-type smokeplates were applied and a number of engines in the three-cylinder groups were converted to roller bearings and to oil firing.

On the East German Reichsbahn, a great deal of locomotive building capacity was removed bodily to Russia, and new steam building was concentrated into the narrow period 1954 to 1960. No very striking developments emerged, and the Iron Curtain did not prevent Bundesbahn features being adopted such as welded I-section plate frames, combustion chambers, and wing type smoke deflectors. The selection of new types to be built was a rather peculiar one, and as Table 25 shows the most numerous were 113 2–6–2s of class 23^{10}, and 92 2–10–0s of class 50^{40}. The former, unlike their Bundesbahn counterparts, were a straight continuation of the original pre-war class 23 of 1941 build, the main difference being the fitting of the pyramidal-shaped feed water heater ahead of the chimney which was standardised on the Reichsbahn. The 2–10–0 was also a version of the pre-war 50 class, and carried a boiler interchangeable with the 2–6–2. Two classes of 2–8–4 tank classes 65^{10} and 83^{10} appeared for main line suburban and for branch line working respectively and there were also two individual 2–8–0 engines of class 25 with 5ft 3in (1600mm) diameter wheels, one arranged for pulverised fuel firing. As in the case of the Bundesbahn there was a fairly widespread reboilering and rebuilding of former G12 50, 52, 39, 01 and 03 classes, these engines becoming new classes 58, 50^{35}, 52^{80}, 22, 01^{5} and 03. It will be noted how carefully the Reichsbahn authorities threaded their way through the former German and latter-day Bundesbahn numbering so as to avoid duplication. Whatever political and human problems might attend the ultimate combination of the two States, confusion in locomotive numbering would not be amongst them.

These short-lived efforts with new locomotive design on both sides of the Curtain were too small in scope to make much impression upon the general level of locomotive practice and performance in their respective halves of the country, which continued to the end of steam to be based upon the main stream of development on the pre-war Reichsbahn. By the same token, they had no discernible influence upon locomotives overseas.

Finally, a word on performance and efficiency. Except for the few experimental types of the later 1930s German design did not step outside the middle of the road in any of the features which bear upon power output, running speeds and economy. The variety of classes was such that ample power was available for the different categories of traffic, and double heading was little resorted to. While admirably simple in their main features, these engines could be rather complex in the design of their details, and anyone who has had the opportunity to study the drawings of a plain bearing axlebox, an inside connecting rod, or even a humble oil box must have marvelled at the wealth of meticulous dimensional detail; such assemblies in turn could only be satisfactorily fitted up and ultimately repaired by a well-trained and highly skilled working staff, and this is perhaps the only real criticism which can be levelled at these engines on a world basis, in that not all countries to which engines of this kind were sent were able to keep to the high standards which the design demanded for its greatest effectiveness. On the Bundesbahn the type 01^{10} in its final form and the newer type 10 with T1A water treatment and oil firing were capable of being rostered up to 150,000 miles (240000km) per annum, and in their last days were worked very hard with train loads up to 590 tons (600 tonnes) on the often severely graded routes of the North to South trunk lines. Economic conditions and the state of the track prevented anything notable in the way of running from emerging from Eastern Germany. As will be seen in Chapter 9 the efficiency of representative German types was up to the best standards of simple expansion in other countries.

Table 21

GERMAN RAILWAYS. STANDARD GAUGE CLASSIFICATION NUMBERS 1920 ONWARDS

Category	*Overall Class Number Allocation*	*Class Numbers for Regional Types taken over by Reichsbahn 1920*	*Reichsbahn Standard Types 1920–1945*	*Post 1945*	
				Bundesbahn	*Reichsbahn*
Express passenger	01-19	12-19	01-06	10	—
Passenger	20-39	33-38	39.23.24	23	23^{10} 25
Freight	40-59	51-59	41-45 50-52	—	50^{40}
Passenger tank	60-79	69-79	61-64 71	65.66. 78^{10}	65^{10}
Freight tank	80-96	88-96	80-81 84-87 89	82	83^{10}
Rack rail	97	97	—	—	—
Secondary lines	98	98	—	—	—

GERMANY. REPRESENTATIVE PRE-REICHSBAHN LOCOMOTIVES 1900–1922

Table 22A

Entry	Classification: Original	Classification: Reichsbahn	Date	Wheel Arrangement	Railway	Cylinders Diameter × Stroke inches / mm	Coupled Wheels Diameter feet / mm	Working Pressure lb/sq in / kg/cm²	Grate Area sq ft / m²	Weight Engine Working Order: Axle tons / tonnes	Adhesive tons / tonnes	Total tons / tonnes
1	P3^{5}	38^{0}	1904/21	4–6–0	Bavarian	(4) $13\frac{3}{8}:22\frac{1}{2}\times25\frac{1}{4}$ 340 : 570 × 640	5′ $4\frac{1}{2}$″ 1640	213 15·0	28·2 2·62	14·0 14·3	42·1 43·0	63·7 65·0
2	S3^{6}	18$^{4-5}$	1908/30	4–6–2	,,	(4) $16\frac{3}{4}\times24:25\frac{1}{2}\times26\frac{3}{8}$ 425 × 610 : 650 × 670	5′ $11\frac{5}{8}$″ 1870	227 16·0	48·4 4·50	17·2 17·5	51·7 52·7	92·1 94·0
3	G5^{5}	57^{5}	1911/24	0–10–0	,,	(4) $16\frac{3}{4}\times24:25\frac{1}{2}\times25\frac{1}{4}$ 425 × 610 : 650 × 640	4′ 2″ 1270	227 16·0	39·8 3·70	15·4 15·7	76·9 78·5	76·9 78·5
4	G4^{5}	56$^{8-11}$	1916/19	2–8–0	,,	(4) $15\frac{3}{4}\times24:24\frac{1}{2}\times25\frac{1}{4}$ 400 × 610 : 620 × 640	4′ $3\frac{1}{8}$″ 1300	227 16·0	35·5 3·30	15·4 15·7	61·8 63·0	74·4 75·9
5	G3^{4}	54$^{15-17}$	1919/23	2–6–0	,,	$20\frac{1}{2}\times24\frac{7}{8}$ 520 × 630	4′ $5\frac{1}{8}$″ 1350	185 13·0	28·6 2·66	15·7 16·0	47·0 48·0	59·3 60·5
6	XI	57$^{1-2}$	1905/18	0–10–0	Saxon	(2) $23\frac{1}{4}:33\frac{7}{8}\times24\frac{7}{8}$ 590 : 860 × 630	4′ $0\frac{7}{8}$″ 1240	185 13·0	35·4 3·29	13·8 14·1	69·1 70·5	69·1 70·5
7	X	14^{3}	1909/13	4–4–2	,,	$20\times24\frac{7}{8}$ 510 × 630	6′ 5″ 1980	171 12·0	30·6 2·84	15·1 15·4	30·3 30·9	68·7 70·1
8	XII	17^{8}	1910/27	4–6–0	,,	$21\frac{5}{8}\times23\frac{5}{8}$ 550 × 600	5′ $2\frac{5}{8}$″ 1590	185 13·0	30·6 2·84	15·4 15·7	46·2 47·1	71·8 73·3
9	XVIII	18^{0}	1917	4–6–2	,,	(3) $19\frac{5}{8}\times24\frac{7}{8}$ 500 × 630	6′ 3″ 1905	199 14·0	48·4 4·50	16·6 16·9	49·7 50·7	91·7 93·5
10	XX	19^{0}	1918/23	2–8–2	,,	(4) $18\frac{7}{8}:28\frac{3}{8}\times24\frac{7}{8}$ 480 : 720 × 630	6′ 3″ 1905	213 15·0	48·4 4·50	16·8 17·1	67·2 68·6	97·9 99·9
11	IId	14^{4}	1902/05	4–4–2	Baden	(4) $13\frac{1}{8}:22\frac{1}{2}\times24\frac{1}{2}$ 335 : 570 × 620	6′ $10\frac{5}{8}$″ 2100	199 14·0	41·7 3·87	15·8 16·1	31·7 32·3	74·0 75·7
12	IVf	18^{2}	1907/13	4–6–2	,	(4) $16\frac{3}{4}\times24:25\frac{1}{2}\times26\frac{3}{8}$ 425 × 610 : 650 × 670	5′ $10\frac{7}{8}$″ 1800	227 16·0	48·4 4·50	16·2 16·5	48·6 49·6	85·6 88·3
13	VIg	—	1912	2–6–2	,,	(4) $14\frac{1}{8}:23\frac{1}{4}\times25\frac{1}{4}$ 360 : 590 × 640	5′ 7″ 1700	227 16·0	40·3 3·75	15·2 15·5	45·7 46·6	70·6 72·0
14	VIc	75^{4}	1914/21	2–6–2T	,,	$21\frac{1}{4}\times25\frac{1}{4}$ 540 × 640	5′ 3″ 1600	171 12·0	22·4 2·06	16·3 16·6	48·7 49·7	72·3 73·8
15	IVh	18^{3}	1918/20	4–6–2	,,	(4) $17\frac{3}{8}:26\frac{3}{4}\times26\frac{3}{4}$ [illegible]	6′ $10\frac{5}{8}$″ [illegible]	213 [illegible]	53·8	17·4	52·2	95·0

Entry	Classification: Original	Classification: Reichsbahn	Date	Wheel Arrangement	Railway		Cylinders Diameter × Stroke (inches / mm)	Coupled Wheels Diameter (feet / mm)	Working Pressure (lb/sq in / kg/cm²)	Grate Area (sq ft / m²)	Weight Engine Working Order: Axle (tons / tonnes)	Adhesive (tons / tonnes)	Total (tons / tonnes)
1	C	18^{1}	1909/21	4–6–2	Württemberg	(4)	$16\frac{1}{2}:24\frac{1}{2}\times24$ $420:620\times610$	5′ $10\frac{7}{8}$″ 1800	213 15·0	42·5 4·57	15·7 16·0	47·1 47·8	85·6 87·0
2	Hh	57^{3-4}	1909/20	0–10–0	,,		$24\frac{1}{2}\times24$ 620×612	4′ $1\frac{1}{4}$″ 1250	185 13·0	27·7 2·58	14·4 14·7	72·3 73·8	72·3 73·8
3	T5	75^{0}	1910/20	2–6–2T	,,		$19\frac{5}{8}\times24$ 500×612	5′ 3″ 1600	171 12·0	20·8 1·93	15·5 15·8	46·6 47·5	73·1 74·6
4	K	59^{0}	1917/24	2–12–0	,,	(4)	$20:30\times25\frac{1}{2}$ $510:760\times650$	4′ $5\frac{1}{8}$″ 1350	213 15·0	45·2 4·20	14·9 15·2	88·5 91·3	101·5 103·6
5	S10	16^{0}	1917	2–6–2	Oldenberg		$22\frac{7}{8}\times24\frac{7}{8}$ 580×630	6′ 5″ 1980	199 14·0	32·3 3·00	14·8 15·1	44·5 45·4	72·4 73·9
6	S4	13^{6}	1904	4–4–0	Prussian		$21\frac{1}{4}\times23\frac{5}{8}$ 540×600	6′ 5″ 1980	171 12·0	24·4 2·27	15·7 16·0	31·4 32·0	54·1 55·2
7	S6	13^{10-14}	1906/14	4–4–0	,,		$21\frac{5}{8}\times24\frac{7}{8}$ 550×630	6′ $10\frac{5}{8}$″ 2100	171 12·0	24·6 2·29	17·0 17·3	34·0 34·7	59·5 60·7
8	S9	14^{0}	1907/10	4–4–2	,,	(4)	$15:22\frac{7}{8}\times23\frac{5}{8}$ $380:580\times600$	6′ 5″ 1980	199 14·0	43·0 4·00	16·2 16·5	32·3 33·0	73·0 74·5
9	P6	37^{0-1}	1902/10	2–6 0	,,		$21\frac{1}{4}\times24\frac{7}{8}$ 540×630	5′ 3″ 1600	171 12·0	24·5 2·25	14·4 14·7	43·7 44·6	55·9 57·1
10	P8	38^{10-40}	1906/24	4–6–0	,,		$22\frac{5}{8}\times24\frac{7}{8}$ 575×630	5′ $8\frac{7}{8}$″ 1750	171 12·0	28·4 2·64	16·9 17·2	50·6 51·6	76·6 78·2
11	S10	17^{0-1}	1910/14	4–6–0	,,	(4)	$17\times24\frac{7}{8}$ 430×630	6′ 5″ 1980	199 14·0	30·8 2·86	16·6 16·9	49·9 50·9	75·6 77·2
12	$S10^{1}$	17^{10-12}	1911/16	4–6–0	,,	(4)	$15\frac{3}{4}:24\times26$ $400:610\times660$	6′ 5″ 1980	213 15·0	34·2 3·18	17·4 17·7	52·2 53·2	81·4 83·1
13	$S10^{2}$	17^{2}	1914/16	4–6–0	,,	(3)	$19\frac{5}{8}\times24\frac{7}{8}$ 500×630	6′ 5″ 1980	199 14·0	30·8 2·86	16·8 17·1	50·3 51·3	79·4 81·0
14	G8	55^{16-22}	1902/13	0–8–0	,,		$23\frac{5}{8}\times26$ 600×660	4′ $5\frac{1}{8}$″ 1350	171 12·0	25·7 2·39	13·9 14·2	56·1 57·2	56·1 57·2
15	$G8^{1}$	55^{25-56}	1913/21	0–8–0	,,		$23\frac{5}{8}\times26$ 600×660	4′ $5\frac{1}{8}$″ 1350	171 12·0	28·2 2·62	16·7 17·0	66·2 67·6	66·2 67·6

GERMANY. REPRESENTATIVE PRE-REICHSBAHN LOCOMOTIVES 1900–1922 (CONT.) Table 22C

Entry	Classification Original	Classification Reichs-bahn	Date	Wheel Arrange-ment	Railway	*Cylinders Diameter × Stroke* inches mm	*Coupled Wheels Diameter* feet mm	*Working Pressure* lb/sq in kg/cm²	*Grate Area* sq ft m²	*Weight Engine Working Order* Axle tons tonnes	Adhesive tons tonnes	Total tons tonnes
1	G10	57^{10-40}	1910/24	0–10–0	Prussian	$24\frac{7}{8} \times 26$ 630×660	4′ $7\frac{1}{8}$″ 1400	171 12·0	28·3 2·63	14·0 14·3	70·1 71·5	70·1 71·5
2	T8	89^{0}	1906/09	0–6–0T	,,	$19\frac{5}{8} \times 23\frac{5}{8}$ 500×600	4′ $5\frac{1}{8}$″ 1350	171 12·0	15·9 1·48	14·9 15·2	44·6 45·5	44·6 45·5
3	T12	74^{4-13}	1902/21	2–6–0T	,,	$21\frac{1}{4} \times 24\frac{7}{8}$ 540×630	4′ 11″ 1500	171 12·0	18·6 1·73	16·4 16·7	50·0 51·0	65·0 66·3
4	T13	92^{5-10}	1910/22	0–8–0T	,,	$19\frac{5}{8} \times 23\frac{5}{8}$ 500×600	4′ $1\frac{1}{4}$″ 1250	171 12·0	18·6 1·73	14·9 15·2	59·6 60·8	59·6 60·8
5	T14	73^{0-12}	1914/24	2–8–2T	,,	$23\frac{5}{8} \times 26$ 600×660	4′ $5\frac{1}{8}$″ 1350	171 12·0	27·6 2·56	17·1 17·5	68·6 70·0	102·0 104·0
6	T16	74^{5-18}	1913/23	0–10–0T	,,	24×26 610×660	4′ $5\frac{1}{8}$″ 1350	171 12·0	24·7 2·30	15·9 16·2	79·2 80·8	79·2 80·8
7	T18	78^{0-10}	1912/27	4–6–4T	,,	$22 \times 24\frac{7}{8}$ 560×630	5′ 5″ 1650	171 12·0	26·0 2·42	15·2 15·5	45·5 46·4	103·0 105·0
8	P10	39^{0-2}	1922/27	2–8–2	,,	(3) $20\frac{1}{2} \times 26$ 520×660	5′ $8\frac{7}{8}$″ 1750	199 14·0	43·0 4·00	18·6 19·0	74·4 76·0	107·8 110·4
9	$G8^{2}$	56^{20-30}	1919/27	2–8–0	,,	$24\frac{7}{8} \times 26$ 630×660	4′ $7\frac{1}{8}$″ 1400	199 14·0	36·8 3·43	17·1 17·5	68·6 70·0	81·8 83·5
10	$G8^{3}$	56^{1}	1918/20	2–8–0	,,	(3) $20\frac{1}{2} \times 26$ 520×660	4′ $7\frac{1}{8}$″ 1400	199 14·0	36·8 3·43	16·6 17·0	66·6 68·0	80·8 82·5
11	G12	58^{10-22}	1917/24	2–10–0	,,	(3) $22\frac{1}{2} \times 26$ 570×660	4′ $7\frac{1}{8}$″ 1400	199 14·0	42·0 3·90	15·7 16·0	78·4 80·0	91·2 93·1
12	$G12^{1}$	58^{0}	1915/17	2–10–0	,,	(3) 22×26 560×600	4′ $7\frac{1}{8}$″ 1400	199 14·0	35·0 3·25	16·6 17·0	83·2 84·9	96·8 98·8

amples of postwar tribution of German orld War II *Kreig-omotiven* of which arly 6,300 were built tween 1942 and 49

Austrian No 52- 57 at Vienna (West) 58. Note effect upon pearance of Giesl stpipe and chimney

[*E. S. Cox*

Russian No T3- 93 on track laying n near Leningrad, 58. Note chimney ension and boxed- cylinders of air pump winter protection

[*E. S. Cox*

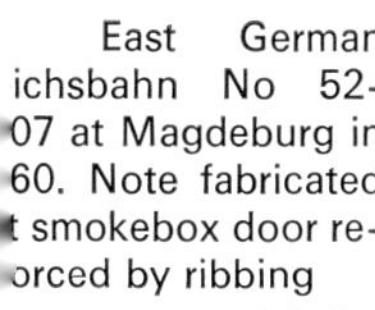

East German ichsbahn No 52- 07 at Magdeburg in 60. Note fabricated t smokebox door re- orced by ribbing

[*E. S. Cox*

73 No 05 002, one of three high speed 3-cylinder simple 4–6–4 engines built in 1934 for the Reichsbahn in fully streamlined form. This view shows the engine as restored to its normal appearance after World War II

[*Archiv Bellingrodt*

74 Last German express passenger design of which only two were built in 1957. Bundesbahn 3-cylinder simple 4–6–2 No 10 002. Note semi-streamlining, American chime whistle and fully enclosed cab [*Archiv Bellingrodt*

75 A 3-cylinder light Pacific Class was built between 1937 and 1940 and rebuilt postwar with an all-welded boiler and other alterations. Here is No 03 1051 at Frankfurt in 1957

[*E. S. Cox*

76 Born too late! No 66 002, a 2–6–4T of Class 66 of which only two were built for Bundesbahn in 1955/56

[*Archiv Bellingrodt*

77 Typical of numerous German exports to South Eastern Europe in the 1926–51 period. Two cylinder simple 2–8–2 passenger locomotive No 46056, built by Henschel in 1927 for Turkish State Railways. Photographed at Ankara in 1958

[*P. Ransome Wallis*

Entry	Class	Date	Wheel Arrange-ment	Total Number Built	Maximum Permitted Speed mph km/hr	Cylinders Diameter × Stroke inches mm	Coupled Wheels Diameter feet mm	Working Pressure lb/sq in kg/cm²	Grate Area sq ft m²	Weight Engine Working Order: Axle tons tonnes	Adhesive tons tonnes	Total tons tonnes
1	01	1925/38	4–6–2	231	81 130	$25\frac{5}{8}\times 26$ 650 × 660	6′ $6\frac{3}{4}$″ 2000	227 16·0	48·4 4·50	19·6 20·0	58·5 59·7	107·6 109·8
2	01[10]	1939/40	4–6–2	55	94 150	(3) $19\frac{5}{8}\times 26$ 500 × 660	6′ $6\frac{3}{4}$″ 2000	227 16·0	46·5 4·32	20·0 20·4	60·0 61·2	111·6 113·8
	02	1925/26	4–6–2	10*	81 130	(4) $18\frac{1}{8}:28\frac{3}{8}\times 26$ 460 : 720 × 660	6′ $6\frac{3}{4}$″ 2000	227 16·0	48·4 4·50	19·6 20·0	58·8 60·0	110·9 113·1
4	03	1930/37	4–6–2	298	81 130	$22\frac{1}{2}\times 26$ 570 × 660	6′ $6\frac{3}{4}$″ 2000	227 16·0	43·6 4·05	17·2 17·5	51·5 52·6	96·8 98·8
5	03[10]	1937/40	4–6–2	60	94 150	(3) $18\frac{1}{2}\times 26$ 470 × 660	6′ $6\frac{3}{4}$″ 2000	227 16·0	42·0 3·90	18·0 18·4	54·1 55·2	101·1 103·2
6	04	1932	4–6–2	2	94 150	(4) $13\frac{3}{4}:20\frac{1}{2}\times 26$ 350 : 520 × 660	6′ $6\frac{3}{4}$″ 2000	355 25·0	44·1 4·10	17·9 18·3	54·9 55·0	102·0 104·0
7	05	1934/37	4–6–4	3	110 175	(3) $17\frac{3}{4}\times 26$ 450 × 660	7′ $6\frac{1}{2}$″ 2300	284 20·0	50·6 4·70	18·8 9·2	56·4 57·6	126·5 129·9
8	06	1938/39	4–8–4	2	87 140	(3) $20\frac{1}{2}\times 28\frac{3}{8}$ 520 × 720	6′ $6\frac{3}{4}$″ 2000	284 20·0	54·2 5·04	19·6 20·0	78·4 80·0	139·0 141·8
9	23	1941	2–6–2	2	69 110	$21\frac{5}{8}\times 26$ 550 × 660	5′ $8\frac{7}{8}$″ 1750	227 16·0	42·0 3·90	17·5 17·9	52·8 53·9	86·6 88·3
10	24	1927/39	2–6–0	95	56 90	$19\frac{5}{8}\times 26$ 500 × 660	4′ 11″ 1500	199 14·0	22·0 2·04	14·8 15·1	44·3 45·2	56·2 57·4
11	41	1936/41	2–8–2	366	56 90	$20\frac{1}{2}\times 28\frac{3}{8}$ 520 × 720	5′ 3″ 1600	284 20·0	44·0 4·09	17·6 18·0	70·6 72·0	100·0 102·0
12	42	1943/51	2–10–0	864	44 70	$24\frac{7}{8}\times 26$ 630 × 660	4′ $7\frac{1}{8}$″ 1400	227 16·0	50·6 4·70	16·8 17·1	84·0 85·7	95·0 96·9
13	43	1927/28	2–10–0	35	44 70	$28\frac{3}{8}\times 26$ 720 × 660	4′ $7\frac{1}{8}$″ 1400	199 14·0	50·6 4·70	19·6 20·0	98·0 100·0	108·7 110·8
14	44	1926/44	2–10–0	1,755	50 80	(3) $21\frac{5}{8}\times 26$ 550 × 660	4′ $7\frac{1}{8}$″ 1400	227 16·0	49·0 4·55	19·6 20·0	98·0 100·0	111·8 114·1
15	45	1937/40	2–10–2	28	56 90	(3) $20\frac{1}{2}\times 28\frac{3}{8}$ 520 × 720	5′ 3″ 1600	284 20·0	51·6 4·80	19·6 20·0	98·0 100·0	125·5 128·0

* Later converted to 01 class

GERMANY. REICHSBAHN STANDARD LOCOMOTIVES 1925–1945

Table 23B

Entry	Class	Date	Wheel Arrangement	Total Number Built	Maximum Permitted Speed mph km/hr	Cylinders Diameter × Stroke inches mm	Coupled Wheels Diameter feet mm	Working Pressure lb/sq in kg/cm²	Grate Area sq ft m²	Weight Engine Working Order: Axle tons tonnes	Adhesive tons tonnes	Total tons tonnes
1	50	1938/44	2–10–0	3,146	50 80	23⅝ × 26 600 × 660	4′ 7⅛″ 1400	227 16·0	42·0 3·90	14·8 15·1	73·8 75·3	85·1 86·8
2	52	1942/49	2–10–0	6,292	50 80	23⅝ × 26 600 × 660	4′ 7⅛″ 1400	227 16·0	42·0 3·90	15·0 15·3	74·8 76·3	83·6 85·3
3	61^{001}	1935	4–6–4T	1	110 175	18⅛ × 29½ 460 × 750	7′ 6½″ 2300	284 20·0	29·6 2·75	18·1 18·5	54·5 55·6	125·7 128·3
4	61^{002}	1938	4–6–6T	1	110 175	(3) 15⅜ × 26 390 × 660	7′ 6½″ 2300	284 20·0	31·1 2·89	18·1 18·5	54·4 55·5	140·5 143·3
5	62	1928/29	4–6–4T	15	62 100	23⅝ × 26 600 × 660	5′ 8⅞″ 1750	199 14·0	37·6 3·50	19·7 20·3	59·6 60·8	121·0 123·6
6	64	1928/40	2–6–2T	520	56 90	19⅝ × 26 500 × 660	4′ 11″ 1500	199 14·0	21·9 2·04	14·9 15·2	44·6 45·5	73·4 74·9
7	71	1934/36	2–4–2T	6	56 90	12¼ × 26 310 × 660	4′ 11″ 1500	284 20·0	14·5 1·35	14·7 15·0	29·4 30·0	57·8 39·0
8	80	1928	0–6–0T	39	28 45	17¾ × 19⅝ 450 × 500	3′ 7⅜″ 1100	199 14·0	16·1 1·50	17·7 18·1	53·3 54·4	53·3 54·4
9	81	1928	0–8–0T	10	28 45	19⅝ × 21⅝ 500 × 550	3′ 7⅜″ 1100	199 14·0	19·2 1·78	16·6 16·9	66·2 67·5	66·2 67·5
10	84	1934/37	2–10–2T	12	50 80	(3) 18⅞ × 26 480 × 660	4′ 7⅛″ 1400	284 20·0	40·5 3·76	17·8 18·2	89·0 90·8	122·5 124·9
11	85	1932	2–10–2T	10	50 80	(3) 23⅝ × 26 600 × 660	4′ 7⅛″ 1400	199 14·0	37·6 3·50	19·6 20·0	98·0 100·0	131·0 133·8
12	86	1928/43	2–8–2T	675	50 80	22½ × 26 570 × 660	4′ 7⅛″ 1400	199 14·0	25·2 2·34	14·7 15·0	58·8 60·0	86·7 88·5
13	87	1927/28	0–10–0T	16	28 45	23⅝ × 21⅝ 600 × 550	3′ 7⅜″ 1100	199 14·0	25·2 2·34	16·8 17·1	83·9 85·6	83·9 85·6
14	89	1934/38	0–6–0T	10	28 45	16½ × 21⅝ 420 × 550	3′ 7⅜″ 1100	284 20·0	15·3 1·42	14·7 15·0	44·1 45·0	44·1 45·0

Entry	Class	Date	Wheel Arrange-ment	Total Number Built	Maximum Permitted Speed mph km/hr	Cylinders Diameter × Stroke inches mm	Coupled Wheels Diameter feet mm	Working Pressure lb/sq in kg/cm²	Grate Area sq ft m²	Weight Engine Working Order: Axle tons tonnes	Adhesive tons tonnes	Total tons tonnes
1	10	1957	4–6–2	2	87 140	(3) $18\frac{7}{8} \times 28\frac{3}{8}$ 480 × 720	6′ $6\frac{3}{4}$″ 2000	256 18·0	42·6 3·96	21·6 22·0	64·7 66·0	113·5 115·3
2	23	1950/59	2–6–2	105	69 110	$21\frac{5}{8} \times 26$ 550 × 660	5′ $8\frac{7}{8}$″ 1750	227 16·0	33·5 3·11	16·7 17·0	50·0 51·0	82·8 84·5
3	65	1951/54	2–8–4T	18	53 85	$22\frac{1}{2} \times 26$ 570 × 660	4′ 11″ 1500	199 14·0	28·6 2·66	16·8 17·1	66·9 68·3	105·8 108·0
4	66	1955/56	2–6–4T	2	62 100	$18\frac{1}{2} \times 26$ 470 × 660	5′ 3″ 1600	227 16·0	21·0 1·95	15·4 15·7	46·3 47·2	92·0 93·9
5	82	1950/55	0–10–0T	41	26 41	$23\frac{5}{8} \times 26$ 600 × 660	4′ $7\frac{1}{8}$″ 1400	199 14·0	25·3 2·35	18·1 18·5	91·7 92·5	91·7 92·5
6	78^{10} *	1951	4–6–4T	—	62 100	$22\frac{5}{8} \times 24\frac{7}{8}$ 575 × 630	5′ $8\frac{7}{8}$″ 1750	171 12·0	28·4 2·64	16·9 17·2	50·6 51·6	110·7 113·0

* Rebuilt from Class 38 4–6–0 engines

EAST GERMAN REICHSBAHN—POST-1950 LOCOMOTIVE DESIGNS

Table 25

Entry	Class	Date	Wheel Arrange-ment	Total Number Built	Maximum Permitted Speed mph km/hr	Cylinders Diameter × Stroke inches mm	Coupled Wheels Diameter feet mm	Working Pressure lb/sq in kg/cm²	Grate Area sq ft m²	Weight Engine Working Order: Axle tons tonnes	Adhesive tons tonnes	Total tons tonnes
1	23^{10}	1956/60	2–6–2	113	69 110	$21\frac{5}{8} \times 26$ 550 × 660	5′ $8\frac{7}{8}$″ 1750	227 16·0	40·0 3·71	17·4 17·8	52·3 53·4	82·4 84·0
2	25	1954	2–8–0	1	62 100	$23\frac{5}{8} \times 26$ 600 × 660	5′ 3″ 1600	227 16·0	41·6 3·87	17·2 17·6	69·6 70·4	84·4 86·1
3	25^{10} †	1955	2–8–0	1	62 100	$23\frac{5}{8} \times 26$ 600 × 660	5′ 3″ 1600	227 16·0	40·5 3·76	17·6 18·0	70·6 72·0	87·2 89·0
4	50^{40}	1956/60	2–10–0	92	44 70	$23\frac{5}{8} \times 26$ 600 × 660	4′ $7\frac{1}{8}$″ 1400	227 16·0	40·0 3·71	14·6 14·9	72·1 73·6	84·1 85·5
5	65^{10}	1954/58	2–8–4T	88	56 90	$23\frac{5}{8} \times 26$ 600 × 660	5′ 3″ 1600	227 16·0	37·1 3·45	17·1 17·5	68·6 70·0	117·5 120·0
6	83^{10}	1955/56	2–8–4T	27	37 60	$19\frac{5}{8} \times 26$ 500 × 660	4′ $1\frac{1}{4}$″ 1250	199 14·0	26·9 2·50	14·7 15·0	58·8 60·0	110·0 103·0

† Fired by pulverised coal

REPRESENTATIVE LOCOMOTIVES IN GERMAN FORMAT EXPORTED TO OR BUILT BY OTHER COUNTRIES — Table 26A

Entry	Date	Wheel Arrange-ment	Railway	Class	Cylinders Diameter × Stroke inches / mm	Coupled Wheels Diameter feet / mm	Working Pressure lb/sq in / kg/cm²	Grate Area sq ft / m²	Weight Engine Working Order: Axle tons / tonnes	Adhesive tons / tonnes	Total tons / tonnes
1	1908	4–6–0	Swiss Federal		(4) 16$\frac{3}{4}$: 24$\frac{3}{4}$ × 26 425 : 630 × 660	5′ 10″ 1780	199 14·0	28·0 2·60	15·0 15·2	44·8 45·5	67·7 68·6
2	1909	4–6–0	Gothard (Swiss)		(4) 15$\frac{1}{2}$: 25 × 25$\frac{1}{8}$ 395 : 635 × 640	5′ 3″ 1600	227 16·0	35·9 3·34	18·0 18·3	54·0 54·8	77·7 78·9
3	1909	2–8–0	,, ,,		(4) 15$\frac{1}{2}$: 25 × 25$\frac{1}{8}$ 395 : 635 × 640	4′ 5$\frac{1}{4}$″ 1350	227 16·0	43·8 4·07	16·3 16·6	65·2 66·2	75·2 76·4
4	1910	4–6–0	Dutch Central		(4) 15$\frac{3}{4}$ × 25$\frac{1}{4}$ 400 × 640	6′ 3″ 1905	175 12·3	37·0 3·43	19·0 19·3	57·0 57·9	78·0 79·2
5	1912	4–6–2	Madrid, Zaragoza & Alicante		(4) 15$\frac{3}{4}$: 24$\frac{1}{2}$ × 25$\frac{5}{8}$ 400 : 620 × 650	5′ 9″ 1750	227 16·0	44·0 4·08	16·0 16·3	48·0 48·8	85·0 86·0
6	1913	4–6–2	Rumanian		(4) 16$\frac{9}{16}$ × 25$\frac{5}{8}$ 420 × 650	6′ 0$\frac{3}{4}$″ 1850	185 13·0	43·0 4·00	16·0 16·3	48·0 48·8	89·0 90·4
7	1940	4–8–2	Bulgarian	03	(3) 19$\frac{3}{4}$ × 27$\frac{1}{2}$ 500 × 700	5′ 5″ 1650	227 16·0	52·2 4·68	16·7 17·0	66·6 68·0	105·8 108·0
8	1928	2–8–2	,,	01	25$\frac{1}{4}$ × 27$\frac{1}{2}$ 640 × 700	5′ 5″ 1650	227 16·0	52·2 4·86	16·6 16·9	66·2 67·6	97·2 99·4
9	1935	2–8–2	,,	02	(3) 19$\frac{3}{4}$ × 27$\frac{1}{2}$ 500 × 700	5′ 5″ 1650	227 16·0	52·2 4·86	16·8 17·1	66·9 68·3	98·1 100·3
10	1940	4–10–0	,,	11	(3) 20$\frac{1}{2}$ × 27$\frac{1}{2}$ 520 × 700	4′ 9″ 1450	227 16·0	52·2 4·86	16·7 17·0	83·3 85·0	107·4 109·6
11	1941	4–6–2	,,	05	(3) 18$\frac{1}{2}$ × 27$\frac{1}{2}$ 470 × 700	6′ 0$\frac{3}{4}$″ 1850	227 16·0	51·5 4·80	17·0 17·4	51·2 52·2	98·6 100·6
12	1931	2–12–4T	,,	46	27$\frac{1}{2}$ × 27$\frac{1}{2}$ 700 × 700	4′ 4$\frac{3}{4}$″ 1340	227 16·0	52·2 4·86	16·5 16·9	99·6 101·7	146·2 149·1
13	1943	2–12–4T	,,	46^{10}	(3) 21$\frac{5}{8}$ × 27$\frac{1}{2}$ 550 × 700	4′ 4$\frac{3}{4}$″ 1340	227 16·0	52·2 4·86	17·6 18·0	106·0 108·0	152·8 155·8
14	1943	2–8–4T	,,	36	(3) 17$\frac{3}{8}$ × 27$\frac{1}{2}$ 400 × 700	5′ 1″ 1550	227 16·0	43·0 4·00	15·3 15·6	61·3 62·6	98·9 100·9

Note:— Entries 1 to 6 include features special to the building firm of Maffei of M

REPRESENTATIVE LOCOMOTIVES IN GERMAN FORMAT EXPORTED TO OR BUILT BY OTHER COUNTRIES — Table 26B

Entry	Date	Wheel Arrangement	Railway	Class	Cylinders Diameter × Stroke inches / mm	Coupled Wheels Diameter feet / mm	Working Pressure lb/sq in / kg/cm²	Grate Area sq ft / m²	Weight Engine Working Order: Axle tons / tonnes	Adhesive tons / tonnes	Total tons / tonnes
1	1922	4–6–0	Polish	Ok22(a)	22⅝ × 24¾ 575 × 630	5′ 8¾″ 1750	171 12·0	43·0 4·00	16·7 17·0	50·0 51·0	77·4 78·9
2	1923	2–10–0	,,	Ty23(b)	25⅝ × 28¼ 650 × 720	4′ 7⅛″ 1400	199 14·0	48·3 4·50	16·9 17·2	84·3 86·0	93·1 95·0
3	1930	4–8–2	,,	Pu29	24¾ × 27½ 630 × 700	6′ 0¾″ 1850	213 15·0	50·7 4·80	18·6 19·0	71·0 72·6	111·2 113·8
4	1932	2–8–2	,,	Pt31	24¾ × 27½ 630 × 700	6′ 0¾″ 1850	213 15·0	48·0 4·50	17·8 18·2	71·6 73·0	103·5 105·5
5	1928	2–6–2T	,,	Okl 27	21¼ × 24¾ 540 × 630	4′ 11″ 1500	199 14·0	28·0 2·60	17·2 17·5	51·5 52·5	80·2 81·8
6	1930	4–6–2	Yugoslavian	05	22¾ × 26 580 × 660	6′ 0¾″ 1850	227 16·0	54·2 5·04	19·5 19·9	58·7 59·9	97·8 99·8
7	1930	2–8–2	,,	06	24¾ × 26 630 × 660	5′ 3″ 1600	227 16·0	54·2 5·04	17·5 17·9	70·4 71·9	99·4 101·4
8	1930	2–10–0	,,	30	(3) 19¾ × 26 550 × 660	4′ 5⅛″ 1350	227 16·0	54·2 5·04	17·6 18·0	88·3 90·1	104·2 106·3
9	1926	4–8–0	Turkish	46.001	24¾ × 26 630 × 660	5′ 5″ 1650	171 12·0	32·5 3·03	15·7 16·0	62·7 64·0	85·3 87·0
10	1933	2–10–2	,,	57.001	24¾ × 26 630 × 660	4′ 7⅛″ 1400	171 12·0	32·5 3·03	13·2 13·5	66·1 67·5	88·7 90·5
11	1937	2–8–2	,,	46.051	25⅝ × 26 650 × 660	5′ 8¾″ 1750	227 16·0	43·1 4·01	18·1 18·5	72·5 74·0	102·5 104·5
12	1937	2–10–0	,,	56.001	25⅝ × 26 650 × 660	4′ 9″ 1450	227 16·0	43·1 4·01	17·9 18·3	90·0 91·8	103·8 105·9
13	1951	2–10–2T	,,	57.01	(3) 22⅜ × 26 570 × 660	4′ 7⅛″ 1400	227 16·0	43·0 4·00	19·6 20·0	98·0 100·0	133·3 136·0

(a) Derived from Prussian P8 Class (b) Derived from Prussian G12 Class

CHAPTER SEVEN

Central Europe

Fifth of our schools of locomotive design is one which originated in the old Austro-Hungarian Empire of pre-1914, and which after two world wars spread over the new countries of South-eastern Europe, Czechoslovakia, Yugoslavia, Hungary, Poland, Rumania and the much diminished Austria proper. This terrain ranged from Bohemia to Italy, from the Swiss border to the Russian Steppes, and included remote territory little trodden by Western feet, the lands of the fictional werewolves and vampires.

From 1900 until 1914, the Austrian and the Hungarian State Railways, working under a combination of central direction and autonomy which it is very difficult now to unravel, produced locomotive designs, some individual and some common to the two systems, but all following an unmistakable and strongly marked layout and appearance as distinctive in their own way as was the case with American, British, French or German products. After the split up into separate states in 1918, and after their rearrangement in 1945, the locomotive stock became distributed and redistributed in a most confusing way, and for those whose interest lies in geographical distribution and numerical details of all the types and sub-types, the industrious researches of A. E. Durrant* paint a most remarkable and well-informed picture. Here, however, we are dealing mainly with technical trends, and of all the countries above named which received this scattered flock, only Czechoslovakia, Hungary and Austria pursued to the end of steam the technical and appearance features of this very distinctive group of locomotives.

It was in these easterly countries of Europe that the more restrictive physical conditions affecting design, and referred to in Chapter 2, particularly applied. Except for the central Danube basin, the whole of the territory concerned was mountainous, and much of it was sparsely populated with little industry so that single tracks of light rails wound their way as economically as possible, round and over the natural features of the land. While there was little call for high speed, good haulage power was necessary, to attain which on the poor coal locally available, ample boiler power and grate area was essential. To save coal, compounding was at first much resorted to, but to meet the class of labour available for driving and maintenance, this was kept to its simplest form, so that its advantages were always marginal, and with the advent of superheating, compounding gradually faded away. Severely limited permitted axleloads, seldom above 14 tons (14·2 tonnes), led to the need for an unusually light construction of main frames and trucks. Ten coupled wheels had appeared for freight by 1900, and twelve by 1911, whilst the only substantial use of Mallet articulated engines on standard gauge in Europe, extended in successive designs from 1898 until 1914 in Hungary. Between the wars eight-coupled engines became standard for principal passenger duties in all three countries. Light bridge construction made it impracticable to crowd these multiple wheels close together, and in spreading them out for low uniformly distributed load per foot run, severe curvature could only be negotiated by special dispositions permitting unusual side play on axle and side rod assemblies. Thus the locomotive designer in this territory had to overcome contradictory obstacles more akin to those facing narrow gauge lines in remote parts of the

* *The Steam Locomotives of Eastern Europe* by A. E. Durrant, David and Charles 1966.

outer world rather than was to be expected in an integral part of Europe. It is small wonder, therefore, that the resulting products did not look quite like anything else.

Both politically and geographically, it is convenient in dealing with these countries to split our story into two parts, before and after 1914. Technically, too, that year formed a natural watershed. Before that time Dr Charles Golsdorf in his own person created one of the most distinctive series of locomotive designs which have ever been produced. Thereafter his successors carried on the same tradition, modified as was natural by the application of modern progress and the impact of their own personalities.

I. Before 1914

Dr Charles Golsdorf is one of the big names of locomotive history. Born in 1861, the son of the locomotive superintendent of the Austrian Southern Railway, he became CME of the Austrian State Railways in 1891 and died in harness in 1916. Early in the twentieth century he was put in charge of all mechanical engineering at the Austrian Railway Ministry in Vienna, where it is to be presumed he had some influence also in what went on in the quasi-autonomous Hungarian State Railways, the other major railway component of the dual monarchy. It is stated that from first to last he was responsible for some 60 locomotive designs,* this large number being partly accounted for by the extreme variety of territory for which he had to cater. From Vienna west to Linz and Passau into Germany, as far as Salzburg towards Switzerland, and eastwards to Budapest, and on to the great Hungarian Plain, main lines were comparatively level and coupled wheels up to 6ft 10in (2100mm) in diameter were not out of place. Over the whole of the rest of Emperor Franz Joseph's uneasy realm, severe grades and curvature were the rule, two international highways in particular posing formidable natural obstacles, the Arlberg route from Salzburg to Buchs on the Swiss border, and the transit of the Semmering Pass south to the Adriatic. For such journeys plenty of sustained steaming capacity was needed, and ample adhesion notwithstanding the 14-ton axleload limitation. Tables 27 and 28 set out in their first parts the principal engine classes built between 1900 and 1914, separated into two groups, those in Table 27 produced directly by Golsdorf, many of which were used on both parts of the system, and in Table 28 those particularly developed for the Hungarian Railways.

Let us look at the kind of locomotives which were designed in this first decade and a half, and then consider what were the particular features which rendered them so unique as to deserve a separate niche in the history of steam locomotion. We are really dealing with three variants of a main theme, the first being Golsdorf's two-cylinder compound phase which had started in 1893, and entered the twentieth century in 4–4–0, 4–4–2, 2–6–2, 2–8–0 and 0–10–0 designs. Characteristics of this phase in outward appearance, were double domes with external connecting pipe and 'flower-pot' spark arresters at the chimney-top. Splashers were still retained where the coupled wheels were of appreciable size. The second phase overlapping the first, and dating from about 1903, introduced four cylinders in place of two, still retaining compound expansion. Greatly increased boiler power was provided by wide grates, and taper boiler barrels in many cases, and the engine outline was much simplified by using only a single dome and eliminating the external spark arrester on the chimney. Splashers and as much external panel work as possible were discarded at the same time. This represented the final stage of Golsdorf's work for the Austrian Railways, covering 4–4–2, 2–6–2 and 2–6–4 passenger engines, 2–6–2 and 2–8–2 mixed traffic and 2–10–0 and 2–12–0 freight. The usual progression in

* There is doubt about this number, some authorities placing it more conservatively at 46.

wheel arrangement for engines of increasing power, first the 4–6–0 and then the 4–6–2, he tended to reject, although with strange inconsistency he did in fact produce two designs of the former. The third phase, again overlapping the other two, were the engines specifically built for the Hungarian lines which, to a bewildering extent, on the one hand accepted Golsdorf's designs *in toto* for certain duties, but, on the other, branched off into entirely independent practice, notably in the more general use of 4–6–0 and 4–6–2 types which Golsdorf had largely eschewed. Later on, a preference for simple expansion began to manifest itself, the latest and largest types being of this kind, while several of the true Golsdorf designs, originally compounds, were subsequently ordered as simples, or were even converted to that state. The keynotes to Golsdorf's design influence which made his products so noteworthy, were simplicity and a high power to weight ratio. The onlooker might at first sight be inclined to question the first of these qualities, since the arrangement of valve gear and external gadgetry produced a somewhat fussy exterior. None the less, the compound engines were provided with what was probably the simplest starting arrangement ever to appear on such locomotives. In the words of Golsdorf himself:

> 'The distinctive feature of the Golsdorf system is that no starting valve is required. In the low pressure port faces two small live steam inlets (in open connection with the steam pipe from regulator to hp cylinder), one at either end of the valve travel, are placed, and are so arranged that when the engine is in full forward or backward gear, as when starting, one or other of the apertures is uncovered and the other closed by means of a rib which is cast in the slide valve. In this way it is only when the valve travel is at its maximum, as at starting, or when the engine is performing heavy duty in full gear, that the inlets are alternately uncovered and the pressure of steam entering the lp cylinder is augmented. Under ordinary conditions of working, with a normal cut-off, neither of the apertures is open to the steam chest, the low pressure cylinders then using solely the high pressure exhaust and the engine working compound.'

No additional valvery of any kind was thus required, and the engine could in all respects be driven as if it were using simple expansion. In the same spirit of simplicity, Golsdorf favoured use of two cylinders only for all his earlier engines, only progressing to four cylinders for his later and larger engines where two cylinders could no longer give the required power even with the prevailing generous loading gauge.

The really remarkable aspect of Golsdorf's genius lay in the way in which he developed locomotives which were large, and even huge, for their time, whilst labouring under the restriction of a 14-ton axleload which would have fatally cramped the style of less imaginative designers. Not only so, but he had to get his products, however spread out as to wheelbase, round main-line curves of frightening sinuosity. The ingenuity with which he accomplished all this is to be seen in a number of individual designs.

At the opening of the century, passenger services were mainly in the hands of 4–4–0 engines, such as are indicated in entry 1 of Table 27. To permit a 54½-ton (55·7-tonne) eight-wheeled engine to achieve an axleload of 14·3 tons (14·5 tonnes), almost half the total weight had to be carried on the bogie, which to gain the required distribution had to be tucked back under the body of the locomotive in such a way that the centre line of smokebox and chimney coincided with the centre line of the leading bogie wheel, giving the engine a 'front heavy' look in appearance but not in fact. In this and in subsequent classes, weight was saved by using built-up plate structures, usually pierced by lightening holes, instead of castings for smokebox saddle and adjacent cross stretchers. As the required boiler capacity increased, weight was again saved, and the necessary space for wide firebox and generous ashpan capacity was won by using the 2–6–2 and 2–6–4 wheel arrangements, eliminating the leading four-wheeled bogie. Even these measures were not enough, and they had to be supplemented by the lightest and most flexible main frames and other mechanical parts which the designer's experience and courage permitted, and the larger-wheeled engines built from 1904 were the first such in Europe to eliminate splashers, to cut foot framing to the very bone, and even to cut away the cab-side sheets at the bottom where the driver was not occupying the space. As the culmination of these developments, Golsdorf's 2–6–4 engine of 1908 was a positive *tour de force*. This powerful machine with a large superheated boiler pitched 9ft 7⅜in (2930mm) above rail, 49·7sq ft (4·62m²) of grate area, 6ft 10⅝in (2100mm) diameter coupled wheels, four cylinders 15⅜in (390mm) and 26in (660mm) diameter for hp and lp respectively, and weighing 84·3 tons (86 tonnes) all up, still only exceeded the statutary weight of 14 tons on each coupled axle by 7cwt (0·4 tonne). In the same idiom, some magnificent 2–10–0 four-cylinder compounds were built for the Arlberg route in 1906 (entry 7), while in 1911 there appeared the pioneer 2–12–0 engine intended to improve still further both passenger and freight haulage over the route through the Tauern tunnel.

As has already been seen, 0–10–0 engines had first begun to appear in 1900, and to get such a wheel arrangement round the horseshoe curves of mountain lines, a graded amount of side play had to be allowed to individual axles, as much as 1½in (38mm) each way in certain circumstances. Since the one axle on any engine to which it is undesirable to give undue side play is the driving axle, Golsdorf had his cylinders on ten-coupled engines drive on to the fourth axle in order to permit the centre (or third) axle to move sideways. To do this involved very long piston rods if the connecting rod was to be of reasonable length, so that crosshead and slidebars were not attached to the cylinder back cover as was usual, but were separately bracketed off the frame in the region of the second pair of coupled wheels. This arrangement looked ungainly but was most effective for its purpose and it was adopted for many engines of this wheel arrangement all over Europe, examples being built as recently as 1940 in the case of 0–10–0 tank engines for the SNCF in France.

On the 2–12–0, due to a geometrical quirk, things were easier, and it was possible to drive the third coupled axle, permitting slidebars and rods in normal disposition. The crankpins at the fifth and sixth axles had, however, to be fitted with universal joints in the side-rod attachment.

After establishing so firmly his family of designs having compound cylinders and two-wheeled leading trucks, Golsdorf reverted in 1912 to simple expansion and a leading bogie in a series of 44 4–6–0s (entry 11, Table 27) built for the Südbahn section of the State Railways. This was one of the designs also to be found working into the Hungarian portion of the old Empire, and after the war many of them were retained by several of the newly-hived-off administrations, MAV, CSD and JDZ.

The Golsdorf design which is least known to Western European enthusiasts is the group of 12 large 2–8–2 engines of class 470 built from 1914 (entry 12, Plate 80). The great man's designing genius would seem to have faltered a little, for unlike his earlier 2–6–2 engines class 110, here trailing coupled and truck wheels were crowded below the wide grate with obvious detriment to ash disposal. In every other respect, however, they retained every typical feature and were a worthy epitome of this most original designer's last work. Some of these engines were rebuilt by the OBB in the early 'twenties with new cylinders having Lentz poppet valves to become class 670, and the last one was withdrawn in 1957.

Very little has come down to us on the performance of this family of engines. Golsdorf was unusually publicity-minded for his day and age, and he showered publications in other countries, such as the *Locomotive Magazine* in England, with copious descriptions of his frequent products. He was less forthcoming when it came to reasoning and background behind his progressive developments, and if there are more than isolated accounts of test results, running experience and maintenance comparisons, this author has signally failed to find them. Applying our technical thinking cap, and drawing conclusions from elsewhere, it seems probable that, as the engines grew larger, wiredrawing and condensation problems robbed them of increase in power proportionally as their size increased, a deficiency likely to be the more acute as piston speed increased. For example, it has been published that the indicated horsepower of the 2–12–0 peaked at a value of 2020 at a speed of 31mph (50kph), whereas a modern design, even with the same small wheels, would, due to better ports and passages, not peak at less than 62mph (100kph). For sheer pulling power at lower speeds, these engines were, however, most effective, and the superheated 2–12–0 worked at a very acceptable economy for its day, being reported to have used a minimum of 16·5lb (7·40kg/cv) of steam per Ihp hour.

The 6ft 10⅝in (2100mm) diameter wheels of the main line 4–4–0, 4–4–2 and 2–6–4 engines were not there primarily for the purpose of attaining very high speeds, which no traveller has reported these engines as ever achieving, but they were provided mainly to keep the piston speed down, and thus give the compound system the opportunity of giving its best horsepower output at the moderate speeds at which all Austrian trains were timed.

Many other features of a highly individual nature were to be encountered on this locomotive family. The use on earlier engines with smaller diameter boilers of two domes with a large diameter external connecting pipe has been mentioned. This arrangement was for the purpose of reducing carry over of water through the regulator to the cylinders. If it is asked why these particular engines required this unsightly provision when countless other machines in other parts of Europe did not, the answer is perhaps to be found by observing that all these engines had a rather large evaporative heating surface for their size. This indicates that the boiler barrels were probably overcrowded with tubes and that the steam volume in the barrel and firebox above the water line was too small, conditions well known to favour priming, This difficulty was overcome in the later and larger Golsdorf engine by increasing the boiler diameter and by use of a steeply tapered back ring in the barrel.

Quality of available water in the days before effective treatment was to hand would also contribute to the priming difficulty, and evidently gave rise to some anxiety regarding firebox safety. All side-stays were hollow at the outward end, and the external firebox clothing plates were drilled opposite each stay head giving the appearance of a large sieve to this locality. The object was to detect instantly by the escaping steam the position and extent of stay breakages. This practice was not particular, however, to Austria alone, being used on a number of other European railways.

In certain localities, particularly in Hungary, the high sulphur content in the available coal had a most deleterious effect upon copper firebox plates. Notwithstanding American experience, suitable material and expertise in the application of steel fireboxes of normal design was not available, and to meet this problem, the Brotan boiler had been developed, the main feature of which was a firebox in which the normal water legs contained between copper inner and steel outer plates were replaced by an arrangement of close-packed vertical steel water tubes encased on the outside by a firebrick casing sheathed in external clothing of normal type. It is understood that over 1,000 Brotan fireboxes in all were built, and that some 25 per cent of engines allocated to Hungary pre-1914 were so fitted. The Emerson firebox used by the Baltimore & Ohio Railroad in the USA was a direct derivative. A high price was paid for this particular solution of water troubles, for this construction was much less rigid than the normal firebox so that leakage was troublesome, while the external firebrick casing soon got into poor condition, and unwanted entry of air in this region could cause defective combustion.

Water troubles also produced another feature which gave a distinctive appearance to many of the engines, again particularly in Hungary. This took the shape of a water purifier mounted in the form of a cylinder some 5ft 8in (1725mm) long by 2ft 3in (685mm) diameter on top of the boiler. Intended to perform something of the same function as the 'Wagner' top feed dome on the German railways, it was thought that incoming scale-forming carbonates should be directed via the internal trays to a sump at the bottom of the purifier whence they could be blown down at suitable intervals.

Still on the subject of boilers, there was another detail which not only appeared on all the stock in the period we are dealing with, but continued on all the derivative engines in Austria, Hungary and Czechoslovakia post-war to the very end of steam. The regulator handle proper, instead of being in the cab as was almost universal elsewhere, was situated on the boiler side below the dome, where it was connected to the regulator head by a cross shaft passing through a stuffing box. The lower end of this regulator handle was connected to the driver's control in the cab by a long external rod suitably bracketed along the boiler flanks. It resulted that a glance inside the cab of these engines failed to sight the handle which was such a prominent feature of the usual locomotive backplate, and indeed until the driver was actually seen to start the engine it was sometimes quite difficult to locate his means for doing so.

Most of the foregoing features were specialties of this particular group of railways, and rarely elsewhere has the appearance of a family of engines been so completely conditioned by the difficult natural conditions they had to meet. To those used to less dramatic looks and particularly English enthusiasts, some of these engines appeared hideously ugly, and even the more seemly amongst them were strange and angular. When, however, the influences which brought them into being are considered, it is possible to detect a certain majesty in the later Golsdorf products, and insular indeed would be the 'railwayac' who could achieve no interest at all in one of these Austrian 2–6–4s or 2–10–0s.

Internally there was one feature initiated by an Austrian engineer which had a widespread application in many countries, and of course in Austria itself. This was the Lentz poppet valve. The author has discussed elsewhere the intractable problem which was presented in earlier times by the lack of steam tightness in the piston valves which the advent of superheating caused to supersede the traditional slide valve. Not only could such leakages double coal consumption after only moderate mileage from servicing, but there were difficulties with the piston valve in attaining adequate inlet and exhaust areas at all cut-offs, and in varying to the best advantage the functions of admission without penalising freedom of steam exit from the cylinders. By using double-seated drop valves, separately for inlet and exhaust, a valuable alternative was provided to the piston valve, and although developments in the latter caused it to remain as the preferred steam distributor over the railways of the world, many were the administrations which made wide use of poppet valves of this kind, usually driven by the existing type of Walschaert valve gear. It will be recalled from Chapter 5 how that great master of steam, Chapelon, found these valves most effective for his purposes.

In Hungary it will be seen from Table 28 that the gospel according to Golsdorf was by no means accepted *in toto* and there was obviously another mechanical engineer in Budapest who claimed a certain measure of independence. Although engines used in Hungary before 1914 closely followed the Austrian style in outward appearance, they had the advantage over many routes of enjoying a 15¾-ton (16-tonne) axleload. Although certain classes, notably a medium-sized mixed traffic 2–6–2, were freely used in both parts of the realm, important Hungarian classes used simple expansion. The two most important passenger types, a 4–6–2 in 1911 (entry 3) and a 4–6–0 in 1912 (entry 2), were initially turned out each in the form of a pair of compounds on the Golsdorf system, four-cylinder in the first case and two-cylinder in the second, accompanied by a pair of simple expansion engines having the same number of cylinders respectively. Since an equal number of working parts existed in each case, compound and simple, there could be little difference in mechanical maintenance costs, but the higher boiler pressures on the former must have outweighed economically any advantage in coal saving, for all subsequent building of both these types continued in simple expansion form. With the advent of superheating there was quite a lot of conversion of two-cylinder compounds to simples, especially in the 2–6–2 medium-powered range. This trend in Hungary supported what was to be deduced from the distribution of compounding over Europe in these pre-Chapelon days. Where hill-climbing was at issue, hard slogging was assured with reasonable economy by retention of compounding. On more level lines, running became sluggish as higher speeds were demanded and the proportion of work done in the lp cylinders became very low. Gradual improvement in train speeds, with introduction of longer locomotive runs embracing both hill and level sections, presently demanded abandonment of a compound system which by its simplicity, unfitted it to meet these more demanding conditions. Thus Hungary before World War I was well on the way towards losing compounding, although the Austrian lines remained faithful to the creed for main line duties.

Another trend in this part of the world was the diminutive tank engine. In a mainly agricultural country where roads were few and poor, a large number of very lightly laid branch and connecting lines was built. Some 450 tiny tank engines were built between 1907 and 1913 having no counterpart in Austria proper. A third of them were two-cylinder compounds with 11-ton axleloads, while the remaining two-thirds were simple expansion with only 9 tons on each axle (entry 5).

In the earlier part of this chapter, reference was made rather frivolously to werewolves and vampires as inhabiting eastern Europe in the imagination of certain authors. Hardly less strange than these mythical creatures, however, are some of the engines which have actually seen the light of day in these regions, engines in which the basic characteristics have become monstrously distorted so as to produce aspects which are difficult to believe, even when presented with the evidence of one's own senses. One such, slightly before our period, and actually illustrated in Durrant's book, combined in one horrifying assembly a Brotan boiler with separate steam drum above, tandem compound cylinders and outside frames. Other strange aspects arose from the agonies of providing ever-increasing diameter for the lp cylinder of two-cylinder compounds, as power demands increased. On the Golsdorf 0–10–0, a numerous and basic type built over many years, the left-hand outside cylinder eventually attained no less than 33½in (850mm) diameter which gave a distinctly ponderous look to the front end on that side. When Golsdorf was contemplating a 4–6–0 type early in the century for use in severe territory, calculation decided that a 31⅞in (810mm) diameter lp cylinder was necessary if the simple two-cylinder compounding was to be retained. Here was a massive problem for the designers since the position of the cylinders further forward as regards the leading coupled wheels than was the case with the 0–10–0, meant that the throwover on curves no longer permitted a cylinder of this size being placed outside. So the pair of cylinders, the hp being 20⅞in (530mm) diameter, had to be placed inside the frames, but outside valves and valve gear were retained. The overall width of the pair of cylinders in a single block made it necessary for the mainframes to be placed outside the wheels. Thus was produced another freak or ingenious solution according to one's attitude (entry 4 in Table 27 and Plate 78).

Finally we come to the Hungarian Mallets. First introduced in 1898 in 0–4–4–0 form, in 1906 a larger 2–4–4–0 appeared which performed mixed traffic duties, and a little later a 0–6–6–0 design for purely freight traffic. In 1914, the series culminated in a really large 2–6–6–0 machine weighing 106 tons (108 tonnes) (entry 7) and equalling if not surpassing in size and power the legendary Austrian 2–12–0. According to Durrant, no less than 90 of these monsters were built up to 1918, and they handled traffic on some of the remoter difficult lines in the Tatra, Carpathian and Slavonian mountains.

Before war shattered the Austro-Hungarian Empire into its component parts, there was thus a strikingly individual and varied locomotive scene; one which is fortunately preserved for us by the archives and photographs of such enthusiastic students of steam as Herr Othmar Bamer of Vienna.

II. After 1914

Whereas after the close of hostilities in 1918, the countries we have so far dealt with entered upon a period of notable locomotive development with many striking new classes of greatly increased power, this was only true of Czechoslovakia, and to a lesser extent of Poland and Yugoslavia, in the newly emergent independent countries which were carved out of the former Austria-Hungary. Of these the last two veered away towards the German school of practice as has been described, leaving the first named as the foremost protagonist of the erstwhile 'Austrian Empire' line of development. Austria and Hungary, now politically separate and greatly shrunken in size and population as a result of the peace treaties, became the poor men of Europe, and only reluctantly was money forthcoming for any rehabilitation of the railways. In each a very small number of new steam designs was forthcoming, but on the whole, for the period between the two world wars and even beyond, they had to make do with the residue of pre-1918 engines left to them after the partition. A vast number of former Austro-Hungarian engines was scattered across the new countries, and besides those mentioned, Rumania naturally acquired a big share by virtue of its taking over Transylvania from Hungary, while isolated groups of Golsdorf-designed products found themselves in Turkey and Greece.

Hungary was first off the mark with a new locomotive design immediately after the war, and we shall deal first with that country's progress. The class 328 of 1918 was a sturdy 4–6–0 mixed traffic engine with 6ft 0in (1826mm) diameter coupled wheels, and two simple expansion outside cylinders of 22·4in (570mm) diameter (entry 8 in Table 28 and Plate 87). This design confirmed Hungary's addiction to this method of using the steam and there were no backward glances towards compounding thereafter. Probably scarcity of copper as well as quality of water led to a final application of the Brotan firebox, and exploiting to the full the 15ft (4570mm) height permitted by the loading gauge, a wide grate was disposed above the coupled wheels. In the current straitened circumstances, any newly built engine had to be able to run anywhere, so 14 tons (14·3 tonnes) again became the permitted maximum axleload, and the designers had to repeat the trick described in respect of the early Austrian 4–4–0s, that is to push the bogie back under the engine with the chimney over the leading axle. Certain other features conspired to make this one of the ugliest machines ever to have been built in quantity. The very high-pitched boiler carried a water purifier cylinder immediately behind a large dome on the sides of which protruded the safety valves. The superheater header broke through the top of the smokebox whence external steampipes ran direct to the cylinders. A conical smokebox door, and on many of the engines a smoke deflector in the form of half of an inverted cone tacked on behind the chimney, combined with the weight-saving absence of any footplating at the front end, to give what was to say the least a most bizarre appearance.

There being no room on the boiler top for the customary sandboxes, these were, very unusually in European practice, perched precariously on the high thin running plate along the boiler side where they must have been extremely awkward to fill. By inspection of the size of the expansion link this engine clearly had only short valve travel, and so was unlikely to be very economical. In spite of these Magyar extravagances, the engine was unmistakably in the Central European tradition as was the next product of Budapest in the form of 424 Class 4–8–0 (entry 9, Plate 88). This excellent design, also two-cylinder simple, had 5ft 3¼in (1606mm) diameter coupled wheels, although the size and lofty pitch of the boiler, which had a normal firebox, made them appear much smaller. With long travel Walschaert's gear, both economy and sprightliness in running were so well served, in conjunction with the inevitable 14-ton (14·3-tonne) axleload, that this single type sufficed for every kind of heavy duty, and construction continued until 1958, by which time over 300 were running. Whoever was responsible for the angularities of the 4–6–0 must have passed on, for on the 4–8–0 the water purifier was now carried in a second dome, there was no conical front or external steampipes and the relative position of chimney bogie and cylinders was restored to normal. The last batches to be built from 1955 had large wing type smoke deflectors of the Reichsbahn type. During two visits to Hungary, the author was increasingly struck by the many ways in which this engine was almost an ideal general utility type, combining simplicity, robustness and versatility to a noteworthy degree. After the second war, in 1946–8 and again as late as 1955, a total of 62 was built for Yugoslavia where they made an interesting variant to the Germanic types in more general use. Some, too, were annexed as war booty by Russia.

Other Hungarian construction consisted of some very nippy small 2–4–2 tank engines with 9·8 tons (10 tonnes) axleload, built from 1928 for branch-line service (entry 11, Plate 89), and four 4–4–4 tanks built 1936–9 which, almost unheard-of in Central Europe, were fully streamlined, presumably to be, however humbly, in the fashion which was sweeping the world at that time in a transient manner. The last act came in 1950 when two prototype 4–6–4 express passenger engines appeared which might have been the harbingers of a new standard series, had traffic warranted and the approach of dieselisation allowed. For the first time 17½ tons (18 tonnes) per coupled axle was permitted, but two simple cylinders were still retained. These engines (entry 10), were something of a curiosity on the European scene in that, unlike their predecessors, there was little which was typically Austro-Hungarian about their appearance. They contained overtones of inter-war Reichsbahn practice but had little of the well-knit symmetry of German engines of that period. On the freight side, the big Mallets were all dispersed to Yugoslavia, Czechoslovakia and Rumania after 1919, and on the more level routes which remained, 2–6–2s of Golsdorf's mixed traffic design sufficed, reinforced by the same designer's 2–8–0s of different vintages. The 4–8–0s when they came after 1924 were well suited for freight duties as well as passenger, and Durrant records that a corresponding design of 2–8–0 using the same boiler and cylinders was prototyped in 1927, but this did not go into further production. As in so many other countries, the bulk of freight duties after the second war was undertaken by foreign engines built initially for wartime purposes. The author can attest the wide distribution of the American WD 2–8–0s of which 500 were at work in the 1950s, and there were also 165 German class 52, 2–10–0s.

Austria was left after 1918 with a small number of the Golsdorf 2–6–4 engines but with little else very suitable for handling the growing passenger traffic post-war. The administration resumed new design also with a general purpose 4–8–0 engine which makes an interesting comparison with the Hungarian version referred to above (entry 14, Table 27, Plate 85). Of almost identical tractive effort, engine weight and grate area, and both having modern valve events, the former with Walschaert-driven Lentz poppet valves, it was unlikely that there could be much difference between them as regards any aspect of performance. The Austrian machine retained a low running plate bracketed from the main plate-frames just above the coupled wheels, whereas on the other the plate was carried high on the boiler flanks with a considerable improvement in accessibility. To an engineer, the layout and details of the Hungarian engine were beautifully thought out, and this was reflected in its altogether better knit and more urbane appearance as seen at work on the road. A minor factor, too, was that the Hungarian engines were spotlessly clean and well kept whereas their counterparts across the border, at any rate in the 1950s, were usually in that sad and neglected-looking condition which so often overtook steam when change to another form of motive power was just around the corner.

Just as Hungarian 4–8–0s were, after World War II, built new for Yugoslavia without affecting that country's general orientation towards Germanic outlines, so in the first phase of rehabilitation after World War I a number, variously reported between 60 and 80, of engines were built in Poland to the designs of the Austrian 4–8–0 for the Polish State Railways, but these were also a stop-gap and had no influence on the main line of development in that country. Other exports of Austrian design consisted of 110 two-cylinder simple 0–10–0 and 2–10–0 engines supplied to Greece between 1924 and 1927.

As the 1920s advanced, the urge to reduce the journey times and increase the weight of important international trains traversing Austria was increasingly felt, and the 4–8–0s with their maximum permitted speed of 56mph (90kph) were becoming out-classed. In 1928 there appeared the first of two prototype engines of 2–8–4 wheel arrangement, the first having two cylinders and the second, three; both simple expansion. Remarkable as the Golsdorf 2–6–4s had been in their day, this development of the earlier theme was no less so, for the same breathtaking ingenuity in design was needed to assemble this 115½-ton (118-tonne) machine within an axleload of 17¾ tons (18 tonnes). Except for compounding, these engines followed directly the central European theme and they were even more impressive in appearance than their forerunners. In service, the two-cylinder version was preferred, and 12 more were built in 1931 and 1936. Just occasionally in locomotive history a class of locomotive becomes more numerous abroad than in its originating country. For example, more 4–4–0s and 0–6–0s to McIntosh design for the Caledonian Railway in Scotland were built for the Belgian Railways than ever ran on their home ground, and reference has already been made to the 50 4–6–0 engines on the État Railway in France to the designs of the Scottish Highland Railway which itself never owned more than 19. So the Rumanian State Railway authorities looked upon the Austrian design and found it good, and no less than 79 of the two-cylinder 2–8–4s were put to good use in that country, the building taking place between 1936 and 1940. After the electrification of the Arlberg route was complete, and that of the Semmering line imminent, the author recalls seeing a few of the Austrian engines of this class in a locomotive graveyard near Vienna. It was explained that negotiations were afoot to sell them to Rumania, where they might be expected usefully to join their sisters in territory not yet launched into other forms of power. Either the price or the condition of the machines cannot have been right, for nothing seems to have come of this apparently sensible proposal.

With an ample supply of Golsdorf inspired 0–10–0 and 2–10–0 engines before 1939, and of German 2–10–0 'Krieglokomotivs' after 1945, no new freight locomotive design was undertaken, but three tank engines appeared in this period, a 2–8–2 for lightly laid lines, a 0–8–0 shunter having the same boiler and mechanical parts, and a 4–6–4 for hauling light fast trains over short distances. After Golsdorf's death in 1916, compounding had been gradually abandoned and all the above engines had two cylinders only, simple expansion, with Lentz poppet valves fitted as standard.

It is fascinating to turn now to the neighbouring country Czechoslovakia (Table 29), which equally inherited the Golsdorf tradition together with a lion's share of the locomotive stock of the old Empire when it was split up after 1918. This administration also turned almost exclusively to simple expansion, using three cylinders for its larger engines, but poppet valves found no favour, and long travel piston valves were retained in their stead. Although track conditions and permitted axleloads slowly improved, anything like a general purpose engine had still to conform to a 14-ton (14·3-tonne) or at most 15-ton (15·3-tonne) ruling, and, like Austria, the largest and latest engines were allowed little more than 18 tons (18·4 tonnes) per axle. The need for economy in weight perpetuated many of the same design features, therefore, whilst the mountainous nature of the country demanded in the same way, eight coupled wheels for passenger services and ten coupled for freight.

Alone of the countries we are now considering, Czech production of new and modified locomotive types was most prolific, and occupied four phases, each technically distinct although overlapping in time. Pure Golsdorf 2–8–0s and 0–10–0s and 4–6–2 tank engines continued to be built, the first two up to 1926 and the latter until 1939, by manufacturing firms which now found themselves under new nationality. Some were built at first as two-cylinder compounds, but later examples were two-cylinder simples to which the former were gradually converted. The second phase began in 1921 with a new design of two-cylinder 2–6–2 passenger engine with wide firebox and 5ft 10⅞in (1800mm) diameter coupled wheels. Although simple expansion, it strikingly carried on the Golsdorf lineaments, and was in capacity a cross between that designer's classes 110 and 310. Complementary to these, there were designed in 1924 some 2–8–0s with 5ft 2in (1575mm) wheels carrying the same boiler, and intended for passenger work on heavier grades. While these engines were not repeated, further new designs of 2–10–0 freight and 2–8–2, 4–8–4 and 2–10–2 tank engines went through stages of development, some of them up to the very end of steam in the mid-fifties. Successive versions of these engines carried higher pitched boilers, sometimes higher working pressures and smaller cylinders, and a general tidying up and modernisation of details, without altering the power classification of the engines materially. Unusual in Europe, they were all adorned with a very attractive design of lipped chimney instead of bearing the ubiquitous stovepipe.

The third phase began in 1925 when the first series 387 Pacific was built. Here the Golsdorf 'line' became much fainter except in so far as the cult of lightness was still enforced by having to design so big an engine within a 17-ton (17·2-tonne) axleload. The trend towards six- and eight-coupled engines with leading two-wheeled trucks was here firmly reversed, and the leading four-wheeled bogie re-established for all fast traffic. Cast vanadium steel bar frames and amazingly light cast steel cylinders and smokebox saddles permitted introduction of three cylinders which in turn opened the way to attaining high power output without sacrifice of main bearing area or driving-crank axle web width. In the same idiom a three-cylinder 4–8–2 class, series 486, with 6ft 0in (1830mm) coupled wheels was turned out in 1934 having an axleload of only 15·4 tons (15·7 tonnes) and characterised by the same remarkably light and very accessible chassis design.

At this same time appeared one of the curiosities of locomotive history in the form of a reversed version of the same engine of 2–8–4 wheel arrangement (entry 9). Cylinder sizes, boiler, coupled wheel diameter, adhesive and total weight were all practically identical, and the two designs were built by the same firm. It baffles the imagination to solve the mystery of what the administration thought it was going to learn from this left-handed version. Whether the design was inspired by the Austrian 2–8–4 of 1928, or the Russian 2–8–4 of 1932, or whether it was just a final looking over the shoulder before throwing overboard a well-established central European format, we shall probably never know.

79 Golsdorf's masterpiece. Austrian 2–6–4 4-cylinder compound design of 1911, type 310. Almost unbelievably this large engine had an axle weight of only $14\frac{1}{2}$ tons

[*O. Bamer*

78 Forty-two of these unusual Class 9 2-cylinder compound 4–6–0s were built for Austrian Railways 1898–1903. Note outside frames and valve gear, $32\frac{3}{8}$in dia (820mm) low pressure cylinder inside frames, cylindrical steam collector on boiler top, unusual means of ventilating cab roof

80 Austrian Class 470 4-cylinder compound 2–8–2 No 470.01 built in 1914. It was Golsdorf's last important design, having many typical features in common with his legendary 2–12–0

81 Austrian 2–8–2 Class 670. This was the former Class 470 rebuilt after World War I with new cylinders and inside driven poppet valve gear. Note Dabeg feed water heating pump rod driven from driving crank pin

82 Golsdorf's basic mixed traffic 2–6–2 design built in both compound and simple form and scattered postwar over South Eastern Europe. Here two Class 354 head a train in Prague station in 1959. Note two domes and connecting pipe [*E. S. Cox*

83 Golsdorf's solution for ten coupled wheels on sharply curved mountain lines; connecting rod drive on to fourth axle permits sideplay on centre axle. Class 524 of Austrian design built 1919 by Skoda for Czechoslovakian Railways [*E. S. Cox*

84 This type of Austrian 4–6–2 was first built during World War I and continued until 1927. No 77.80 at Vienna (South) in 1956. Unusually in later Austrian practice, this engine retains piston valves [*E. S. Cox*

85 First post-World War II Austrian design for passenger service; 4–8–0 No 33.121 in original condition at Vienna (South) in 1956. Note Walschaert gear driving Lentz poppet valve [*P. Ransome Wallis*

Only three of these engines were built against ten of the 4–8–2s and, as will presently be seen, it was the latter which proliferated in further developments. Within the third phase also may be included the application of three cylinders and bar frames to the 4–8–4 tank design series 464 first built in 1934 (entry 14).

The engines of phase three carried large wing type smoke deflectors, a very neat combined dome and sandbox casing, and their 'Coale' type safety valves also had their own little casing, a refinement not often seen anywhere else. Double-window cabs of more German than Austrian appearance were introduced, but the external regulator handle below the dome was staunchly continued. Copper fireboxes were still the order of the day, and three separate light and elegant sets of Walschaert's gear were provided for the three cylinders, the inside expansion link being driven from a separate outside return crank, another imported German feature.

The fourth and last phase came with the resumption of development after 1945. No less than four further stages in the 4–8–2 theme began with the construction in 1946 of Class 498 with slightly lower tractive effort, but more adhesive weight than the preceding series 486, in other respects they were close counterparts, but were distinguishable from them in having a running plate set much higher up the boiler flanks, separate sandbox, steam dome and top feed dome on the boiler-top, and shorter chimney. In the next version, series 476 (entry 7), one would dearly love to know the thinking which led to the production of a small batch of three-cylinder compounds having one hp cylinder inside and two lp outside in the manner of the Deeley compounds in England and similar to French developments after 1946. A boiler pressure of 284lb/sq in (20kg/cm^2) was adopted and a starting valve controlled by the driver admitted steam at 200lb/sq in (14kg/cm^2) to the lp cylinders. Here there is an interesting and somewhat unexpected inter-connection with French practice. It will be remembered that politically Czechoslovakia was a protégé of France between the two wars, but after the events of 1938, it was to be imagined that no Czech would be much enamoured of any Frenchman in the post-war aftermath. Nevertheless in the short period before the Communist *coup*, there is evidence of some collaboration, or at least emulation. The double Kylchap blastpipe and piston valves with double admission and exhaust, both Chapelon specialties, were introduced on this compound engine. The cylinder and starting-valve arrangements, too, were the same as the SNCF had been working on during the war as an alternative to the de Glehn arrangement culminating in the appearance in 1946 of Engine 242A1 as described in Chapter 5. However, of these features, only use of the Kylchap blastpipe was widely extended, and compounding after this brief spurt on five engines once more lapsed. A two-cylinder simple version of the above, having the same boiler and 5ft 8⅞in (1750mm) coupled wheels, but with 227lb/sq in (16kg/cm^2) boiler pressure, became from 1948 the mixed traffic maid of all work of this system (Class 475). By now, world developments were lapping at the doors of the very aware Czech designers. With the experience from German wartime production, welded steel fireboxes became standard using the American Nicholson thermic syphon and mechanical stoker. Roller bearings too began to be applied to all axles, including the coupled, while the Franklin type of self-adjusting axlebox wedge as also adopted. The last stages of development reverted to the three-cylinder version with 6ft 0in (1830mm) diameter coupled wheels, and in series 498.0 and 498.1, the latter appearing in 1954, the ultimate in this striking progression arrived. Now the boiler barrels were all welded, inside and outside big ends had roller bearings, and the time-honoured regulator arrangement was replaced by a multiple valve front end throttle, again of American origin. In the last series the deep wing plates of earlier German origin were replaced by the Bundesbahn type. In all, some 212 4–8–2s were built from first to last.

In this post-war phase, the basic 4–8–4 tank was also taken in hand, and in its last stage as series 476 and 477, built from 1951, all of the above-mentioned developments were introduced, including the stokers and roller bearings. In all there were about 60 of these huge machines, and in no other country of the world was the tank engine developed to anything like the same degree of sophistication. Last of all, mention must be made of the 556 class of 2–10–0 of 1952. This was an entirely new design having all of the features of the later 4–8–2s, excepting the roller bearings. It retained two outside cylinders only, however, and was in every way a most successful and economical machine, over 500 having been built. Unlike its German counterparts, it does not seem to have been used for important passenger work, but visitors to the country may well have been hauled by one of them, as the author was, tender first over the short connecting line through the barbed wire and the watchtowers between Schrinding in Germany and Cheb the entry point behind the Curtain. Alone amongst Czech or indeed European engines since the days of the McIntosh engines in Belgium these 2–10–0s had a pure Caledonian whistle and once more one can only wonder why and by whom it was selected for this single class.

From the international point of view there was a rather striking fact about this brilliant culmination to the mid-European school of design—it found little favour abroad, none outside Europe. Although, as we have seen, versions of American, British, German and French engines have been built for many other countries about the world, with the sole and rather insignificant exception of six Pacifics for Lithuania in 1939, no recognisably Czech design was built for any country outside the homeland. The renowned firm of Skoda at Posen exported locomotives all over the world, but a glance at their last and very comprehensive catalogue confirms that while they produced engines in the British, German and even American idiom, none was based upon the family of native Czech designs produced since 1921. So far as Austrian and Hungarian designs are concerned, we have seen above what isolated quantities were built specifically for service in neighbouring European countries if one excludes accretions due to the explosion of war and its aftermath. This is a strange circumstance, not easily explained when not only the excellence but the variety and modernity of the later Czech designs in particular are considered. Absence of any one-time colonial or current financial interest in overseas railways would be one factor. A second might be that so absorbent of world trends had Czech practice become that it it had no separate advantage to offer (other than light axleloads) over the German and American schools of design which were already so well established in other continents.

If then, so little influence was exerted upon locomotive design as a whole, from any of these countries what, if anything, was exported in principles or details? Apart from the Lentz poppet valves already mentioned, and the Dabeg system of feed water heating whose pump assembly was driven by linkage from the side-rods, and which was fairly widely, but unsuccessfully, tried out in the early 'twenties, only the Giesl ejector remains as something which has made a wide impact outside its native land. Dr Giesl-Gieslingen, one-time Locomotive Designer in the Vienna Locomotive Works at Florisdorf, realising the varied and haphazard manner in which blastpipe and chimney proportions were arrived at, made it his life interest to study the air/gas/steam cycle of the locomotive boiler, and by 1951 had ready for demonstration the novel arrangement which bears his name. Others before him had discovered the value of ejecting the exhaust steam from the cylinders through multiple nozzles, ranging from plain double blastpipe and chimney, through single and double and even triple Kylchap arrangements having four and eight or twelve dividers respectively, to the Le Maître which exhausted the steam through a number of small nozzles set in a circle, in conjunction with a large diameter chimney. Giesl's experiments led him to the conclusion that greatest suction for least exhaust steam pressure and highest pumping efficiency to entrain the hot gases through the tubes was obtained by multiple jets, as many as seven in number, set in line along the centre line of the smokebox, exhausting into a chimney whose length was many times its width. After some initial scepticism, the Austrian Federal authorities took it up enthusiastically, and although plans for electrification promised the remaining steam a relatively short life, they decided in 1956 to equip all road locomotives due to remain in service for five years or more. Since then it has been tried out in a dozen other countries, including India, Australia and East Africa, and has found much acceptance in Czechoslovakia. Nevertheless, like compounding, it remains at the end of the steam era as one of the unresolved question marks. Was it, as its supporters so vehemently upheld, one of the last great developments of the steam age, ranking with the work of Schmidt and Chapelon, or was it, as others who had tried it without notable success claimed, just a link in the chain of events from ashpan to chimney-top, an important link it is true, but one which might take many other forms according to the completeness with which the other components of the whole air/gas/steam cycle were understood and provided for? We shall never know now, but as in so many other locomotive inventions, it was vitally necessary to know what was being compared to what. We do know from work done by Ell in England and other sources, how deficient many, if not most, of the draughting systems in being up to 1950 really were. In the atmosphere of rule of thumb and empiricism in which blastpipe and chimney proportions were arrived at, not only single chimneys, but other arrangements, not excluding those such as the Kylchap, could be most inefficient, if there had been no opportunity to investigate them and tune them up with the aid of knowledgeable experiment. There were many locomotive types coming to the end of a long and acceptable career in which it was found that steam production could be doubled by no more than a change in the dimensions of plain single blastpipe and chimney, once it was known scientifically and not guessed as to what needed to be done. Giesl offered a compact, easily applied, and relatively cheap means of getting more draught out of a given back pressure, or of getting the same draught at lower back pressure or any combination in between. It was immediately successful in replacement of less efficient devices where air entry, combustion conditions, free area through tubes and in-built capacity to boil water, were such as to leave a substantial margin for improvement. What there has not been time before the end of steam to establish beyond the shadow of a doubt, was whether the fitting of the Giesl arrangement as distinct from any other, could be justified where the limits of steaming capacity had already been reached due to factors other than draught alone, a condition by no means infrequent in modern power. Thus England, France and Western Germany, large steam users after 1951, did not take it up, and the final rundown of steam everywhere leaves the two aspects of acceptance and rejection set against each other in unresolved confrontation.

Technically, the Giesl ejector formed one road, but not the only road, to optimum combustion and evaporation. Aesthetically it was a disaster which disfigured the appearance of a large number of locomotives in the final stages of their lives.

CENTRAL EUROPE. REPRESENTATIVE AUSTRIAN LOCOMOTIVES 1900–1938

Table 27

Entry	Date	Wheel Arrange-ment	Railway	Class	Cylinders Diameter × Stroke inches mm	Coupled Wheels Diameter feet mm	Working Pressure lb/sq in kg/cm²	Grate Area sq ft m²	Weight Engine Working Order: Axle tons tonnes	Adhesive tons tonnes	Total tons tonnes
1	1898/1900	4–4–0	Austrian pre-war	106	(2) $19\frac{5}{8}:29\frac{7}{8}\times26\frac{3}{4}$ 500 : 760 × 680	6′ $10\frac{5}{8}$″ 2100	185 13·0	32·3 3·00	14·3 14·5	28·1 28·7	54·6 55·7
2	1897/1918	2–8–0	,, ,,	170	(2) $21\frac{1}{4}:31\frac{1}{2}\times24\frac{7}{8}$ 540 : 800 × 632	4′ $1\frac{1}{2}$″ 1258	185 13·0	42·1 3·91	14·1 14·3	55·8 57·0	67·3 68·5
3	1900/08	0–10–0	,, ,,	180	(2) $22:33\frac{1}{2}\times24\frac{7}{8}$ 560 : 850 × 632	4′ $1\frac{1}{2}$″ 1258	171 12·0	32·3 3·00	13·1 13·3	64·4 65·7	64·4 65·7
4	1898/1903	4–6–0	,, ,,	9 later 409	(2) $20\frac{7}{8}:31\frac{7}{8}\times28\frac{3}{8}$ 530 : 810 × 720	5′ $11\frac{5}{8}$″ 1820	199 14·0	33·3 3·10	13·8 14·0	41·2 42·0	68·4 69·8
5	1901/10	4–4–2	,, ,,	108	(4) $13\frac{3}{4}:23\frac{5}{8}\times26\frac{3}{4}$ 350 : 600 × 680	6′ $10\frac{5}{8}$″ 2100	213 15·0	38·0 3·53	14·3 14·5	28·4 29·0	67·0 68·3
6	1905/07	2–6–2	,, ,,	110	(4) $14\frac{1}{2}:24\frac{3}{4}\times28\frac{3}{8}$ 370 : 630 × 720	5′ 10″ 1780	213 15·0	43·1 4·00	14·1 14·3	42·1 42·9	67·7 69·1
7	1906/07	2–10–0	,, ,,	280	(4) $14\frac{1}{2}:24\frac{3}{4}\times28\frac{3}{8}$ 370 : 630 × 720	4′ $7\frac{1}{2}$″ 1410	227 16·0	49·5 4·60	13·3 13·5	66·0 67·4	75·6 77·2
8	1907/09	2–6–2	,, ,,	329	(2) $17\frac{3}{4}:27\frac{3}{16}\times28\frac{3}{8}$ 450 : 690 × 720	5′ 2″ 1575	213 15·0	32·3 3·00	14·1 14·3	42·1 43·0	58·5 59·7
9	1911/16	2–6–4	,, ,,	310	(4) $15\frac{3}{8}:26\times28\frac{3}{8}$ 390 : 660 × 720	6′ $10\frac{5}{8}$″ 2100	213 15·0	49·7 4·62	14·4 14·7	43·2 44·1	84·3 86·0
10	1911	2–12–0	,, ,,	100	(4) $17\frac{3}{4}:29\frac{7}{8}\times26\frac{3}{4}$ 450 : 760 × 680	4′ $7\frac{1}{2}$″ 1410	227 16·0	53·8 5·00	13·5 13·7	80·5 82·2	94·0 95·8
11	1912/14	4–6–0	,, ,,	109 later 209	$21\frac{5}{8}\times25\frac{1}{2}$ 550 × 650	5′ $8\frac{1}{2}$″ 1740	185 13·0	38·0 3·55	14·2 14·4	42·3 43·2	65·6 66·9
12	1914/18	2–8–2	,, ,,	470	(4) $17\frac{3}{4}:27\frac{1}{8}\times26\frac{3}{4}$ 450 : 690 × 680	5′ 2″ 1575	213 15·0	49·7 4·62	14·3 14·5	56·8 58·0	85·0 86·7
13	1917/27	4–6–2T	,, ,,	629	$18\frac{3}{4}\times28\frac{3}{8}$ 475 × 720	5′ 2″ 1575	185 13·0	29·1 2·70	13·0 13·2	38·8 39·6	78·6 80·2
14	1923/28	4–8–0	Austrian post-war (OBB)	113	$22\times28\frac{3}{8}$ 560 × 720	5′ $8\frac{1}{2}$″ 1740	213 15·0	48·0 4·46	14·7 15·0	58·8 60·0	83·6 85·2
15	1928/36	2–8–4	,, ,,	214	$25\frac{5}{8}\times28\frac{3}{8}$ 650 × 720	6′ $4\frac{3}{8}$″ 1940	213 15·0	50·4 4·71	17·7 18·0	69·6 71·0	115·6 118·0

CENTRAL EUROPE. REPRESENTATIVE HUNGARIAN LOCOMOTIVES 1900–1950 — Table 28

Entry	Date	Wheel Arrangement	Railway	Class	Cylinders Diameter × Stroke inches / mm	Coupled Wheels Diameter feet / mm	Working Pressure lb/sq in / kg/cm²	Grate Area sq ft / m²	Weight Engine Working Order: Axle tons / tonnes	Adhesive tons / tonnes	Total tons / tonnes
1	1906	4–4–2	Hungarian pre-war	203	(4) $12\frac{5}{8}:24\frac{3}{8}\times 26$ 320 : 620 × 660	6′ $10\frac{5}{8}$″ 2100	227 16·0	42·0 3·90	15·6 15·9	31·1 31·7	72·9 74·4
2	1912	4–6–0	,, ,,	327	$21\frac{5}{8}\times 25\frac{5}{8}$ 550 × 650	6′ 0″ 1826	171 12·0	33·2 3·09	13·8 14·1	41·5 42·4	61·7 62·9
3	1911	4–6–2	,, ,,	301	(4) $16\frac{7}{8}\times 26$ 430 × 660	6′ 0″ 1826	171 12·0	52·0 4·84	15·4 15·7	46·3 47·2	83·0 84·7
4	1909	2–6–2	,, ,,	324	$20\frac{1}{16}\times 25\frac{5}{8}$ 510 × 650	4′ $8\frac{5}{8}$″ 1440	171 12·0	33·9 3·15	13·8 14·1	41·5 42·3	58·9 60·1
5	1910	2–6–2T	,, ,,	376	$14\frac{1}{2}\times 21\frac{1}{4}$ 370 × 540	3′ 5″ 1040	171 12·0	17·2 1·60	9·1 9·3	27·3 27·8	45·0 45·9
6	1906	2–4–4–0	,, ,,	401	(4) $15\frac{3}{8}:25\times 25\frac{5}{8}$ 390 : 635 × 650	4′ $8\frac{5}{8}$″ 1440	227 16·0	37·4 3·55	16·0 16·3	64·0 65·3	73·8 75·3
7	1914	2–6–6–0	,, ,,	601	(4) $20\frac{1}{2}:33\frac{1}{2}\times 26$ 520 : 850 × 660	4′ $8\frac{5}{8}$″ 1440	213 15·0	53·9 5·10	15·7 16·0	94·4 96·2	105·8 108·8
8	1919	4–6–0	Hungarian post-war (MAV)	328	$22\frac{1}{2}\times 25\frac{3}{8}$ 570 × 650	6′ 0″ 1826	171 12·0	35·0 3·25	14·0 14·3	42·0 42·9	67·6 69·0
9	1924	4–8–0	,, ,,	424	$23\frac{5}{8}\times 26$ 600 × 660	5′ $3\frac{1}{4}$″ 1606	185 13·0	47·9 4·45	14·0 14·3	56·1 57·2	81·6 83·2
10	1950	4–6–4	,, ,,	303	$21\frac{5}{8}\times 27\frac{1}{2}$ 550 × 700	6′ $6\frac{3}{4}$″ 2000	256 18·0	59·1 5·50	17·6 18·0	53·0 54·0	107·4 109·5
11	1928	2–4–2T	,, ,,	22	$14\times 18\frac{1}{8}$ 355 × 460	4′ 0″ 1220	185 13·0	13·4 1·25	9·8 10·0	19·6 20·0	33·7 34·4

CENTRAL EUROPE. REPRESENTATIVE CZECHOSLOVAKIAN LOCOMOTIVES 1921–1954

Table 29

Entry	Date	Wheel Arrange-ment	Railway	Class	Cylinders Diameter × Stroke inches / mm	Coupled Wheels Diameter feet / mm	Working Pressure lb/sq in / kg/cm²	Grate Area sq ft / m²	Weight Engine Working Order: Axle tons / tonnes	Adhesive tons / tonnes	Total tons / tonnes
1	1921	2–6–2	Czechoslovakia (CSD)	365	$22\frac{7}{16} \times 26\frac{3}{4}$ 570 × 680	5′ $10\frac{7}{8}$″ 1800	193 13·5	43·0 3·99	15·1 15·3	45·3 46·0	73·2 74·4
2	1930	2–8–0	,,	445	$23\frac{5}{8} \times 28\frac{3}{8}$ 600 × 720	5′ 2″ 1575	185 13·0	47·3 4·39	15·2 15·5	60·8 62·0	72·6 74·1
3	1925	4–6–2	,,	387	(3) $20\frac{1}{2} \times 26\frac{3}{4}$ 525 × 680	6′ $4\frac{3}{4}$″ 1950	185 13·0	52·1 4·84	16·9 17·2	50·5 51·5	90·8 92·6
4	1934	4–8–2	,,	486	(3) $21\frac{5}{8} \times 26\frac{3}{4}$ 550 × 680	6′ 0″ 1830	227 16·0	52·1 4·84	15·4 15·7	61·5 62·7	103·0 105·1
5	1946	4–8–2	,,	498	(3) $19\frac{5}{8} \times 26\frac{3}{4}$ 500 × 680	6′ 0″ 1830	227 16·0	50·8 4·72	17·7 18·0	70·6 72·0	104·0 106·0
6	1948	4–8–2	,,	475.1	$20\frac{7}{8} \times 26\frac{3}{4}$ 530 × 680	5′ $8\frac{7}{8}$″ 1750	227 16·0	46·7 4·34	15·0 15·3	60·0 61·2	97·6 99·6
7	1950	4–8–2	,,	476	(3) $19\frac{5}{8} : 22\frac{7}{8} \times 26$ 500 : 580 × 660	5′ 4″ 1624	284 20·0	46·7 4·34	17·8 18·1	70·7 72·1	106·3 108·4
8	1954	4–8–2	,,	498.1	(3) $19\frac{5}{8} \times 26\frac{3}{4}$ 500 × 680	6′ 0″ 1830	227 16·0	52·2 4·85	18·2 18·6	73·0 74·4	111·3 113·5
9	1934	2–8–4	,,	486.1	(3) $21\frac{5}{8} \times 26\frac{3}{4}$ 550 × 680	6′ 0″ 1830	227 16·0	53·8 5·00	15·7 16·0	62·6 63·9	95·6 97·6
10	1923	2–10–0		534	$22\frac{7}{8} \times 24\frac{7}{8}$ 580 × 630	4′ $3\frac{1}{2}$″ 1310	227 16·0	43·9 4·08	14·1 14·4	70·7 72·1	81·1 82·7
11	1952	2–10–0	,,	556	$21\frac{5}{8} \times 26$ 550 × 660	4′ $7\frac{1}{8}$″ 1400	256 18·0	46·7 4·34	15·7 16·0	78·4 80·8	93·1 95·0
12	1922	2–8–2T	,,	423	$18\frac{7}{8} \times 22\frac{1}{2}$ 480 × 570	3′ $9\frac{1}{4}$″ 1150	185 13·0	30·9 2·87	11·9 12·1	47·4 48·3	70·4 71·8
13	1926	2–10–2T	,,	524.1	$22\frac{1}{2} \times 24\frac{7}{8}$ 570 × 632	4′ $3\frac{1}{2}$″ 1309	185 13·0	41·6 3·87	13·2 13·5	65·8 67·2	96·2 98·2
14	1934	4–8–4T	,,	464	$23\frac{5}{8} \times 28\frac{3}{8}$ 600 × 720	5′ 4″ 1624	185 13·0	47·1 4·38	13·0 13·3	51·9 53·0	112·2 114·5
15	1951	4–8–4T	,,	477	(3) $17\frac{3}{4} \times 26\frac{3}{4}$	5′ 4″	227	46·7	16·9	67·4	128·0

CHAPTER EIGHT

The Others

WE HAVE NOW DEALT with the five countries whose locomotive practice has had the widest influence outside their own borders, and regarding which a guess has been hazarded that they account for around 80 per cent of the locomotives which have ever been constructed, for standard or broad gauge. Although containing examples of considerable technical interest, the remaining countries which have built up a recognisable school of design of their own have not for one reason or another made much impact on their neighbours, and, again, with certain isolated exceptions, where they have had an exporting industry it has built to the designs of the customers rather than to those of the home railways. Six further territories, Belgium, Holland, Italy, Russia, Scandinavia and Spain, enter this category; the remaining standard or broad gauge administrations having had steam locomotive studs which were almost wholly derivative.

It is not to be thought that, by compressing reference to the above into a single chapter, they are without interest or importance. Excellent books have been written about several of them, the perusal of which would instantly dismiss such a thought. Here we shall confine ourselves to pointing out those features of technical content and appearance which achieved their individuality and the limited extent to which they influenced others, and were in their turn influenced from outside.

I. Belgium

Although one of the smallest countries in Europe, Belgium has by virtue of its industrialisation had a high density of rail transport, and lying as it does athwart important international highways, it has had to provide motive power appropriate to membership of the comity of 'Grandes Lignes'. Within a rich locomotive tapestry in the present century it has not, however, achieved the same uniformity of practice as has been the case with the other countries, so far dealt with, such as would cause the intelligent but technically unaware traveller to say of any given engine, 'That is typically Belgian'. Rather it has passed through a series of design periods, some deploying native ideas, others chameleon-like, taking their colour from one or other of the practices of the 'Big Five'. And of course it has, more severely than anywhere else in Europe, had to bear the brunt of two wars with total occupation by the enemy, followed by painful reconstruction. Table 30 sets out the highlights of Belgian design since 1900.

As the century opened, Belgium had just entered on its 'British' period. A Caledonian Railway 'Dunalastair' class 4–4–0 to the design of J. F. McIntosh had been exhibited at the Brussels Exhibition of 1897, and besides being awarded a gold medal, had claimed the rapt attention of the State Railway engineers, who were so struck by its elegant simplicity, and its record of excellent performance at home, that five identical engines were ordered from Neilson, Reid & Company of Glasgow in 1898. Some 200 more engines of this kind were built by Belgian firms between 1900 and 1905, known as types 17 and 18, while construction began in the former year of the corresponding 0–6–0 freight engine type 32, and this also had proliferated by over 300 units in the same period and ultimately attained 500. A third type of Caledonian lineage, a 4–6–0 mixed traffic engine (type 35), ran to 42 units from 1903. There was also a 4–4–2 tank engine, type 15, of which 115 were built between 1900 and 1903, which was like what a Caledonian 4–4–2 tank engine would have been if the Caledonian Railway had ever possessed such a type.

It was rather an odd circumstance that to see McIntosh design in real quantity it was to Belgium that the student must go, but if he did so he would discover that underneath an apparent identity of appearance, there was one very important difference. Caledonian engines on their home ground were notorious coal-eaters even for their day and this was largely due to insufficient grate area giving rise to excessive rates of combustion even at moderate output. The Belgians had evidently rumbled this weakness for their series production of 0–6–0s had 27¼sq ft (2·53m²) of grate instead of 20·6sq ft (1·91m²) on the corresponding Scottish engine, and the 4–6–0 no less than 30·6sq ft (2·84m²) instead of 21sq ft (1·95m²). Only on the 4–4–0s did the grate remain the same at 22sq ft (2·04m²). There were in all over 750 engines built to the three types mentioned above, and it is interesting to recall that the Caledonian Railway itself never had more than 57 4–4–0s, 21 4–6–0s and 100 0–6–0s to the corresponding McIntosh design.

This massive restocking of the railway with what were essentially British designs was apparently based purely upon technical appreciation, for British manufacturers played no part in this provision other than the first five 4–4–0s as already mentioned. Later engines had superheaters, while the cabs soon departed from McIntosh's cut-away sides, and sported two and even three side-windows. Much later the shapely Caledonian chimneys were replaced by native designs of less pleasing appearance as is to be seen in Plates 31 and 32.

By 1904 these engines were becoming overburdened on international services and particularly on the heavily graded Luxemburg lines, and a second phase of design was born, this time displaying a strong local individuality. In that year studies were commenced upon a four-cylinder simple expansion 4–6–0, and in 1906 the first of type 9 appeared a really large engine for its day, and in having all its cylinders driving on to the leading axle it was the prototype of class S10 in Germany, and of the Claughton class on the LNW Railway in England. The first few engines carried a fantastic complication never seen before or since in that outside Walschaert's gear drove the inside valves through rocking shafts disposed behind the cylinder blocks, the inside valve spindles being continued through their front covers to drive the outside valves through additional rocking shafts placed this time in front of the cylinders. Engineering sanity returned with later builds and only one set of rockers was employed in the ordinary way (entry 4, Plate 93).

In 1910 the Belgian designer J. B. Flamme produced his masterpieces, a 4–6–2 type 10 and a 2–10–0 type 36, both having, once more, four simple cylinders but this time associated with a huge taper boiler whose wide firebox carried 54sq ft (4·98m²) of grate area. A total of 58 of the Pacifics was built by various Belgian firms between 1910 and 1914 and they are certainly the most extraordinary-looking Pacifics ever to have taken the rails. With the smokebox set behind instead of above the leading bogie, and with the massive firebox it is small wonder that there was trouble at first with bad weight distribution. On the later engines this was redressed by a reduction in grate area to 49sq ft (4·55m²) and of total engine weight by 4 tons. In 1922 a considerable rebuilding took place with strengthened frames, increased superheat, improved steampiping and double blastpipe and chimney. Plate 94 shows one of the engines in its improved state which brought the maximum Ihp on test up to 2,700, and reduced the coal consumption.

These were to the author's mind almost terrifying-looking engines, and to see one

86 Austrian masterpiece: a 2-cylinder simple 2–8–4 No 12.10 at Gloggnitz in 1956. Note the water feed pump on the footplating in front of the cab, and the complexity of the associated feed piping [*P. Ransome Wallis*

87 First postwar Hungarian design for passenger service; 4–6–0 No 328.029 at Budapest, 1958. Note built up construction of smokebox saddle, outside steam pipes, cylindrical water delivery drum behind dome [*E. S. Cox*

89 Lightweight Hungarian 2–4–2T for branch lines permitting only 10ton axle loads; Class 22 built 1928–39. This example was photographed at Siofok (Balaton) in 1958 [*E. S. Cox*

88 Hungarian general purpose locomotive Class 424 4–8–0 of 1956-build at Budapest. The first dome contains distributing trays for incoming feed water [*E. S. Cox*

92 Czech maid of all work; 2-cylinder simple 4–8–2 No 475 168 at Prague. Introduced in 1948, these engines have roller bearings throughout, arch tubes and thermic syphon in firebox, Kylchap double exhaust and mechanical stokers [*E. S. Cox*

90 Czech 2-cylinder simple 2–6–2 of the first postwar period. No 365 039 of 1923-build at Pilsen in 1959. Note the lipped chimney and "cleaning-up" of the basic Austrian design [*E. S. Cox*

91 Czech 3-cylinder simple 4–8–2 No 498 007 at Cheb in 1959. Note the external regulator handle, curious chimney cowling, and lightweight tubular trailing truck construction [*E. S. Cox*

93 Belgian 4-cylinder simple Type 9 4–6–0 design of 1906; No 4055 at Liège in 1931. The ACFI feed water heater system was a later addition [*C. Shorto*

94 Belgian 4-cylinder simple Type 10 4–6–2 designed by Flamme and built in 1910. Modified in 1922 with double blastpipe and chimney. Note unusual disposition of smokebox behind leading bogie [*C. Shorto*

95 The French phase in Belgian design is shown in this 4-cylinder de Glehn compound 4–6–0 No 4659 of Type 8 *bis* at Liège in 1931 [*C. Shorto*

96 Belgian 4-cylinder simple 2–10–0 design of 1914—Type 36; No 4478 at Brussels in 1931. Note unusually wide spacing of coupled wheels [*C. Shorto*

97 No 3798 of Dutch 3700 Class 4-cylinder simple 4–6–0, most numerous passenger series. The earliest examples were supplied by Beyer, Peacock (England) in 1910. Construction was continued by Continental firms until 1928

[*C. Shorto*

98 Tank engine version of Dutch 3700 Class 4-cylinder simple, 4–6–4T No 6101 at Roosendaal. Note the copper capped chimney and polished brass dome [*C. Shorto*

approach with its vast capuchon chimney, and the formidable battlements of its inside cylinder covers, coupled with the muffled roar of its exhaust, was certainly something without parallel in any land. In spite of their somewhat chequered career on the technical plane, some of them were still performing main-line duties forty-five years after building.

Just as the 4–6–2 was foreshortened the 2–10–0 was elongated, with the wheelbase spread out in a manner unusual in ten-coupled machines. Similar modifications to those of the Pacifics were applied to these engines after the war, and here the compliment was nearly returned, for this time it was visiting English railway engineers who studied the Belgian design and thought they found it good, for the Lancashire & Yorkshire Railway in England proceeded to work out proposals and a similar engine adapted to the British loading gauge which might have been built but for the onset of war. It was World War I which brought various adventures to these 'big boys'. Sent to France to escape the invasion, the Pacifics were overweight for those lines, and except for a few captured by the Germans, they remained inactive until the war's end when 49 were returned. Of the 136 2–10–0s, 113 similarly escaped to France, but then in 1915, 60 were sold to the Russian Government for working over the standard gauge lines in captured territory in Austrian Galicia. This latter batch evaporated in the mists of war, and only the 76 remaining in France came home to Belgium afterwards. Seventeen more were built new in 1921–2 with the later improvements.

There was evidently within the Belgian administration a French-inspired resistance movement against these typically Flamme products, for as early as 1905, 4–4–2s and 4–6–0s began to appear having a very different cut of the jib. In particular the type 8 4–6–0 with 5ft 11in (1800mm) diameter coupled wheels was in all respects a typical de Glehn compound totally Gallic in layout, and experience with 42 examples built up to 1907, encouraged the rebels to prepare the very similar type 8 *bis* for production in 1914, but due to the war, building was deferred until 1919 when orders were placed for 75 engines from 8 Belgian firms. A corresponding compound 2–8–0 began to appear in 1921, and nothing could be further design-wise from the Flamme series than these engines so congruous with what was to be seen south of the border (Table 20, entries 12 and 13).

A sidelight on the Belgian scene, then as now, was the large number of locomotive building firms in so small a country. No fewer than eleven makers shared the first 100 of the 2–10–0s, and this commercial independence, which must have inflated costs, remained to plague even the new world of the electric and the diesel, as was lamented to the author by the Belgian Chief of Motive Power not so very long ago.

In the period of reconstruction the 'wheels within wheels' aspect of Belgian outlook was exemplified by the ordering in 1922 of a considerable number of 2–8–0s from Armstrong Whitworth in England, again as unlike the 'Flamme' or 'French' schools as they could well be. This time there resulted a massive two-cylinder simple design with 24in × 28in (610 × 712mm) cylinders, a Belpaire firebox unusual in the land of Belpaire himself and 18·8-ton (19·1-tonne) axleload.

By the end of the first decade after the war two things had occurred. The main lines had now been largely reconstructed to take a 22½-ton (23-tonne) axleload, and a lot of experience had been gained with various American features on engines imported from the USA to supplement the big influx of German reparation engines which was referred to in Chapter 6. There now appeared in 1929–30 two very large engines which might be described as of Americanised Belgian design. These were a 2–8–0 freight (type 35) and a 2–8–2 mixed traffic engine (type 5) both having a 22½-ton (23-tonne) axleload and both destined more particularly for the difficult Luxemburg line with its 1 in 62 grades in places. Both engines had two outside cylinders, 28⅜in × 28⅜in (720 × 720mm) in the case of the Mikado, bar frames and compensated spring gear, and both had double blastpipes and chimneys. The 2–8–0 with its high axleloading was designed to have as much adhesive weight as the older and more complex 2–10–0, while the 2–8–2 was allocated to take 614-ton (625-tonne) trains in the timings to which the four-cylinder 4–6–2s took only 430 tons (438 tonnes). When the later success of the SNCF American 2–8–2 engines is considered, it could have been imagined that these Belgian counterparts might have become equally successful and have proliferated, but for some reason they did not. Thus in 1935 there was brought out another, and as it turned out the last, Belgian design for important heavy passenger traffic, namely the type 1 Pacific; 35 engines built by four local firms retained the bar frames and 22½-ton (23-tonne) axleload of their predecessors, the 2–8–2s, but now a return was made to four-cylinder propulsion with two outside long-travel valve gears. This time the boiler assumed a normal position on the chassis, and the front end was encased in a cowling arrangement very similar to that of Gresley *Cock o' the North* engine in England.

For their last indigenous steam class of any kind the Belgians repeated their unpredictability in design matters by making a most surprising *volte-face*, namely, a return to four-coupled wheels and inside cylinders. Influenced like other administrations by the onset of diesel and electric traction which could so easily provide fast services over short distance inter-city routes, the six 4–4–2 engines of 1940 had coupled wheels 6ft 10⅝in (2100mm) diameter and were intended to be very fast indeed, and to this end they were covered by a most unsightly aerodynamic casing which hid from view what could have been quite a handsome engine. With 14in (355mm) diameter piston valves for 18⅞in (480mm) diameter cylinders and 7⅞in (200mm) valve travel they were economical as well as fast, but they never really got a chance due to the rapid change to new motive power on those lines for which they were best suited. The author encountered them in their later days on the regular Brussels–Amsterdam service with normal heavyweight stock which was rather like putting a racehorse to do haulage around the farm and was just about as effective. After World War II, apart from a short-term use of British and American WD types the only influx of new construction was the purchase of 300 typically American 2–8–0s from the United States and Canada, which took over secondary passenger and freight duties for as long as steam lasted (Table 7, entry 12 and Plate 16).

There must, of course, be a story behind the various changes in design direction which have been outlined, but to the best of the author's knowledge nobody has chronicled the personal factors, the test results, and the experience on the line and in the workshops which led to such frequent and complete changes. The only constant factor was that all Belgian engines were very massively built for their power, in which respect they were the antithesis of the French and Middle European schools.

II. Holland

Unlike Belgium, Holland, first in its constituent railways and then in the unified State system, since 1900 has sustained a remarkably consistent line of locomotive development both in content and appearance. Like Belgium it opened the century with the residue of strong British ties, and the influence of the firm of Beyer Peacock was far-reaching. Unlike its neighbour to the south, however, it never pursued strange gods, but continued to the end of steam with a basically British outline, even if this latterly became slightly tinged with ideas from Germany by whose manufacturers most of the Dutch engines were latterly built. There was a small home industry, the firm of Werkspoor indeed being world famous, but its exports were usually to customers' designs, whilst, unlike the case of Britain in India, design on the railways of the colonial East Indies, narrow gauge it is true, seemed to have nothing whatever to do with that at home. The Dutch terrain was almost entirely flat, and those who remember journeys into Germany before the last war will recall the extreme leisureliness of the progress across the plains towards the border. Thus 4–4–0s and 0–6–0s had a longer innings than in most other countries on the Continent and nothing larger than a 4–6–0 was ever developed for passenger work. Copper-capped chimneys and brass domes lasted surprisingly, while excrescences such as sand-boxes on the boiler-top appeared only fitfully and were absent in both the earlier and later periods. If feed water heaters were employed they and their pumps were tucked discreetly along the running plate, and never sprouted from the smokebox top. Although Walschaert's gear was common it was rarely if ever carried outside, and where four cylinders were employed it was the outside valves which were driven through rocking shafts rather than the other way round as was customary elsewhere. All this maintained a decorous appearance on the part of the home team, only interrupted by the various outsiders which from time to time brought in the ruder aspects of their originating countries.

Tables 15 and 30 set out the dimensions of a selection of the principal types. The 4–4–0s of 1914 (entry 7 of Table 15 and Plate 33) were a well-advanced design of their kind whose inside cylinders and orderly appearance would not have disgraced any British railway of the period. This was only the last of a family of such engines progressing out of the previous century with corresponding 0–6–0s in being at each stage. A departure from the line of near-British development was provided by the Dutch Central Railway between 1910 and 1914 which had a number of 4–6–0s built by the German firm of Maffei containing all of the special features which made that firm's products famous, except only that the four cylinders driving the leading coupled axle were simple expansion (Tebla 26A, entry 4). Bar frames and outside Walschaert's gear were used and there was a single steamchest to each pair of cylinders having two valves mounted on the same spindle. With cylinders of 15¾in × 25¼in (400 × 640mm), coupled wheels 6ft 3in (1905mm) diameter and 37sq ft (3·43m²) of grate area, these engines were worthy competitors to the Beyer Peacock type of four-cylinder 4–6–0s being developed at the same time as referred to below, but it was the latter which won the day for future proliferation. Thus a wobble in the direction of a more European form was nipped in the bud, again by agencies and policies of which it would be interesting to learn.

The centerpiece of the Dutch locomotive scene was the 3700 class of four-cylinder 4–6–0s (Plate 97). These simple expansion engines were largely designed by Beyer Peacock of Manchester who supplied 36 between 1910 and 1914. Eighty-four more were built by Werkspoor and three German firms from 1911 to 1928. With 15¾in (400mm) diameter simple expansion cylinders, 6ft 0⅞in (1850mm) diameter coupled wheels and 31sq ft (2·88m²) of grate area, they were not very dashing machines either in appearance or performance, the latter being circumscribed by a steam lap of only ⅞in (22mm) and a valve travel of 4·3in (110mm). Their maximum permitted speed was 62mph (100kph).

The 3900 class of 1929 was considerably larger and was the final expression of purely Dutch passenger engine (Plate 100). Still retaining drive of all four cylinders on to the leading axle, a departure was made in the use of bar frames, whilst retaining the standard practice of placing the valve gear inside. It was on these engines that the author first encountered the North European practice of locating the mechanical lubricators bracketed from the firebox backplate inside the cab. Occupying the fireman's seat, the rapid up-and-down motion just before the eyes of the linkage which connected the drive off the trailing crankpin to the lubricators themselves was rather startling. There were 22 of this class.

For each passenger-tender class there was usually a corresponding tank class for the short runs and inside cylinder 4–4–4 and 4–6–4 tank classes were followed by the 6100 class of the latter wheel arrangement which carried the same four cylinders, but a rather smaller firebox than the 3700 class 4–6–0s (Plate 98). The culmination of this kind of engine lay in the 4–8–4 tanks of 1930, which carried the identical boiler, cylinders, motion and type of framing of the 3900 class 4–6–0. Since these engines, also 22 in number, were intended for heavy mineral haulage, the German system was adopted of carrying the whole fuel supply, water as well as coal, over the trailing bogie, so as to minimise changes in adhesion as supplies were used up during a journey. Apart from these latter engines, freight work was still being catered for in new construction as late as 1920 by 0–6–0 engines, although the 2–8–0 in limited numbers had made its appearance earlier.

In World War I Holland was neutral and the tenor of its motive power procedure was hardly affected. In World War II things were different, and the devastation of the railways following the German withdrawal was almost total. Dutch engineers had to scour the far recesses of Europe to locate and bring back units of rolling stock of all kinds, and the recovered steam stock was far from sufficient to serve the country. Under the energetic leadership of F. Q. Den Hollander, a drive was initiated to electrify and dieselise the whole system. No new steam engines were developed or built post-war, and interim needs were met by use of British WD 2–8–0s and 2–10–0s taken over from the Army, by importation of some new Swedish 4–6–0 and 0–8–0 locomotives referred to later and even by purchase of a number of Swiss four-cylinder compound 4–6–0s built between 1907 and 1915, and released by the extending electrification in that country.

Throughout the years we are considering Dutch locomotive development remained entirely conservative, and just as its engines had no special obstacles to overcome of gradients, speeds or loads, of lightly constructed track or unsuitability of coal supplies, so this happy medium was reflected in absence of any heroics in design, and while superheating was accepted in its due time, compounding and long travel valve events were alike eschewed.

III. Italy

Until 1905 there were three major independent railways in Italy, but from their fusion into the Italian State Railways in that year, a very consistent 'line' in locomotive development was pursued so far as outward appearance was concerned, not quite so consistent as regards technical content. Before amalgamation compounding was general, in two-cylinder form on the Mediterranean Railway and with four-cylinder on the Southern Railway. A 4–6–0 of the former company of 1903 was straightforward but a 4–8–0, built in the same year and the first of its wheel arrangement in Europe, carried a wide firebox having 47sq ft (4·37m^2) of grate area set so low over the coupled wheels, that at least a third of it must have become ineffective after a small mileage due to build-up of ash below the bars on the shallow ashpan shelf above the wheels. In many countries there has been a yearning to reverse the conventional steam locomotive so that the cab might be carried in front with the greatly improved vision that this must bring. One of the earliest examples was the very unorthodox 4–6–0 of Table 31, entry 1 designed by Plancher, Locomotive Superintendent of the Southern Railway. Cab and firebox were over the leading bogie, with cylinders behind the 6ft 3⅝in (1920mm) diameter coupled wheels. Only oil firing made such an arrangement possible, and a cylindrical oil tank on three axles was coupled to the engine at the smokebox end. Water was carried in short side-tanks behind the cab. These curious features were never repeated, but the equally odd system of compounding on the engines was quite widely extended over Italian locomotives generally for some time afterwards. In this arrangement two high-pressure cylinders were disposed on one side of the engine, outside and inside the frames respectively, and there were two low-pressure cylinders on the other side similarly disposed. One piston valve driven by outside Walschaert's gear was situated above each outside cylinder, and distributed steam to each pair of cylinders. The starting mechanism was akin to that of the Deeley compounds in England in that the first portion of the movement of the regulator handle across the gradient uncovered in the dome an auxiliary steam supply to the lp cylinders which was shut off as the regulator was further opened.

In the very individual school of design which followed amalgamation of all the railways on the peninsula there were many curious features. Much of Italy was then, as now, poor country with industry concentrated in a relatively small area in the North. Only light axleloads 14·7 tons (15 tonnes) and below were permissible over much of the system with 18·6 tons (19 tonnes) as an exceptional value on a few main lines only. Coal was almost entirely imported, and although often of good, if dusty, quality, it was so relatively expensive as almost to count as a precious mineral. Lightness in construction and economy in fuel were thus sought as avidly as in the neighbouring countries of south-eastern Europe, but in a different manner. One immediate result of all this was skeleton footframing and an absence of splashers. The Plancher system of compounding was persisted in until superheating came along, but thereafter, with one notable exception, simple expansion was adopted, using four cylinders in the larger applications. Bogies were banished for long years, the 'Zara' truck connecting leading guiding wheels with leading coupled axle being preferred in the manner of the Krauss truck common in Germanic countries. The bogie only returned with the introduction of Pacifics in 1911. 2–6–0s and some 2–8–0s used inside cylinders with outside valves and Walschaert's valve gear. At first a single square sandbox was mounted separately on the boiler-top, but all larger and later types had a very neat combined dome and sandbox in a single unit. The spring balance safety valve, rarely retained into the present century elsewhere, had a considerable vogue in Italy, being present on engines built as late as 1921. Appearance was rounded off by uncompromising stovepipe chimneys, coned smokebox doors, and cabs with cut-away sides and without side-windows in the English style, a layout possibly more suitable for the hot Mediterranean climate than it was for the mists and rain of Albion. Where a wide firebox was used, as was common on the larger engines, the obvious ploy of setting the trailing carrying wheels well behind the firebox to allow ample ashpan capacity, the arrangement so widely used in Germany for example, was ignored, and trailing radial axles were placed fairly and squarely under the middle of the firebox to make the very worst of all possible worlds alike in air entry, ash disposal, and the well-being of trailing axleboxes.

Most numerous were the 2–6–0, 2–6–2 and 2–8–0 classes, and on these permutations and combinations of inside and outside cylinders and simple and compound expansion were played. The 2–6–0s had uniformly inside cylinders with outside steamchests and valve gear as shown in Plate 101, whilst the 2–8–0s for freight working carried two outside cylinders, those of 1907 being compound merging into simple expansion from 1911. Another breed of 2–8–0 carried larger wheels, 5ft 4½in (1630mm) diameter instead of 4ft 5½in (1360mm), for passenger work on heavily graded routes and for fast perishable traffic from the fruit-growing areas. Those of Group 745 built from 1914 to 1919 had, like the 2–6–0s, inside cylinders with outside valves. There was, however, trouble with the big ends and axlebox journals as could be well imagined with cylinders 23⅝in (600mm) in diameter, and a later version, Group 744, had two outside cylinders. The 2–6–2 Group 685 was the principal passenger type, and it was built from 1907 to 1927 at first in Plancher compound form, but later as four-cylinder simple, but still retaining the single steamchest per pair of cylinders of the former arrangement. With only a 14¾-ton (15-tonne) axleload these engines could traverse all the principal routes.

Pacifics were first introduced in 1911, Group 690 having trapezoidal grates in the French manner. Later series Group 691 had wide firebox and, unlike the case with previous trailing trucks, had outside bearings at this position. Four simple cylinders, again with two-valve spindles only, all drove the second coupled axle, wheel diameter being 6ft 7¾in (2030mm), the largest in Italy. These engines, with 18·6-ton (19-tonne) axleload, were intended mainly to speed the through trains over the level terrain of the Po valley from Venice to Milan, but because they suffered from the disability of all Italian engines with Walschaert's gear, they were very sluggish machines. Not only were short lap short travel valve events obstinately clung to, but the crossed ports and narrow steam passages involved in the use of a series of valve heads on a single spindle serving each pair of cylinders, added itself to the initial defect to cause near steam strangulation at the very hub of the whole power-producing circuit. Why, with so many examples in neighbouring countries of better ways of doing, all this was persisted in, must be added to our list of mysteries. The end of domestic Italian steam development came in 1921–3 with the appearance in the former year of fifty large 2–8–2s of Group 746 having 6ft 2in (1880mm) diameter coupled wheels. Here a reversion was made to compounding, the four cylinders this time, however, being disposed in rational manner with both lps outside. Four valves were used, but again valve travels, ports and passages were deficient, and although their 16¼-ton (16·5-tonne) axleload should have made these engines of universal value, they largley gravitated to the south with undistinguished performance. Similarly the 2–10–0s of Group 480 of 1923, intended for the Brenner Pass section of the international route into Austria, although two-cylinder simples, fared no better and ended their days in Sicily.

Due to abundant water power and absence of coal, Italy was one of the first countries in Europe to introduce extensive main-line electrification, so that steam development was always a Cinderella in that administration. Its designers remained apparently blind to what was going on around them, nor did the influx of American, German and Austrian engines during and after World War I have any visible effect upon home thinking. There was in the later 'twenties a project for a larger and more modern Pacific having three simple cylinders 21¼in × 26¾in (540 × 680mm), three independent valve gears, 6ft 8¾in (2050mm) diameter coupled wheels, bar frames and a bigger boiler with 199lb/sq in (14kg/cm^2) pressure and a grate area of 51sq ft (4·30m^2). Whether with this effort Italian steam design would have burst its bounds and achieved modernity we shall never know, for the scheme was shelved. But if thus non-absorbent of outside influence, Italian engineers produced two novelties which did have an international application, the Caprotti poppet valve gear and the Franco-Crosti boiler. The first of these, initially applied in 1921, used vertical poppet valves, operated from rotating cams, which, by an ingenious scroll arrangement, could be varied in relative angular position so as to give a range of admission and exhaust events, the two being independent of one another in a manner which allowed the designer to seek optimum efficiency. The drive to the cross shaft operating these cams was usually by an automobile type cardan shaft from a bevel gearbox located on one of the driving axles inside the wheels. The Caprotti and the Lentz poppet valve systems have chased one another round the world in many applications and continuing development. They made a tremendous impact at first by correcting the deficiences of short travel short lap normal gears, but after the gap was closed by introduction of long laps, choice between Caprotti and Lentz on the one hand, and between either of them and normal piston valves became inconclusive and was not resolved one way or the other by the end of steam. It can only be said that as mentioned in Chapter 4 the use of Caprotti valve gear in its final perfected form enabled the British Railways' 4–6–2 engine of the 71000 class to attain the lowest steam consumption per 1hp hour of any simple expansion engine in the world of which we have record. In the land of its origin, Caprotti gear, although fitted to a considerable extent, was by no means so widely used as was the Lentz in Austria, and it is to be feared that the native version retained certain mechanical imperfections which concessionnaires in countries such as Britain were able to overcome.

The Crosti boiler was in essence a normal Stephenson boiler, the number and diameter of the tubes in which were manipulated to release the hot gases at a higher temperature than usual, the products of combustion then passing back through what was in effect a giant feed water heater lying below the boiler proper and discharging through a chimney placed towards the rear end. Boiler efficiency was increased by thus wringing the last calorie out of transferable heat, but the low temperatures of the escaping gases caused corrosion in smokebox and chimney. Belgium, Germany, Britain and Spain applied this boiler to small numbers of engines but in Italy 2–6–0, 2–8–0 and 2–6–2 types were extensively fitted. The Italian engines were beheaded by removing completely the chimney at the front which so lends identity and character to any locomotive. Plate 104 indicates the extraordinary effect. Appearance-conscious designers in England and Germany found means of retaining a false chimney in the usual position.

Of purely Italian designs exported in our period to other than narrow gauge railways, the sole example of any importance was the 2–10–2 class built by the firm of Breda for the Greek railways in 1954. How an order for such a vast machine so late in the day of steam came to be placed in a country whose own development had ceased thirty years before, and which even then lagged behind contemporary achievement, must be sought, one imagines, in the jungle of commercial enterprise. Technical trouble was the almost inevitable result, and the Greeks hardly received a return on their outlay before the diesel removed the *raison d'être* of these fantastic machines, so normal in some respects, so blind to world experience in others.

IV. Russia

Russian locomotive development merits a place in this chapter by virtue of its domestic designs produced up to about 1935 which had characteristics particular to their country of origin. Commencing with the acquisition of large numbers of engines of pure American design from the United States from 1915 during and after World War I, a second phase appeared, overlapping the first, so that from 1931 certain designs, and from 1937 all new effort, became derivative, in that what were produced were simply versions of basic transatlantic thinking.

At the opening of our period there were still being built in large numbers two principal engine classes, a 2–6–0 for passenger traffic with a 14½-ton (14·7-tonne) axleload and a 0–8–0 having a 13-ton (13·2-tonne) axleload for universal freight working. On particular railways within the Imperial domain small groups of 4–4–0s and 4–6–0s began to appear soon after, although in small quantities in comparison with the first two types mentioned above. Between them these four classes exhibited many of the features with which Russian designers entered the twentieth century. Compounding was at this time wellnigh universal, using two or four outside cylinders, the latter being arranged in tandem form. The crank axle was something which was studiously avoided throughout Russian design history, only having appeared on less than 150 engines all told. Joy's valve gear arranged outside was another speciality, being at first standard on the 2–6–0, 0–8–0 and 4–6–0 engines. The very light axleloads permitted in those years produced the same effect which we have already seen in Austria, namely the pushing of the bogie where fitted, far back under the locomotive in order to get a more even division of weight over all the axles. Stovepipe chimneys were particularly unsightly, having a flared base with the upper part connected by a flanged joint. Very large domes carried spring balance safety valves, and even on the smallest engines cabs were large and well protected as became the need to travel in one of the worst winter climates in the world. In the same context and by Government decree, double railings supported by stout stanchions ran round the whole perimeter of the running boards, which themselves were carried clear of the coupled wheels. This feature, which above all others marked out a Russian engine, was ostensibly to make it safe for personnel filling sandboxes and doing other chores up top, when the footplating was covered in ice and snow. Such solicitude towards the *hoi polloi* was not common in the land of the Czar, and one would like to know a little more about the circumstances which made it obligatory. In any case, with the adoption of the American style its use was dropped after the early 1930s for all new construction. Ten years later a full array of Russian railings appeared on some 4–6–2s of typically Reichsbahn appearance built by Krupp for Bulgaria, such comradely zeal seeming out of place in a country sharing the milder zephyrs of southern Europe. Nowhere else, including the Canadian North, were such appendages thought to be necessary.

In 1907, a 2–8–0 of rather rambling appearance and having a 15-ton (15·3-tonne) axleload was turned out, again as a two-cylinder compound, but all of the types above mentioned, except the 4–4–0, changed over to two-cylinder simple expansion for later construction. A feature of this administration was the large number of locomotives which were built to particular designs and the long manufacturing runs. Thus the 0–8–0s continued to be built until 1923 and the 2–8–0 until 1918, reaching totals of 9,000 and 2,200 respectively.

This characteristic was greatly exaggerated in the next two Russian classes to appear, the 2–6–2 S class for passenger work and the 0–10–0 E class for freight, starting in 1911 and 1912 respectively. With gradual improvement in details and increases in size and weight within the same essential design, both types were built continuously over a period of forty years, attaining numbers of 13,000 for the 0–10–0 and nearly 4,000 for the 2–6–2, both world records as to quantity in their individual categories.

The design of the 2–6–2 is stated by some authors to have been inspired by the Italian engines of the same wheel arrangement, but a close examination of the two designs shows this connection to be somewhat tenuous. Certainly there was little which was Italian left on the 'Su' version of 1925 onwards, and by the final 'Sum' series of 1951 the axleload had risen from 15·8 to 20 tons (16·1 to 20·3 tonnes). The 0–10–0 began life in 1912 on the Vladikavkaz Railway in the Caucasus area, but introduction of so eminently suitable a type for Russian conditions was delayed by inability of many routes to take even a 16·2-ton (16·5-tonne) axleload, and by bickering amongst the authorities as to whether anything better than the rather mean 'Shch' 2–8–0 was in fact needed. Through the impenetrable veil which covers so much in that country, it can dimly be discerned that in Russia, not chief mechanical engineers, not motive power superintendents, not even general managers, but university professors had the principal say in locomotive design. Certain types were even designed by two of these gentlemen in double harness, and without disrespect to the breed, the long periods of gestation, and occasional 'prima donna-ish' behaviour are hardly to be wondered at. Like the 2–6–2, the Decapod passed through a number of stages. To meet desperate transport needs after the first war, 1,200 were ordered together from Germany and Sweden, while after the second, Czechoslovakia, Poland and Hungary contributed large numbers.

The small number of locomotive classes in so vast a country is astounding, Le Fleming identifying only 24 such over a probable total of 36,000 locomotives. The author travelled 4,000 miles in 1958 in that country on a visit specifically for the purpose of studying the railways, and he saw only nine steam classes in all. Thus the last class which can be called wholly Russian also attained some 5,000 units, namely the S.O. class 2–10–0, built between 1934 and 1954. This engine had the same cylinders and wheels as the 0–10–0s, it retained a plate frame when design was already veering off for American-inspired classes towards the bar frame, and it had a similar boiler but with a larger grate. These big brutes were common in the Stalingrad region and the author's photograph (Plate 106) taken at the station in that city indicates something of their vast proportions by reference to the two men to be seen in cab and along the foot framing respectively.

The rest of Russian development was pure American, as has been stated and referred to in Chapter 3; later designs are listed in Table 8. Although strongly derivative in the design of their later engines it would not perhaps be quite fair to say the Russians copied US practice *in toto*. The bones of the carcass were there, but they were dressed up in flesh which experience had shown would best stand Russian conditions. In the first place they had to work within axle weights far lower than the American, while their long distances and lack of alternative transport demanded exceptional reliability, reflected in massive and even clumsy moving parts. The climate, too, required specialised attention to lubrication, feed water system, and protection of the engine crew. In one remarkable *tour de force* Russian designers did, however, outshine their mentors, and a single 4–14–4 engine built about 1934—its actual construction was surrounded by much secrecy—was a kind of gargantuan caricature of American layout. Undoubtedly the largest non-articulated locomotive ever built, the idea is understood to have been sparked off in 1930 by study of certain American and European 12-coupled engines, and a Stalin-like resolve to go one better than the effete 'West'. Starting as a 2–14–4 it achieved massive dimensions, with an adhesive weight of 138 tons (140 tonnes) and an engine weight of 249 tons (253 tonnes). The boiler was pitched with its centre line almost 12ft (3650mm) above rail within an overall height of 17ft (5182mm). Two exhaust and two live steam injectors supplied this boiler which had 129sq ft (12·0m²) of grate area. Two cylinders 29⅛ × 31⅞in (740 × 810mm) drove 4ft 4in (1320mm) diameter coupled wheels through connecting rods 13ft 1½in (4000mm) long and had 13in (330mm) diameter valves having 2in (50mm) steam lap and 7 15/16in (2000mm) travel. Cast steel side frames were 5½in (140mm) thick and to get this caterpillar of a machine round the curves, first and second coupled axles had ± 11/16in (27mm) side play each, and the seventh ± 1⅜in (35mm). The other four axles were allowed only nominal side clearance, but Nos 3, 4 and 5 were flangeless. In what way it was a failure is unknown but based upon the fun and games which it is possible to have with one pair of flangeless tyres within a wheelbase, it is perhaps not guessing too hard to assume that three pairs together must have made the engine very liable to leave the road when traversing networks of points and crossings. It was never perpetuated, diagrams of it are few indeed, and one might almost doubt that it had ever existed in the flesh at all were it not for a single published photograph taken from the front end, clouds of escaping steam conveniently masking some of its technical details.

And what of Russian influence outside its own borders? Except possibly to China, in the days before the ideological split, very little if anything seems to have been exported by way of actual locomotives. In two of the post-war satellite countries there have appeared, however, two modern engine classes which could possibly owe something to Russian thinking, whether political or technical. The first is the Polish 2–6–2 passenger engine (Table 31, entry 16) of which 116 were built by Polish firms when manufacture was able to recommence after the last war. These engines have many points in common with the 'Sum' Russian engines and collaboration between the technical forces of the two countries seems probable. Less certain is the Russian influence which may or may not have caused the Czechoslovakian authorities to produce in 1934 a 2–8–4 version of their already established 4–8–2s (Table 29, entry 9), just two years after the appearance of the first Russian J.S. class 2–8–4. There was little design similarity between the two machines other than the wheel arrangement, but, as mentioned in Chapter 7, infiltration of Russian ideas cannot be ruled out at a time when zealous emulation might bring political advantage to some.

If there was little to show in hardware about the world of Russian origin, academically Russian scientists did a lot of work on steam locomotive theory, which was studied in many other countries. Borodin and Lomonosoff are well known names, the latter in particular having contributed to the technique of locomotive testing on the line as well as publishing profound treatises on the elements of rail transport as a whole. A lot of work was also done on combustion air preheating, use of exhaust fans instead of blastpipes to create draught, and adaption of normal fireboxes to burn oil fuel. Then with steam, as now with the diesel and electric, there always seemed to be a considerable gulf between the professor in his laboratory, and the man in the depot who ran the engines, and the machines which were to be seen hauling the trains only appeared to reflect some, but by no means all, of the industrious work which took place in academies and universities.

V. Scandinavia

Norway, Sweden, Denmark and Finland each achieved a distinctive style in appearance without differing from one another to any great degree in technical content. If they leaned more towards the practice of any one of the 'Big Five' it was from Germany that most of the external inspiration came, but mountainous territory in the first two, and a severe winter climate in all four naturally introduced individual features. Traversing sparsely populated territory with little industry many long tenuous routes partook almost of the nature of light railways and 15·7-ton (16-tonne) axleloads could rarely be exceeded even on the main line while it was necessary to design some engines with under 10·8-ton (11-tonne) limits. Standing away from the main streams of international traffic, they found little call for locomotives of high power or speed, and sure-footed tractive effort was the most prized attribute.

As can be imagined from the topography of the country, no four-coupled engines were built for the Norwegian Railways in the present century, and 2–6–0s and 4–6–0s worked both passenger and freight in its opening years. It was the 4–8–0, however, which, as in Spain, became the most characteristic feature of the locomotive scenery, and a number of variations gradually increasing in size were produced from 1910 until 1926. The earlier engines having axle weights of only 11·4 tons (11·6 tonnes) had four cylinders in both simple and compound form; the largest and more recent were compound only with 13·7-ton (14-tonne) axleload. In all these engines a single piston valve with multiple heads served a pair of cylinders. This of course saved considerable weight, and while, as similarly in Italy, steam ports and passages were not good, such an arrangement was not so deleterious where speeds were low. This was one of the administrations which found difficulty in making up its mind about compounding, and in many of the smaller classes also, there were both simple and compound versions. Compounding can perhaps be said to have won the day in the building in 1935 of the last and biggest Norwegian steam engine, a very compact 2–8–4 weighing 96·5 tons (98·5 tonnes) but having an axleload of only 15·3 tons (15·6 tonnes). As in the case of the Austrian engine of the same wheel arrangement referred to in the last chapter, very skilful design was needed, and a big boiler was achieved by scaling down the scantlings of the mainframes to a daring extent. Nevertheless a piston valve was provided for each of the four cylinders, outside long travel Walschaert's gear driving the outside lp valves direct, and the inside hp valves through pendant rocking shafts, in typical German style. There were seven in all of these remarkable engines, five built in Norway and two in Germany.

Norwegian practice never influenced any other administration and itself received little from outside. One of the 2–8–4s was tried out with an American booster, later removed, and a few Baldwin-built tank engines were imported in 1918. It was the German wartime 2–10–0 of class 52 which was the most extensive foreign invader, and more than 60 of these engines were introduced during the occupation to give exceptionally good service here as elsewhere in the remaining days before alternative forms of motive power took over.

In Sweden rail traffic was shared between private companies and the State, the latter only taking over the former gradually throughout the past sixty years. There were thus a much larger number of engine varieties than in Norway, but as befitted local traffic in sparsely populated areas, many were of small size and power. Inside cylinders were quite common but outside return cranks to actuate the inside Walschaert's link and high running plates above the coupled wheels made the 4–6–0s, 0–6–0s, 2–6–4 tanks and even 2–8–0s so arranged look rather odd. Compounding was practically unknown for the generality of classes, but an exception of the middle period is that shown by entry 10 in Table 32. This 4–6–0 of 1914 with compound cylinders, 30sq ft (2·78m²) of grate and an adhesive weight of 46·2 tons (47·1 tonnes) out of a total of 70 tons (68·9 tonnes), was very typical in appearance with totally enclosed windcutter cab, conical smokebox door, stovepipe chimney, combined dome and sandbox and, a common feature on many classes, a bogie having outside axleboxes and springs. In 1930 the three-cylinder simple arrangement was introduced on some 4–6–0s for the Bergslagernas Railway using the same arrangement of front drive with three separate valve gears as had been introduced in Denmark in 1922. Three cylinders were also used on the last steam engine design produced in 1947 in the form of a 4–8–0, the only time Sweden used this type, so prevalent in Norway next door. The most striking Swedish design was undoubtedly the 4–6–2 introduced in 1914 (entry 11; Plate 110) carrying every typical aspect of their country of origin although these engines were departures from much of previous practice in that they were compounds, with all four cylinders driving the intermediate coupled axle. The outside lp cylinders were steeply inclined and the German scheme of multiple piston valve heads on a single spindle serving adjacent pairs of cylinders was again used, but generous dimensions and narrow valve rings helped to give reasonable facility for the passage of steam. This very massive-looking engine had only a 15·7-ton (16-tonne) axleload, and a good feature in its design was the ample free space allowed below the grate for adequate ashpan provision. In 1936, due to electrification, the 11 engines of this class were sold to Denmark, where they became the principal express passenger type, and they with others built new in that country, lasted on important services until the 1960s.

The Swedish firm of Nydquist & Holm, which built large numbers for home service, was well known in the exporting field, and in a few cases it sent abroad adaptations of typical Swedish designs. Of such were some three-cylinder 2–8–2s for Iran in 1937 (entry 12) and 15 4–6–0s and 35 0–8–0s (entries 13 and 14), also three-cylinder machines, to meet the urgent need for motive power in Holland after the last war. The first of these latter classes was ordered by the exiled Dutch Government in London in 1942, although delivery did not take place until 1946. It was tragic that some of these fine engines were eventually grounded by corrosion troubles on their most modern feature, namely coupled axle roller bearings, and the effective life of the 4–6–0s at any rate was regrettably short.

Denmark like Holland is mostly flat, and like that country also it entered the twentieth century with small four- and six-coupled engines for passenger and freight respectively, and its own home-inspired designs never exceeded 4–6–0s and 2–8–0s for these duties. Although the 4–4–0 continued for some time, the 0–6–0 for some reason never 'caught on' and the 2–6–0 was the basic freight type until 1923. Outside Stephenson valve gear persisted longer on the main line in this country than it did elsewhere. A handsome 4–4–2 design, having Maffei overtones, was brought out in 1907 (entry 1, Table 32; Plate 107) being a four-cylinder compound of the classic South German arrangement having outside lp cylinders and two multi-headed piston valves. This engine had no subsequent influence, for in the immediate post-war years, the final purely Danish design took the form of three-cylinder simple 4–6–0, 2–8–0 and 2–6–4T classes built in 1922, 1924 and 1925 respectively (entries 2, 3 and 4). Separate Walschaert valve gears were used, the motion for the inside link being derived from outside return cranks in the case of the two latter. All three used the very neat detailing of their valve gear initiated by the firm of Borsig, and used also by the Reichsbahn. This consisted of carrying the expansion link on the same bearings as pivoted the reversing arm in the manner shown in Plate 108, an arrangement very economical of space and weight. A minor but happy detail of Danish practice was to surround the chimney by a band bearing the colours of the national flag, but although the band remained, the colours had disappeared by the 1950s. Last phase of steam in Denmark was the purchase of the 11 Swedish Pacifics already referred to, and the building of 25 more by the domestic firm of Frichs in 1943–7. During and after the last war, the ubiquitous German class 52 2–10–0s also took a hand until dieselisation swept the steam fleet into the discard.

That remote country Finland with its sturdy independence and unpronounceable language having only 3,000 miles (4800km) (route) of 5ft 0in gauge railway in its 130,000 square miles (333,000km^2) of territory, managed to sustain a very individual breed of straightforward simple expansion engines, which if they partook little from their Scandinavian neighbours, owed nothing at all to Russian influence from the East, especially after 1917 when independence was won. The presence of almost limitless forest required exceptional precautions against lineside fires, to which the bulbous spark-arresting chimneys of the earlier engines, and the more discreet wire netting at the chimney top of the later engines, bore witness. The same ample supply of softwood caused wood burning to be resorted to on the smaller engines on remoter lines. Most numerous engines were two classes of very neat little 2–8–0s built at intervals from the liberation in 1917 right up to 1950. The first had axleloading under 10·8 tons (11 tonnes) and the second between 10·8 and 13·7 tons (11 and 14 tonnes), indicating the very light nature of the track over much of the country. There were seven classes of 4–6–0 but the most interesting types technically were a Pacific and corresponding 2–8–2 built to the numbers of 22 and 67 respectively between 1937 and 1957. These were in every way abreast of modern times, having steel fireboxes with arch tubes and bar frames. Later Mikado engines even had roller bearings on all axles. Engines generally were built in Germany, Sweden and Finland itself, and American influence came in with a class of 2–10–0 built by Alco and Baldwin which were much akin to those being supplied in much larger quantities to Russia.

IV. Spain

The Spanish, or rather the Iberian scene, for we must include Portugal here, is illuminated for us by that excellent but elusive book by L. G. Marshall* and one can only salute the industry which has identified, engine by engine, so various a kaleidoscope in the Spanish part of the peninsula. Here at the western tip of the Euro-Asian land mass seem to have accumulated examples of nearly every school of steam locomotive design. Mountainous territory and a policy of few but heavy trains have called for large and powerful units;

* *Steam on the RENFE*, by L. G. Marshall, Macmillan, 1965.

chronic shortage of funds, and the effects of a destructive civil war have hampered renewal and upgrading of the permanent way, and have led to the retention of ancient lightweight engines far beyond the stage at which in other lands they would be consigned to the scrap heap. Where in the 1950s but in Spain could one start a journey on an important international Wagon-Lits train behind a powerful Chapelon-inspired 4–8–2 piloted by a British-built 2–8–2 containing all the final developments of the century in locomotive design, only to finish its passage over Spanish territory, with reduced load it is true, behind a pair of diminutive 0–6–0s of Belgian and Saxon build, dating from 1897 and 1901 respectively?

Marshall lists no fewer than 55 locomotive builders from ten different countries which have supplied the engines still existing at his time of writing, but here we must confine ourselves to building after 1900, and in the first place to the identification of a more especially Spanish trend in design. This trend expressed itself on the one hand through the need for eight-coupled engines, 4–8–0s and 4–8–2s, to carry heavy loads across the mountains, and on the other hand through the emergence of a substantial indigenous locomotive building industry in the 1920s, and the unification in 1941 of the separate railways into the RENFE, both of which events rationalised what had hitherto been alien designs into a recognisable Spanish school. Table 33 displays a cross section of Spanish locomotive development, and in entries 1, 2 and 4 can be discerned the reaching out towards the utmost in adhesion which the limited permitted axleloads could provide, culminating in the establishment in 1912 of the 4–8–0 which was to play such a big part in future steam traction. Of these engines the first Norte 4–6–0 and the MZA 4–8–0 were built in Germany, and the Norte 2–8–0 in Belgium and Germany. How far the designs were basically German and what part the Spanish railway administrations took in formulating the main features or details cannot be discerned today, but it was clearly from these beginnings that the purely Spanish design entity emerged when domestic design and construction began. By 1920 a Spanish-designed version of the 4–8–0 (entry 5) was turned out by the indigenous firm of Maquinista of Barcelona, and further variations, all built by one or other of the five Spanish firms which eventually set up in this business, took upon themselves an increasingly Spanish aura.

The 505 such engines of five groups were the centrepiece of modern motive power on these railways and were characterised by outside simple expansion cylinders, plate frames, coupled wheels no larger than 5ft 4¾in (1630mm) diameter and low running plates. Different batches carried Lentz poppet valves, ACFI feed water heaters, sideplate wind deflectors and double chimneys. Large sandboxes were mounted on top of the boiler, and as befitted so warm a country, cabs carried a cut-away section at the sides behind leading side-windows.

As more power still became necessary it was a logical step to the 4–8–2, and 95 such engines built for the MZA line from 1925 to 1931 (entry 7) were a development of the previous 4–8–0s for the same system, and looked much alike. An interlude was provided in 1939 by the building by Maquinista of 10 rather similar engines but having a streamlined casing over boiler and smokebox, the frontal appearance being much akin to Gresley's streamlined engines in England. By no stretch of the imagination were speeds ever attained by these engines which were likely to give rise to any benefit, and this phase can only be taken as a salute to a widespread but short-lived fashion. Last in this wheel arrangement came the 51 largest engines of this kind built for the RENFE after 1944 (entry 8) and these were accompanied by 22 2–10–2 engines having the same boiler. The final achievement of Spanish design was the quite magnificent 4–8–4 engines, 10 in number built in 1955–6 which, in their attractive green livery, have been so admired by visitors to Spain in recent years (entry 9).

As in the case of the 4–8–0s already mentioned two outside cylinders only were employed, except in the case of the 2–10–2s (entry 10) where three cylinders were used to develop the tractive effort required to grapple with heavy coal trains over the mountains in the north-western part of the country. Unlike the case in most other lands, here the 4–6–2 wheel arrangement found little lodgement. Only 44 were built in this century, but this little group of engines typified the variety of influences at work. Ten engines for the Andaluces Railway (entry 3) were home built and displayed all the typical features of the developing 4–8–0s referred to above. Fourteen were pure American design, built by Alco in 1920, and four were characteristic German Maffei, the leading particulars of which have already been shown in entry 5 Table 26A. The remaining 16 engines were built in France and were as typical French de Glehn compounds as ever ran upon the Nord or Paris and Orléans (entry 9, Table 20).

This latter manifestation draws attention to a massive splinter movement within the Spanish scene. Somewhat like the Great Western Railway in England, the Norte Railway was rather a law unto itself, and from 1911 until 1948, well after the formation of RENFE, it used the de Glehn compound system and where it did not actually import complete engines from France, it made the various German or Spanish builders conform to typically French practice for its orders. In the first years of the century it had been the MZA and Andaluces Railways which had introduced the de Glehn system on to two designs of 4–6–0s while at that time the Norte operated with two-cylinder simple expansion engines on the main line. However, around 1911 the MZA abandoned the system and the Norte took it up in a long series of 4–6–2, 4–8–0, 4–8–2 and 4–8–4 tank classes, any one of which could have worked without remark into any of the Paris stations had the gauge permitted. The best known were the Norte class 4601 4–8–2s (RENFE class 241.4001) of which the first 6 were built strangely enough in Germany in 1925 and 60 others by Spanish firms up to 1927. It was one of these engines which was converted to include Chapelon features which caused 28 more of them to be built new as late as 1946–8 (Table 20, entries 9, 10, 11 and 14).

British practice has likewise made a periodic appearance. The North British Locomotive Company built some very typically English 4–6–0s in 1907 having outside cylinders, which found their way on to the Oeste system, and some 2–8–0s in 1919. Its biggest contribution came, however, in 1953 when it was largely responsible for the design of a 2–8–2 mixed traffic engine which became a RENFE standard type. This engine expressed to the full all the improvements and know-how which British design had acquired through the years and although having plate frames, it included all those other features of American origin which had proved themselves so well in India. The first 25 engines were built in Scotland, and the firm provided material for the construction in Spain of 100 more. In all 232 units of this excellent maid-of-all-work were built (Table 14, entry 15). Other British importations were six 4–6–2 + 2–6–4 Garratt locomotives for passenger service and sixteen 2–8–2 + 2–8–2 engines for freight built by Spanish firms between 1930 and 1961 under licence from Beyer Peacock, ten of the latter being the last steam locomotives built in Spain.

Pure American design on engines built in USA was to be seen in a number of classes, mostly imported between 1917 and 1920 when no other source of supply was available. Fifty-two 2–8–2s of moderate size were supplied to the Norte in 1917–18 for mixed traffic working, and as referred to above ten Pacifics were built by Alco for the MZA in 1920.

It was German builders, however, who got the lion's share of the orders before the setting up of a Spanish manufacturing industry, and amongst a large number of engines of all kinds, many with no specially distinguishing features, may be mentioned besides the pioneer 4–8–0s for the MZA in 1912, some 4–6–4 tank engines of 1903 which, with their successors, were the inspiration for considerable numbers of home-built 2–8–2 and 4–8–4 tanks, 72 of the latter having been constructed up to 1927. All of these were two-cylinder simples, and compounding on the German as distinct from the French system found very sparse lodgement.

Finally there were 13 0–6–6–0 compound Mallet engines built between 1906 and 1928 by Esslingen and Henschel. They were still working in the 1960s on heavily graded lines out of Valencia.

In Portugal before 1927 there was one large privately owned railway, and a number of smaller state-owned lines. Unlike the trend in most other countries the former swallowed up the latter and from 1948 there was only one broad gauge system. Because a lot of French capital had been employed for the construction of the line, French firms were building the principal types in the first decade of the century, of which three classes of de Glehn compound 4–6–0s were the principal. Thereafter German builders supplied most requirements even although the de Glehn system was retained for 4–6–2 engines with narrow fireboxes in 1924 and for the really striking 4–8–0 engines which until the end of steam took the international train which had traversed Spain, from Vilar Formoso on the border to Pampilhosa on the Lisbon main line (Table 20, entry 15). There was nothing which could be identified as of purely Portuguese form, and besides those mentioned above, including some 4–8–0s from Spain, the scene was diversified by 20 oil-burning 2–8–2 engines of one of the US wartime designs, built by Alco in 1944, and by a series of 2–6–4 tanks for the Lisbon suburban system, built in Switzerland to Swiss design, one of he very few design exports from that country.

Thus on the Iberian peninsula it was possible to see together not only the products of many design schools, but to see each of them spread over a time scale which extended rom the mists of the mid-nineteenth century until the 1960s. That perhaps, more than any individuality of design or appearance, was the true speciality of Spain and Portugal.

We must now take a final look round the remaining countries which have not been mentioned, or have only been barely mentioned in this chronicle in order to assure ourselves that we use the word 'derivative' as a fair description and not as an unjustice to native endeavour.

Switzerland, lying at the crossroads of so many European trunk routes, might be expected to reflect something of the locomotive practice of the countries which surrounded it, and in fact its design was almost wholly based upon French and German precepts in principle, its national flavour being confined to an economical but graceful exterior appearance. An unexpected feature having regard to the very mountainous nature of the land was the comparatively small size of the engines employed for as long as steam was in use. Unlike its neighbours, its largest passenger engines were no more than 75·4-ton (77-tonne) 4–6–0s and 2–8–0s while 83·3-ton (85-tonne) 2–10–0s did not appear until 1914 and were the end of steam development, for extending electrification thereafter cut off steam in that country earlier than in most others. While steam lasted, nearly all of the main line engines were compounded either on the de Glehn or Maffei systems, and the grinding task of surmounting the heavy grades up to the St Gotthard tunnel for example, was undertaken by moderately sized 4–6–0s in pairs, the advantages or disadvantages of either form of compounding mingling indistinguishably in a common effort. Smaller engines used simple expansion but there was one breed of 2–6–0 dating from around 1905 and attaining over 100 units which took the form of a three-cylinder compound on the same layout as the English Deeley engines. Italy and Portugal received some tank engines of Swiss design, but exports by Swiss industry were usually to customers' requirements.

In Greece no attempt was made by the railway authorities to impose any domestic style, and their locomotives bore the features and appearance of the countries from which they were ordered. After the two wars, in 1916 and again in 1947, pure American designs of 2–8–2 and 2–10–0 wheel arrangement respectively were introduced, the latter being supplemented by a number of US Army 2–8–0s of the type already referred to which was scattered all over Europe. Between the wars a batch of Austrian-looking 2–10–0s of pure Golsdorf design, but of simple expansion, were built in Czechoslovakia and of course at the very end there were the huge but ill-starred 2–10–2s of Italian build referred to earlier in this chapter. At the other side of the Continent, Esthonia, Latvia and Lithuania, those tiny Baltic States liberated after 1919 and bludgeoned into submission again after 1940, showed some glimmerings of embarking upon a modest locomotive development, culminating in some Pacifics ordered for Lithuania from Skoda in 1939 but never delivered.

Outside Europe, in Asia the Netherlands East Indies and Japan had locomotive styles of their own, but entirely for the narrow gauge. China received upon its several pre-1939 railways the typical products of American, British, French, German and other European manufacturers without any vestige of a purely Chinese 'line', and since the last war took such further steam input as it required from Russia, ideological rather than technical considerations being paramount. In the New World although Canada possessed many most admirable locomotives designed and built in that country, there was nothing to distinguish them, except in detail, from those of the USA, and the same could be said of Mexico, Chile and those railways in Argentina and Brazil which had not, through finance, come under the influence of British entrepreneurs.

99 Dutch 2-cylinder simple 2–8–0 freight engine No 4617 at Haarlem, 1930. Outside valve gear was unusual in Dutch practice [*C. Shorto*

100 Final phase of Dutch design. No 3906 of 3900 Class of 4-cylinder simple 4–6–0 built 1929. Note continuance of British "line", and absence of outside valve gear [*C. Shorto*

106 Last purely Russian design without American influence, No C017–2314 of Class SO 2–10–0 at Stalingrad. Some 5000 units of this class were built between 1934 and 1954. Note large size of engine in relation to men on footplate and in cab

[*E. S. Cox*

101 Italian mixed traffic 2–6–0 with inside cylinders. No 630 027 at Orta in 1926. Note outside piston valves and valve gear [*C. Shorto*

102 Italian 4-cylinder simple 2–6–2 No 685 097, built 1912, in Rome (Termini) in 1961. Note one piston valve serving two adjacent cylinders and combined dome and sandbox [*E. S. Cox*

691 031

104 A locomotive beheaded! Italian 2-cylinder simple 2–8–0 No 743 433 of a class originating in 1911, as fitted later with Franco–Crosti boiler. Note preheating drum below boiler and blastpipe and chimney alongside firebox. The plain cab without side windows was typical

[*Italian State Rlys*

103 Italian 4-cylinder simple 4–6–2 No 691 031 built in 1914 and photographed at Milan (Greco depot) in 1957. Note same characteristic features as on 2–6–2s (previous page) [*P. Ransome Wallis*

107 Danish 4-cylinder compound 4–4–2 No 906 built 1907, standing in Copenhagen station in 1956. Note band round chimney which originally carried national colours

[*E. S. Cox*

108 Danish 3-cylinder simple 4–6–0 No 958, Class R1 of 1921. Note double return crank providing motion for Walschaert link for inside cylinder, also compact arrangement of lifting arm embracing outside expansion link

[*P. Ransome Wallis*

Nr 958
R

109 Largest of several classes of Norwegian 4–8–0s both simple and compound with 4-cylinders. Compound No 418 of Class 31b designed in 1921, pictured at Oslo in 1954

[*P. Ransome Wallis*

110 Swedish 4-cylinder compound 4–6–2, design introduced in 1914. Sold to Denmark in 1936 where others of same class were built new. No 980 leaving Copenhagen, 1956

[*E. S. Cox*

112 Locomotive cocktail! French de Glehn compound system, favourite Iberian 4–8–0 wheel arrangement, built in Germany, 1931. Portuguese Beira-Alta Railway No 103 at Pampilhosa in 1949 [*E. S. Cox*

113 Puzzle picture—simple or compound? Portuguese 4–6–0 No 282 at Vilar Formosa on Spanish border, 1949. Note de Glehn position of cylinders, and double link driving outside valve from inside valve gear [*E S. Cox*

111 One of 505 4–8–0s, the arch-type of Spanish locomotives. Originally MZA 1400 Class of 1920, by 1962, when photo was taken at Valencia, it had become No 240.2257 of RENFE [*P. Ransome Wallis*

Entry	Date	Wheel Arrange-ment	Railway	Type	Cylinders Diameter × Stroke inches mm	Coupled Wheels Diameter feet mm	Working Pressure lb/sq in kg/cm²	Grate Area sq ft m²	Weight Engine Working Order: Axle tons tonnes	Adhesive tons tonnes	Total tons tonnes
1	1902	4–4–0	Belgian State	17	19 × 26 483 × 660	6′ 6¾″ 2000	199 14·0	22·0 2·04	17·7 18·0	35·5 36·1	49·5 50·3
2	1902	0–6–0	,, ,,	32	18½ × 26 470 × 660	4′ 11⅞″ 1520	185 13·0	27·2 2·53	17·0 17·3	46·8 47·5	46·8 47·5
3	1903	4–6–0	,, ,,	35	20½ × 26 520 × 660	5′ 7″ 1700	199 14·0	30·6 2·84	17·9 18·2	53·8 54·6	73·3 74·4
4	1906	4–6–0	,, ,,	9	(4) 17½ × 25⅛ 445 × 640	6′ 6″ 1980	199 14·0	32·4 3·01	19·1 19·5	55·8 57·0	82·2 83·9
5	1910	4–6–2	,, ,,	10	19⅝ × 26 500 × 660	6′ 6″ 1980	199 14·0	53·8 4·98	19·3 19·6	58·0 58·9	104·0 105·6
6	1910	2–10–0	,, ,,	36	(4) 19⅝ × 26 500 × 660	4′ 9″ 1450	199 14·0	54·5 5·06	17·6 18·0	88·2 90·0	103·9 106·0
7	1922	2–8–0	,, ,,	37	24 × 28 610 × 712	4′ 11⅞″ 1520	199 14·0	35·1 3·26	18·8 19·1	70·0 71·2	80·2 81·4
8	1929	2–8–2	,, ,,	5	28⅜ × 28⅜ 720 × 720	5′ 7″ 1700	199 14·0	59·2 5·50	22·5 23·0	90·1 92·0	128·3 131·0
9	1930	2–8–0	,, ,,	35	25⅝ × 28⅜ 650 × 720	4′ 9″ 1450	199 14·0	54·6 5·07	22·5 23·0	90·1 92·0	105·8 108·0
10	1935	4–6–2	,, ,,	1	(4) 16½ × 28½ 420 × 725	6′ 6″ 1980	256 18·0	53·8 5·00	22·6 23·1	69·0 70·5	119·5 122·0
11	1940	4–4–2	,, ,,	12	18⅞ × 28⅜ 480 × 720	6′ 10⅝″ 2100	256 18·0	40·0 3·72	22·8 23·4	44·9 45·8	87·4 89·2
12	1910	4–6–0	Dutch	3700	(4) 15¾ × 26 400 × 660	6′ 0⅞″ 1850	171 12·0	31·0 2·88	15·7 16·0	47·0 48·0	70·6 72·0
13	1929	4–6–0	,,	3900	(4) 16½ × 26 420 × 660	6′ 0⅞″ 1850	199 14·0	34·0 3·16	17·9 18·3	53·9 55·0	82·4 84·0
14	1930	4–8–4T	,,	6300	(4) 16½ × 26 420 × 660	5′ 1″ 1550	199 14·0	34·0 3·16	17·6 18·0	70·5 72·0	123·6 126·2

For other Belgian engines see Tables 15 and 20

For other Dutch engines see Tables 15 and 32

THE OTHERS. REPRESENTATIVE LOCOMOTIVES OF ITALIAN AND RUSSIAN DESIGN

Table 31

Entry	Date	Wheel Arrangement	Railway	Approx. Number Built	Type	Cylinders Diameter × Stroke inches / mm	Coupled Wheels Diameter feet / mm	Working Pressure lb/sq in / kg/cm²	Grate Area sq ft / m²	Weight Engine Working Order: Axle tons / tonnes	Weight Engine Working Order: Adhesive tons / tonnes	Weight Engine Working Order: Total tons / tonnes
1	1903	4–6–0	Italian State		Southern Ry.	(4) $14\frac{1}{4}:23\frac{1}{4}\times25\frac{5}{8}$ 360 : 590 × 650	6′ $3\frac{5}{8}$″ 1920	213 15·0	32·5 3·02	13·8 14·0	41·3 42·0	69·0 70·0
2	1908	2–6–0	,, ,,		640	$21\frac{1}{4}\times27\frac{1}{2}$ (A) 540 × 700	6′ $0\frac{7}{8}$″ 1850	171 12·0	26·0 2·42	14·5 14·7	43·5 44·2	53·7 54·5
3	1912	2–6–2	,, ,,		685	(4) $16\frac{1}{2}\times26$ (A) 420 × 650	6′ $0\frac{7}{8}$″ 1850	171 12·0	38·0 3·53	14·7 15·0	44·1 45·0	69·4 70·8
4	1914	4–6–2	,, ,,		691	(4) $17\frac{3}{4}\times26\frac{3}{4}$ 450 × 680	6′ $7\frac{3}{4}$″ 2030	199 14·0	46·3 4·30	18·6 19·0	52·9 54·0	88·7 90·5
5	1911	2–8–0	,, ,,		740	$21\frac{1}{4}\times27\frac{1}{2}$ 540 × 700	4′ $5\frac{1}{2}$″ 1360	171 12·0	26·9 2·50	13·4 13·7	53·9 55·0	64·7 66·0
6	1914	2–8–0	,, ,,		744.745	$23\frac{5}{8}\times28\frac{3}{8}$ (B) 600 × 720	5′ $4\frac{1}{4}$″ 1630	171 12·0	37·6 3·49	14·5 14·8	58·0 59·2	70·4 71·8
7	1921	2–8–2	,, ,,		746	(4) $19\frac{1}{4}:28\frac{3}{8}\times26\frac{3}{4}$ 490 : 720 × 680	6′ 2″ 1880	199 14·0	46·3 4·30	16·2 16·5	64·7 66·0	91·1 93·0
8	1923	2–10–0	,, ,,		480	$26\frac{3}{8}\times25\frac{5}{8}$ 670 × 650	4′ $5\frac{1}{2}$″ 1360	171 12·0	49·3 4·57	14·7 15·0	73·5 75·0	85·6 87·3
9	1954	2–10–2	Italian built for Greek State Rys.		—	$26\times27\frac{1}{2}$ 660 × 700	5′ 3″ 1600	256 18·0	60·3 5·60	19·6 20·0	98·0 100·0	129·3 132·0
10	1892/1913	2–6–0	Russian	1,000	N	(2) $21\frac{1}{4}:29\frac{1}{2}\times25\frac{5}{8}$ (C) 540 : 750 × 650	5′ 7″ 1700	171–199 12·0–14·0	23·6–28·0 2·19–2·60	14·5–16·0 14·7–16·3	43·5–48·0 44·2–48·8	54·0–62·0 54·8–63·0
11	1901/23	0–8–0	,,	9,500	O	(2) $19\frac{5}{8}:28\frac{3}{4}\times25\frac{5}{8}$ (C) 500 : 730 × 650	3′ $11\frac{1}{4}$″ 1200	156–213 11·0–15·0	19·9 1·85	13·0–13·7 13·2–13·9	52·0–55·0 52·8–55·8	52·0–55·0 52·8–55·9
12	1907/18	2–8–0	,,	2,200	Shch	(2) $21\frac{1}{4}:30\times27\frac{1}{2}$ (C) 540 : 762 × 700	4′ $3\frac{3}{16}$″ 1300	199 14·0	30·0 2·78	15·0–16·0 15·3–16·3	60·0–64·0 61·0–65·0	77·0–78·0 78·2–79·2
13	1911/51	2–6–2	,,	3,750	S. Su Sum	$21\frac{5}{8}$ or $22\frac{5}{8}\times27\frac{1}{2}$ 550 or 575 × 700	6′ $0\frac{3}{4}$″ 1850	185 13·0	40·8–50·9 3·79–4·75	15·8–20·0 16·1–20·3	47·4–60·0 48·3–61·0	76·0–90·0 77·2–91·4
14	1912/52	0–10–0	,,	13,000	E. Eu Em Er	$25\frac{5}{8}\times27\frac{1}{2}$ 650 × 700	4′ 4″ 1320	171–199 12·0–14·0	45·2–54·7 4·20–5·08	16·2–17·5 16·5–17·8	80·0–87·2 81·3–88·6	80·0–87·2 81·3–88·6
15	1934/54	2–10–0	,,	5,000	SO	$25\frac{5}{8}\times27\frac{1}{2}$ 650 × 700	4′ 4″ 1320	199 14·0	64·5 5·99	17·5 17·8	87·5 88·9	97·0 98·6
16	1947	2–6–2	Polish		Ol 49	$19\frac{5}{8}\times24\frac{7}{8}$ 500 × 630	5′ $8\frac{7}{8}$″ 1750	227 16·0	39·8 3·70	16·8 17·1	50·4 51·4	81·8 83·5

THE OTHERS. REPRESENTATIVE LOCOMOTIVES OF DANISH, NORWEGIAN AND SWEDISH DESIGN Table 32

Entry	Date	Wheel Arrangement	Railway	Type	Cylinders Diameter × Stroke inches / mm	Coupled Wheels Diameter feet / mm	Working Pressure lb/sq in / kg/cm²	Grate Area sq ft / m²	Weight Engine Working Order: Axle tons / tonnes	Adhesive tons / tonnes	Total tons / tonnes
1	1907	4–4–2	Danish State	PI	$13\frac{3}{8} : 22\frac{7}{16} \times 23\frac{5}{8}$ 340 : 570 × 600	6′ $6\frac{1}{8}$″ 1984	213 15·0	35·0 3·25	16·0 16·3	32·0 32·5	66·0 67·0
2	1922	4–6–0	,, ,,	R2	(3) $18\frac{1}{2} \times 26\frac{3}{8}$ 470 × 670	6′ $1\frac{1}{2}$″ 1866	171 12·0	28·0 2·60	18·0 18·3	51·0 51·8	74·0 75·2
3	1924	2–8–0	,, ,,	H	(3) $18\frac{1}{2} \times 26\frac{3}{8}$ 470 × 670	4′ $7\frac{1}{4}$″ 1404	171 12·0	28·0 2·60	16·2 16·5	64·9 65·9	75·7 76·9
4	1925	2–6–4T	,, ,,	S	(3) $16\frac{7}{8} \times 26\frac{3}{8}$ 430 × 670	5′ $8\frac{1}{8}$″ 1730	171 12·0	25·8 2·40	15·7 16·0	47·0 48·0	90·2 92·0
5	1914	4–6–0	Norwegian State	30a	(4) $15\frac{3}{8} \times 23\frac{5}{8}$ (A) 390 × 600	5′ 3″ 1600	171 12·0	25·8 2·40	13·5 13·7	40·2 41·1	59·0 60·2
6	1919	4–8–0	,, ,,	26c	(4) $15\frac{3}{8} : 23 \times 23\frac{5}{8}$ (A) 390 : 585 × 600	4′ $5\frac{1}{8}$″ 1350	206 15·5	28·0 2·60	11·4 11·6	45·5 46·4	62·7 64·0
7	1921	4–8–0	,, ,,	31b	(4) $16\frac{1}{2} : 24\frac{7}{8} \times 23\frac{5}{8}$ (A) 420 : 630 × 600	4′ $5\frac{1}{8}$″ 1350	227 16·0	32·3 3·00	13·7 14·0	54·8 56·0	71·7 73·2
8	1935	2–8–4	,, ,,	49c	(4) $17\frac{3}{8} \times 25\frac{1}{2} : 25\frac{1}{2} \times 27\frac{1}{2}$ 440 × 650 : 650 × 700	5′ $0\frac{1}{4}$″ 1530	242 17·0	53·8 5·00	15·3 15·6	61·2 62·4	96·5 98·5
9	1908	4–4–2	Swedish	—	$19\frac{11}{16} \times 23\frac{5}{8}$ 500 × 645	6′ 2″ 1880	171 12·0	28·0 2·60	15·3 15·6	30·7 31·2	59·4 60·3
10	1914	4–6–0	,,	—	(4) $15\frac{3}{16} : 23\frac{1}{4} \times 27$ 410 : 590 × 685	6′ $0\frac{7}{8}$″ 1850	199 14·0	30·0 2·78	15·7 16·0	46·2 47·1	68·9 70·3
11	1914	4–6–2	,, (B)	—	(4) $16\frac{1}{2} : 24\frac{3}{4} \times 26$ 420 : 630 × 660	6′ 2″ 1880	185 13·0	38·7 3·59	15·7 16·0	47·0 48·0	86·0 87·8
12	1937	2–8–2	Swedish design for Iranian State		(3) $19\frac{11}{16} \times 26$ 500 × 660	4′ $5\frac{1}{8}$″ 1350	171 12·0	45·0 4·17	15·7 16·0	62·7 64·0	84·2 86·0
13	1946	4–6–0	Swedish design for Dutch State	4001	(3) $19\frac{11}{16} \times 26$ 500 × 660	6′ $2\frac{3}{8}$″ 1890	171 12·0	35·0 3·25	17·9 18·3	53·8 54·9	81·6 83·3
14	1946	0–8–0	,, ,,	4701	(3) $19\frac{11}{16} \times 26$ 500 × 660	4′ $5\frac{1}{8}$″ 1350	185 13·0	32·3 3·00	18·1 18·5	71·5 73·0	71·6 73·0

(A) Variants built with four cylinders in both simple and compound form (B) Sold in 1936 to Danish State Railways

THE OTHERS. REPRESENTATIVE LOCOMOTIVES RUNNING IN SPAIN AND PORTUGAL — Table 33

Entry	Date	Wheel Arrangement	Railway	Type	Cylinders Diameter × Stroke inches / mm	Coupled Wheels Diameter feet / mm	Working Pressure lb/sq in / kg/cm²	Grate Area sq ft / m²	Weight Engine Working Order: Axle tons / tonnes	Adhesive tons / tonnes	Total tons / tonnes
1	1904/13	4–6–0	Norte	1950	$19\frac{5}{8} \times 25\frac{5}{8}$ 500 × 650	5′ $8\frac{7}{8}$″ 1750	171 12·0	29·0 2·69	15·0 15·3	44·3 45·0	61·0 62·0
2	1909/43	2–8–0	,,	401	$24 \times 25\frac{5}{8}$ 610 × 650	5′ $1\frac{5}{8}$″ 1560	171 12·0	32·8 3·05	14·1 14·4	56·4 57·5	68·4 69·8
3	1930	4–6–2	Andaluces	3301	$20\frac{1}{2} \times 26$ 520 × 660	6′ $2\frac{3}{4}$″ 1900	227 16·0	43·0 4·00	15·7 16·0	47·0 48·0	82·0 83·6
4	1912/21	4–8–0	Madrid, Zaragoza & Alicante	1101	$22\frac{7}{8} \times 26$ 580 × 660	4′ $7\frac{1}{8}$″ 1400	171 12·0	41·7 3·87	14·2 14·5	56·8 58·0	77·0 78·5
5	1920/31	4–8–0	,, ,	1401	$24\frac{3}{8} \times 26$ 620 × 660	5′ 3″ 1600	199 14·0	49·1 4·56	15·6 15·9	62·3 63·6	84·9 86·6
6	1935/53	4–8–0	Oeste and RENFE	240–2471	24×28 610 × 710	5′ $4\frac{3}{4}$″ 1630	242 17·0	56·0 5·2	19·1 19·5	74·5 76·0	94·1 96·0
7	1925/31	4–8–2	Madrid, Zaragoza & Alicante	1701	$24\frac{3}{8} \times 28$ 620 × 710	5′ $8\frac{7}{8}$″ 1750	199 14·0	53·8 5·0	15·7 16·0	62·7 64·0	101·0 103·0
8	1944/52	4–8–2	RENFE	241–2201	$25\frac{3}{16} \times 28$ 640 × 710	5′ $8\frac{7}{8}$″ 1750	227 16·0	57·0 5·3	20·6 21·0	82·4 84·0	130·3 133·0
9	1955/56	4–8–4	,,	242–2001	$25\frac{3}{16} \times 28$ 640 × 710	6′ $2\frac{3}{4}$″ 1900	227 16·0	57·0 5·3	19·6 20·0	78·4 80·0	142·2 145·0
10	1942/45	2–10–2	,,	151–3101	(3) $22\frac{7}{16} \times 29\frac{1}{2}$ 570 × 750	5′ $1\frac{5}{8}$″ 1560	227 16·0	57·0 5·3	20·6 21·0	103·0 105·0	137·2 140·0
11	1903/26	4–6–0	Portugal (Sul-e-Sueste)		(4) $14\frac{3}{4} : 21\frac{1}{2} \times 25\frac{5}{8}$ 375 : 545 × 650	5′ 1″ 1550	199 14·0	31·0 2·88	14·0 14·2	42·0 42·7	58·5 59·4
12	1914	4–6–0	Portugal		$21\frac{1}{4} \times 26\frac{3}{4}$ 540 × 680	5′ 7″ 1700	171 12·0	32·8 3·05	14·7 15·0	44·0 45·0	63·0 64·3
13	1914	2–8–0	,,		$22 \times 24\frac{7}{8}$ 560 × 630	4′ $4\frac{3}{8}$″ 1330	171 12·0	30·6 2·85	13·7 14·0	54·8 56·0	64·2 65·5
14	1916/44	2–6–4T	,, (A)		$20\frac{1}{2} \times 25\frac{3}{16}$ 520 × 640	5′ 0″ 1525	171 12·0	27·5 2·56	15·9 16·2	47·6 48·6	79·6 81·2

CHAPTER NINE

Summary and Conclusions

THE TOTAL NUMBER of steam locomotives which have been built is almost beyond computation. No one to the author's knowledge has done sufficient research to ascertain even the number built within the present century, on properly constituted public railways, let alone the further stock acquired by industrial concerns of all kinds, always supposing that investigations of this nature were in any case considered worth the effort. Although there were a few locomotive designs which have been built to the extent of thousands, there have on the other hand been innumerable cases which have never proliferated beyond single figures, with every variety in numbers in between. Thus the amount of design work, and the making of patterns and templates, jigs and fixtures, for manufacture, which have been undertaken in countless offices and workshops all over the world, staggers the imagination. None was undertaken without good reason at the time, and yet the total effort would seem to the impartial observer to be somewhat disproportionate to the result, for nothing has so impressed the author in gathering the material for this book as the general similarity of dimensions and basic form of engines destined for the same kinds of duties on railways within a single country, having a number of different administrations within its borders, or as between one country and another having roughly similar limiting conditions as regards size and weight. The detailed diversity which did actually obtain, however, represents an almost bottomless mine of interest to the engineer, to the historian and to the enthusiast, any of whom could consider themselves fortunate indeed that they lived in or could visit countries where such profusion reigned.

Having examined so vast a canvas in as much detail as space will allow, and having attempted to trace something of the random manner in which national design practices have become intermingled, it remains to stand away, if we can, from the great mass of steam locomotive production since 1900 and see what, if anything, can be said to summarise the broadest trends. We are not here reporting a Eurovision Song Contest, and we do not have to try to distinguish an absolute best, whether by consensus or in the opinion of this fallible author. It must suffice, therefore, if we attempt in conclusion, no more than some general reflections upon a scene which is rapidly passing away, has indeed already vanished in some parts of the world.

Apart from the various natural controlling conditions outlined in Chapter 2, locomotive design was, of course, most influenced by the men responsible for it, whether they were world figures in their own particular sphere, such as du Bousquet, Churchward, Garbe, Golsdorf, Gresley, Lomonosoff or Chapelon, or whether, faceless and unseen, they evolved their designs behind the façade of some chief mechanical engineer, works director or traffic operator, whose main interests lay elsewhere. It was such men who decided whether there should be many types or few to deal with the available or potential traffic, and who were prepared, or were not prepared, as the case might be, to continue and develop the well established content and appearance of their predecessor's engines, or on the other hand to ignore the past and start again. These men too, determined the extent of standardisation, if any, both as to complete locomotive types and as to their details. Consciously following their national trend towards order and authority, it was the Germans who seemed able to pursue the most consistent 'line' in locomotive design over all the vagaries of this century. Unconsciously, the Americans produced almost as consistent a line of development, scorning general standardisation, or identity of dimensions and details with those of their fellow superintendents, but achieving all the same an overall similarity, much as continues to be the case with their automobile development over succeeding years. At the end of World War I, an American series of twelve standard types was rapidly produced for general service throughout the country and was just as quickly abandoned when Government control ceased. The British series, also of twelve standard designs, was short lived, due to the elimination of steam traction as a policy. The Russians standardised in a rather different manner by the multiplication to huge numbers of a very small variety of separate designs, each widely differing from the others. On the whole, the steam locomotive proved a difficult subject for standardisation due to its long life, small annual production for any one administration, and the succession of often strong-minded individuals who were responsible for its continued development.

Looking at particular design features, the use of two cylinders placed outside the frames was preponderant, as much in the last examples before the end of steam power, as at any other time during the century. This arrangement best satisfied the twin desirabilities of simplicity and accessibility and the alternatives of three and four equal cylinders, using a crank axle, were in some cases a deliberate design preference for the sake of some technical advantage, real or imagined, but were more often simply for the sake of obtaining a required increased tractive effort where loading gauge had brought the permissible size of outside cylinders alone to a full stop.

Preference for simple or compound expansion was one of the major variables throughout the whole history of the Stephensonian locomotive, and this chronicle has already tried to explain something of the pros and cons, to indicate where compounding was enthusiastically received and where little regarded, who were the renegades, who discarded it after previous adoption, and where, most curious of all, successive batches of the same basic locomotive were in certain periods, indifferently built as simples or as compounds. As Chapter 5 has explained, lower steam and fuel consumptions were always achievable by the compounding provided like was strictly compared with like, and this appealed strongly to those with a more academic or logical background to whom theoretical advantage was unanswerable. A compound too, designed to bring out the best efficiency of which the system was capable, was also able to achieve running performance rather more brilliant than that of its single expansion counterpart. The design of the usual form of steam locomotive was, however, more often in the hands of practical rather than of theoretical engineers, and to the former it was the general rather than the particular aspect which counted, the lowest total cost per mile including servicing and maintenance as well as fuel, and the ability of an engine to give acceptably good service in the hands of not specially skilled driving and maintenance staff. To these the simple expansion engine made a powerful appeal, an appeal which became well-nigh unanswerable as the human and economic conditions of post-World War II began to mature.

Accepting as valid, however, all of the advantages put forward on behalf of compound expansion, this system of propulsion was reaching limits determined neither by opinion nor economics. To gain increasing power within the ceiling of around 300lb/sq in (21·1kg/cm^2), which was the greatest pressure at which experience had found the normal locomotive boiler capable of working at satisfactorily, the diameter of the cylinders had to be progressively enlarged, and the power transmitted through the crank axle consequently increased. But the dimensions of this axle and in particular the width of the crank webs could not be increased in proportion, so that the integrity life and maintenance costs of this component deteriorated progressively with each increase in power. Below is a composite diagram showing the cylinder and bearing centres and sizes for a projected British compound locomotive, designed by the English engineer Fowler, which never matured, but a study of its features will illuminate the nature of the problem. Assuming a four-cylinder system, inside lp cylinders could be increased in diameter by arranging for their outer walls to protrude through or over the main frames, but only at the expense of increasing the distance between their vertical centre lines. The left-hand side of the diagram will suggest how crank web widths and inside crank and main bearing widths had correspondingly to be decreased, remembering that the rail gauge and consequently the distance between the backs of the tyres was inescapably fixed. Latter day French compounds had inside lp cylinders 25$\frac{5}{8}$in (650mm) diameter which so widened the centres that there was room for crank webs only 4in (103mm) wide, even when dishing of the wheel centres and the dimensions of the bearings had been designed down to the outside edge of what was permissible. From well attested experience elsewhere, acceptable service from crank axles, such as 180,000 miles (288000km) service without loosening or cracking or the need for attention of any kind, would require a web width of some 6$\frac{1}{2}$in (165mm) for the level of power transmitted from the French cylinders, and this was clearly just not attainable. On the other hand, placing the smaller hp cylinders inside would do something to ease the crank axle problem, but now the difficulty would be transferred to the outside driving crank pin. The more generous continental loading gauge permitted outside cylinders of 26$\frac{3}{8}$in (670mm) diameter, but only at the

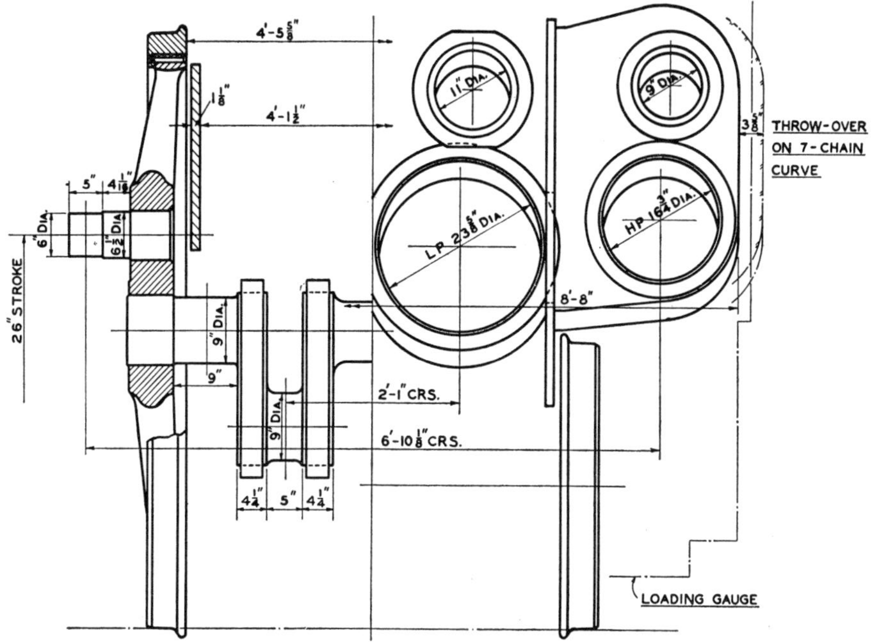

COMPOSITE DIAGRAM SHOWING CYLINDER & BEARING CENTRES
FOWLER COMPOUND PACIFIC

expense of reducing the spacing of their centre lines so as to crowd the connecting and coupling rod bearings against the wheel centre in such a manner as again to render their sizes insufficient to cope with the power transmitted. This latter limitation to ultimate power remained even when the crank axle problem could be once again pushed back by substituting only a single in place of two hp cylinders inside the frames, thus turning over to the three-cylinder system as the SNCF showed every intention of doing had steam continued.

Bearing and crank axle defects coupled with poor mileage between repairs had been a major trouble on many locomotives of all kinds earlier in the century, but better design, materials, manufacture and repair had pretty well exorcised them all as time went on, so long as they were not overloaded. To repeat in different words what has been said before, it was the possibility of re-introducing these much feared troubles caused by increasing unit loadings, which more than anything else turned the face of engineers all over the world, other than in France, from the undoubted thermal advantages of compounding.

Whether using compound or simple expansion, the practice of European countries differed from that in England and America in the general use of larger cylinders for a given nominal power output, and in relation to the weight available for adhesion. To take a single example of two contemporary designs, one German and one English, the well-known and numerous Prussian State G8 class 0–8–0 had 23⅝in (600mm) diameter × 26in (660mm) stroke cylinders with 4ft 5⅛in (1350mm) diameter wheels and 171lb (12kg/cm²) working pressure, which assuming 85 per cent boiler pressure available at starting, gave 39,650lb (18000kg) nominal tractive effort on an adhesive weight of 56 tons (57 tonnes). The Great Central Railway 04 class 2–8–0 having 20in (533mm) diameter × 26in (660mm) stroke cylinders, 4ft 8in (1422mm) diameter wheels and 180lb (12·7kg/cm²) pressure, gave 31,400lb (14280kg) tractive effort for 66 tons (67 tonnes) adhesive weight.

This example illustrates in extreme form the case where one school of design thought, such as the British, called for a relationship between adhesive weight and starting tractive effort of nearly five to one, whilst in German practice, a relationship of little more than three to one was accepted, in both cases in respect of heavy freight service. Many similar examples could be extracted from the tables, the significance of which is the differing attitude towards two complimentary but conflicting factors, the desire for the highest power to weight ratio on the one hand, and the desire on the other hand for a locomotive which will grip the rails at all times and start reliably without slipping. Locomotive weight is a drug on the market in that the effort required to move it has to be subtracted from the cylinder power, before the effort available for moving the commercially valuable train can be applied. In countries where rail and bridge conditions severely limited axle weights, there was a double temptation to crowd power on to the driving wheels to the very limit of reliable adhesion. There is no absolute criterion of the term 'reliable' in this context, but only a broad acceptance for steam traction that a tractive effort corresponding to a quarter of the weight on the coupled wheels gave a good all-round compromise, and that the 25 per cent adhesion thus represented was adequate for all but the worst rail conditions. To the extent therefore that lower factors of adhesion than four to one were tolerated for the sake of a good power to weight ratio, as was usual continental practice, so to an increasing extent reliance had to be placed upon sensitive regulators, good sanding and a gentle application of power, in order to endeavour to maintain reliable starting and acceleration.

As against this in England and more especially in America, more generous axleloading removed the absolute necessity of teetering on the very edge of reliable adhesion, and there a locomotive was well liked which would start its load under the most adverse conditions without slipping or stalling, and without anything fine-fingered about the way the regulator was handled. Two extreme positions have been illustrated in the foregoing, and there were in all countries, as always, exceptions to the general rule. From the broadest aspect, however, these two divergent trends have been interwoven through the design practice of the century.

A major difference in boiler design was the use of narrow or wide firebox, the latter becoming obligatory beyond a certain capacity. The considerable intermediate range of output in which either type could be used equally effectively, provided a large area of argument between engineers as to which was best, but decision one way or the other usually depended upon the quality of fuel available. Use of the superheater based upon the work of Schmidt, became universal and further improvements such as use of the stoker, of arch tubes or syphons in the firebox, and of welding extensively applied, although originating in America, became widely used in other countries in later developments. Reference has been made at several points in preceding chapters to the problem of ash disposal and free entry of air for combustion under the grate. Absolutely vital to good performance as the utmost freedom in these matters could be, they seem to have been something of an after-thought to many designers. The excellent back end design in this respect of many German engines in which the trailing carrying wheels were moved back clear of a wide ashpan, has only been sporadically followed, and other arrangements of trailing frames and trucks have often precluded any satisfactory solution. In America this factor was a definite bar to the introduction of long non-stop locomotive runs. The utmost ashpan capacity which could be worked in between firebox bottom and trailing truck on a typical 4–8–4 engine was about 100cu ft (2·83m^3). Burning average coal at 15,000lb (6830kg) per hour would produce 37cu ft (10·5m^3) of ash per hour, so that after about three hours, or anything from 100 to 200 miles (160 to 320km) according to the duty being performed, a stop had to be made for ash disposal, if air entry to the underside of the fire was not to become entirely choked. Even so advanced a designer as Chapelon seemed strangely insensitive to the importance of this factor, for in the several designs he produced for 6,000hp locomotives at the end of his great book, none appeared to have any but the most rudimentary provision for this very important design factor. On the other hand the British invention of the Garratt principle of articulated engine made a clean sweep of all the difficulties surrounding this problem.

It is naturally of some interest to review the greatest and the least—which were the biggest and most powerful steam engines ever produced, and which attained the lowest steam and coal consumptions in relation to work done, thus reaching the highest efficiencies of which the Stephensonian locomotive proved capable. Maximum size and power are not necessarily synonymous, but on any count the palm under these headings must go to the United States, made possible by the natural and traffic conditions of that great country. As Chapter 3 has pointed out, no one machine attained maximum dimensions on all counts, so that according to this or that criterion it is possible to stake a claim on behalf of several engines as being the 'biggest ever'. On balance it would seem that this distinction must go to the Union Pacific 4–8–8–4 engines affectionately called the 'Big Boys' (Table 5, entry 15), although the Northern Pacific 2–8–8–4s of the 5000 Class (entry 13) ran them very close. The huge grate of the latter having an area of 182sq ft (16·9m^2) was fitted, however, for the special purpose of burning especially low grade Montana coal, and although a most remarkable production for the year 1928, this engine had not quite the potential of the 'Big Boys' of 1941. As to which engine was actually the most powerful, we have no fully reliable information for no Mallet articulated engines were experimented with at the Altoona Test Plant. The Pennsylvania Q2 Class 4–4–6–4, which was a rigid frame 'Duplex' locomotive, is known to have evaporated 137,476lb (62500kg) of water per hour, and to have produced 8,000 1hp, but whether

'Big Boy' or any of the other dimensionally bigger monsters could have exceeded these figures in a strictly scientific comparison must remain for ever unknown.

Before seeking candidates for the position of the most economical engine in fuel consumption, it is necessary to find a sound criterion, for a fascinating fact regarding the steam locomotive is how little can be said about its performance without ample qualification. Coal is one of the most variable substances known to man. What it consists of and its resultant heating value per unit of weight can vary from different parts of the same mine, or even from the same part with the passage of time. From different coalfields a much greater range of product emerges, so that from an international point of view, pounds of coal per horsepower recorded on test is just about valueless as a means of comparing the efficiency of one engine with another, unless qualifications of a complex kind are available. The other ingredient of power production, water, only varies from place to place and from country to country in aspects which do not affect the amount of steam required to produce a given power, so water consumed and formed into steam forms a much sounder comparative basis. The horsepower at the drawbar, although the commercial end product which the locomotive provides to the traffic department, is subject to a number of influences which are not necessarily connected with the essential technical design of the machine, such as overall weight, including that of the tender, whose capacity is an operating and not a technical consideration. So it finally comes down to water and steam used per Indicated Horsepower in the cylinders as the safest 'international' comparison if, as here, a single figure is sought which best epitomises the level of thermal efficiency which has been designed into given engines.

Table 34 lists the lowest values attained on test for pounds of steam per lhp hour in France, Britain, Germany and America, as made available to the author from particulars supplied by the engineering departments in the different countries, and although there seems to be no data to prove it, it is unlikely that materially lower figures have been attained elsewhere. The French 'Chapelon' compounds head the list, and at 11·2lb steam/Ihp/hr (5·02kg/cv/heure) must be acclaimed as the most economical steam engines ever to have taken the rails. With the aid of many of Chapelon's ideas regarding high superheat, good draughting and freedom for flow of steam through ports and passages in conjunction with poppet valves, simple expansion in the form of the British Railways' 4–6–2 Class 8 design came next with a figure of 12·2lb (5·84kg). Figures from 13 to 14lb (5·83 to 6·28kg) broadly encompassed the best which might be attained with 'normal' design including piston valves and radial valve gears, much liked for their robust and trouble-free nature, and it is of interest that techniques independently arrived at in the principal locomotive-producing countries gave so uniform a level of efficiency in the last days of steam. Leaving out the 'star turns' a representative locomotive of this era using 13½lb (6·05kg/cv) of steam per Ihp hour, would attain a cylinder efficiency bordering on 14 per cent in conjunction with a 72 per cent boiler efficiency and a 90 per cent efficiency for the final transmission from pistons to road wheels, giving 9 per cent overall, whilst the Frenchmen would just manage to top 10 per cent. Feeble as these efficiency figures might appear, a half-century of global development had succeeded in doubling the optimum values obtainable anywhere in 1900, and the final best cylinder efficiency with compounding represented the attainment of some 90 per cent of what was theoretically possible using the heat cycle appropriate to the reciprocating steam engine in the form in which it was, in other respects, found to be most generally satisfactory as a machine tool to produce traction ton/miles.

The locomotive boiler was one of the most remarkable producers of energy of its day, not only for its steam output in relation to size, weight and cost, but also because of its extreme adaptability in that it could still produce steam in spite of the utmost variation in its proportions and in the kind of fuel it was called upon to digest. Short and fat, or long and thin, having anywhere from four to eight cubic feet of firebox volume for each square foot of grate area, with deep or shallow firebox, with or without combustion chamber, and with a proportion of free area through the tubes to grate area of from 9 to 16 per cent, an acceptable measure of performance was obtainable from them all. As to the best proportions, each designer developed his own ideas from his own experience, and although the stationary testing plants, and particularly the work done by Dr Nordmann in Germany, helped, they never got round to testing sufficient variations in the proportions of any one boiler to establish beyond question which were preferable. It would perhaps have been a rather academic exercise, for boiler proportions in any given case were more or less forced upon the designer by loading gauge, available length, disposition of wheels and permitted weight, and with these points settled his room for manœuvre was often restricted. Given moderate rates of combustion such as sufficed for much of European railway operation, the locomotive boiler achieved smokeless and cinderless combustion, with an overall efficiency from heat content in the fuel to energy in the steam produced of 75 to 80 per cent. Forced to its utmost in high power operation such as could be demanded in the New World over 200lb (982kg/m^2) of coal per square foot of grate area per hour might be fired with the products of combustion entering the tube bank at a velocity of over 200mph (320km) such that a given particle of coal caught in the draught would pass through the furnace in less than one-tenth of a second. In such cases, efficiency could fall below 50 per cent, and the surrounding countryside become blackened by a torrent of cinders ejected unburned from the chimney top. Whatever good cylinder efficiencies might be attainable by careful design, they would always be undermined where boiler operation of this kind was called for. If maximum boiler size was fixed by physical limits, there was bound to arrive a power demand where that size of boiler could only supply the steam required by frantic and uneconomical performance of the kind outlined above, and this was a major factor in bringing steam traction to its end.

What, in conclusion, is to be said to summarise the main theme of this book, the cross-fertilisation of ideas from one country to another? It will have been noted that every such influence which has been identified was concerned with some component or some detailed aspect of layout or appearance. What was most remarkable was the way in which all countries nevertheless remained true to the basic Stephensonian concept for the locomotive as a whole. Another book could be written about the attempts in all lands to abandon it in the direction of marine and power station practices, water tube boilers with higher pressures, turbines, condensers, but none survived. In a similar manner many were the attempts to twist even the Stephensonian pattern into other shapes, back-to-front engines with the cab leading, high speed multi-cylindered engines geared to the driving axle, strange and exotic alternative rod drives, and a multitude of water tube firebox designs attached to a normal boiler barrel. None lived in any one country long enough for it to become normal practice in any other. Nothing has been so criticised in railway practice by non-railway engineers as this adherence to such an 'old-fashioned' composition as sufficed for the entirety of the steam age. But error is seldom universal, and the manner in which independent mechanical engineers all over the world remained true to the first principles of Stephenson's masterpiece, even while adapting it to the most varied human and natural conditions, and learned from one another the various ways in which it could be improved in detail, is surely a lasting tribute to the essential rightness of the concept for as long as fire, water and steam was able to provide the most effective and economical form of rail traction.

LOWEST RECORDED STEAM CONSUMPTIONS ON TEST. FRANCE BRITAIN GERMANY AMERICA — Table 34

Entry	Country of Origin	Wheel Arrangement	Administration and Class	Means of Propulsion	Steam Distribution		Working Pressure lb/sq in kg/cm²	Minimum Steam Consumption lb per ihp/hr kg per cv/hr	Reference in Previous Tables	
					Valves	*Valve Gear*			*Table*	*Entry*
1	France	2–8–2	SNCF 141P	4-cyl. Compound	Poppet	Walschaert	284 20·0	11·2 5·02	19	8
2	,,	4–8–0	SNCF 240P	4-cyl. Compound	Poppet	Walschaert	284 20·0	11·4 5·11	19	7
3	Britain	4–6–2	BR 71000	3-cyl. Simple	Poppet	Caprotti	250 17·6	12·2 5·48	13	1
4	,	4–6–2	BR 70000	2-cyl Simple	Piston	Walschaert	250 17·6	13·3 5·96	13	2
5	,,	2–6–2	LNER Gresley	3-cyl. Simple	Piston	Walschaert	220 15·5	13·4 6·01	11	7
6	,,	4–6–0	GWR 'King'	4-cyl. Simple	Piston	Walschaert	250 17·6	13·8 6·19	11	11
7	Germany	4–6–2	DB 04	4-cyl. Compound	Piston	Walschaert	355 25·0	12·6 5·65	23A	6
8	,,	2–6–2	DB 23	2-cyl. Simple	Piston	Walschaert	227 16·0	13·2 5·92	24	2
9	,,	4–6–2	DB 01	2-cyl. Simple	Piston	Walschaert	227 16·0	13·4 6·01	23A	1
10	America	4–4–4–4	PRR T1	4-cyl. Simple	Poppet	Franklin	300 21·1	13·6 6·10	5	7
11	,,	2–8–2	SNCF 141R	2-cyl. Simple	Piston	Walschaert	220 15·5	14·1 6·32	7	7
12	,,	4–6–4	NYCRR J3A	2-cyl. Simple	Piston	Baker	275 19·3	14·7 6·59	5	3

Bibliography

List of publications consulted by the Author

BOOKS

Yoder and Wharen, *Locomotive Valves and Valve Gear*, Van Nostrand, New York, 1917
R. P. Johnson, *The Steam Locomotive*. Simmons Boardman, 1942
Locomotive Cyclopedia. Simmons Boardman, 1945
A. W. Bruce, *The Steam Locomotive in America*. Norton, New York, 1952
C. S. Lake, *The World's Locomotives*. Percival Marshall, 1904
Lord Monkswell, *French Railways*. Smith Elder, London, 1911
E. L. Ahrons, *British Steam Locomotives 1825–1925*. Loco. Publishing Co., London, 1927
World's Railways. Sampson Low, 1951 onwards
Edited P. Ransome-Wallis, *Encyclopedia of World Railway Locomotives*. Hutchinson, 1959
H. M. Le Fleming and J. H. Price, *Russian Steam Locomotives*. Marshbank, 1960
O. S. Nock, *Continental Main Lines*. Allen & Unwin, 1963
J. N. Westwood, *Soviet Railways To-Day*. Ian Allan, 1963
P. Ransome-Wallis, *Last Steam Locomotives in Western Europe*. Ian Allan, 1963
L. G. Marshall, *Steam on the R.E.N.F.E.* Macmillan, 1965
P. B. Whitehouse, *Steam in Europe*. Ian Allan, 1966
A. E. Durrant, *The Steam Locomotives of Eastern Europe*. David & Charles, 1966
O. S. Nock, *British Steam Locomotives 1925–1965*. Ian Allan, 1966
G. Marié, *Traité de Stabilité des Chemins de fer*. Béranger, Paris, 1924
A. Chapelon, *La Locomotive à Vapeur*. Baillière, Paris, 1938
E. Sauvage and A. Chapelon, *La Machine Locomotive*. Béranger, 1948
L. Niederstrasser, *Leitfaden für den Dampflokomotivdienst*. Reinhold Rudolph, Leipzig, 1941
Meineke and Rohrs, *Die Dampflokomotiv*. 1949
Janusch, Parski and Pavlov, *Konstruktionen und Berechnung von Lokomotiven*. Fachbuchverlag, Leipzig, 1954
Madel, *Deutschlands Dampflokomotiven*. VEB. Verlag Technik, Berlin, 1957
V. A. Rakov, *Locomotives of the Railways of the Soviet Union*. Transheldorisdat, Moscow, 1955

PERIODICALS

Engineer.
Locomotive Magazine.
Railway Engineer.
Railway Magazine.
Railway Age.
Railway Mechanical Engineer.
Revue Générale des Chemins de fer.
Trains Illustrated.
Henschel Review.

PROCEEDINGS

Institution of Mechanical Engineers.
Institution of Locomotive Engineers.
Transactions, American Society of Mechanical Engineers.

CATALOGUES

Beyer Garratt Articulated Locomotives.
Skoda Catalogue of Steam Locomotives.
Vulcan Locomotives.

Index

Index

INDEX